Public Management in Britain

Edited by
Sylvia Horton
and
David Farnham

First published in Great Britain 1999 by
MACMILLAN PRESS LTD
Houndmills, Basingstoke, Hampshire RG21 6XS and London
Companies and representatives throughout the world

A catalogue record for this book is available from the British Library.

ISBN 0–333–73740–7 hardcover
ISBN 0–333–73741–5 paperback

First published in the United States of America 1999 by
ST. MARTIN'S PRESS, INC.,
Scholarly and Reference Division,
175 Fifth Avenue, New York, N.Y. 10010

ISBN 0–312–22634–9

Library of Congress Cataloging-in-Publication Data
Public management in Britain / edited by Sylvia Horton and David
Farnham.
p.   cm.
Includes bibliographical references and index.
ISBN 0–312–22634–9 (cloth)
1. Administrative agencies—Great Britain—Management.   2. Great
Britain—Politics and government.   I. Horton, Sylvia.   II. Farnham,
David.
JN318.P824   1999
351.41—dc21   99–28095
                                                              CIP

Selection, editorial matter and Chapters 1, 2 and 15 © Sylvia Horton and David Farnham 1999
Individual chapters (in order) © Stephen Cope; Kester Isaac-Henry; John Rouse; Richard
Christy and Jill Brown; David Farnham; Christine Bellamy; Sylvia Horton; Chris Painter
and Kester Isaac-Henry; Susan Corby; David Holloway, Sylvia Horton and David Farnham;
Barry Loveday; Margaret May and Edward Brunsdon 1999

This book is printed on paper suitable for recycling and made from fully managed and
sustained forest sources.

10   9   8   7   6   5   4   3   2   1
08   07   06   05   04   03   02   01   00   99

Printed and bound in Great Britain by
Creative Print & Design (Wales), Ebbw Vale

Contents

PART III   CASES

PART IV   CONCLUSION

List of Figures and Tables

Figures

Tables

Abbreviations

ACPO	Associations of Chief Police Officers	EMS	European Monetary System
ADP	Automatic Date Processing	ERA	Education Reform Act (1988)
AHA	Area Health Authority	ERM	Exchange Rate Mechanism
AUT	Association of University Teachers	ESD	Electronic Service Delivery
BCU	Basic Command Unit	EU	European Union
BMA	British Medical Association	FE	Further Education
BPR	Business Process Re-engineering	FEC	Further Education Corporation
BV	Best Value	FEFC	Further Education Funding Council
CBI	Confederation of British Industries	FHEA	Further and Higher Education Act (1992)
CC	Chief Constable	FMI	Financial Management Initiative
CCT	Compulsory Competitive Tendering	FTE	Full Time Equivalent
CE	Chief Executive	G7	The G7 now G8 Group of Industrial Nations
CIHE	Colleges and Institutes of Higher Education	GCHQ	General Communications Headquarters (Cheltenham)
CITU	Cabinet Central Information Technology Unit		
CMPS	Centre for Management and Policy Studies	GDP	Gross Domestic Product
CPS	Crown Prosecution Service	GGE	General Government Expenditure
CSC	Civil Service College	GMS	Grant Maintained Status
CSP	Chartered Society of Physiotherapists	GMTS	General Management Training Scheme
DfEE	Department for Education and Employment	GP	General Practitioner
		HC	Health Commission
		HE	Higher Education
DHA	District Health Authority	HEC	Higher Education Corporation
DoH	Department of Health		
DSS	Department of Social Security	HEFC	Higher Education Funding Council
EAZ	Education Action Zone	HMI	Her Majesty's Inspector
EC	European Community	HMIC	Her Majesty's Inspectorate of Constabulary
EEC	European Economic Community		
EFTA	European Free Trade Area	HRD	Human Resource Development

HRM	Human Resources Management	PEST	Political, Economic, Technological, Social
IBIS	Integrating Business and Information Systems (a project in the criminal justice system)	PFI	Private Finance Initiative
		PI	Performance Indicator
		PIU	Performance and Innovation Unit
ICT	Information and Communication Technology	PM	Performance Management
		PMCA	Police and Magistrates Courts Act (1994)
IiP	Investors in People		
INSET	In Service Training	POST	Parliamentary Office of Science and Technology
IS	Information System		
LEA	Local Education Authority	PRB	Pay Review Body
		PRP	Performance Related Pay
LFM	Local Financial Management	PSA	Public Service Agreements
LMS	Local Management of Schools	PSBR	Public Sector Borrowing Requirement
MCI	Management Charter Initiative	RAE	Research Assessment Exercise
MIS	Management Information Systems	RCN	Royal College of Nursing
		RCM	Royal College of Midwives
MSF	Manufacturing Science and Finance Union	RHA	Regional Health Authority
NATFHE	National Association of Teachers in Further and Higher Education	RMI	Resource Management Initiative
NCB	National Collective Bargaining	SCS	Senior Civil Service
		SEU	Social Exclusion Unit
NDA	Non-Departmental Agency	SSD	Social Services Department
NDPB	Non-Departmental Public Body	SSI	Social Services Inspectorate
NHS	National Health Service	STG	Special Transition Grant
		STRB	School Teachers Review Body
NPM	New Public Management		
NSA	Next Step Agency	SWOT	Strengths, Weaknesses, Opportunities, Threats
NVQ	National Vocational Qualification	TECS	Training and Enterprise Councils
OFSTED	Office for Standards in Education	TQM	Total Quality Management
OPS	Office of Public Service		
OSCE	Organisation for Security and Co-operation in Europe	TUPE	Transfer of Undertakings (Protection of Employment Regulations)
PCFC	Polytechnics and Colleges Funding Council	UFC	University Funding Council
PA	Police Authority	UGC	University Grants Commission
PAM	Professions Allied to Medicine		
		VFM	Value for Money
PCEF	Polytechnics and Colleges Employers Forum	WEU	Western European Union
		WIRS	Workplace Industrial Relations Survey

List of Contributors

Christine Bellamy is Professor of Public Administration, Nottingham Trent University.

Jill Brown is Senior Lecturer in Marketing, University of Portsmouth.

Edward Brunsdon is Principal Lecturer in Social Policy, London Guildhall University.

Richard Christy is Senior Lecturer in Marketing, University of Portsmouth.

Stephen Cope is Principal Lecturer in Public Policy, University of Portsmouth.

Susan Corby is Senior Lecturer in Human Resources Management, University of Greenwich.

David Farnham is Professor of Employment Relations, University of Portsmouth.

David Holloway is Principal Lecturer in Education, University of Portsmouth.

Sylvia Horton is Principal Lecturer in Public Sector Studies, University of Portsmouth.

Kester Isaac-Henry is Professor of Public Management, University of Central England in Birmingham.

Barry Loveday is Principal Lecturer in Criminal Justice, University of Portsmouth.

Margaret May is Principal Lecturer in Social Policy, London Guildhall University.

Chris Painter is Professor of Public Policy and Management, University of Central England in Birmingham.

John Rouse is Professor of Public Services Management, University of Central England in Birmingham.

Preface

The election of New Labour to office in May 1997, with a commitment to modernise and make Britain better, triggered a number of contradictory expectations. One was that there would be a reversal of many of the changes introduced by Conservative governments during their 18 years of uninterrupted office. Another was that change would continue but that it would take a different direction and remedy many of the problems that earlier changes had produced. A more sanguine view was that the new government would continue to steer in the same direction as its predecessors, whatever the rhetoric, because all governments are constrained by the system of international capitalism and forces of globalisation and technological transformation over which they have no control. In other words governments do not make a lot of difference, whatever they might say.

The previous editions of this book mapped the structural, organisational and managerial changes associated with Conservative governments between 1979 and 1996 (Farnham and Horton, 1993, 1996). Here we argued that the British state had been transformed from a welfare model to a contract one. There had also been a revolution in the way in which public organisations were being managed. All public services had been affected by the adoption by successive Conservative governments of neo-liberal or New Right ideas and all had been managerialised. The services were described as 'new', because they had been subjected to changes shifting them from traditional, administered bureaucracies to managed public 'businesses'. By 1997 the impact of the reforming governments had been internalised and it was possible to describe 'New Public Management' as the norm.

The election of a Labour government committed to further change has prompted the need to revisit the public services and describe and assess whether the neo-liberal paradigm is being challenged. New Labour stated in its election manifesto that: 'Some things the Conservatives got right. We will not change them. It is where they got things wrong that we will make change. We have no intention or desire to replace one set of dogmas by another' (Labour Party, 1997: 1). This book assesses the legacy of 18 years of reform of the public services under both Margaret Thatcher and John Major and the impact of the New Labour Government under Tony Blair.

The book is in four parts. Part I examines the changing political contexts within which organisational change and public management in Britain have emerged and developed over the last 20 years. In Chapter 1, the editors examine the rationale for the changes, first under the Conservatives and more recently under New Labour. It describes the ideology of the New Right which informed the policies of Conservative governments under

Margaret Thatcher and John Major and identifies the goals and objectives
to which they were committed. These are contrasted with the ideas, goals
and objectives associated with Labour's so-called Third Way, described by
Prime Minister Tony Blair, as 'a modernised social democracy . . . founded
on the values [of] – democracy, liberty, justice, mutual obligation and
internationalism'. Chapter 2, by the editors, revisits the debate about the
increasing convergence between the way that public and private organisations are managed and whether managers can move effectively between the
two sectors. Chapter 3, by Cope, explores the wider contexts of globalisation
and Europeanisation which are impacting on the ways in which the state is
being managed. It also examines the debates about the 'hollowing out' and
'filling in' of the state and integrates these seemingly contradictory trends in
an explanation of the changing anatomy of the British state.

Part II focuses on five major aspects of public management. Chapter 4, by
Isaac-Henry, provides an account of the strategic management process and
the reasons why it is considered both necessary and difficult to operate in
public organisations. He highlights its growing importance throughout the
public services but points out that there are critics who question its private-
sector origins and its relevance to the public sector. He concludes, however,
that the imperative to act strategically is likely to increase under New
Labour rather than to decrease. Rouse, in Chapter 5, traces the introduction
of performance management and quality management systems under successive Conservative governments and the challenges these have posed to
public organisations, because of their distinctive characteristics and their
multiple stakeholders. In the absence of real markets, profits and competition, which are the means of stimulating and measuring performance in the
private sector, substitutes have had to be found. Contracts, performance
indicators and quasi-markets are all surrogates that have their limitations.
He notes that the approach to performance and quality management under
New Labour shows signs of both continuity and change with earlier
Conservative administrations. Chapter 6, by Christy and Brown, examines
the relevance of marketing theory and practice to public services. They
illustrate how marketing techniques are being applied in public organisations to assist in the delivery of services to meet consumer and user needs.
Farnham, in Chapter 7, focuses on the management of people within the
public services. He argues that under the Conservatives there was a shift
away from a centralised, standardised, welfare-oriented system of personnel
management, and a collectivist system of industrial relations, towards a new
'human resources management' model and dualist system of employment
relations. He concludes that New Labour's employment policies in the
public services are unlikely to reverse that trend. In Chapter 8, Bellamy
focuses on one of the most radical aspects of the Blair government's agenda
for public services – its proposal to exploit information and communication
technologies (ICTs) to 're-engineer' government. After tracing the application of ICTs over the last 20 years, she explores the implications of the Blair

administration's white paper on *Better Government*, with its commitment to 'joined up government'. She raises questions about its social and political implications and, in particular, the vexed question of public accountability.

Part III consists of six cases of public management in key public services. Each summarises how management changed under the Conservatives and examines the impact of the New Labour government on them so far. Horton, in Chapter 9, discusses how the 'quiet revolution' in the civil service came about under the Conservatives and what New Labour inherited. She identifies the major differences of emphasis and priorities under New Labour, which are likely to ensure a continuation of organisational and cultural change rather than further radical reform. Painter and Isaac-Henry, in Chapter 10, demonstrate how changes introduced into local government during the 1980s and 1990s brought about a transformation of its role. This was away from a traditional service-provider role to a 'community leadership' one, which also created a fragmented system of local governance. New Labour is contributing to the momentum towards the 'community leadership' role but is committed also to replacing the system of fragmented and often adversarial governance, which it inherited, with a more holistic, joined-up one, and to eliminating poorly performing local councils through closer monitoring and control. Corby, in Chapter 11, shows how Conservative governments from 1979 to 1997 sought to resolve the inherent tensions within the NHS by structural and managerial reforms. She asserts that these tensions remain under New Labour and are unlikely to be removed by Labour's proposals for further structural reform and minor increases in public expenditure.

Holloway *et al.* demonstrate in Chapter 12 how all sectors of public education have experienced relentless change since the 1980s. The high profile given to education by New Labour, and the spate of legislation and policy documents produced since 1997, ensure that further change is inevitable. They conclude, however, that Labour's innovations tend to reinforce the Conservative emphasis on greater central control and improved management and that the legacy of 18 years of Conservative government is safe in Labour's hands, even though there are more students and more money in the system. Loveday, in Chapter 13, describes how management reforms comprehensively embraced the police service under the Conservatives, driven by both the Audit Commission and Her Majestys Inspectorate. New Labour's interest in performance management appears to be as strong as its predecessor's and is continuing to challenge any residual resistance within police organisational cultures to managerial changes. Greater emphasis on joined-up government in policing, however, is likely to place new demands on police managers to which they will have to respond. In the final case, in Chapter 14, May and Brunsdon explore the challenges facing social services in managing the transformation of community care. They trace the unprecedented changes in the structure and management of social services over the last decade and conclude that the

Blair government has accepted the basic principles on which they rest. New Labour is committed to a mixed economy of service provision but where it differs is in its approach to service allocation, regulation and performance management, and in its emphasis on partnership. Social service managers face further challenges of meeting more rigorous targets, controlling more costs and service activities and developing effective human resources strategies.

In Part IV, the editors identify and discuss the elements of continuity and change in management of the public services since 1997 and the election of New Labour to power. They conclude that manageralism is still firmly in place although markets and competititon no longer go unchallenged and the citizen has in part displaced the consumer.

Finally, completion of this book would not have been possible without the collaboration and cooperation of its contributors. In spite of competing work pressures and some personal difficulties, they still delivered their chapters and we thank all of them for making this book possible. Special thanks are due to John Rouse who stepped in at very short notice to write his chapter. Our thanks are also due to Irene Burrows, Nadine Wilson, Frances Jordan, Peter deLara and Joe Tuck who assisted with the various technical problems in compiling the manuscript. We would also like to thank Steven Kennedy for his support in commissioning this new book.

University of Portsmouth   SYLVIA HORTON
January 1999   DAVID FARNHAM

PART I

The Changing Contexts of Public Management

1

The Politics of Public Sector Change

SYLVIA HORTON and DAVID FARNHAM

The mid-1970s was a watershed in the development of the British state. These years marked the breakdown of the postwar settlement established after 1945, which was based on Keynesian economics and Beveridge social welfare policies, and rejection of the social democratic principles and values which had underpinned the modern welfare state. A new set of political and economic principles, values and policies emerged. These were associated with the New Right and influenced the transformation of the state, from a welfare to a contract model, over 18 years of uninterrupted Conservative government from 1979 to 1997. The Conservatives succeeded in redrawing the boundaries of the state, substituting markets for politics in the allocation of resources and modelling the remaining public sector on private business approaches to organisation and management. The hegemony of New Right ideas, which were at their most influential during the Thatcher administrations (1979–90), continued largely unchallenged under the premiership of John Major. However, when the Labour party led by Tony Blair was elected to office in May 1997, some claimed that 'New Labour' stood for a 'Third Way' in British politics. New Labour's approach was seen as a Third Way because, Labour reformers argued, the party had moved 'beyond an Old Left preoccupied by state control, high taxation and producer interests; and a New Right treating public investment, and often the very notion of "society" and collective endeavour, as evils to be undone' (Blair, 1998: 1). According to Giddens (1998: 26), the Third Way transends 'both social democracy and neoliberalism' and is presented as an alternative to both state socialism, associated with the postwar Labour party, and market-liberalism advocated by the Conservatives in the 1980s and 1990s.

These political and economic changes, in turn, are taking place in an increasingly turbulent and uncertain international environment. This is associated with the spread of corporate capitalism and globalisation, on the one hand, and the creation of supra-national political formations, such as the European Union (EU), and international systems of cooperation such

3

as the World Trade Organisation, on the other. Both sets of environmental changes are being accompanied and fuelled by a technological revolution, based on advanced computer systems, which is transforming the means of communication across the world, concentrating space and time and creating an information and knowledge explosion.

This chapter provides the political and ideological backgrounds to the book. It puts the changing British state and its critics into context and sets the scene against which changes in the managing of public services in the last 25 years are discussed and analysed in subsequent chapters. It also outlines developments in the size and scope of the British state, as it has moved from a social democratic consensus created after 1945 to a new consensus associated with Thatcherism and Majorism after 1979. Finally, it explores the extent to which the claimed Third Way is refashioning the state still further, by offering a 'new' political economy which contrasts with the orthodoxies and legacies of both the postwar settlement and the New Right.

Growth and decline of the state sector in Britain

In retrospect, Margaret Thatcher's Conservative administration, from 1979 to 1990, heralded a new stage in the development of the British state. During her premiership, and that of her successor John Major, significant changes took place both in the size and composition of the public sector and in the ways public organisations were structured and managed. However, in spite of the rhetorical commitment to roll back the state and reduce public expenditure, in 1997 the state sector still accounted for over 40 per cent of Britain's Gross Domestic Product (GDP), defined as the value of the goods and services produced by its residents annually, and it still employed over five million people.

The boundary between the state and non-state sectors is difficult to define, as we demonstrate in Chapter 2. The state sector includes central and local government, the armed forces, National Health Service (NHS), nationalised industries and an array of public fringe bodies with administrative, regulatory, advisory and adjudicatory functions. During the nineteenth and early twentieth centuries, the role of the state was essentially a regulatory one, regulating the dominant private sector and providing law and order and defence in the public domain. After the First World War, the state became more interventionist and collectivist as governments accepted greater responsibility for housing, education, health and social insurance and, in the 1930s, assisted regions hardest hit by the depression. Some public corporations were created, such as the British Broadcasting Corporation and Electricity Generating Board in 1926 and the London Passenger Transport Board in 1933. The amount of General Government Expenditure (GGE) rose from an average of 12.2 per cent of GDP (1904–14) to 25 per cent in the decade 1928–38.

During the Second World War, GGE rose dramatically to over 60 per cent as government planned and controlled the whole war economy. Immediately after the war, GGE fell as the country returned to a peace-time economy. Between 1945 and 1979, however, GGE rose steadily, never falling below a third of GDP and peaking at 48.8 per cent in 1975 (Farnham and Horton, 1996a). This reflected the catalytic effect of the war in changing social expectations about the role of the state in the economy and it provided the basis upon which the modern welfare state was created and extended (Marwick, 1968). It also enabled both Labour and Conservative administrations to sustain higher taxes and transfer expenditure to social welfare without any strong resistance from the electorate.

There was significant growth in all parts of the public sector after 1945. The Labour governments (1945–51), elected on a programme of radical economic and social reforms, embarked upon nationalisation of key in-dustries, economic and physical planning and a full programme of social welfare provision. Public-sector employment expanded rapidly with natio-nalisations adding over one million to the state payroll. The civil service grew to a peak of 740,000 staff by 1976 and local government grew at an even faster rate, since it was the key provider of new and extended services in housing, education and personal social services. Local government also had responsibility for environmental, physical and infrastructural development. Over one million people were employed in local government by the late 1940s and over three million by 1979. The creation of the NHS also brought doctors, health practitioners and ancillary workers into the public sector. By 1979, there were some seven million officials employed in public organisa-tions and many millions of private-sector workers were dependent for their employment on governmental contracts and state subsidies.

Alongside the increase in public employment went a corresponding increase in GGE. Government expenditure on goods and services, approxi-mately 13 per cent in the inter-war years, had doubled to nearly 27 per cent by the mid-1970s. Transfer payments, the second element in GGE, fluctu-ated although the trend was generally upward from the mid-1950s. This was due to a number of factors including changes in the numbers claiming benefits, increases in the range of benefits and increases in payment levels. Transfer payments rose from 11 per cent of GDP in 1954 to 23 per cent in 1975 (Farnham and Horton, 1996a).

Since 1979 patterns within GGE have changed, although there has been no significant reduction in the share of GDP that it represents. GGE averaged around 43.5 per cent of GDP throughout the 1980s, excluding revenues from privatisation, and remained consistently around that level during the 1990s despite governmental attempts to reduce it. State spending on goods and services varied by only 2 per cent throughout the period 1945–91, remaining fairly steady at about 23.5 per cent of GDP. Increases in government expenditure in the early 1980s were due in part to substantial pay increases in some public services and increased spending on law and order and defence, but primarily to the cost of supporting three million unemployed during the economic recession at that time. Marginal falls in GGE in the late 1980s coincided with an upturn in the economy and falling unemployment. With the onset of a second recession in 1990, the upward trend in GGE returned. When the Conservatives left office in 1997, GGE as a share of GDP was almost the same as when they had entered office in 1979. Actual spending over the period was partly concealed by the practice of financing public expenditure with proceeds of sales of nationalised industries, which accounted for some £64 billion between 1979 and 1996 alone. This was used to fund expenditure, reduce the public-sector borrowing requirement (PBSR) and, in the period 1987–8, repay national debt. Government public expenditure policy between 1979 and 1997 was tied closely to its economic policy which aimed to keep inflation down and stimulate economic growth through transferring resources from the public to the private sector. Its limited success in doing the latter was because of external demographic and economic pressures (Flynn, 1997).

The change of government to New Labour in 1997 appears to have made little difference to the situation inherited from the Conservatives. Labour committed itself to keeping within the public expenditure plans of the Major government for its first two years in office and not to increase income taxes in the life of its first Parliament. This essentially locked it into the existing Conservative framework, although there was scope for redistributing expenditure and resorting to other sources of funding. The current government's aims, however, are to continue seeking to reduce GGE as a percentage of GDP through controlling expenditure, particularly transfer payments, and to extract greater efficiency and 'best value' from the remaining public services.

The Postwar Settlement

It was the experiences of the interwar depression and the Second World War which eclipsed the economic orthodoxy of *laissez-faire*. This doctrine rests upon the belief that the economic affairs of society are best left to the market with the minimum of state intervention. As indicated above, there was a shift in economic thinking in the 1930s which supported a role for the state in economic planning, whilst the extensive intervention of the wartime government (1940–5) in managing the economy demonstrated that planning could work. The levelling effects of the war experience also led to a demand for more equality and acceptance of greater collectivism. These paved the way for a new economic and social role for the state which was the basis of the 'postwar settlement'.

The postwar settlement comprised three interrelated elements: a mixed economy and Keynesian economic policies; a welfare state, with universal social services; and a political consensus. The Keynesian approach involved governments assuming prime responsibility for managing and fine-tuning the economy and ensuring that there was a high level of aggregate demand for goods and services in order to maintain 'full employment'. Governments relied on a combination of fiscal, monetary and prices and incomes policies aimed at attaining four economic goals: full employment; price stability; balance of payments equilibrium; and economic growth. To achieve these goals, governments consulted widely with industry and the trade unions in the policy process. This system was called 'bargained corporatism' (Crouch, 1979).

The welfare state component of the postwar settlement is described by Marwick (1990: 45) as 'the totality of schemes and services through which the central government, together with the local authorities, assumed a major responsibility for dealing with all the different types of social problems which beset individual citizens'. A wide range of publicly and universally available services was provided including: social security payments and pensions, designed to ensure a minimum safety net for the unemployed, sick and elderly; a comprehensive NHS, free at the point of use; compulsory education up to the age of 15 (later 16); and public housing. This set of citizenship and social rights was the legacy of the Beveridge Report (1942), which was supported by all political parties in the wartime coalition.

The political consensus is described by Marquand (1988: 18) as the 'set of commitments, assumptions and expectations, transcending party conflicts and shared by the great majority of the country's political and economic leaders, which provided the framework within which policy decisions were made'. There was a high level of agreement across political parties and elites about the substance of public policy, especially on the mixed economy and the welfare state. The political consensus also referred to the tendency of new governments to accept their predecessor's legislation, even when, in opposition, it had opposed it (Kavanagh, 1987). Further, there was also an agreement on the nature of the political system and its key institutions. The political consensus did not go unchallenged but the minority who opposed it was overshadowed by widespread support for it.

By the 1970s, cracks were appearing in the consensus and opposition to it grew louder. It was the slowing down of economic growth in the 1970s which eventually undermined the Keynesian–Beveridge edifice and a turning point was the onset of the long world recession triggered by the sharp rise in oil prices after the Arab–Israeli war in 1973–4. Steady economic growth in the postwar period had reduced internal political tensions and eased the problem of governing the Keynesian welfare state, with increased taxation and rising government spending going hand-in-hand with rising standards of living and higher consumption. With recession and the slowdown of economic growth, political decisions became more difficult and the postwar consensus was weakened. This opened the way for new political and economic ideas to take its place.

It fell to Labour governments to deal with the economic crisis in the mid-1970s. Significant cuts in planned expenditure were imposed each year between 1974 and 1977 and GGE fell from 48.8 per cent of GDP in 1975–6 to 43.0 per cent in 1978–9. Unemployment was allowed to rise and real incomes allowed to fall. This weakening of Keynesian economic orthodoxy was paralleled by growing challenges to the welfare state. Some blamed the welfare state for Britain's economic problems, arguing that the high taxes required to sustain it fuelled inflation, reduced incentives and diverted scarce resources out of the 'wealth creating' private sector into the 'wealth consuming' public sector (Bacon and Eltis, 1976). Others accused the welfare state of being professionally dominated, lacking client involvement, acting as unaccountable monopolies and being poorly managed.

These critiques were mirrored in the breakdown in the social democratic consensus in politics, as the centre ground in British politics crumbled. A polarisation was emerging with the right wing of the Conservative party repudiating Keynesianism and welfarism in favour of the free market and personal responsibility, whilst the Labour party was moving to the left with proposals for more nationalisation and more socialism. With the Liberals – and later the Social Democratic Party formed in the early 1980s – filling the centre ground, it was the Conservatives, taking political power in 1979, who finally broke with the postwar consensus and introduced a new politics based on the ideas of the 'New Right'.

The New Right

The New Right critique of the postwar settlement contained elements of economic liberalism, anti-collectivism and social authoritarianism. It drew on the works and ideas of economic liberals such as Friedman (1962) and Hayek (1944 and 1973), public choice theorists, such as Buchanan (1975), Niskanen (1971) and Mueller (1979), and political economists such as Lindblom (1977). The influence of American thinkers on the New Right was dominant but the main outlets of New Right ideas in Britain were the Institute of Economic Affairs, Adam Smith Institute, Centre for Policy Studies and *The Salisbury Review*.

The key values underpinning New Right thinking were those of individualism, personal freedom, choice and inequality. These contrasted with the values of collectivism, social rights and equality which were associated with supporters of the Keynesian welfare state. The New Right emphasised the virtues and creative possibilities of the free market economy and attacked Keynesianism and Beveridgism. Markets were preferred to politics, both as means of producing and distributing goods and services in society and as institutional arrangements for providing social organisation and social control. Political systems, they argued, were particularly unsuited for creating economic welfare because of the inherent complexity of coordinating centrally planned economic decisions and the lack of knowledge of what people want. Markets, in contrast, were seen to facilitate economic prosperity through their efficiency in allocating scarce resources, whilst offering choice to consumers and producers in determining their own well-being and welfare. In addition the market was seen as an effective allocator of resources, an efficient coordinating mechanism and a rational decision-making process. Markets also encourage resourcefulness and enterprise, are flexible and allow room for invention and improvisation (Lindblom, 1977). Through the market, societal welfare can be obtained, without the state and politicians imposing specific values or prioritising economic wants or needs. The result is a 'spontaneous order' where the consumer is sovereign (Hayek, 1973). For the New Right, markets generally are believed to serve the public interest better than politics, with the main function of government being to make the best use of markets by letting them develop spontaneously to serve the public interest.

Although New Right economic liberals prefer markets to politics, some concede that there is a role for the state in providing public and merit goods such as defence, clean air, street lighting, policing and highways, as these are socially necessary but there are no economic incentives for individuals to participate in funding or providing them, unless forced to do so (Mueller, 1979). Other cases for state intervention are where the commodities produced within the market have externalities and social costs; where the market fails; or where the market is a monopoly. Finally, there is a case for supplying merit goods such as health and education where it is socially desirable that individuals have them, because they need them to function as active and purposeful citizens. However, New Right theoreticians disagree about where the boundaries of 'public goods' begin and end.

Public choice theorists claimed that the contradictions inherent in the social democratic, mixed economy were demonstrated by likening politics to a marketplace in which politicians are the 'producers', voters the 'consumers' and votes the 'currency'. Unlike the economic market, however, there is no cash nexus, so voters can make irreconcilable demands on politicians, such as wanting both lower taxes and more public goods, whilst politicians can promise what voters will 'buy', since they do not bear the economic costs of those choices (Downs, 1957). Just as in the economic market, monopolies also appear and a maldistribution of resources results from irrational power politics amongst interest groups. Public bureaucrats in particular, in pursuing their own self interests, promote growth and expansion of governmental functions which become overextended. A coalition of politicians and bureaucrats fuels the extension of political activities, leading to inefficiency, lack of democratic control and concentration of power in the hands of the monopolistic public suppliers. This 'overloaded government' thesis was not exclusive to the New Right (Rose and Peters, 1978) but gave support to the creative possibilities of the free market economy and the need to roll back the frontiers of the social democratic state.

New Right critics of the British welfare state drew heavily upon these American ideas and theories, arguing that the Keynesian welfare state created personal dependency, weakened individual responsibility, was led by professionals and bureaucrats and was unresponsive to individual needs and personal choice. There was no effective democratic control over monopoly suppliers of state services, whilst alternative sources of social welfare such as the family, local communities, voluntary bodies and the market were neglected and enfeebled. The New Right claimed that Keynesian welfarism was fundamentally inefficient, because macroeconomic management was inflationary and monopoly providers of welfare services were expensive. Only through market competition could economic efficiency be achieved. Their solution was free market choice.

The Politics of Thatcherism and Majorism, 1979–97

Conservative governments post-1979 were not simply vehicles for the New Right but radicals in the Conservative party were sympathetic to New Right proposals such as educational vouchers, private health insurance, abolition of child benefit and workfare. All these proposals were initially rejected as politically impracticable but privatisation in its many forms was introduced and internal market mechanisms became the centrepiece of major pillars of the state sector, such as in health and education, by the early 1990s.

There is no evidence that the Conservative government in 1979 had a blueprint or strategic plan which it consistently followed through. Rather it appears to have adopted an incremental and pragmatic approach and its policies unfolded as circumstances and opportunities permitted or as failures and problems called for new responses. What is clear, is that New Right ideas and values informed the strategic policy choices and implementation of programmes which all four Conservative administrations pursued between 1979 and 1997. The early policies made throughout the 1980s came to be associated initially with 'Thatcherism' and were described as 'New Right' to signify the difference between traditional and 'new' Conservatism. Although Thatcherism is difficult to define precisely and there are many different meanings attached to it (Gamble, 1988; Hall and Jacques, 1983 and 1989; Riddell, 1983), it is usually identified with the objectives and policies pursued by Conservative governments led by Margaret Thatcher between 1979 and 1990 and John Major subsequently. Their policies incorporated macro, meso and micro objectives.

The macro objectives included reversing Britain's relative economic decline, improving the efficiency of the economy, creating conditions for economic prosperity, 'destroying socialism' and reasserting Britain's world role in politics. Improving the efficiency of the economy was the core objective. Keynesian demand management policies and governmental *dirigisme* were abandoned in favour of monetarism, supply-side economic policies and deregulation of markets. Linked with these were the aims of removing the 'dependency culture', rolling back the frontiers of the state, creating a dynamic 'enterprise culture' and moving to an open, free market economy. Elimination of socialism, which was identified with social and economic equality, suppression of personal initiative, excessive bureaucracy and trade union power, was a necessary condition for free enterprise to thrive.

Making Britain 'Great' again had nationalistic undertones, emphasising Britain's international role in influencing foreign policy initiatives, defending the interests of the 'free world' and protecting her position in the European Community and subsequently in the EU. Paradoxically, free market policies aimed at opening up and internationalising the British economy were paralleled by governmental attempts to protect and safeguard the UK's political sovereignty.

The meso objectives were to revitalise private enterprise, increase the competitiveness of British businesses and strengthen the right to manage. Revitalising private enterprise was linked with reducing public enterprise and increasing business competitiveness. These were seen as fundamental in counteracting the growing competitive advantage of foreign firms, both domestically and internationally. Only by remaining competitive, it was argued, could British businesses survive and prosper and raise their share of European and world trade.

The Conservative's commitment to an enterprise culture meant strengthening the right to manage. This complemented their aim to weaken the trade unions both in collective bargaining and corporatist politics, as well as providing managers, in both private and public organisations, with greater authority and autonomy in enterprise decision-making. This would enable managers to react swiftly to changing product markets, obtain flexibility from their human resources and increase workforce productivity. In these ways, companies could become more efficient and more competitive in the marketplace, thus boosting the economy and leading to economic growth. Within public organisations, managers would replace administrators and professionals in taking responsibility for using resources efficiently and effectively in the pursuit of government's overall policy goals and objectives.

The micro objectives of successive Conservative governments included increasing consumer choice and consumer sovereignty in the marketplace, freeing individuals from the 'dependency state' and motivating individuals to take personal responsibility for themselves and their families. These objectives were at the heart of governmental economic and social strategy throughout the 1980s and early 1990s (Walker, 1990). The state's role was to be limited to encouraging individual freedoms, market opportunities and private enterprise. The tenets of market individualism within an enterprise culture were clearly set out in the first Thatcher government's budget statement (*Hansard*, 1979) and the themes were restated in successive election manifestos. As Walker (1990: 32) points out, such strategies were aimed at transforming economic and social life permanently, not just for the lifetime of a single Parliament.

The tactical means by which successive Conservative governments attempted to implement their strategic objectives consisted of three main sets of measures. The first was economic and designed to increase market competition, foster enterprise and create a 'business' culture. Government deregulated financial capital markets by removing exchange controls in 1979 and gradually deregulated the labour market with a series of Employment Acts (1980, 1982, 1988, 1989 and 1990), the Trade Union Act 1984 and Trade Union Employment Rights Act 1993, most of whose provisions were incorporated in the Trade Union and Labour Relations (Consolidation) Act 1992). Government also weakened trade unions by abandoning the postwar commitment to full employment, allowing unemployment to rise and encouraging market determination of wages. In addition, government paved the way for a bigger role for the market and private enterprise, first, by creating enterprise zones and development corporations to encourage business expansion and later by privatising the major public industries. Cuts in income tax were also made to encourage more spending, saving and investment.

Another major initiative was reducing the size of the public sector. As later chapters in this book illustrate, various means of rolling back the frontiers of the state were attempted. These included both selling off public enterprises to private shareholders and introducing competition into the remaining public sector. These policies had the triple effects of transferring the supply of services to the private sector, providing them through the market, or at least quasi-markets, and limiting government expenditure. Privatisation had the further advantage of raising additional revenue from the sale of state assets, thus avoiding increases in general taxation to fund government spending. By 1997, more than 90 public enterprises had been sold to the private sector. Competitive compulsory tendering (CCT) and contracting out in the public services, although limited in the early 1980s, was widespread by the 1990s (Greenwood and Wilson, 1994; Rao and Young, 1995). All these activities were associated first with monetarist and subsequently supply-side economic policies. Monetarism is predicated on the belief that governmental management of the rate of growth of money supply controls inflation. Supply-side economics posits that governmental intervention should be limited to improving the supply side of the economy, by creating the conditions enabling markets to function efficiently.

Other measures aimed at liberalising the British economy included reducing planning and development controls by local authorities, strengthening the role of the Monopolies and Mergers Commission and encouraging self employment and the small business sector. All these were directed towards facilitating economic competition and enterprise. Many statutory monopolies, such as local authority bus services, telecommunication and opticians services, were removed in the 1980s but the Deregulation and

Contracting Out Act 1994 was a major step in removing legal obstacles to involving the private sector in areas previously reserved for the state, such as administering public-sector pensions and transferring prisoners. A main advantage of expanding job opportunities to small businesses and self-employment was that this flagged up the ideologies of enterprise, wealth creation and self help. It was also a useful but limited means of reducing unemployment.

In order to achieve their economic objectives, Conservative governments had to create a strong state which could carry its policies through without political constraint from either local authorities or powerful pressure groups. Strengthening the role of central government involved using a range of policy instruments, including legislation, administrative directives and financial controls. After 1979, there was an explosion of legislative initiatives, aimed at strengthening central government, weakening local government and making local authorities and other public bodies agents of central government policy (Horton, 1990). A whole range of new public bodies appointed by central government was created to carry out government policies. This 'new magistracy' was not democratically elected or accountable. Central government also asserted its control over local government and other public bodies by using administrative directives and circulars. These covered managerial changes in the NHS and imposition of the national curriculum on schools. Perhaps the most important set of controls over local government and other bodies was financial. Conservative governments introduced over 20 changes in local government finance between 1979 and 1997 which effectively removed a great deal of independence of local government and resulted in central government controlling, directly or indirectly, the expenditure of individual authorities. 'Over-spending' authorities were initially rate-capped and then community-charge capped. The rating system was abolished and replaced, first, by the community charge and national business rate and, subsequently, by the council tax. By 1997, less than 20 per cent of local government tax revenue was raised locally. Further, local government capital expenditure was subject to ceilings. The financing of the NHS was cash limited and the few remaining nationalised industries were controlled by financial targets and borrowing controls to keep their expenditure within planned limits.

Conservative governments after 1979 also dispensed with many of the consultative political mechanisms which had characterised the corporatist, participative styles of previous governments. Tripartism in economic policy-making, involving government, the Trades Union Congress and the Confederation of British Industry, was abandoned. Major constitutional changes, like the abolition of the Greater London Council, were carried out without public enquiries, whilst radical legislative proposals were introduced with a minimum of time for interested parties to respond. In industrial relations, a series of Green Papers was used as the basis for definitive legislation, not for consultative purposes.

Strengthening the traditional responsibilities of the state in law and order and policing, as well as shedding some of its welfare and public service functions, were other tactical means for achieving governmental political and economic objectives during the 1980s and 1990s. Prior to 1979, law and order policy reflected the consensus politics of the postwar settlement but this changed after 1979, when it was placed high on the government's agenda (Savage, 1990). Whilst many other areas of government expenditure were subjected to a restrictive if not reductionist policy, the law and order budget was increased. There were increases in police staffing, pay and prison buildings and a major programme of legislation, reflecting a much harder line on law and order, giving more powers to the police. In parallel with these developments, government introduced a series of reforms in welfare and public service provision aimed at: encouraging the voluntary sector; making public services more efficient through internal and external competition; forcing public services to prioritise and ration what was provided to citizens; and encouraging individuals to assume personal responsibility for themselves through private insurances.

Government priorities changed in the early 1990s, although their direction remained the same. Police and the criminal justice system were submitted to the financial disciplines associated with the three 'Es' of 'economy', 'efficiency' and 'effectiveness' and were forced to adopt CCT and market testing, whilst competition was strengthened in other public services. There was greater concern for managing quality and citizens became the focal point of government's new rhetoric for the need to make it more responsive and accountable to the public it claimed to serve.

At international level, successive Conservative governments wanted to re-establish a powerful role for Britain, as part of their drive towards a strong centralised state. On taking office in 1979, government committed itself to making defence the first charge on public resources. This policy was reviewed, however, in the 1990s, with the ending of the 'Cold War' and collapse of the Communist regimes in Eastern Europe. This coincided with a change of leadership in the Conservative party and, under John Major a greater focus on Britain's role in the EU. Conservative governments remained committed to retaining the nuclear deterrent, partly to reinforce the claim that Britain was a world power and partly to reinforce Britain's 'special relationship' with the United States. Britain's relationship with the European Community and, after 1992, the EU was consistently ambivalent, with Conservative governments resisting attempts to suppress the nation state and British political sovereignty, whilst welcoming the single market and the opening of trade with an expanding membership. Britain's reluctance to join European Monetary Union and its refusal to sign the Social Chapter of the Maastricht Treaty led to the provision of 'opt outs'. Overall, there was a tendency to conservatism in foreign affairs.

The third set of tactical measures used by successive Conservative governments was linked to the goal of popular capitalism. Popular capitalism is 'the term applied to a variety of policies aimed at widening property ownership and consumer choice' (Gamble, 1988: 138). The objective was to weaken individual attachment to the welfare state and collectivist values and raise public consciousness of the ideas associated with the 'enterprise culture'. Widening property ownership was facilitated by the sale of council homes to tenants, encouraging individual shareholdings in denationalised industries, and employee share ownership schemes and profit sharing in the private sector. The policies of contracting out and deregulation of public services afforded opportunities for private companies to compete with public bodies in new areas such as refuse collection, policing, hospitals, nursing homes and professional services. Assisted places gave access to private schools, whilst tax relief on health insurance encouraged use of the private health sector. All these market initiatives were aimed at increasing competition and providing choices for 'consumers'.

The Emergence of 'New Labour'

Just as the 'New Right' under Margaret Thatcher drew its ideas and values from theorists and ideologists identified with it, so the ideas and values of New Labour can be found in the writings of sociologists, political scientists and political economists such as Giddens (1994, 1998), Marquand (1988) and Hutton (1995, 1997). The origins of New Labour thinking, however, lie as much within the party as outside it and are the result of a process of transformation which dates from the party's third consecutive electoral defeat in 1987. Following the post-mortem after this election, the Labour party began reforming itself. The first initiatives had been under Neil Kinnock, who had been elected leader in 1983, then under John Smith and finally under Tony Blair. Labour shifted to the right in the political spectrum, modified its political values and modernised its internal organisation in response to the party's need to be trusted by the electorate and become electable.

The concept of New Labour can be found in an article, written in *The Guardian* in June 1987, by a young Labour MP, Tony Blair, first elected to the House of Commons in 1983. Blair stated that the Labour party needed to rethink its attitudes to society and its institutions. He argued that 'whether it is education, or public ownership, or housing, it is not our values that are open to doubt . . . . It is (our) effectiveness that is in question'. He saw Labour's task as expressing its traditional values through new policies in which the country could believe. 'It is the Tories who say you have to choose between efficiency and social justice, that you can only have one at the expense of the other. It is Labour's historic task to show that the two, in fact, are essential partners.' To succeed, he wrote, 'we must have not just the appearance but the reality of being modern'. A modernised Labour party, in short, had to have both image and substance. And, according to early chroniclers of New Labour, the party's 'ideology, policies, membership and organisation all had to be transformed to give it the essential modern thrust it needs to be an effective governing party' (Mandelson and Liddle, 1996: 41).

In retrospect it is possible to see the stages through which the transformation took place. First there was a radical restructuring of the party organisation which reduced the power of trade unions, gave individual members and constituencies more influence and raised the profile of the party leader. Second, there was a major constitutional change with the rewriting of clause IV which signified not only a break with the past but also a symbolic rejection of traditional Labour party commitment to socialism through 'common ownership' of the means of production, distribution and exchange. This opened the way for different interpretations of what the Labour party stood for. Third, the reformed Labour party, under the leadership of Tony Blair, set about creating a new image and vision and developing policies on all aspects of social, economic and international affairs with the overriding aim of winning the 1997 general election (Farnham, 1997).

By the mid-1990s, the party was projecting itself as 'New Labour' and disassociating itself from 'old' Labour with its images of class-based politics, nationalisation, trade union control and state monopolies (Gould, 1998). It sought to present itself as a renewed, social democratic party but still loyal to the fundamental values which underpinned old Labour. What then does New Labour stand for? Certainly, it is different from old Labour. Mandelson and Liddle (1996), for example, identify seven main attitudinal differences between the two which relate to: the private sector, incentives, public ownership, public expenditure, the role of the state, Europe and the trade unions. Old Labour preferred indicative, centralised planning, whereas New Labour accepts free, dynamic markets. Old Labour supported high taxes on incomes, whereas New Labour favours low taxes and believes that incentives are necessary for risk taking. Old Labour supported public ownership, whilst New Labour believes that social objectives can be met through properly regulated markets. Old Labour equated high public spending with more equality, whereas New Labour recognises the importance of how public money is spent, not just how much is spent. Old Labour believed in statist solutions to people's problems, whereas New Labour aims to help people achieve things for themselves. Old Labour was divided on Europe, whereas New Labour wants to participate in Europe. Old Labour supported the corporatist concept of politics and legitimised the union block vote in party affairs; New Labour supports a 'stake-holder' concept of the economy and seeks to involve individual trade unionists in party affairs. However, the messages and evidence which New Labour provides, in terms of its values and policies, are somewhat ambiguous and are open to differing interpretations. There is little or no agreement about what New Labour stands for.

One interpretation of New Labour is that it is essentially a continuance of the 'new' politics initiated by Margaret Thatcher and John Major in the 1980s and early 1990s. New Labour fought and won the 1997 election largely on policies which, less than 10 years earlier, were associated with the New Right and repudiated by the old left. According to Hay (1997: 373 and 377) Britain is witnessing the 'unfolding of a new state regime' and a 'new consensus' which has moved from a Keynesian welfare settlement 'towards a neo-liberal post-Thatcher settlement'. For him, 'Blajorism' has replaced 'Butskellism' and is a 'one-vision' form of politics providing a new convergence between the two main political parties which reflects 'Labour's accommodation to the newly ascendant and seemingly unassailable neo-liberal economic and political paradigm'. Indeed the 1997 general election 'may well mark a symbolic transition from a one-party state to a one-vision polity'.

A second interpretation of New Labour is that it epitomises the revival of a 'one nation' political economy. Although rooted in Labour values, New Labour's political project is perceived as being based on 'the middle way' in politics which builds upon moderation, compromise, commonsense and national unity in political affairs. It is a 'conservative' approach to politics as practised by Stanley Baldwin in the interwar years, argued for by Harold Macmillan (1938) in the 1930s and Ian McLeod (1950) in the immediate postwar period and supported by postwar Conservative governments in the pre-Thatcher years. This view of New Labour's political position posits that the party now represents a wide coalition of interests in Britain, drawing its political support from across all social strata including some old Labour, blue-chip Tories and traditional political liberals as well as Labour modernisers. It was highlighted in the party leader's preface to Labour's manifesto at the 1997 election, where he wrote (1997: 1): 'I want a Britain that is one nation, with shared values and purposes . . . . And I want . . . to govern in a way that brings our country together, that unites our nation in facing the tough and dangerous challenges of the new economy and changed society in which we must live.' Like one-nation Toryism, one-nation New Labourism can be interpreted as unitarist, pragmatic and rejecting ideology in favour of 'what works'.

A third interpretation of New Labour is that its values and policies represent a renaissance of collectivist, social liberalism. This defines New Labour as a 'new, progressive liberal coalition, committed to *laissez-faire* economics and a loose notion of social justice' (Hutton, 1998: 29). It is epitomised by not only the differences within the party between traditionalists and modernisers but also the similarities in policy between New Labour and the Liberal Democrats, and the close personal links between Tony Blair and Paddy Ashdown, Leader of the Liberal Democrats. This concept of New Labour perceives the party as shifting towards a modernised version of Gladstonian liberalism. To critics such as Hutton (ibid.), a political economy of this type rests on the assumption that interventionist initiatives by government in the contemporary economy obstruct the natural course of markets and entrepreneurship and are therefore to be avoided. It is epitomised by the view that 'we must accept capitalism as it is and equip individuals better to adjust to it.'

A fourth interpretation of New Labour's political project, and the one which has been most richly commented upon, is that it represents a 'Third Way' in British politics. By this view, New Labour's historic mission is to revive social democracy in Britain and provide the basis of a new politics for the millenium. For Tony Blair (1998: 1):

> The Third Way stands for a modernised social democracy, passionate in its commitment to social justice and the goals of the centre-left, but flexible, innovative and forward-looking in the means to achieve them. It is founded on the values that have guided progressive politics for more than a century – democracy, liberty, justice, mutual obligation and internationalism. But it is a *third* way because it moves decisively beyond an Old Left preoccupied by state control, high taxation and producer interests; and a New Right treating public investment, and often the very notions of 'society' and collective endeavour, as evils to be undone.
>
> My vision for the 21st century is of a popular politics reconciling themes which in the past have wrongly been regarded as antagonistic – partiotism *and* internationalism, rights *and* responsibilities, the promotion of enterprise *and* the attack on poverty and discrimination . . . .
>
> The Third Way is not an attempt to split the difference between Right and Left. It is about traditional values in a changed world . . . uniting the two great streams of left-of-centre thought – democratic socialism and liberalism – whose divorce this century did so much to weaken progressive politics across the West.

Giddens (1998: vii, 26, 64, 66 and 70) argues that the 'Third Way' refers 'to a framework of thinking and policy-making that seeks to adapt social democracy to a world which has changed fundamentally over the past two or three decades.' For him, the overall aim of Third Way politics 'should be to help citizens pilot their way through the major revolutions of our time: *globalisation, transformations in personal life* and our *relationship to nature*'. Giddens identifies seven sets of values with which New Labour is identified: 'equality', 'protection of the vulnerable', 'freedom as autonomy', 'no rights without responsibilities', 'no authority without democracy', 'cosmopolitan pluralism' and 'philosophic conservatism'. He goes on to refer to a 'programme in the making', incorporating ten elements: 'the radical centre', 'the new democratic state (the state without enemies)', 'active civil society', 'the democratic family', 'the new mixed economy', 'equality as inclusion', 'positive welfare', 'the social investment state', 'the cosmopolitan nation' and 'cosmopolitan democracy'. For Giddens the Third Way is 'an attempt to transcend both old-style social democracy and neoliberalism . . . and to appeal to all classes and sections of society'.

The Politics and Values of New Labour

New Labour's electoral victory in 1997 was thought by many to mark the end of the domination of New Right ideology in Britain and the beginning of a 'new' era of politics. The evidence, after Labour's first two years in office, suggests that although there is a different tone in government and New Labour's basic values and policy priorities are different from those of the Thatcher and Major administrations, there is also a great deal of continuity. New Labour occupies a 'middle ground' in politics which has shifted to the right over the last 20 years and, because of this, it has had to embrace the new neo-liberal consensus which has replaced the old postwar settlement. As Hay (1997: 373) suggests, Blairism is perhaps best described as a 'neo-liberal post-Thatcher settlement'.

The macro economic and social objectives of New Labour differ little in substance from those of its Conservative predecessors. They are clearly rooted in an acceptance of market-based capitalism, the inevitability of economic globalisation and the need to ensure that Britain is able to compete in a rapidly changing, technologically-driven world economy. The Labour government is committed to strengthening the British economy, making it more efficient and competitive, and 'working together with industry to achieve key objectives aimed at enhancing the dynamics of the market, not undermining it' (Labour Party, 1997: 3). It seeks 'personal prosperity for all', stable economic growth, low inflation and a dynamic and competitive business and industry at home and abroad. This is largely a commitment to the same economic objectives as the Conservatives. Similarly, Labour's aim to build a modern welfare state based upon individual rights and responsibilities and eliminate the culture of dependency echoes Conservative pledges of the past. Labour is also pledged to reinstate Britain in a leadership role internationally (Labour Party, 1997: 37).

> Britain will be strong in defence; resolute in standing up for its own interests; an advocate of human rights and democracy the world over; a reliable and powerful ally in the international institutions of which we are a member; and will be a leader in Europe.

Although New Labour's emphasis on human rights and its more positive attitude towards Europe is a significant difference between the parties, Blair's special relationship with President Clinton and his strong and resolute stand in Middle Eastern affairs suggest a re-run of Thatcher's interpretation of being a key player in international relations. Two macro aims of New Labour which are different from the Conservatives, however, are its commitment to constitutional reform and a revitalised democracy and its determination 'to clean up politics' and renew people's trust and confidence in government and politicians.

An analysis of New Labour's meso objectives also reveals close resemblances to those of the Conservatives, as it seeks to increase the competitiveness of British business, encourage enterprise, raise general educational standards and the skills of the labour force, reduce unemployment by providing opportunities to become employable and achieve better government through more efficient and effective management of public services.

The basic micro objectives of the Conservatives also appear to underpin those of New Labour. These include a commitment to freeing individuals from dependency on the state and motivating them to take personal responsibility for themselves and their families; increasing personal choice; rewarding hard work, ability and success; not increasing income taxes, promoting self-help; and encouraging entrepreneurialism.

What has changed are the values and core beliefs that are informing Labour's policies and priorities. In contrast to the crude possessive individualism of the New Right, its unquestioned belief in the superiority of private enterprise and the market and its negative assumptions about state provision, public services and abuse of power by professions and trade unions, New Labour offers an alternative set of values. One of these is the belief in a strong civil society, in which individuals can thrive, 'comprising strong families and civic institutions and intelligent government' (Blair, 1998: 3). Another is the belief that individual and collective interests have to be accommodated through cooperation and partnership so that all are included within the social and political fabric. Competition is not rejected but is only one means of achieving economic ends. A third belief is the 'drive to "reinvent" national government' to promote the 'common good'. This aims to find new ways of enabling citizens to share in the decisions affecting them through active government nationally and partnerships at local level, incorporating national standards but local freedom to manage and innovate (ibid.: 15).

Justice is a key value of New Labour and Blair claims that there are four elements essential to promote a just society, that is one seeking to maximise the freedom and potential of all its people. These are equal worth, opportunity for all, responsibility and community. Equal worth means eliminating all forms of discrimination and prejudice based on other than individual ability and effort. Opportunity for all means seeking the widest spread of wealth, power and opportunity by tackling the obstacles which limit access to these resources. Responsibility must balance rights, since 'rights and opportunity without responsibility are engines of selfishness and greed' (Blair, 1998a: 4). Thus whilst people should take responsibility for their own health, education and long-term security and for their children, they need to be helped when they are unable to do so. Strong communities are essential to individual and family well-being and are the bulwark against social exclusion, social disintegration and alienation. Although markets are an effective mechanism for allocating resources, they have imperfections which only the state can regulate and control. There is a role for the state as owner, provider, enabler and promoter but the test of who does what must be 'best value'. This puts 'pressure on the public sector to raise its game, and encourages public–private co-operation' (ibid.: 17). It is these sorts of values and ideas, then, which underpin the policies of New Labour which, as its manifesto claimed, 'is a party of ideas and ideals but not of outdated ideology' (Labour Party, 1997: 4).

New Labour in Action

The Labour party's manifesto in 1997 set out 177 pledges, arguing that it had entered into a contract with the people to deliver on 10 major commitments. After 18 months in office it claimed 'that 50 of its pledges had been carried out, 119 were under way and only eight had yet to be timetabled' (Labour Party, 1998: 3). This was an impressive record for any government and reflected in part the high state of preparedness of Labour when they assumed office. Many Labour shadow ministers and political advisers had been in talks with civil servants for up to a year before the election and so departments were prepared for Labour's policy programme. Labour's immediate priorities were education, crime and law and order, the NHS, a 'New Deal' for the unemployed and constitutional reform.

Constrained by its commitment not to increase income taxes or value added tax, and to operate within the public expenditure targets of its predecessor for two years, Labour had limited scope for extra spending in its early period of office. Extra money was raised, however, by imposing a 'windfall tax' on the privatised public utilities and this enabled government to find £2.3 billion for education, an extra £1.2 billion for the NHS and to make progress on its New Deal and Welfare to Work programmes. It also reduced corporation taxes to encourage business investment and released £900 million of impounded local authority funds from council house sales for housing investment. Other major developments in its first year of office were relatively 'low cost' initiatives, including passing legislation to hold referenda on devolution for Scotland and Wales, reform of local government in London, signing the Social Chapter of the Maastrict Treaty and setting up an array of public enquiries and consultative exercises to underpin developments of new policies.

By late 1998, the tactics and strategies of the Labour government became clearer after publication of its Comprehensive Spending Review (HM Treasury, 1998). This set out government's plans for securing its key objectives of increasing sustainable growth and employment, promoting fairness and opportunity in the economy and society and modernising public services. Public spending is being directed, first, into delivering high and sustainable levels of economic growth and employment. This is to be achieved by compensating for past under-investment in Britain's labour force, its economic infrastructure and transport system and its scientific and technological base. Improving educational achievement is a top priority of government, as it sees higher skills as the means of achieving higher productivity, innovation and improved employability. Investing in schools is the key to improving long-term prospects for economic growth, whilst investment in further and higher education is aimed at improving the skills of people of working age (see Chapter 12). Government's Welfare to Work and New Deal programmes are designed to support a number of objectives including getting the under-25s and the long-term unemployed back into work, assisting lone mothers and the disabled who want to work to do so and modernising the structure and management of the national employment service so that it becomes more 'user focused, flexible and responsive to local labour markets. Coupled with the reform of the social security and income support system it is intended to make work pay ' (Finn, 1998). In the longer term, this is expected to reduce public expenditure, as people are weaned from dependency upon state benefits whilst ensuring that Britain has a modern skilled workforce.

In order to be successful in the new global economy, companies need a first-class research base and the ability to translate good ideas into market-able products. Government is therefore investing in strengthening Britain's science base, in partnership with the private sector, by equipping universities with laboratories and hardware and providing money for research councils to fund new projects (see Chapter 12). Further tactics for stimulating economic growth include working closely with business to meet its needs and provide it with advice. A policy of low inflation, prudent public expenditure and a low PSBR, which is restricted solely to financing investment and not current expenditure, is designed to win business confidence. Government is also reforming subsidies and encouraging capital investment by increased use of public–private partnerships and the Investing in Britain Fund. The latter is aimed at providing for the renewal and modernisation of Britain's public sector capital stock and is specifically aimed at improving the transport system. This is all designed to support industry and commerce.

Government's second spending priority is to enhance fairness and op-portunity, which overlaps with its first priority of creating a modern, dynamic economy. Access to work and work opportunities are seen as the key to individual autonomy and personal well-being. But the Welfare to Work programme has to be complemented by investing in major social services. This includes putting money into the NHS to ensure that high-quality health care is available on the basis of need, not ability to pay. Investing in education is necessary so that problems of deprivation are tackled at source, with children at risk of social exclusion being especially targeted. A 'sure start' programme, aimed at the under-threes, is to help children get a better start in life, whilst a wide range of associated educational reforms are aimed at attacking truancy, poor educational performance and failing schools. At the other end of the educational spectrum, help is to be made available to those who have traditionally missed out on opportunities for further and higher education. New educa-tional maintenance allowances are designed to encourage young people to stay on at school or college and become better qualified.

New investment in public housing, coupled with housing management reforms, is designed to lever up standards in all local authorities to those of the best. Some £3.6 billion is committed to refurbishment and maintenance of council housing, whilst a new housing inspectorate will be responsible for ensuring high-quality service from local authority housing management. Investment in communities is to be the means of tackling poverty and social exclusion at grass-roots level. Also as part of its reform of social services, government is making priority investment in services for children in care and young people leaving care (see Chapter 14). Government states that 'the NHS, education and other key services which form the basis of the welfare state, are the bedrock of a fair society and affect the quality of all our lives.' These investments in reforms are designed to ensure that 'these services meet the changing demands of the modern world' (HM Treasury, 1998: 27). A distinctive approach underlies government committment to be 'tough on crime and tough on the causes of crime'. Reforms of the criminal justice system are aimed at eliminating duplication and lack of coordination of the agencies involved (see Chapter 13) but there is also investment in tackling the underlying causes of crime, which government identifies as social exclusion, lack of skills and drug dependency. Greater emphasis is now being placed on crime prevention and rehabilitation.

Most poverty is, however, the result of unemployment or lack of skills. Here government is tackling the problem with a series of programmes including the New Deal, introduction of a statutory minimum wage, reform of social security and introduction of the Working Families Tax Credit. Welfare to Work is aimed at making work pay, enabling people to rise out of poverty, and is targeted particularly at lone mothers, young unemployed and long-term unemployed. Once again education and training are to be the major vehicles for tackling poverty, as they are designed to provide people with the skills to enable them to work. Government also has a New Deal for Communities which is providing funding and integrated help in innovative ways for small, extremely deprived neighbourhoods. In addition to tackling multiple barriers to employment and investing in improving the fabric of these communities, there is also commitment to involving local people in the management of their communities and delivery of public services, to empower them to take control.

Investing in reform for efficient and modern public services is the third spending priority of government and involves new public service agreements between departments and the Treasury, new systems of monitoring and audit, cross-departmental budgets to facilitate joined-up government, higher quality standards and efficiency targets and procurement reform. All government departments are encouraged to 'invest to save', with the aim of both improving services and reducing costs. Government has no dogmatic view of how public services should be delivered and sees its bottom line as ensuring delivery of high quality services to taxpayers. It believes that this can be done through the public, private or voluntary sectors or in partnership. Choice of delivery depends largely on what works best. A key priority of government, however, is that the work of its departments and agencies should be coordinated and integrated and that they should focus on the needs of 'clients' receiving their services.

Conclusion

It is generally accepted that 18 years of Conservative rule from 1979 to 1997 brought about a transformation of the British state and its electoral geography. Informed and guided by a neo-liberal ideology, successive governments redrew the boundaries of the state, changed public expectations about the functions of government and restructured and managerialised public organisations. The former postwar consensus resting on Keynesian economics, Beveridge concepts of universal social services and a political elite which accepted existing liberal democratic institutions had been replaced by the mid-1990s with a new consensus, based on a renewed neo-liberal economic orthodoxy. This consists of an acceptance of the superiority of the market over state provision and of neo-classical economic ideas on the causes of inflation and unemployment. The role of the state is to assist the private sector in wealth creation which ensures employment and the rising standards of living of the population. Welfare becomes largely the responsibility of individuals for themselves and their families, although the state has to ensure that those unable to provide for themselves are provided with basic rights. Rights, however, have to be balanced by responsibilities, with dependency a residual option.

The question dominating current political discourse is whether New Labour has embraced the new political consensus and neo-liberalism, by offering adjustments and adaptations to an essentially post-Thatcherite terrain, or whether it represents a radically new response to the core political issues of the day. A secondary question is whether a second period in office would allow New Labour to develop 'the Third Way' into a more coherent social democratic ideology and thereby begin to evolve another consensus, in true dialectical fashion, which would synthesise Keynesian–Beveridgism orthodoxy with neo-liberalism.

Some early political judgements are that New Labour has failed to break with neo-liberalism. Hobsbawm (1998) argues, for example, that New Labour could not be expected to reverse what the Conservatives had done nor should they have tried, as many of the electorate believed that much of what happened needed doing. New Labour is also constrained by the dominance of neo-classical academic economists who dream of a nirvana of an optimally efficient and frictionless economy and of a self-adjusting global market, that is to say, an economy with minimal interference by states and other institutions (ibid.: 5). Furthermore, New Labour accepts the inevitability of globalisation, growing world markets and the inability of governments to control national economies. Finally, New Labour believes that it can only win elections if it appeals to the middle ground of politics and, in particular, to those of the middle classes who have embraced Thatcherism and benefited from it. This constrained New Labour's project and ensured that much of the neo-liberal consensus was reflected in Labour's Manifesto in 1997.

Hall's (1998: 9) judgement also is that 'stripped of its hyperbole the continuities with Thatcherism are all too obvious'. In his view, Blair has set out to model himself in the Thatcherite mould and project his populist style of leadership through the media directly to the people by continual exposure and walk-abouts. But unlike Thatcherism, which was a project with a strategy and an underlying social and economic philosophy, 'the Third Way' appears to be little more than a projection of sociological trends on to the political screen and lacks a strategic framework or ideology. For Jacques (1998: 3) too, New Labour does 'not usher in a new era but more properly belongs to the end of the previous one'.

On the other hand, Mulgan (1998: 15), challenges critics who argue that New Labour 'is obsessed with presentation to the exclusion of content [and that it] has sold out to a right-wing agenda'. He points out that the New Labour project is about an agenda for change, it is about creating a humanised capitalism, a regulated international world economy and a fairer and more equal society. True to its social democratic credentials, it is committed to redistributive justice and removing inequalities in wealth, income and opportunities which have grown over the last 20 years. Passionately committed to democracy, the party and government have set out not only to introduce major constitutional changes to extend democracy and bring government closer to the people but also to reinvent a new corporatism in which all stakeholders are involved in formulating and influencing government across the policy spectrum. For Mulgan then, a member of Blair's Number 10 Policy Unit, Britain is experiencing 'a very rare period of radical transformation' (ibid.: 16).

After only two years in office, it is too soon to know which analysis of New Labour will prove to be correct. Looking to North America, however, where the Third Way was first projected by Bill Clinton, New Labour may learn some lessons. Robert Reich (1998), a member of the Clinton cabinet from 1993 till 1997, states that the 'Third Way doesn't have a chance unless political leaders are willing to devote serious political capital to making it happen.' Economic change has traditionally produced winners and losers and the Third Way aims to create a 'win-win' situation. This can only be achieved if government spends money in providing support systems to ease change. For Britain, fiscal prudence may appear necessary to maintain the support of the financial and business sectors and meet the criteria necessary for eventual entry into European Monetary Union but it possibly dooms the Third Way to failure. As Reich suggests: 'For the Third Way to succeed it has to be turned into a political movement, based on a new social contract between winners and losers. In return for the winners gaining what they need to do even better, they must agree to apply a portion of the added booty to the things that give the others a fair shot at joining the winners' circle.' Failure to do this in the USA hobbled the Third Way. Tony Blair and New Labour modernisers need to learn this lesson if the Third Way is to become a political reality in Britain.

2

Managing Public and Private Organisations

DAVID FARNHAM and SYLVIA HORTON

The debate about markets and politics and the role of the state in producing goods and services, which dominated the 1970s and 1980s, raised the issue of whether there are differences between the ways that organisations located in the 'public' and 'private' domains are structured and managed. One view was that there were significant differences reflected in the use of different terms to describe the processes of running organisations in the public and private sectors. 'Management' described the way that private businesses were run, whilst 'administration' was a description of the approach to running public bodies. The former was associated with a so-called rationalist approach to organisational decision-making, with managers seen as the agents for achieving organisational goals and corporate growth with the most efficient use of resources. In the public sector, by contrast, public officials, employed by state agencies, implemented and executed governmental policies determined by the political authorities within a framework of law, where efficient use of resources was of only secondary importance.

An alternative view was that 'management' and 'administration' are simply different terms for describing similar activities and that the words are used interchangeably (Self, 1965: 8). The implication here is that the practices and activities of managing are generic and that private-sector managerial practices are wholly transferable to public organisations and vice versa. A third view, which emerged in the 1980s, was that recent changes in public organisations had led to a 'new public management' which was different from both traditional 'public administration' and private 'business management'. Perry and Kraemer (1983) claimed that the new public management (NPM) was merging traditional public administration with the instrumental orientation of business management. This new model of management reflected both the unique nature of public organisations, stemming from the scope and impact of their decisions, and their fundamental political character. The purpose of this chapter is to examine these views and consider whether managing public organisations is similar to or different from managing in the private sector. It contrasts managing private businesses with traditional administration in the public services as a basis for assessing the nature of the managerial changes that have taken place in Britain since the 1980s.

Private and Public Organisations

Organisations are social constructs created by groups in society to achieve specific purposes by means of planned and coordinated activities of their technical systems and those working in them. These activities include using human resources to act in association with other inanimate resources to achieve the aims of the organisation. Private organisations are those created by individuals or groups for market or welfare purposes. They are ultimately accountable to their owners or members. Private organisations take the forms of unincorporated associations, companies, partnerships and voluntary bodies. Private organisations are normally businesses or non-profit organisations. Businesses vary widely in size and scope, from small scale, local enterprises to large, multinational companies and provide a wide range of goods and services in the primary, secondary and tertiary sectors of the economy. Private not-for-profit organisations are even more heterogeneous, varying not only in size and ownership but also in function, ranging from trade unions, friendly societies and sports clubs to charities and self-help groups. What distinguishes private businesses from public organisations, in addition to their goals, ownership and accountability, are their criteria for success which are largely economic or market in nature. There is less distinction between public and private not-for-profit organisations because neither are dominated primarily by market and economic factors. However, in recent years it can be argued that there has been a convergence not only within the not-for-profit sectors but also between them and the for-profit business sector.

Public organisations are created by government for primarily political purposes. They are ultimately accountable to political representatives and the law for achieving the objectives set for them. Their criteria for success are less easy to define than those of private organisations, since they include social and market measures as well as political ones. Public organisations cover a wide range of activities and encompass all those public bodies which are involved in making, implementing and applying public policy throughout the British state. They include the Post Office – which is the only remaining nationalised industry – other public corporations, central departments, local authorities, non-departmental agencies, the National Health Service (NHS) and a multiplicity of fringe bodies which are collectively known as the machinery of government or governance.

In practice, when it comes to establishing a dividing line between the public and private sectors, the distinction is blurred and it is difficult to determine where public organisations end and private ones begin. Tomkins' (1987) spectrum of organisational types, ranging from the 'fully private' to the 'public without competition', illustrates the interdependence and inter-relationships which exist between the private and the public spheres. His typology is as follows:

1   Fully private
2   Private with part state ownership
3   Joint private and public ventures
4   Private regulated
5   Public infrastructure, operating privately
6   Contracted out
7   Public with managed competition
8   Public without competition.

Tomkins adds to the debate about the relative merits of 'markets' and 'politics' by suggesting reasons why organisations might be located at particular points in the spectrum. Where there are no social issues and no specific social needs to be protected, and ability to pay for the organisation's goods or services is seen as a fair mechanism for distributive purposes, fully private organisations are appropriate providers. Where there is potential for social issues to arise, and where governmental action may be needed to protect the public interest, part state ownership is appropriate. Joint private and public ventures are found where there are commercial risks involved. In the past it was because the private sector was unwilling to bear them that government stepped in. In recent years, however, the private sector has stepped in to bear the risks that the public sector does not want to, largely because government investment and policies have been used to make private provision an attractive proposition.

Private regulated organisations exist where the private sector operates within a legal framework imposing requirements and limits on their activities. Regulatory bodies such as the Office of Telecommunications and Office of Gas Supply monitor British Telecommunications and British Gas respectively. They control standards of provisioñ, examine prices and in some areas ensure supply of the service. Private regulated organisations are generally found where there are monopolistic or near-monopolistic suppliers and where there is a need to protect consumers and the public interest from possible abuse of market power.

Some sectors of industry rely upon a public infrastructure, with private organisations supplying and operating a service. Examples are found in transport where government builds and maintains roads or supplies air-ports, with private bus companies, haulage contractors and airlines operating the services. This mode of private/public provision is used to facilitate a wider adoption of market mechanisms but with the state guaranteeing the necessary investment to ensure that markets respond to public needs. Historically, underwriting or subsidising of the private sector has been a key feature in Britain and most other states.

Contracting out public services to private suppliers has always been open to governmental organisations. Central and local government, for example, have traditionally used private construction companies to build state schools, hospitals, roads and so on. They have also obtained supplies of goods and services from private wholesalers or manufacturers and negotiated research contracts with private firms and establishments. This type of market relationship enables public bodies not only to avoid overheads and use the specialised expertise of the private sector but also to monitor the contractor. It is in this area that major changes have occurred in recent years as government has moved from being the provider of services to the manager of a 'contract state'.

There is also the option of internal markets or 'managed competition'. This is where public organisations provide services but are encouraged to compete with one another for either contracts or individual customers. The 'purchaser-provider' system introduced into the NHS in 1990 is an example of this. Finally, there are public organisations which provide public goods or services without competition such as defence, policing and the administration of justice, although even here some market elements are appearing. There are no *a priori* economic reasons why some goods or services should be provided exclusively by private organisations or public ones. Ultimately the relative configuration of private and public organisations in society reflects political choices and priorities, not economic ones. Tomkins (ibid) suggests the focus should be on the appropriate form of management for each activity rather than ideological support for its location in either the private or public sector.

Management in Private Organisations

The distinctive feature of the private sector model of management is that it is largely market driven. This means that the ways in which private organisations are managed reflect the market environment in which they operate. Success, growth or even survival for private businesses depend on the ability of their managerial cadres to manage effectively the dynamic economic environment facing them. Ultimately, it is 'meeting the bottom line' which counts. Unless, over time, private businesses are able to satisfy customer demand in the marketplace, provide a surplus of revenues over costs and ensure capital investment programmes for the future, they cease to trade as viable economic units. Private businesses, in short, must be both profitable and economically efficient to survive in the market place. The managerial function within them derives from these basic facts of economic life.

Goals and Accountabilities

Every organisation is set goals to achieve by those governing it. Goals establish the reasons for an organisation's existence. They are important because they act as guides for decision-making and a reference standard for evaluating success. Goals are translated by senior management into objectives and policies which provide the framework and parameters within which operational managers, and their subordinates, are expected to carry out their job tasks. Private businesses in general tend to have less complex, more easily stated and less-disputed goals than those of public organisations. This is because they are market-centred enterprises and must have the economic goal of creating a profit, for distributing as dividends to shareholders and for reinvesting in the business. Second-order goals such as organisational growth and expansion, business reputation, market domination, brand leadership and product diversification may be set by managers but these goals are also largely market driven. Private businesses, in short, are for-profit organisations.

Large businesses generally have corporate plans detailing how their goals are to be operationalised into specific objectives, over three, five or even ten-year periods. It is this planned, rational approach to objectives and target setting, within the boundaries of business goals, which is often singled out as the distinctive feature of the large business sector and the way it is managed. Other managerial activities associated with business organisations include: identifying the total business and its markets; forecasting likely changes in the environment; acting to take advantage of market opportunities or averting market threats; and focusing on the needs of the organisation's customers (Johnson and Scholes, 1999).

Not-for-profit private organisations, or voluntary bodies, have goals generally concerned with mutual self-help, the interests of their members, or social welfare. Their managements have to ensure a surplus of revenue over costs or at least break-even and are normally actively involved in generating funds to finance their organisational activities. Like their profit-centred counterparts, they have to be organised and managed efficiently and effectively. But their criteria for success are not profit related. In this sense, they have more in common with 'not-for-profit' public services than private commercial organisations (Hudson, 1995)

All organisations, whether private or public, are ultimately responsible, through their governing bodies, for the actions they take, in seeking to achieve their goals and objectives. They have a duty to use the resources they employ efficiently and provide goods or services to their customers, taking account of their obligations to a variety of organisational stakeholders. In private businesses these include, in addition to their customers, shareholders, employees, suppliers and the community. The principle of organisational or corporate accountability is that the collective responsibilities of private businesses may be enforced by a mixture of market, legal, social and moral imperatives.

Private businesses are held accountable in a number of ways. They are legally accountable to their shareholders who may attend meetings and vote on issues affecting company policy. Shareholders – who are increasingly other companies – also have rights to appoint and remove directors, receive annual reports and accounts and share in corporate profits. Private businesses are also legally accountable, in part at least, to their employees, suppliers and consumers. Employees, for example, have a set of common-law and statutory employment rights. The legal obligations of private businesses to their suppliers are embodied in the law of contract which provides a legal framework around which these organisations build their mutual commercial activities. As far as consumers are concerned, corporate legal accountability is largely through consumer protection law and the Office of Fair Trading, which publishes information, proposes new laws and takes action on behalf of consumers.

Legal accountability of private businesses to the community incorporates a variety of measures, such as controls over land use and development, pollution control and noise abatement. The law covering land use and development, for example, attempts to achieve a satisfactory balance between the interests of people within the community and those of business organisations. Pollution control is aimed at minimising the potentially hazardous impacts of effluents and noxious substances released into the air, land or waterways. Legislation is also geared to preventing the damage done to individuals and households by excessive noise levels from factory machinery, motor vehicles, aircraft and so on.

The social and moral accountabilities of private businesses have become more important in recent years as businesses have increasingly accepted that they have social and ethical responsibilities, partly in response to pressure-group lobbying. These have to be taken into account when their managements take decisions about production, pricing, resource utilisation, distribution of profits and payments to themselves. Private businesses are becoming increasingly customer aware and environmentally conscious. Not to do so can result in lost customers, fines and loss of reputation. Ultimately, however, the accountability of for-profit organisations is to the market. If they do not satisfy the market place, they eventually go bankrupt and go out of business.

The Managerial Function

In response to their needs to meet the market demands placed upon them, private businesses tend to have a managerial function based on a combination of 'economistic', 'rationalist' and 'generic' principles. The economistic nature of business management is reflected in its market goals, accountabilities and the dominance of economic efficiency as its criterion of success. It also explains why functional areas of management, such as finance, production and marketing, have such high status and standing within the private sector. It is these which are seen as providing the keys to: profitability, efficiency, cost control, productivity, product design, product quality, product innovation, sales growth, market share and market potential. It is success – or failure – in the market which is ultimately the measure of effective private business management, nothing else.

The rationalist nature of business management derives from the ideas of 'scientific management' and classical management theory, where managers and appropriate managerial techniques are allocated a special and crucial role in organisations (Taylor, 1911; Urwick, 1944; Fayol, 1949). That role is to achieve the organisation's goals and objectives through planning, organising, staffing, directing, coordinating, reporting and budgeting. Managers are expected to take decisions ensuring that the resources needed to achieve market goals and objectives are used economically and efficiently. They claim the right to take these decisions because of their superior technical skills and the right to manage. The rationalist approach to management also claims that there is a body of managerial knowledge and skills which managers need to apply to make their organisations successful. Armed with this knowledge and these skills, managers can determine appropriate organisational structures, technical systems and the division of work into its fundamental parts. They are also responsible for creating the necessary communication, coordination and control systems, integrating the organisation and providing measures of performance. In the rationalist approach, managers are the systematic planners and controllers of organisations. As Drucker (1989) writes, management expresses the belief in the possibility of controlling humankind's livelihood through systematic organisation of economic resources.

The view of management as largely a generic set of activities and structures common to all organisations had its origins in the early classical school of management theorists (Sheldrake, 1995). But a range of American and other writers in the postwar period created a body of modern management principles which they applied to both private and public organisations (Drucker, 1954 and 1974; Herzberg *et al.*, 1959; McGregor, 1960; Rice, 1963; Lawrence and Lorsch, 1969; Mintzberg, 1973). They asserted that management is a universal activity, across organisations. It does not take the same form in all situations and there is no 'one best way' of organising businesses. However, all managers are faced with similar tasks and problems and perform similar roles which involve a mix of rational decision-making, problem solving and intuitive judgements. This generic approach to managing dominated management theory from the 1950s, and has been reflected in managerial practice in much of the market sector, in Britain, North America and the anglophone countries ever since.

A 'new wave' generic management, however, emerged in North America in the 1980s, finding its way into some leading-edge British companies during the decade. This focused on the managing of 'culture', 'quality' and 'excellence'. It derived from ideas articulated by a number of American managerial 'gurus' who were seeking to provide sets of prescriptive answers to managers desperately looking for corporate and personal success in increasingly competitive world product markets. Their ideas have had a major influence on business education and business literature. One focus, on corporate culture, developed by writers such as Deal and Kennedy (1982) and Schein (1985), argues that 'strong culture' is an important element in business success and that companies with clearly articulated values and beliefs are outstanding performers. The concept of total quality management, borrowed heavily from Japan, is basically a simple one. It asserts that all work processes are subject to variation which reduces quality and, if the level of variation is managed and decreases, quality standards improve.

The emergence of excellence as a managerial philosophy is associated particularly with the writings of Tom Peters (Peters and Waterman, 1982; Peters and Austin, 1985; Peters, 1987). In analysing what constitutes 'excellent' companies, Peters and Waterman identified: getting on with the job; believing that customers come first; encouraging innovation; treating people as a source of quality and productivity; having leaders who tell employees about corporate values; staying close to the business they know; having simple structures with small corporate centres; and inculcating 'core values'. Peters (1987) also addresses the problem of change, arguing that companies require flexibility and 'love of change' to replace mass production as a driving force. The latter was based on stable, mass markets which have now vanished. His recipe for corporate success is quality and flexibility, supported by training of the highest order.

Variants of the economistic, rationalist and generic views of management are observable in many private businesses, rooted in the belief by their managers that these precepts are soundly based in managerial theory and good managerial practice. These approaches are necessary, it is believed, to meet the market demands of economic efficiency and optimise the chances of organisational success. They derive from the predominantly market goals and market accountabilities of private organisations. To what extent these prescriptive approaches to the managing of resources within businesses actually deliver what they promise has yet to be satisfactorily demonstrated. Managerial practice in the private, for-profit sector may well be a much more pragmatic and contingent set of activities than the theoretical literature leads us to believe.

Management in the Public Sector

The public sector consists of many diverse organisations and it is difficult to generalise about their goals, structures and styles of management. What they have in common is their creation by governments to achieve political goals in support of political objectives and policies. This political context is the driving force behind public bodies and is reflected in how they are managed.

Goals and Accountabilities

Managing in the public sector contrasts with the market-driven nature of management in private businesses in a number of ways. First, organisational goals are set by politicians. Second, the criteria of success are relative to those goals and cannot be reduced to a 'bottom line' of profit or loss. Public organisations cannot go bankrupt because they do not rely on the market for revenue. Governments command taxation and public bodies are generally financed wholly or partly from these funds. There is no cash nexus between the suppliers of most public goods and services and their consumers. Commercial public bodies like the Post Office, and trading agencies which charge the public directly like the Passport Office, can still be subsidised if they incur deficits. It is this absence of market discipline which, it is claimed, results in inefficiency and waste and the management function in public bodies is, therefore, a dilution of the private model (Flynn, 1997).

Public organisations are given goals which reflect the purposes for which they exist but, in contrast to those of private bodies, they tend to be complex, vaguely defined and often conflicting. The goals of public organisations are also sometimes unattainable. The reasons for this are identified by Pollitt (1990, p. 121):

> First, there is the need to build and maintain coalitions of support . . . . Second, a broadly-based objective is less likely to give immediate hostages to fortune . . . [and] it is easier to argue that it has been, at least in part, successful . . . . Third, vague wording . . . [or] 'woolly wording' is . . . attractive in the sense that it provides endless opportunities for defence, evasion and apparent innovation during the process of political debate.

In a liberal democracy, politicians have the task of trying to satisfy many different and disparate interests and integrating these into the policies which public bodies pursue. Therefore, the more general the stated goals, the wider their appeal. It is because of the many different areas of concern for government that the goals of public bodies may sometimes conflict. For example, a government may be committed to reducing taxation and at the same time increasing expenditure on education and health. Governments pursue multiple goals which are also continuously disputed as sectional interests challenge them. Public officials, unlike private-sector managers, are also faced with frequent changes of goals, as either political pressures force a new negotiated order or changes in political leadership result in new priorities.

Division of responsibilities amongst public organisations is also a consequence of political considerations rather than of logic, economics or organisational principles. It is not uncommon for one level of government to set goals and policies and for another level to implement them. Policies developed by the Department for Education and Employment, for example, are carried out by universities, colleges, local education authorities and schools. The size and complexity of public organisations, and the frequent separation of goal setting and policy implementation, means that there is often a lack of control by policy makers over those carrying out policy. Here a 'power-dependency' relationship emerges in which skill in exploiting political resources replaces any rational process of decision-making or direct form of control.

A further consequence of the multi-functional nature of public organisations is their complex structures. Central and local government are characterised by complex systems of interdepartmental committees and multiple consultative and communication channels. Those responsible for managing these systems are often managing the interface between their own organisation and others. This has increased in recent years with the growth of inter-agency networking (Rhodes, 1997) and will be extended further with the Labour Government's commitment to joined-up government. For public managers this is much more of a political than a technical role.

Public organisations are ultimately accountable to the public they serve. The public are especially interested in what these organisations do and how they do it. This is because, first, public bodies are often monopoly providers, leaving the public no choice but to take what they supply. Second, public bodies can exercise power to ensure compliance with public laws, by fining people or even depriving them of their liberty. Third, they provide public and merit goods which directly affect the quality of people's lives. Fourth, they levy compulsory taxation to fund governmental activities. Fifth, they regulate many areas of social life such as licensing drinking, driving and entertainment or controlling building designs and land use. Therefore as citizens, consumers and taxpayers, the public are interested in the use of public power, the values reflected in the decisions made, the efficiency with which public money is used and the quality of the services provided.

It is this exercise of public power that necessitates public organisations being held accountable in a democratic society. Public officials are expected to act as stewards of the public interest and the public purse, as well as being providers of goods and services. The forms that public accountability takes vary according to the type of agency, the political salience of its activities, the level of government and its particular functions. As Lawton and Rose (1991: 17) state, it is difficult to generalise about the process of accountability in the public sector. 'The mechanics of accountability in local authorities are different from those in central government, which in turn vary from those in the NHS.' In practice four types of public sector accountability exist; legal, political, consumer and professional.

All public bodies operate within a strict legal framework. Unlike private organisations, which can do anything which the law does not specifically forbid or prevent them from doing, public ones can only do what the law permits and prescribes for them. This legal rule of *ultra vires* means that public officials must be able to point to legal authority for their actions. Failure to exercise their legal responsibilities, or actions which are in excess of their legal authority, can be mandated or restrained by the courts. Unlike most European countries, there is no system of public courts in Britain. It is the ordinary courts that hold public organisations to account, both for their actions and the procedures they use. Public officials are required to demonstrate that they have complied with the substantive law, procedural law and rules of natural justice.

Political accountability manifests itself in a number of ways. All public officials are directly or indirectly accountable to a political person or body. Civil servants are accountable to ministers, local government officers to elected councillors and non-departmental agencies to appropriate ministers. This model assumes that powers are vested in ministers who are responsible for what public servants do and are accountable, in turn, to Parliament for their actions. Similarly, power is vested in the elected local authority council which is responsible to the public for the actions of its officials. The reality of ministerial responsibility has long been disputed and there are claims of an accountability gap (Barker, 1996: Barberis, 1998) which is only partly filled by making civil servants, including the chief executives of Next Steps Agencies, more directly accountable to Parliament, through its specialist committees (Drewry, 1989). Local officials are also increasingly dealing directly with the public. In both central and local government ultimate accountability to the public, as the electorate, is through periodic elections and the ballot box. Between elections, the press and pressure groups keep public organisations alert and inform the public of what is going on.

Accountability to consumers and clients of public organisations is through institutions established for dealing with complaints and grievances and, more recently, for consulting consumers. Various tribunals deal with appeals against administrative decisions but complaints of maladministration are dealt with by the Parliamentary, Health Service or Local Government Commissioners. In addition to these external institutions, each public body has its internal complaints procedures. Since the 1980s, the rights of consumers and service users have come to the fore and all public organisations now have to look at ways in which they are responsive to and accountable to the public. The *Citizen's Charter* (Prime Minister, 1991) led to much more accountability to consumers and users of public services. Many public organisations have their own charters or charter standards, providing mechanisms for holding them to account (see Chapter 9). The relaunch of the Charter under the title of *Service First* (Cabinet Office, 1998e) has reinforced the obligation of all public organisations to respond to customers and clients and consult them.

Professional accountability is particularly pertinent to the public sector, since many public organisations are staffed by professional workers such as doctors, nurses and teachers (Farnham and Horton, 1996b). Professionals seek not only to control entry to their occupations but also determine their own methods of work and police their members. They claim professional autonomy, clinical freedom or academic freedom (Johnson, 1973) It has been argued they are not accountable to their clients, their managers or the politicians responsible for the policies they carry out, although professionals claim they are accountable to their professions and their internal codes of ethics. Complaints against doctors are dealt with by the British Medical Council and against lawyers by the Law Society. Since the 1980s, there has been an attack on public professional bureaucracies, with the imposition of internal managerial structures subordinating professionals to hierarchical controls. Professional workers are now held increasingly accountable to public managers, who may or may not be drawn from among the professionals they supervise. They are also increasingly subject to audits to control and monitor their use of resources (Clarke *et al.*, 1994).

Administration or Management?

A dominant perception is that public organisations are administered, whilst private organisations are managed. Both types of organisations have goals, use resources to achieve those goals and are held accountable to their various stakeholders for the decisions they take and for the ways they use resources. The people responsible for taking the decisions and carrying out the policies and objectives, in both types of organisation, are clearly performing the same role: they are planning, organising, coordinating and controlling – in other words, managing. Administration in both types of organisation involves establishing procedures which are designed to link policy with practice, to ensure consistency and facilitate control. In public organisations, it is these administrative processes that have tended to dominate. This gives public organisations their distinctive nature, although this varies from one organisation to another.

An early analysis by Keeling (1973) identified a large number of systems within public organisations. Only a minority, however, had the primary task of making the best use of resources. These he called 'management systems', and they were found notably in the nationalised industries. He classified other systems as 'judicial', 'diplomatic' and 'administrative', all of which differed in their structures and operational styles from management systems. The latter bore a closer resemblance to business organisations than the other systems. The key contrasts between administrative and management systems which he observed were that:

1   Objectives tend to be expressed in very general terms in administrative systems and are rarely reviewed or changed. Management systems, in contrast, have more clearly identified goals and objectives, with specific time scales and targets.

2   The main criteria of success for administrative systems are avoiding mistakes and getting things right. In management systems, the criteria are achieving targets, usually expressed quantitatively.
3   The economical and efficient use of resources are secondary tasks in administrative systems but of primary importance in the creation of effective management systems.
4   Administrative systems tend to have role cultures where responsibilities are precisely defined and there is limited delegation; structures tend to consist of long hierarchies and there is a tendency to caution and to refer problems upwards. In management systems there is more of a task culture, shorter hierarchies, more delegation and a willingness to take decisions.
5   The role of the administrator is more one of arbitration and rule interpretation. In contrast the manager is a protagonist, looking for opportunities, fighting for resources and taking initiatives.

The key features of administrative systems which Keeling highlighted were mechanistic structures, long chains of command, narrow spans of control, extensive bureaucratisation and defensive and passive behaviour. Role and status are routinised to constrain discretion. Managerial systems, on the other hand, tend to have more flexible structures with less hierarchy, are task oriented, maximise individual discretion, have high levels of decentralisation and wider spans of control. The criteria of success in public administrative systems are mistake avoidance, satisfying public expectations of equity and fairness, averting political controversy and achieving consensus, conformity and consistency in practice. The criteria of success in management systems, in contrast, hinge around achieving the goals set for the organisation. Making the right decision is less important than making an appropriate decision, given the elements of risk and uncertainty involved. Managers are judged by their ability to recognise and seize opportunities, react quickly to changed circumstances and make profits or avoid losses.

Administrative systems traditionally dominated public organisations because historically the public services emerged as administrative bodies, supporting political policy makers and law makers and ensuring that the law was implemented. The civil service is still dominated by an elite whose perception of their role is that of policy advisers to ministers and guardians of the public interest rather than managers. The administrative culture is also a consequence of traditional systems of public accountability identified above. Public bodies still have monies appropriated by Parliament or local authorities for specific purposes annually and until the late 1990s were required to account for the regularity of their expenditures each year. This invites a cautious attitude to the use of funds and close scrutiny over each commitment of resources. Any decision to change the use of funds has traditionally required to be vired by the finance department.

Bureaucratic administrative structures and systems are in part a consequence of the size of public bodies, their dispersal throughout the country and the need to ensure standard and uniform practices. The law requires that all those entitled to social or welfare rights should receive equal treatment. It also sets down rules and procedures to be followed. Only bureaucratic practices can ensure that this occurs. Administrative systems are concerned about the use of resources in so far as they constrain what can be done but they do not assess success in terms of a narrow economic definition of efficiency – the ratio of resource inputs to product outputs. They do so in terms of goal effectiveness. As Dunsire (1973) argues, public organisations have to achieve a balance between resource efficiency and goal effectiveness. Those public organisations operating in the market can use 'resource tests' of efficiency whilst those not operating in the market have to use 'goal tests'. For some operating in the market, but committed to political goals, a mix of policy/resource tests is appropriate. Policy tests are ultimately qualitative and judgemental. They imply a qualitative judgement about not only the goals but also the relative priority given to different goals. It is politicians in the final analysis who decide on both the goals and resources to be used in pursuing them. There is no objective way of determining what the right policies or right amount of resources are. In the market it is the price mechanism which arbitrates, in the public domain it is political choice.

How public organisations are managed is affected by those fundamental facts of political life. Traditionally, their management systems have emerged out of their administrative systems, not vice versa. In the private sector, the management function precedes the administrative one. In public organisations, because of their primarily political goals and accountabilities, and the priority given to procedures, it is the administrative function which is prior to the management one.

The Managerial Function

The managerial function in most public organisations has tended to be 'bureaucratic', 'incrementalist' and 'particularist'. The characteristics of bureaucratic management are specialisation and hierarchy, impersonality and expertise. Those in managerial positions have clearly defined roles within a specialised, hierarchical and horizontal division of labour. Their responsibilities are narrowly defined and circumscribed by rules, and officials have limited discretion. The implications are that individual managers do not control the resources used to carry out managerial tasks and responsibilities. Managers in a bureaucratic structure cannot vary the mix of resources and are bound by human resources allocations and appropriation budgets determined centrally. Bureaucratic management leads to narrow spans of control and decisions are taken at a high level in the organisation, leading to centralisation. All these features result in slow decision-making and delays in responses, including to the demands of public consumers and citizens.

The impersonal nature of bureaucratic management is reflected in the ways that managerial tasks are carried out according to prescribed rules. This is done without arbitrariness or favouritism, with records being kept of each transaction. Public managers are expected to ensure that employees, suppliers and members of the public are treated fairly, equitably and within 'the rules'. This results in predictability and standardisation of procedures and outcomes, although it also produces inflexibility and unresponsiveness to particular needs.

The expertise of public managers has traditionally derived from their skills as either generalist administrators or specialist professionals. The civil service, for example, has always been dominated by the administrative generalist, whose expertise has been rooted in understanding the machinery of government and the political process. This has been acquired through experience in various parts of the service as their careers progress. Lower-level managers have also tended to be generalists, with the managers of professional groups, such as lawyers, economists or statisticians, accountable to generalists. In contrast local government managers, at all levels, have tended to be specialist professionals with chief officers normally drawn from the professional groups they manage. In the NHS, it has traditionally been the professionals, especially doctors, who have dominated the managerial processes. In both sectors, administrators have provided supportive roles to managers of professionals.

The incrementalist nature of public management reflects the fact that the perspective of public managers is short term. Planning takes place through small changes and limited adjustments to existing policies (Hogwood and Gunn, 1984), including financial planning which is based upon the annual budget cycle. Although most public bodies have produced three-year expenditure surveys since the 1960s, these tended to be little more than forecasts and were not binding. External changes of policy and intra-organisational changes of priorities are constantly confronting public managers. Public organisations work in a context in which they are interdependent and rely on other public bodies. Local authorities, for example, depend upon the Department of the Environment Transport and the Regions and Parliament to grant them money each year and determine the powers and responsibilities they have. Operating in a politically dynamic environment also makes rational, long-term planning difficult for public managers (see Chapter 4).

Changes in political leaders often mean substantial changes in policies. Attempts by public organisations to adopt rational decision-making strategies and longer-term plans have been short lived and unsuccessful. The introduction of planned programme budgeting (PPB) and policy analysis reviews (PAR) in the civil service during the early 1970s, for example, fell victim to the new Labour government and the International Monetary Fund after 1974. The movement to corporate management in local government, following its reform in 1974, was abandoned within a few years of the introduction of cash limits. The problem of rational, long-term planning is greatest where the process of strategic choice and strategic implementation are separate.

Public management is particularist in the sense that there has traditionally been a notable absence of general managers in public organisations. Although managerial structures in the former nationalised industries bore a closer resemblance to those in the private sector, and a general management orientation was more evident, this was particular to these more market-oriented, commercial bodies. Management in the civil service, local government and the NHS is particular to those bodies. In local government, for example, there is the tradition of both specialist management in departments like social service and general management in the chief executive's department. Specialist management structures, based on particularist traditions, have made coordination, planning and rational use of resources difficult in local government and resulted in managerial fragmentation. Professional managerial bureaucracies also tend to put service to their clients above resource considerations and resist external controls infringing their autonomy. This is especially evident in the NHS, where doctors have traditionally managed the use of resources and claimed clinical autonomy in doing so.

The New Managerialism

Widespread criticism of managing public organisations because of their alleged inefficiency and ineffectiveness built up during the 1970s and 1980s. It was the election of the Conservative government in 1979 which provided the political impetus to bring about a new-style public management sometimes referred to as managerialism. There is no generally agreed and precise definition of the term 'managerialism' but a succinct one is provided by Pollitt (1990: 1). He sees 'managerialism [as] a set of beliefs and practices, at the core of which burns the seldom-tested assumption that better management will prove an effective solvent for a wide range of economic and social ills.' Five axioms of managerialism are that: social progress requires continuing increases in economic productivity; productivity increases come from applying sophisticated technologies; the application of these technologies can only be achieved through a disciplined workforce; business success depends on the professionalism of skilled managers; and to perform their crucial role managers must have the right to manage.

The new managerialism which has emerged in Britain since the early 1980s pervades both private and public organisations. As the then Secretary of State for the Environment wrote: 'Efficient management is a key to the [national] revival. . . . And the management ethos must run right through our national life – private and public companies, civil service, nationalised industries, local government, the National Health Service' (Heseltine, 1980). In the private sector, growth of the new managerialism has been essentially market driven. With the exposure of British industry to increasingly fierce European and global competition, the corporate sector had to adapt to these new market conditions. In response to these forces, private businesses looked to increases in productivity, greater job flexibility, more investment in new technologies, more job restructuring and better management to help them cope with turbulent, global market conditions.

These changes have sometimes been forced upon reluctant workforces by macho styles of management whilst in other cases, managements have used more sophisticated styles of managing aimed at getting greater employee commitment to corporate goals and enterprise success, through improved business performance and quality programmes. It is the skills and competences of their professional managerial cadres which are seen to be the key to organisational survival and success. Management control was strengthened during the 1980s and 1990s by high unemployment, weakened trade unions and changes in employment law, which shifted the balance of bargaining power away from employees towards employers (see Chapter 7).

In the public sector, the thrust towards managerialism has been politically driven and predicated on the view that private-sector economistic, rationalist and generic management was the ideal model of management to be aimed at. It is seen as being superior to the public administration model and, if the efficiency and quality of public service provision are to be improved, then business management practices and ideologies need to be imported into public organisations to make them successful. There was also a political agenda underpinning public service managerialism in the 1980s. As Pollitt (1990: 49) writes:

> better management provides a label under which private-sector disciplines can be introduced to the public services, political control can be strengthened, budgets trimmed, professional autonomy reduced, public service unions weakened and a quasi-competitive framework erected to flush out the natural 'inefficiencies' of bureaucracy.

The new managerialism, in short, was a distinctive element in the policies of New Right Conservative governments, under Margaret Thatcher and John Major, towards the public services, and has been built upon by New Labour under Tony Blair since 1997. Since the early 1980s, there have been three main managerialist thrusts in the public services, although there have been variations within each service. First, there was tighter control of spending, involving cash limits and 'manpower budgets', and cuts in spending on staff. Second, there was a movement to decentralise managerial responsibilities and functions through more devolved budgetary systems and giving more responsibility to line managers. Third, management has become more

rational with the introduction of management by objectives and performance management systems, including use of performance indicators and
merit pay.

With the shift towards managerialism in the public services there has been
a weakening of the bureaucratic, incrementalist and particularist style of
management in favour of the economistic, rationalist and generic model.
The economistic nature of the new managerialism is reflected in the
increasing importance paid to the three Es of economy, efficiency and
effectiveness, and value for money. The introduction of compulsory competitive tendering and market testing across the public services has also
sought to move the public sector closer to the private business model and the
marketplace. Now most middle and lower-level public officials have responsibilities for identifying costs, monitoring the way that money is spent
and accounting for the financial performance of their units or sections.
Efficient use of resources has become a dominant concern. Public managers
also have to devise criteria for measuring and evaluating the efficiency of
their organisations. The rationalist nature of the new managerialism is
demonstrated by the introduction of mission statements and corporate and
business plans into all public service organisations. Mission statements set
out an organisation's ground rules for doing business, whilst corporate and
business plans provide targets to be aimed at and performance measures to
be used.

The shift from particularist management to generic management in the
public services is demonstrated by four key changes: first, public management is increasingly dominated by general managers, rather than specialist
managers or professionals, although there is some evidence of colonisation
of management positions by professionals in some sectors; second, it is more
objective-driven, rather than problem-driven; third, managers are now
prepared to facilitate change, rather than resist it; and, fourth, managers
behave as if the public are their main concern, rather than their staff. In
1998, chief executives headed 137 'Next Steps' agencies in the civil service;
general managers with programme or directorate responsibilities populate
the new-style local authorities, whilst general managers have been appointed
throughout the NHS since 1984. Headteachers are managers of their
schools, rather than administrators, and university vice-chancellors are
designated chief executives of university corporations, with salaries to
match. Although many of these general managers are members of professions they are appointed for their general management skills. Mobility
between public sector organisations and between the public and private
sectors is more common than in the past, although it has not been as great as
governments have wanted.

General managers are driven by objectives, plans, budgets, performance
indicators and quality standards. All public organisations are using benchmarking against private business standards to evaluate their own performance whilst individual performance reviews and performance pay ensure

that staff focus on agreed objectives. Although managers still respond to problems, they are now expected to be proactive in anticipating and avoiding them. Managers today are at the centre of managing change in the public services. Without changing the values, beliefs and expectations of those working in public services, managers cannot achieve the objectives set for them. There is evidence that the culture of the public services today is a managerially led one and that a new public service ethos is pervading them. The emphasis is on doing things right and providing services which meet the needs of the customer, not of the organisation. Public service managers are now much more customer aware and client oriented, and less concerned with worker-related problems. It is at the point of delivery, where citizens come directly into contact with public workers, that a new service-oriented culture is most evident.

Conclusion

This chapter has set out to demonstrate the similarities and differences between managing private and public organisations. The similarities are that managing each type of organisation involves operating within strategic choices, determining goals, providing means to achieve them, using resources efficiently and ensuring the quality of their outputs. Both have their administrative systems and both are held accountable to their principal stakeholders. Public service management has traditionally been seen as distinct and separate from much of private sector practice because it is contingent on factors which are unique to public organisations. These include control by elected politicians; the legal framework of the public services; their relative openness; and their accountability to a diverse range of public watchdogs. All these factors constrain managerial discretion, structures and styles in the public services. In contrast private businesses are market driven, not politically driven. Private business orientation is towards meeting consumer demands, as a means of making profits, whilst public sector orientation is towards satisfying political demands, as a means of achieving political integration and social stability. Outputs are, therefore, more qualitative and less easily measured in the public domain.

Although contextual differences remain, some convergence between managing private businesses and public organisations has occurred since the early 1980s. This is ascribed to the new managerialism and new public management (NPM) introduced by successive governments. Business management techniques are now widely used in the public services and business language and practices are common to the sector. Public service managers are increasingly concerned with marketing services, measuring efficiency, achieving customer satisfaction and ensuring financial viability. NPM is distinctly managerialist in the sense that responsibility for achieving organisational efficiency and success, and carrying out public policy, is now firmly placed upon public managers, especially the new genre of general managers. Public managers are increasingly seen by political policy makers as agents of resource efficiency, enterprise initiatives and business effectiveness. They are trained alongside private managers and are expected to demonstrate the same competencies as their private counterparts. A report of a benchmarking exercise to assess how close public organisations come to the business excellence model stated (Cabinet Office, 1998c: 3ff):

> Their experience suggests that much of the language and approach of the private sector applies equally to public services . . . [and] it is apparent that the best public sector organisations are within striking distance of world class performance in many areas most notably customer satisfaction and people satisfaction.

The appropriateness of the business excellence model has been challenged (Talbot, 1998) and the effect of managerialism on public sector ethics is of widespread concern (Lawton, 1998). The managerial role of public officials is still limited by the fact that they are constrained by overall resource decisions and policy boundaries made by the politicians, although this is less the case in areas where agencies can generate revenues and operate under market conditions. It is their ultimate subordination to politics rather than to the market which is the essential distinction between public and private organisations. Managing public organisations can never be exactly the same as managing market-driven companies. Convergence is demonstrated through the ways in which resources are being managed, with public services becoming more customer centred and financial and staffing decisions being devolved to managers. It is these themes which are explored in Part II and Part III of the book.

3

Globalisation, Europeanisation and Management of the British State

STEPHEN COPE

This chapter examines the wider, and largely external, developments that are influencing public management in Britain. In particular, it assesses the impact of globalisation, Europeanisation and new public management (NPM) upon the capacity of the British state to manage public service provision. It is not easy to unravel the impact of these wider developments upon the managing capacity of the state, not least because the state itself has promoted many of the developments and also exercises significant latitude in how it responds to these wider pressures.

Globalisation and the State

Globalisation reflects 'the increasing interdependence of world society' (Giddens, 1993: 528). It embodies a complex set of processes – economic, financial, technological, political and cultural – that increasingly connect the local with the global. For Held and McGrew (1993: 262):

> Globalization can be conceived as having two interrelated dimensions: scope (or 'stretching') and intensity (or 'deepening'). On the one hand, the concept of globalization defines a universal process or set of processes which generate a multiplicity of linkages and interconnections which transcend the states and societies which make up the modern world system. . . . On the other hand, globalization also implies an intensification in the levels of interaction, interconnectedness or interdependence between the states and societies which constitute the modern world community.

There are considerable disputes about the meaning of globalisation, its causes and its effects. Lash and Urry (1994: 280), for example, suggest globalisation 'is really advanced capitalist globalisation' caused by the inherent dynamics of capitalist economic systems and consequently it is not experienced uniformly across the globe. Hirst and Thompson argue (1996: 1,195).

> Globalization has become a fashionable concept in the social sciences, a core dictum in the prescriptions of management gurus, and a catch-phrase for both journalists and politicians. It is widely asserted that we live in an era in which the greater part of social life is determined by global processes, in which national cultures, national economies and national borders are dissolving.

Writers mesmerised by its image, believe that states can do little in the face of increasing globalisation as the world economy

> is dominated by uncontrollable global market forces, and has as its principal actors and major agents of change . . . transnational corporations . . . which owe allegiance to no nation state and locate wherever in the globe market advantage dictates.

This view has led many to believe that the nation-state is increasingly a 'hollow' state, hollowed-out by the dynamics of global markets (Martin, 1993; Ohmae, 1995).

The 'hollow state' thesis is challenged by Hirst and Thompson who make a useful and subtle distinction between globalisation as transnationalisation and globalisation as internationalisation. They argue that the world economy is far from being genuinely global but instead is at present highly internationalised (as it has been in the past) and that dominant states 'have the capacity, especially if they coordinate policy, to exert powerful governance pressures over financial markets and other economic tendencies' (1996: 2–3). Consequently, it is wrong simply to read off from the global to understand what is happening locally. And it is wrong to assume the local is detached from what is happening globally; rather, what is happening needs to be increasingly understood as glocalisation involving 'the simultaneity and the interpenetration of what are conventionally called the global and the local' (Robertson, 1995: 30).

Globalisation has had profound, though uneven, effects upon states worldwide. As Dunleavy observes, economically (1994: 50):

> We have progressively established a kind of 'Macworld' capitalism, where product choices whether for hamburgers or computers are increasingly homogenized and standardized across all countries, and where systems and tastes are alike controlled and developed in a proprietary mode by large corporations. . . . The scale of markets and competition has decisively escalated in some areas, screening out local solutions and corporations in favour of transnational companies, dominant brands and standardized solutions. Cultural barriers to product acceptance have crumbled even in areas where they once seemed insurmountable.

Politically, as a result of increasing interconnectedness and interdependence, the policy-making capacity of states has been both constrained and enhanced. Globalisation creates 'spreading networks of subtle and direct interconnection and interdependence that enmesh public officials at all levels of government, from one part of the planet to another' (Luke and Caiden, 1989: 83). Policy-making in government is shaped by an increasingly complex interplay of global and local pressures, resulting from 'the substantial internationalisation or regionalisation of an activity previously handled in a single-country context' (Dunleavy, 1994: 37). As a result 'events, decisions and activities in one part of the world can come to have immediate significance for individuals and communities in quite distant parts of the global system' (Held and McGrew, 1993: 262). For example, in 1995 the collapse of the merchant bank, Barings, resulting from substantial unauthorised dealings in Singapore, affected many British local authorities which consequently faced losses of more than £50 million.

There is a paradox within the processes of globalisation as states have both pushed for and been pulled along by globalisation. Dominant western states have authored many developments leading to increasing globalisation, such as the creation of the United Nations; the free-trade missions of both the International Monetary Fund and World Bank; successive free-trade agreements as part of the General Agreement on Tariffs and Trade now under the auspices of the World Trade Organisation, European states have created and launched the common market and single market programmes within the European Union (EU); the United States (US) government has sponsored the Internet and satellite technology; established the North American Free Trade Agreement; and supported the proposed Multilateral Agreement on Investment negotiated by the Organisation for Economic Co-operation and Development. However, these same states, along with others, have been increasingly affected, sometimes adversely, by such moves towards globalisation. The key question is whether states, either singlehandedly or collectively, can control the processes of globalisation that they largely promoted.

Globalisation is challenging the autonomy of states and the ability of governments to govern and manage their economies. As a result governments are restructuring themselves and the societies they govern to remain competitive in 'the global marketplace' (Dahrendorf, 1995: 41), where goods, services, capital and persons can move more freely than before. Generally states have moved away from being welfare states, towards becoming competition states, less concerned with satisfying the welfare needs of their citizens and more concerned with retaining and attracting business to their territories in the face of competition from other states (Cerny, 1993; Jessop, 1993). In Britain successive governments, whether Conservative or Labour, have attempted to shed their responsibilities for providing welfare by encouraging private (including voluntary) sector provision in the belief that they cannot afford, either financially or politically, to maintain the welfare state if they are to preside over a thriving economy in global markets. Governments have given priority to creating the conditions necessary for economic growth with government policies increasingly directed towards low inflation, low taxation, skilled and flexible labour markets and curbs on public expenditure. The shift in Britain from a 'welfare state' to a 'competition state' has led to significant restructuring involving Europeanisation, privatisation and NPM, which collectively have reshaped its capacity to manage public services.

Europeanisation and the State

Europeanisation is a shorthand term denoting the increasing influence of the European Union (EU) upon its member states and those states aspiring to member status. There are other forms of Europeanisation including the Council of Europe, the Organisation for Security Cooperation in Europe (OSCE) and the Western European Union (WEU) but the EU is by far the most dominant regional actor within Europe, as well as an increasingly significant actor worldwide. Indeed the EU represents the most advanced form of regionalisation in the world. The origins of the EU can be traced back to the aftermath of the Second World War when the six founder states, West Germany, France, Italy, Belgium, the Netherlands and Luxembourg, committed themselves to specific forms of economic and political cooperation as a way of rebuilding their war-torn economies and preventing further war between themselves. The states signed the Treaty of Paris in 1951 establishing the European Coal and Steel Community, and the Treaties of Rome, establishing the European Economic Community (EEC) and the European Atomic Energy Community in 1957; these were later merged to become the European Community in 1963 and the European Union in 1992. The EEC committed member states to establishing a common market whereby tariffs on trade between member states would be gradually abolished and to setting a common external tariff on trade between member and non-member states. The common external tariff, along with a Common Agricultural Policy which was quickly established, were largely protectionist measures insulating member states from outside competition. Politically, the treaties were attempts to allay fears of German resurgence and to reintegrate Germany into the new Europe. In the words of Taylor (1996: 14): 'From the beginning, therefore, the European Community was as much about state creation as about integration.'

Further, the US government was keen to support economic and political cooperation between western European states in the belief that a more politically coherent, economically strong and ideologically friendly western Europe would contain Soviet influence (Carr and Cope, 1994a). Indeed the US government hoped that Britain would join the EC from its inception, not least because it believed that the British government could safeguard American interests more effectively inside than outside it. However, Britain declined to join in 1951 and again in 1956, arguably suffering from delusions of grandeur and preferring instead to maintain its relations with the US and its 'Empire' over those with Europe. The British government was also wary of the political designs of the EC with its treaty commitments towards 'ever closer union'.

The decision of British governments not to join the EC soon began to be questioned as a result of a combination of political and economic pressures: continued American pressure upon British governments to join, Britain's diminishing world role and declining Empire, growing pressure from domestic business wanting better access to larger EC markets and dismay at EC economies outperforming the British economy. After two failed attempts to join in the 1960s, Britain eventually became a member of the EC in 1973. Since joining Britain's relations with the EC have frequently been troubled and it has been dubbed 'an awkward partner' (George, 1990). A root cause of Britain's sometimes stormy relations with the EC is undoubtedly its late entry: it joined a club late, thus having to accept rules – the EC's *acquis communautaire* – that it had no influence in making and some of which did not work in Britain's favour for example, the common agricultural policy and the formula for calculating member states' budgetary contributions (Engel, 1998).

Since its establishment, the EC has both widened and deepened. It has expanded from the six founding member states to the present 15, with a growing queue of mainly Eastern European states currently seeking membership. Furthermore, the EC has greatly expanded its policy briefs which now embrace agricultural, social, environmental, economic, monetary, foreign, security and policing policy. In 1992 the Maastricht Treaty established the EU, which comprises three pillars or policy fields – the EC, Economic Pillar, Common Foreign and Security Pillar (CFSP) and Justice and Home Affairs Pillar (JHA) – which together represent a significant integrationist push towards both economic and political union (Carr and Cope, 1994b). As a consequence of widening and deepening, there has been a significant, and increasing, Europeanisation of policy-making within all member states.

The process of 'widening' and 'deepening' the EU reflects growing interdependence within Europe and also between Europe and the rest of the world. The development of the EU can be seen as a response to managing such interdependence. The EU originated in attempts by member states to engage in relatively limited forms of cooperation (for example, coal and steel production, agriculture) but these moves, providing economic and political benefits for participating member states, led to further moves to cooperate in interconnected policy sectors. This neo-functionalist account of European integration explains, for example, why moves creating a free-trade area within the EC led to moves to launch a single currency within the EU, and why moves creating a large EC-wide market in which goods, services, capital and persons can move about freely led to moves (albeit embryonic) to develop a common foreign policy and a common policing policy. These 'spill-over', deepening effects of policy cooperation are manifestations of policy interdependence, in that what happens in one policy sector affects other connected policy sectors.

The effects of successive moves towards policy cooperation amongst member states within the EU spill over on to non-member states, often prompting them to seek membership of the EU, as inside they can at least exercise more influence over the forms of cooperation than if they remained outside. For example, most members of the European Free Trade Association, a free-trade association largely set up in 1960 to rival the EEC by countries (including Britain) not wishing to sign up to the EEC's commitment towards political union, have now joined, recognising that their national interests can be protected and indeed furthered better inside than outside the EU.

In the EU's drive towards economic and monetary union, most member states signed up to the launch of the single currency in January 1999, which is managed by the European Central Bank setting a common interest rate for all those in this 'euro-zone'. If the latter is successful, there will be considerable pressure upon those non-participating member states (including Britain) to sign up to the single-currency project, as they will be able to exercise more (if only limited) influence over this project as insiders.

As well as being a way of managing increasing interdependence between intra-European policy sectors and states, European integration is a response to the perceived challenges of globalisation (Giddens, 1998: 141–2). The EU has both sponsored and been shaped by the processes of globalisation. Business, particularly big business, within the EU is highly dependent on free trade worldwide to buy imports and sell exports and consequently the EU has been at the forefront generally in pushing for the liberalisation of world trade, which has made states and societies more interconnected and thus more interdependent. It is increasingly difficult for national governments to manage their domestic economies and pursue significantly distinctive economic-policy goals in isolation. Therborn argues (1995: 191):

> The importance of states began to decline in the 1980s, when capitalist states began to drift in the high seas of global financial markets, when the EC gathered momentum in the second half of the decade. The change was consummated in the early 1990s, when the multinational states of the USSR and Yugoslavia broke up into chaos, as well as into new, fragile states, and when private financial operators brought down the monetary system of Western Europe states.

In the early 1990s many central banks of EU member states, including the Bank of England, struggled and even failed to manage exchange rates of national currencies within the prescribed bands of the EU Exchange Rate Mechanism (ERM) against a tide of considerable speculation in foreign exchange markets. The ERM, launched in the late 1970s as part of the European Monetary System, was itself an attempt to 'establish a zone of monetary stability in Europe at a time of international monetary instability' (George, 1996: 25). However, the chastening experience of the ERM crises in the 1990s prompted many member states, led by Germany, to pursue economic and monetary union further in the belief that member states collectively can manage the single currency more effectively within increasingly globalised financial markets largely devoid of capital controls. Though individual member states may compromise on their preferred policy stance, collectively they will exercise more influence over economic and monetary policy than if they acted singlehandedly. The recent development of the EU therefore can be seen partly as a manifestation of globalisation (Gamble and Payne, 1996).

Increasing Europeanisation of policy-making within Britain has led many, particularly the so-called Europhobes, to argue that the autonomy of the national government has been severely constrained as a result of membership of the EU and that Britain is being increasingly governed from Brussels. This view generally misunderstands how policy is made within the EU and underestimates the opportunities for Britain to promote policies and in some instances veto policies in terms of its national interest. Policy-making in the EU contains elements of both supranationalism and inter-governmentalism. Of the three pillars of the EU only the EC can be regarded as both intergovernmental and supranational. Both the CFSP and JHA pillars are intergovernmental, with the Council of Ministers and the European Council, representative bodies of member states, firmly in control of policy-making. Ministers serving on the Council of Ministers are 'concerned about the impact of any decisions made in Brussels on the people back home and about the impact of those decisions on any upcoming elections' (Peters, 1992: 79). Although for some proposals the Council must legislate on the basis of qualified majority voting (where votes cast by each member state are weighted according to population size) and the European Parliament may veto the Council's decision, these tend to be in areas where there is a high degree of consensus amongst member states, such as the single market. The European Council, comprising the political leaders of member states, has the major task of setting the agenda for the EU and resolving disputes that cannot be resolved in the Council of Ministers.

Policy-making in the EU is largely characterised by the striking of intergovernmental bargains between member states within supranational processes and structures of policy-making. For example, the Amsterdam Treaty, signed in 1997, proposes to introduce *de jure* forms of flexible integration, permitting some core member states to further cooperation between themselves that cannot be vetoed by non-core member states but does not bind non-core member states to pursue such forms of flexible cooperation (Duff, 1997). Such flexibility represents an intergovernmenal agreement by all member states to pursue differentiated integration within the EU, allowing some member states to integrate further and more quickly than others. The EU is more about the pooling of national sovereignty than the loss of national sovereignty. Milward (1994: 447, 19) argues that the EU represents a European rescue of the nation-state that 'marked some limits of the state's capacity to satisfy by its own powers and within its own frontiers the demands of its citizens'. Member states, constrained by increasing global interdependence, 'pursue integration as one way of formalising, regulating and perhaps limiting the consequences of interdependence, without forfeiting the national allegiance on which its continued existence depends'. Further reading of Nugent (1999) will explain the institutional and procedural framework within which EU decision making takes place.

Privatisation and the State

Privatisation has been, and remains, a prominent policy pursued by government since 1979, though pursued more vigorously by previous Conservative governments than the present Labour government. It has taken three main forms: the selling-off of government assets, the increased private-sector role within the public sector, and commercialisation of the public sector. First, the selling-off of government assets involves the transfer of ownership from the public to the private sector. Since 1979 more than 60 nationalised industries and state companies have been privatised, local authorities have sold over one million council homes to their former tenants and other public bodies have sold land and other assets. Second, the increased private-sector role within the public sector involves private businesses and voluntary organisations providing public services still under government control. Conservative governments launched the Private Finance Initiative (see Chapter 9), now warmly embraced by the Labour government, as a way of injecting private finance into the running of government projects; government bodies have increasingly contracted-out service provision to private contractors; and central government has appointed many business people on to the boards of quangos that are responsible for providing public services.

Third, commercialisation of the public sector requires public sector bodies to imitate allegedly more efficient private sector bodies in the way they manage themselves. For example, government bodies have levied more charges on consumers of their services; performance management has been increasingly entrenched in the public sector; and government reforms of public services have often asserted the right to manage with public managers being given more freedom locally to deploy resources in pursuit of centrally set policy goals.

The effect of privatisation has been a major shift away from state to market provision, and globalisation is a significant contextual factor in explaining this move. Martin argues (1993: 1) that: 'the roles of the state and society in defining, protecting and promoting the public interest are being whittled away by a global campaign of privatization and public sector commercialization driven by the needs of transnational business.' As capitalist states have reinvented their role away from being welfare states towards competition states, governments have been increasingly keen to shed responsibilities for providing public services, reduce tax-funding of remaining public services and exert greater centralised control over the management of public services. The push towards privatisation in Britain (and other countries), however, cannot be simplistically understood solely as a response to globalisation; there existed also more local pressures to privatise, though such pressures were framed within the context of globalisation.

The British government's privatisation programme can be understood more particularly as a threefold strategy. First, privatisation is an ideological strategy – a manifestation of New Right ideology that believes the market is superior to the state in providing goods and services. Nigel Lawson, a former Chancellor of the Exchequer in the Thatcher government, said the Conservative party 'has never believed that the business of government is the government of business' (Steel and Heald, 1982: 333). Second, privatisation is a financial strategy. The previous Conservative government's privatisation programme did not take off until its second term despite its ideological commitment to 'roll back the frontiers of the state'. From 1979 onwards the Conservative government was committed to cutting income tax and hoped that public expenditure cuts would finance tax cuts. It failed to cut public expenditure but by privatising 'profitable' nationalised industries it financed tax cuts and thus kept an election promise. The privatisation of nationalised industries raised vast sums of money for the Conservative government. The present New Labour government sees privatisation largely as a financial strategy; privatisation monies are used to finance its public expenditure commitments without having to raise taxes. Third, privatisation is a political strategy. Privatisation enhances support for the party in government from voters who have bought cheap shares and sold them quickly, the City which has made lots of money from handling the sales of nationalised industries, and business which bought many industries cheaply and have been awarded profitable contracts to provide public services.

Government's privatisation programme has been accompanied by the formation of regulatory regimes within which privatised utilities, private contractors and private operators within government must act. Regulation 'is the new border between the state and industry' (Veljanovski, 1991: 4). For example, many regulatory bodies have been established to watch over privatised utilities, for example, Office of Telecommunications, Office of Gas Supply and Office of Electricity Regulation. Generally they 'have the power to monitor performance, prices, and the quality of service, and to ensure that the consumer is afforded protection' (Veljanovski, 1990: 301).

There is a paradox behind these simultaneous moves towards privatisation and regulation. Nationalised industries were privatised mainly to be freed from government control yet regulation of these privatised industries represents government control in a different guise. Nicholas Ridley (1989), a former Secretary of State for Trade and Industry in the Thatcher government, claimed that privatised industries are more easily controlled when they are in the private sector. Many privatised utilities have complained that the 'tightening corset of regulation' is impeding their performance (Veljanovski, 1991: 4), whilst others complain that the regulatory bodies are too weak to check the monopoly power of privatised utilities and are thus unable effectively to 'protect the consumer from exploitation' (National Consumer Council, 1989: 2–5). For government, regulation represents a relatively cheap way to control the private sector.

For the present Labour government, now committed to partnership (a disguised form of privatisation), regulation offers the promise of government control without having to embark on an expensive programme of nationalisation. However, successive government moves to privatise pose the question of whether government can effectively regulate those activities it has privatised. There is also the prospect of a further loss of national control as public utilities are bought and sold in the international capital market to foreign companies.

New Public Management and the State

The rise of NPM is 'one of the most striking international trends in public administration' (Hood, 1991: 3). It is no accident that the spread of NPM worldwide corresponds with increasing globalisation. As states have responded to globalisation, NPM has been a prominent form of restructuring in most western governments, though its impact has been uneven between countries and even between policy sectors within the same country (Farnham *et al.*, 1996; Flynn and Stehl, 1996). Britain is very much on the crest of the NPM wave, as successive governments have sought not only to cut public expenditure and redraw the boundaries of the state but also to increase the efficiency and effectiveness of public services. Essentially NPM rests on the twin doctrines of removing differences between the public and private sectors and of shifting 'methods of doing business in public organizations' away from complying with procedural rules towards 'getting results' (Hood, 1994: 129). While recognising the variety found within NPM (Hood, 1995b), it has manifested itself generally as a series of interconnected managerial traits.

First, NPM often embodies an ideological commitment asserting the superiority of the market over the state, underpinned by no more than a simplistic and dogmatic 'private good, public bad' faith. With its emphasis on injecting market forces into government, it represents the New Right way of managing the public sector by 'reorganizing public sector bodies to bring their management, reporting, and accounting approaches closer to (a particular perception of) business methods' (Dunleavy and Hood, 1994: 9). Second, NPM centralises the making of policy strategy, especially policy goals and budgets, increasingly in the hands of the core executive at the heart of government, embracing a closely knit network of senior ministers and officials (especially those in the Prime Minister's Office, Cabinet Office and Treasury). It separates 'steering from rowing', leaving the centre to steer while other agencies row (Osborne and Gaebler, 1992: 34).

Third, NPM decentralises the delivery of public policy to a plethora of agencies, local authorities, quangos and private contractors, that exercise managerial and operational discretion within the limits of policy strategy set by the centre. These delivery agencies, regulated by the centre, thus possess 'freedom within boundaries' (Hoggett, 1991:251). Fourth, NPM reflects the view that greater competition between the public and private sectors and within the public sector promotes greater efficiency by making public sector agencies more consumer-responsive.

NPM involves 'the separation of purchasing public services from their provision or production' (Foster and Plowden, 1996: 46). Policy strategy (involving provision, purchasing and regulating decisions) is increasingly centralised and policy delivery (involving production, management and operational decisions) is increasingly decentralised. By providing centralised leadership, it is argued, governments can decentralise policy delivery as a way of empowering consumers of public services, as a 'remote agency is less likely to give customers the public services they want' (ibid.: 52). Savas argues that the role of government 'is to steer, not to row the boat' because 'government is not very good at rowing' (cited in Osborne and Gaebler, 1992: 25). Policy-making in government has become simultaneously centralised and decentralised (Richards, 1994). Steering agencies, such as central government, increasingly, both directly and indirectly, regulate rowing agencies, such as executive agencies, local authorities and quangos, by setting policy goals for rowing agencies to achieve, fixing budgets within which rowing agencies must operate, awarding contracts (or quasi-contracts) to competing rowing agencies, making key appointments to ensure the 'right' people head up the rowing agencies to do the 'right thing', and establishing regulatory agencies, such as the Audit Commission, to monitor the performance of rowing agencies.

NPM seeks to enhance the capacity of steering agencies to manage rowing agencies under their jurisdiction. It is all about managerial surveillance – the ability of steering agencies to monitor and direct rowing agencies more effectively and, within rowing agencies, the ability of managers to control workers more effectively. Regulation of public services is thus central to NPM and such regulation has expanded rapidly within government (Hood *et al.*, 1998). However, whether NPM has increased the managing capacity of government needs to be empirically tested. It is likely that the degree of regulatory control varies between policy sectors, largely reflecting the different levels of professional and political power of those being regulated, the political salience of activities being regulated, and the legal and political power of those regulating. For example, Hughes, Mears and Winch (1997: 309) compared the regulatory regimes of education, health-care and policing and found 'considerable, although not unexpected, diversity given the very different historical trajectories of these services, their differing political profiles and the extent to which they have been regulated at a local or national level and whether regulation has relied on formal or informal mechanisms'.

In the policing policy sector, Savage, Cope and Charman (1997) suggest that, rather than the Audit Commission auditing the police service, the Association of Chief Police Officers (ACPO), a professional association of senior police officers, were policing the Audit Commission, reflecting a significant degree of regulatory capture. The rise of NPM, and the consequent restructuring of regulatory relations between steering and rowing agencies, may both enhance the capacity of government to manage public services if there is regulatory control, and diminish its capacity if there is regulatory capture, thus representing a recasting of the regulatory bargains struck between central steering and local rowing agencies.

Managing the State: Hollowing-out or Filling-in?

This chapter has examined the impact of globalisation on the British state's capacity to manage the public sector and surveyed significant forms of state restructuring – Europeanisation, privatisation and NPM – in response to increasing globalisation. Its argument is that these forms of restructuring cannot be deterministically and simplistically read off from the structural forms of globalisation. Governments of states, including Britain, actively sponsor many of the conditions and developments leading to further globalisation and they possess considerable latitude in their responses to globalisation; government reforms represent political choices and are not purely the result of exogenous forces. States have shaped and reshaped globalisation and, in turn, have been shaped and reshaped by globalisation. As Smith points out (1998: 55): 'There is . . . a core problem that runs through the globalization literature: it is unclear whether globalization is an explandan or explandum. Is the process of globalization the result or the cause of change?' The answer is both.

There is another emerging, increasingly fashionable and slightly hyperbolic view that states are being hollowed-out by the forces of globalisation and becoming less capable of governing societies and managing economies within their national borders (Crook *et al.*, 1992; Dunleavy, 1994; Peters, 1993; Rhodes, 1994, 1997). Payne and Gamble argue that 'control of the world order [has] slipped beyond the capacity of any single state and perhaps even any group of states' (1996: 5), whilst Tony Blair admitted that governments can do little to influence the 'twists and turns of world markets' in the wake of an announced microchip plant-closure in his parliamentary constituency (Hetherington and Atkinson, 1998: 2). Jessop posits (1993: 10) that 'hollowing out' of the state:

> does not mean that the national state has lost all importance; far from it. Indeed it remains crucial as an institutional site and discursive framework for political struggles; and it even keeps much of its sovereignty – albeit primarily as a juridical fiction reproduced through mutual recognition in the international political community . . . [however] its capacities to project power even within its own national borders are becoming ever more limited due to a complex triple displacement of powers upward, downward, and, to some extent, outward.

Consequently the state appears to be hollowing-out as it seeks to retain core functions but sheds peripheral functions (Painter, 1994: 245). Jessop's observed triple displacement of powers appears to capture what is happening within British government with the prominent trends of Europeanisation (upward displacement), privatisation (outward displacement) and NPM (downward displacement).

A note of caution is called for, however, as this analysis too readily assumes that states are unable to reverse these trends and, moreover, states may not be hollowing-out but rather filling-in. Panitch (1994) argues that globalisation is authored by states and is primarily about reorganising, rather than bypassing them. Similarly Mulgan (1995: 14) argues that 'what has happened in recent decades is not a whittling away of a once supreme state, and intact virgin sovereignty, but rather a series of shifts in what governments can do.' Such reorganising or shifts as Europeanisation, privatisation and NPM may actually enhance the managing capacity of the state. British government arguably manages interdependence more effectively inside, rather than outside, the EU by striking intergovernmental bargains; it arguably exerts more influence over regulated privatised industries operating within a greater (though not great) competitive environment than if it owned them. And it arguably controls public services more tightly by introducing NPM reforms. Rather than these trends representing a displacement of state powers, they may represent a reconfiguration and even rejuvenation of those powers. What may be happening is not the hollowing-out of the state but rather the filling-in of the state. It is perhaps premature to argue definitively what is happening and more particularly whether the endgame is the hollowing-out or filling-in process. Whatever the endgame, the ongoing restructuring of the British state, in response to the wider challenges of globalisation, Europeanisation, privatisation and NPM, is significantly, albeit unevenly, impacting upon its capacity to manage public services and the way in which it does it.

PART II

Managerial Functions

4

Strategic Management in the Public Services

KESTER ISAAC-HENRY

The 1980s and 1990s witnessed dramatic changes in the way public services are managed, not only in Britain but also in a number of other countries. Many of these changes have taken on a decidedly private-sector flavour and, for this reason, have occasioned a fierce and sustained debate concerning their appropriateness for the public sector. Strategic management itself sits within this debate, with critics of its use viewing it as one more concept and practice imposed from the private sector to complicate and frustrate management in public service organisations. Others take the opposite view, arguing that strategic management is generic to all organisations, helping them to understand their environment, identify their aspirations and objectives and set the direction in which they wish to go. This chapter briefly examines the concept of strategic management, explores the arguments for and against its use in the public sector and discusses, with examples, some of its uses, developments and problems in public service organisations.

What is Strategic Management?

Attempts to define strategic management have been likened to walking through a terminological minefield with different writers and organisations using 'the same terms to describe different things or different terms to describe the same thing' (Smith, 1994: 13). There is confusion over terms and concepts such as strategic management, corporate strategy, corporate planning and strategic planning. Whilst some writers attempt to make clear distinctions between them, others take the view that they convey similar meanings and are interchangeable. There is some agreement, however, that from the 1940s managers and organisations have experimented with different methods of applying systematic approaches to managing organisations: from budgeting and control through to long-range planning and strategic (corporate) planning and now to strategic management. Despite differences of definitions and interpretations, the common element in 'strategy' is the attempt by managers and organisations, through a thinking process, to plan and make decisions that are strategic in the sense that such decisions:

- relate the organisation to aspects of both its internal and external environment which might impact on key issues of the organisation in the future;
- consider issues which generally span the whole organisation and are expected to have some important impact on it;
- allow for strategic choice as, for example, concern with the purpose of the organisation and the direction in which it should be heading;
- facilitate effective implementation of policy and strategy.

Strategic management is concerned with the process of formulating, implementing, monitoring and controlling organisational strategies (Thompson, 1995). The objective of practising strategic management is to reap the reward of greater effectiveness by matching the organisation to its environment and by managing change, the very essence of contemporary management, more easily. For Johnson and Scholes (1997) strategic management is involved with and based around three core areas of strategic analysis, strategic choice and strategic implementation.

Strategic analysis is predicated on the basis that for an organisation to be effective it must understand the nature of its internal and external environment including its markets, the power, influence and wishes of its stakeholders and the extent of its resources, competencies and capabilities. Strategic analysis is concerned with scanning the environment to ascertain the key influences likely to impact on the organisation, and especially to gauge the strengths and weaknesses as well as the opportunities and threats (SWOT) which might affect it. For example Figure 4.1 is the result of a SWOT analysis conducted by the City of Birmingham in the early 1990s.

Strategic choice is essentially the core of strategic management because it is concerned with decisions about the purpose and future of the organisation and 'the way in which it responds to the many pressures and influences identified in the strategic analysis' (Johnson and Scholes, 1997: 235). Strategic decisions involve the generation of options and their evaluation, influenced by the mission and objectives of the organisation and the findings of the SWOT analysis. It is also influenced by the suitability of options for addressing the situation in which the organisation operates, the acceptability of such options to stakeholders and the feasibility of successful implementation, given the resources and competencies the organisation possesses.

Decisions on the strategies having been made, the next step in strategic management is to arrange their implementation. This involves ensuring that objectives to be met are clearly set out with responsibilities and resources appropriately allocated. It may also be necessary to attempt to change the behaviour, beliefs and assumptions of those working in the organisation in order to achieve these objectives. In short this part of the process of strategic management may (and often does) call for the management of strategic change.

FIGURE 4.1   *SWOT analysis*

STRENGTHS
Improvement in services
Comprehensive networks of NO*
Majority of contracts won in-house
National and international recognition
Retention of a core manufacturing base

OPPORTUNITIES	SWOT ANALYSIS	THREATS
Maximise benefits of the NCC**		Loss of control over finance
The creation of a European market will facilitate Birmingham becoming a truly international city,		Population loss
		Recession
Exploiting government initiatives		Social tensions
Refashioning the city centre		Lack of investment
Census Information will help the city to review polices		Deteriorating environment
Strength of a multi-cultural city		Decreasing role of the council
		Continued extension of CCT

WEAKNESSES
Inadequate communication with citizens
Lack of real citizen access to the council
Negative image of the city
Deteriorating infrastructure
Mismatch of staff skills with new skills needed

* Neighbourhood offices;
** National Convention Centre

Source: Adapted from Birmingham City Council (1992) *City Strategy and Report, 1992/93*, Birmingham: The Council House.

Since strategies should be regularly modified and adjusted to take account of a constantly changing environment, strategic management is a reiterative process, unlike its forebears, long-range and corporate planning, which were criticised for their formality and inflexibility. It is now conventional wisdom to distinguish between three levels of organisational strategies, namely corporate, business and functional levels, as shown in Table 4.1. In discussing levels of strategy there is an assumption (not necessarily borne out in practice) that organisations are generally divided into discrete and fairly autonomous strategic business units which have distinct markets, services or clients. Although it is considered important to separate such units to avoid confusion in strategy making, all three levels must be linked and co-ordinated if strategic objectives are to be achieved. Business level strategies, for example, have to reflect corporate mission and objectives, whilst functional level strategies must underpin those at business level.

TABLE 4.1   *Levels of strategy*

Levels of strategy	Responsibilities and Activities	Public Service example
Corporate	Decides: What business the organisation should be in; How the organisation should be structured; How resources should be allocated to sub units; Whether the organisation should be involved in mergers, acquisition or divestments.	Cabinet/ Department of State e.g. DfEE, DSS
Business	Develops competitive strategies; Explores key trends in the business/industry; Identify opportunities; Decides how customer/client needs are to be met; Ensures consistency amongst functional strategies.	Local authorities
Functional	Decides how the business level strategies can be delivered. (Functional strategies include those relating to marketing, human resources, production, information systems, financial.)	Education dept Social services dept

The use and effectiveness of strategic management, both as a technique and a process, are not uncontested. There are those who argue that the popular concept of strategic management is too simplistic and linear to explain the outcomes hoped for by managers and organisations (Mintzberg, 1994; Stacey, 1992, 1996). It is too much to expect that the precise intentions, set out in such a rational manner, will emerge as intended outcomes, buffeted as they would be by external forces outside a manager's control and subject to internal dissensions and resistance. Strategies are more likely to emerge from actions and interactions within organisations and between organisations and their environments. Hence organisations are likely to follow an umbrella strategy where the broad outline may be deliberate but the details are allowed to emerge. Thus, when well-managed organisations make significant changes in strategies, the approaches used bear little resemblance to the rational/analytical system so often lauded in planning literature. Strategies 'originate in many varied and hard-to-control ways, some of which are more about implementation than about strategy development' (Campbell and Alexander, 1997: 42).

There is yet another objection to the 'design' school's approach. Strategic management, with its search for certainty, continuity, control and equilibrium, is an inadequate concept and process to cope with a world of turbulence, complexity and unpredictability. In such an environment the effect of a small action can, in the end, be magnified out of all proportions (the butterfly effect) to the extent that it causes instability, changes behavioural patterns and renders strategies ineffective. In a state of 'chaos', analysis loses its primacy, contingency loses its meaning, long-term planning becomes impossible, visions become illusions and consensus becomes dangerous (Stacey 1992). It is better for organisations and managers to be pluralistic, flexible, questioning and self-learning. Nevertheless, despite agreement that there is some validity in these arguments, mainstream writers on management continue to believe that analysis and planning still have a role to play, even if it is that strategy' 'walks on two feet, one deliberate the other emergent ' (Mintzberg and Waters, 1994: 12).

Strategic Management in Public Services

The development of new public management (NPM) has been a source of controversy. Some observers believe that many of its practices, coming as they do from the private sector, are often used out of context, demand inappropriate processes and responses and run counter to the culture and values of public organisations. So, while the Thatcher and Major governments viewed NPM as the grit in the system helping to deliver the pearl of effective management, others regard it as the irritation of a foreign body causing frustration, fragmentation and lack of organisational focus. The language of strategic management, dotted as it is with terms such as 'mission' and 'vision', 'competitive advantage', 'value chain' and 'scenario planning', is often met with scepticism and cynicism and dismissed as management-speak by its critics (Midwinter and McGarvey, 1995).

But public service organisations are not immune from the fads and fashions of management theories and ideas. Although usually a step or two behind their private counterparts such organisations have, over the last 40 years or so, experimented with a number of management developments including management by objectives, corporate planning, the search for excellence in the 1980s and the quality movement of the 1980s and 1990s. Enthusiastically supported by both the Maud (1967) and Bains (1972) reports, the majority of local authorities attempted to adopt a corporate or strategic planning approach to management after 1974. Based on 'rationalistic' principles, corporate planning was intended to impart internal unity and consistency of purpose in decision-making to a local authority as an entity, and at the same time encourage top managers to take a broader and a longer-term view of the authority's purposes and objectives. By the beginning of the 1980s the corporate planning experiment is said to have failed (Caulfield and Schultz, 1989). This was a result of:

- too uncritical an acceptance of other people's ideas by local authority managers;
- lack of commitment from both councillors and officers, suggesting that the system was imposed on a resistant culture with no sustained effort to change that culture;
- inflexibility and unresponsiveness to the management needs of organisations;
- its development at a time of relative stability, whereas by the mid-1980s the environment was becoming increasingly turbulent and uncertain.

There are many objections to the practice of strategic management in public services organisations. Its lineage is suspect, coming as it does from private sector roots. But there are more substantial objections. Public service managers, it is argued, are given little room to manoeuvre since strategies are often handed down by politicians, whether as continuous policy decisions or, in the case of Next Steps executive agencies, in the framework documents. The emphasis seems to be on operational rather than strategic issues, especially in recent times when governments have attempted to make hard and fast distinctions between policy and administration. It has been suggested, for example, that the creation of executive agencies has reinforced the prominence of 'predominantly operational concerns of public management reform, downgrading strategic issues such as management of environmental change' and effective networking (Painter, 1995: 30).

It is also argued that the management of public services is too complex a matter to lend itself to the simplistic promptings of private sector management. Public services managers have to deal not only with the vagaries of elected politicians and their short-term perspectives but also with public involvement and networking with dominant stakeholders. Clear objectives and goals are difficult to come by, since there is often no clear 'means–end relationship' (McKevitt, 1992: 36). Governments' stated policy aims are usually general and vague and even when made more explicit 'do not necessarily correspond to what government really has in mind: it may have a hidden agenda' (Baggott, 1997: 284). One of the many problems of such managers is simply to know what is to be done in an environment 'where goal ambiguity is rampant' (Bozeman and Straussmann, 1990: 37) and where fundamental policies are determined by actions external to the organisation. Yet a common criticism of traditional public administration is its failure to implement the 'will-o'-the wisp' of policy, with critics erroneously treating the policy process as unambiguous and certain. Many factors influence effectiveness of implementation. They include how the issue is defined; whether implementation was ever intended or was merely a sop to placate stakeholders and other interests; and how the implementation stage is resourced. Quite often issues are defined in such a way as to guarantee failure, while the lack of adequate resources often leads to the same result.

One of the major objections to strategic planning in public service organisations is that the rationalist scientific approach and the tools used to generate and evaluate key issues and choices appear to downgrade the political processes. In the political arena, many major decisions are based on political judgements which fall prey to the illusion of objective 'scientific' decision-making (Ranson and Stewart, 1994: 188). Public management is involved with public and political discourse, public access, interest groups and activists. The apparent rational approach of strategic management does not fit well into this environment, where policies and decisions nearly always appear to be negotiable as a result of public discourse.

Two factors immediately come to the fore when making a case for strategic management in the public services organisation,. First, if the concept is interpreted as a process which helps managers to think through aspects relating to their organisation's purpose and objectives, directions and implementation, then it appears to be generic to all sectors. Second, concern with management and strategy in the public sector is not merely a recent phenomenon. The Fulton Committee (1968) expressed the anxiety that the civil service, under constant pressure to deal with the needs of the moment, was not giving enough attention to strategy and planning for the long term. This also applied to local government, where the Maud (1967) and Bains (1972) reports made similar points.

But perhaps the most important reason for incorporating strategic management in public service organisations is a recognition that these organisations have been transformed in recent years. In local government, for example, the once-simple role of service provision supported by self-sufficiency, direct control and uniformity has been supplanted by new ones. These have been fashioned in a period of uncertainty as to what powers and services would remain in its possession, amidst calls for a more entrepreneurial culture. This also applies to other public services. The collective impact of these changes opened up 'a number of fundamental choices regarding role and processes, thus strengthening the case for a more corporate strategy' (Leach, 1996: 7). Too many commentators in the 1990s tend to ignore such changes and continue to treat the public services as if they were dealing with institutions of the 1970s and 1980s. The result is that they are fighting battles long lost or won and using arguments that have seen better days.

Changes in recent years, in terms of competitiveness, market orientations and freedom to take decisions in their own spheres of activity, have resulted in a public sector of very diverse institutions. The development of executive agencies, NHS trusts, quangos, the modified position of local authorities and the general breaking up of large bureaucracies, have resulted in a wide variation amongst institutions in their freedom to act and make strategic choices. Whilst some agencies complain of choices and actions being heavily circumscribed by central government (Painter, Isaac-Henry and Rouse, 1997), others appear to have wide discretion to make decisions which can have an important impact on the organisation itself, the people who work for it and on the service delivered. It is as wrong to treat the public sector as a uniform whole as it is to view the private sector as an entity managed by a set of predetermined prescriptions.

Bryson (1988: 94) asserts that organisations either 'believe they are more tightly constrained in action than they are; or they assume that if they are not explicitly told to do something, they are not allowed to do it'. He suggests that one way of beginning the strategic thinking process is to have a mandate analysis to find out what must be done, what must not be done and what could be done. If organisations do not explore what can be done, they become rule bound, negative and get out of kilter with their environments. Most organisations appear to have some choice in determining the direction in which they would like to go. A common criticism of local government of the 1970s and 1980s was that the assumption of self-sufficiency and service delivery was so ingrained in its thinking and culture, that it:

- encouraged an 'enclosed organisation' which provided services for people, not with or by them;
- failed to utilise the skills, resources, experience and knowledge outside its own narrow administrative and managerial boundaries;
- led to neglect of community, community leadership and responsiveness.

Of course public service organisations cannot decide to go out of business or refuse to provide services, nor can a local authority move to another area. However, public services can, by using a variant of portfolio analysis, choose to do things differently or concentrate more resources on one activity and less on another. In response to the impact of CCT many local authorities made key strategic decisions about their roles. They chose between the residual, market oriented and community-based enabler roles (Leach *et al.*, 1994). In so doing they are responding differently from one another according to their political, economic and cultural circumstances. Such decisions can have enormous implications for the services provided and the way an authority is managed. In any case organisations developing a strategic approach need not necessarily be involved in aspects as fundamental as deciding 'what business' they are in. Most public service organisations appear to be at the business level of strategy. Financial constraints make deciding on priorities a necessity with 'enough hard choices to be made as to what services to be protected and which reduced or even discontinued' (Leach 1996: 8). Nor should the argument that private sector organisations are always free to make strategic choices be taken at face value. Freedom and discretion, as in the public sector, varies amongst organisations. Rosemary Stewart (1982), analysing the work of managers, argued that their work can be divided into demands (what they have to do), constraints (what they cannot do) and choices. In private as in public services, organisations develop multiple goals, have multiple stakeholders and deal with complex and intractable problems. As such, the 'real world of private sector management is both murkier and closer to some issues present in the public service organisations than the ideal would suggest' (Newman and Clarke, 1994: 2).

Strategic Management Practice in Re-invented Public Services

There is now hardly a self-respecting public service organisation which has not succumbed to the blandishments of developing strategic management and planning, whether referring to primary schools, local authorities or executive agencies. Almost every public body now trumpets abroad its mission and vision, accompanied by its core values, goals, key strategic issues and strategic choices. SWOT and PEST analyses are commonplace and stakeholder analysis is regarded as relevant to both the public and private sectors. But there are many who are sceptical of such approaches. Mission statements and visions come in for particular criticisms, not least because of their evangelistic outpourings of good intentions, often without demonstrating the means or processes to achieve them. Nevertheless the collective impact of changes in the public sector over the last 20 years demand different ways of managing. Strategic management can be viewed as a process which is attempting to transform public organisations from the bureaucratic management model to 'a more progressive model displaying greater managerial freedoms and incentives, devolution of power and the constitution of a vision for a better future' (Morley, 1993: 77–8).

The extent to which such claims for strategic management can be justified is a matter of some debate. It can be admitted, however, that it presents an attempt at mediation between the organisation and its environment 'enabling it to clarify and judge the significant changes of purpose and priority in policy that will determine the future of the organisation' (Ranson and Stewart 1994: 189). Pettigrew *et al.* (1992), in examining and evaluating the management of change in the NHS, contend that the type and effectiveness of change is influenced by and varies according to the content, context and processes involved. Content refers to the 'what' of change – the particular area or activity under consideration; context concerns the 'why' of change – the driving forces produced by the external and internal environments giving rise to thoughts of change; while processes relates to the 'how' of change – the actions, reactions and inter-reactions.

Differences in context produce different reasons for organisations attempting strategic management. In some cases institutions are forced into its adoption by government actions, as in the case of executive agencies, where framework documents generally set out the strategies for organisations, whilst they are obliged to provide business plans to demonstrate how those strategies are to be effectively implemented. In other cases, organisations feel the need to concentrate on key strategic issues and priorities as the drive towards efficiency gathers pace and as decreasing financial support from governments reduce their financial capacity. In addition, as in local government, where the very existence of the organisation is threatened, questions relating to its purpose, the business it is in and the way it conducts that business are being posed and answered. For many, part of the solution lies in the adoption of strategic management. Still others have adopted a strategic management stance to demonstrate to sections of their stakeholders the extent of their fitness and legitimacy to manage 'by the adoption of the latest management totems whether or not they are effective or have any real impact' (Leach *et al.*, 1994: 51). Young (1996: 358) argues that preparing and adopting a corporate strategy is regarded by the district auditor and external consultants 'as the *sine qua non* of serious management'. In 1992 the strategic framework document of the city of Birmingham won high praise from the Audit Commission for the way the city documented its strategic objectives and the clear way it presented a sense of purpose. The praise coming from such a source was gratifying to those responsible but the extent to which such a document and strategy influenced the actions and activities of the city, or helped it to achieve its objectives of a more corporate approach, is highly debatable (Isaac-Henry, 1999: forthcoming).

The 'how' of strategic management appears to be as important as the 'what'. It is generally accepted that the way the new management styles and processes are introduced are crucial to eventual implementation and outcomes. Effectiveness depends on the extent to which people in the system – middle managers and other employees – ' buy' into the new ways. Change is not just about directing what is to be done: it is also about convincing those involved that it is the 'correct' thing to do – hence the emphasis on changing cultural values. Public service organisations attempting to introduce strategic change face a number of problems and obstacles including:

- the extent to which people in the organisation are receptive to such changes;
- the difficulty of changing the culture of the organisation and building organisational capacity for change;
- the appropriate process to employ;
- lack of autonomy;
- predominance of the efficiency factor and lack of resources.

Receptivity and Culture

The introduction of strategic management in public services requires basic rethinking of the beliefs, values and behaviour of managers and workers. In short, for such management to succeed culture has to change. Culture has been long thought to have a major impact on corporate strategy. A change of culture generally takes a long time and is often difficult. In public services where the values of established and defensive professional groups are deep-rooted they are likely to survive for some time. Attempts by managers at top-down restructuring over the last 20 years have had limited success (Pettigrew *et al.*, 1992: 22). Fifteen years after reforms were introduced to create an internal market and a more entrepreneurial NHS culture, an observer argued that neither the medical nor the nursing professions had changed their attitude towards management (Baggott, 1997: 295).

A general criticism of the attempt to change management philosophy and practice is that although government and public services managers acknowledge the importance of culture, they have not been prepared to invest the resources of time, effort and money in bringing about change (McHugh, 1997). Indeed at times it could be argued that culture is often treated as something which can be turned on and off by managers at their whim 'the construction of instant designer culture' (Pettigrew *et al.*, 1992: 23). One local chief executive having taken up his post in 1997 was reported to have set himself the task of obtaining effective corporate leadership, sound finance, organisational change, performance review and community involvement, all within his first nine months in office (*Local Government Chronicle*, 1997 (July): 12). Often much effort is spent on the 'what' of change and little on the 'how'. As a result culture, which is considered of such significance to effectiveness of outcome, has been neglected in favour of efficiency and meeting targets.

Allied to the need for paying attention to changing culture and increasing receptivity in an organisation is the need to develop what Collinge and Leach (1995) call the 'capacity' of the organisation. While context, content and processes are crucial to the outcome of change, those factors can themselves influence and be influenced by the organisation's capacity for taking strategic direction and organisation. Capacity refers to the framework and processes put in place for identifying, formulating and making strategic change, regardless of any particular strategy. Thus to 'develop and refine strategic direction, a council must strengthen this capacity for strategy formulation' (ibid.: 344). Capacity is concerned more with the conditions for effective development of strategy than with the substantive strategy itself. In developing such capacity some of the following component are needed:

- the articulation by leaders (politicians as well as officials) of the need for such a strategic capacity;
- the creation of conducive bodies, structures and communication systems at corporate level, to facilitate greater co-operation and breakdown duplication;
- the development of a culture which rejects short-termism and departmentalism and is more conducive to a more integrated approach (Collinge and Leach, 1995: 345– 6).

Building capacity for strategy formulation is part of a wider argument, which suggests that for effective change to take place, an organisation must possess a receptive context. A context characterised by a more integrative structure and culture is more receptive to change and innovation than one which is segmented.

It is recognised that there is no one best way of introducing change in organisations. Conventional wisdom suggests that effective change involves consideration of stakeholder interests, participation, effective communication and development, and learning as some of the various means of changing attitudes and behaviour. A strategy 'formulation process which begins and ends with a board level document is doomed to fail, so far removed is it from the ideal defined by those in the organisation below' (Hay and Williamson, 1996: 654). In many public organisations, strategy is

CASE STUDY 4.1   *Building strategic capacity*

Kirklees Metropolitan Council (KMC) has been one of the most talked-about local authorities'in recent years because of its move away from a rampantly fragmented structure and decision-making process to embrace the more holistic approach of strategic management. It exhibited a more-than-typical local authority fragmented committee structure and political infighting. Its newly appointed chief executive of 1988, Robert Hughes, observed that it lacked corporate leadership, failed to address corporate issues, demonstrated little or no strategic thinking and did not deliver on policy decisions. Following a number of recommendations from INLOGOV in 1989, the council decided to go down the path of strategic management and started the process by attempting to

- clarify and understand the challenges and opportunities presented by the environment;
- identify key issues, goals and objectives;
- consider the implication such changes would have on management structures.

The objective was to strengthen the organisation's capacity for strategic decision-making by the creation of an Executive Board, with the five members chosen not only for their skill and experience but also for their ability to think strategically. The traditional directorate (heads of services) would cease to exist and each functional service would have a head of services reporting to the appropriate executive director. Alongside the Executive Board there would be a Policy Board consisting of senior elected politicians from the majority party with the Executive directors in attendance.

Source: Adapted from Davies and Griffiths, 1994

---

imposed from above either by politicians or by 'heroic management parachuted in by charismatic chief executives' (Pollitt and Harrison, 1992: 283). There are examples in local government, where newly appointed chief executives arrive with ready-made strategic plans which often are not discussed within the organisation as a whole and sometimes bear little reality to the organisation's work or culture (Isaac-Henry, 1999: forthcoming). In executive agencies too, there are complaints that in formulating strategic plans 'individual employees on whom performance of the organisation is highly dependent have been largely ignored' (McHugh, 1997: 37).

In developing change in Kirklees (see Case Study 4.1) the process certainly was top down and there was little participation by those further down the hierarchy, although employees were kept informed by road shows conducted by the chief executive and, in the 1990s, by an internal newspaper. The concept of changing culture was considered important. Hence the management development programme of the 1990s was designed to help deal with cultural change. Nevertheless it was argued in 1994 that until a

CASE STUDY 4.2 *Process and strategy formulation in the Civil Service College*

The Civil Service College (CSC) became an executive agency in 1989 and by 1995 a full cost organisation (Framework Document 1995, p. 1). Its Chief Executive is appointed by the Chancellor of the Duchy of Lancaster and is responsible for the efficient management of the College and *for achieving the strategies, objectives and targets set by the Minister* (Ibid., p. 5). A Management Board consisting of eight directors (of Business Groups) and the Head of Facilities Services and Finance aid the Chief Executive in his management. An Advisory Council consisting of civil servants, industrialists and academics also aids him.

Obliged to produce a strategic plan every three years, in 1992 the CSC began the process by gathering and evaluating information from former students as well as evaluating trends in the external markets. It was thought such information would focus the debate on strategy and help to develop strategic issues. The Management Team held a two-day meeting to discuss a number of key strategic issues and to decide on core objectives. Both a PEST and SWOT analysis as well as scenario building were used to weight and rank objectives.

Participation by members of the college (outside the Management Team) was facilitated by the formation of six groups to discuss strategy, each conducting a PEST and SWOT analysis as well as building scenarios which were later compared with those of the management team. This resulted in the majority of staff working for the College taking part in the exercise. At the same time, each business group as well as service providers was asked to produce strategy statements to demonstrate how they would contribute to the chosen scenarios.

Source: Adapted from Smith (1996)

---

performance culture was more widely developed, the authority would find it difficult to prove that its management revolution had succeeded (Davies and Griffiths, 1994).

Managers of course may be acutely aware of the importance of changing organisational culture but might feel powerless to influence those values and behaviour, especially in the short run. In a survey of emerging changes in local government in the early 1990s, Isaac-Henry and Painter (1991) found some chief executives who were conscious of the necessity of promoting ownership of changes. However, size of authorities and depth of belief of staff were inhibiting factors. The process employed by the Civil Service College (CSC) was different from that of Kirklees and followed almost precisely Bryson's (1988: 5) definition of strategic planning as requiring 'broad scale information gathering, an exploration of alternatives, an emphasis on the present implication for future decisions'. The level of stakeholder participation in the CSC (see Case Study 4.2) was much higher and more direct than is customary in public organisations but such participation might not have been feasible in a larger organisation.

In dwelling too long on the problems faced by the public sector in effectively introducing and developing strategic management, one may become too defensive and negative about this experiment. Strategic management is a dynamic process. It changes and develops over time in the same organisation. A 'good' strategy is one that is flexible and allows objectives to be changed and new ones come on-stream in response to the changing environment. Often public service managers and organisations do not get their strategies right first time. This is in part because many of them have been 'bureau-professionals' and need time to change and think more strategically. As they gain experience, their touch becomes surer. The chief executive of the Child Support Agency (Northern Ireland), for example, considered that only after four years of operation had the agency become sufficiently knowledgeable about the business to be able to plan effectively over the next three to five years (Online, 20/11/98, http://ssa.nics.gov.uk).

Criticisms of strategic management in public sector services organisations must be tempered by the fact that organisations develop, learn, and adapt through their life cycle. 'Young' organisations behave differently from 'middle-aged' or 'mature' ones. In the prison service, for example, the first attempt to develop strategic management and planning was, according to a former deputy governor, no more than a paper exercise – 'a comfort blanket' – where responsibility for developing and writing the strategic plan was given to one middle-ranking officer (Wilson, 1998). However, as managerialism became more pronounced, finances became more scarce and as the prison service moved into agency status, the importance of strategic management took on a much greater significance and status.

Conclusion

It is understandable that the practice of strategic management should be caught up in the political backlash of 'managerialism' and the debate about the distinctiveness of the public services. Increasingly it is being recognised, however, that managerialism has gone hand-in-hand with restructuring of the state and that, given its salience across international boundaries, it has a volition of its own. It is not simply the creation of an ideological Thatcherite and Majorite agenda. Thus while the eyes of many have been firmly fixed on the lineage and style of NPM, some have missed the substance – that of seeing these management changes as a means of transforming the public sector, giving it new meanings, purposes and roles. The lines between public and private organisations are becoming blurred. Certainly, whatever criticisms may be made of NPM, it is questioning and changing perceptions, power relationships and organisational boundaries. Within this changed public service environment, strategic management sits quite comfortably if it is thought of as a process 'which helps key decision makers to think and act strategically' (Bryson, 1988: 46). This is not to say that the tools of analysis and language used are applicable to all organisations and all sectors. While some are pertinent to both private and public organisations, others are more appropriate to one form of organisation than to another. Neither must it be regarded as a panacea for public service managers. It certainly has not been so for the private sector.

The New Labour administration seems to have accepted the tenets of NPM, albeit giving some of them a softer edge. Although there is no turning back to the pre-Thatcher era, the language has been modified. Competition, the watchword of Conservative governments, has slipped from its pre-eminent position. CCT is giving way to 'best value', although contracting out is still an option. Much more is being heard of joint workings, networking, multi-agency approaches and 'joined up government'. None of this lessens the need for strategic management and indeed its use seems certain to increase for a number of reasons. First, as Elcock (1993: 76) indicated, developing coherent longer-term strategies has proved useful to many managers in meeting governmental and other environmental demands and is therefore unlikely to be abandoned. It could be argued that after a lengthy period of experiment with strategic management it is becoming part of the culture of public management. Second, the turbulent environment, in which priorities have to be determined and hard choices made, is set to continue for the foreseeable future. Third, government shows no sign of lessening the pressures it exerts on public services organisations to act strategically. It still continues to demand strategic plans from an increasing number of public service bodies, against which performance is judged. The imperative to act strategically is even more firmly imposed on local government. Government envisages a new role for local authorities – that of community government. This entails them taking the 'lead in developing a clear sense of direction for their communities'; ensuring at all times that they 'consider the longer-term well-being of their area' based on clear and understandable strategy (DETR, 1998a: 80–1). Hence the necessity of finding answers to such fundamental questions as: 'What are our essential functions? Who is our public? How are we to serve them? What are the implications for the way we are organised?' (Ranson and Stewart, 1994: 189) will not diminish. What is likely is that government's emphasis on democratic renewal, increased participation by 'customers' and a more 'networked' and organised public service is likely to put greater demand on obtaining effective information. Much of this will be dependent on the use of information and communication technologies (ICTs). The new government has pledged to use ICTs to revitalise the delivery and quality of public services (Online, 11/19/98, http://www.opem.gov.uk.). What should not be forgotten is the huge benefits which could be obtained from the effective use of ICTs in the provision of information in making strategic choices.

5

Performance Management, Quality Management and Contracts

JOHN ROUSE

Improving performance in public service organisations has been described as a 'wicked problem' since it is inherently complex, ambiguous and intractable (Jackson, 1998). A key characteristic of the Conservative years in office was to move the focus of public services from the traditional public administration model of organisation and accountability to a new managerialism most frequently described as the New Public Management (NPM) (Hood, 1991). This approach shifted the emphasis from the traditional concerns of political, bureaucratic and professional values to performance and quality service delivery, judged essentially from the perspective of the customer. This chapter explores the performance management and quality movement associated with the new managerialism and the developments most recently introduced by New Labour, with its claimed commitment to social democratic renewal and the participation of citizens as shapers of public services, rather than simply customers.

The Challenge of Performance and Quality Management in the Public Domain

Performance and quality management is important both for providing accountability to the public for public funds spent and producing better and more effective services. At the broadest level, it is concerned with the overall approach taken to establishing and implementing performance and quality systems to achieve success. At micro level, it is about enhancing the value adding process within organisations. This process defines the relationship between the inputs used by an organisation, the activities it undertakes to transform these inputs into delivered outputs, and ultimately to the outcomes achieved, where the latter can be interpreted as the value placed by society on the public service. For example, a university employs lecturers and uses buildings and learning materials (inputs) to deliver classes, library access, assessment (activities) in order to produce graduates (output) who become more educated and able citizens (outcome). Performance and quality management is concerned with maximising the value added through this process such that the initial 'costs' are exceeded by the subsequent 'benefits' by as wide a margin as possible. It involves the simultaneous achievement of economy, efficiency and effectiveness – 'value for money' (VFM) – in the delivery of a quality service.

VFM as an indicator of successful performance is most easily defined as the economic acquisition of resources and their efficient utilisation in the realisation of the purposes of the organisation (Rouse, 1997). Economy is about the cost of inputs used and entails the purchasing of inputs of a given quality specification at the lowest possible cost. Efficiency relates to the costs involved in producing outputs and is concerned with ensuring the maximum possible output – service delivered – from a given level of inputs. Hence, economy and efficiency are concerned with doing things right. Effectiveness is concerned with outcomes and is about producing desired results – doing the right thing. Figure 5.1 illustrates the relationships.

In the private sector, value added between inputs, activities, outputs and outcomes is measured by the profitability of the organisation, since costs and benefits are translated via prices into financial returns through the processes of market exchange. It is claimed that market competitive forces ensure that economy, efficiency and effectiveness are achieved. The fact that public services are rarely characterised by full market transactions is the first fundamental reason why the application of value chain analysis, though still conceptually relevant, is more complex in the public arena. Without the process of market exchange in a competitive environment there are no

FIGURE 5.1 *The Value Adding Process*

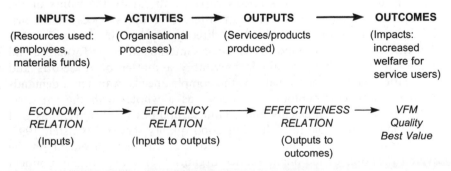

INPUTS →	ACTIVITIES →	OUTPUTS →	OUTCOMES
(Resources used: employees, materials funds)	(Organisational processes)	(Services/products produced)	(Impacts: increased welfare for service users)

ECONOMY RELATION →	*EFFICIENCY RELATION* →	*EFFECTIVENESS RELATION* →	*VFM Quality Best Value*
(Inputs)	(Inputs to outputs)	(Outputs to outcomes)	

Source: Rouse (1997)

simple and reliable monetary measures of value chain components, particularly of outputs and outcomes, with the result that values must be imputed by more indirect means. Therein lies the real difficulty, since public service organisations are characterised by a complex array of stakeholders – current and potential users, voter-citizens, elected members, professionals and other employees – each with a different set of values and ideas about good performance and a quality service experience. For example, those on probation may see the probation service as an intrusion, magistrates may see it as preventing re-offending and the Home Secretary as punishment (Flynn, 1995). 'Value', and consequently performance, in this context of conflicting objectives is deeply contested, defies a simple equivalence such as the bottom line of profitability and is necessarily a matter of political judgement (Stewart and Walsh, 1994). Moreover, political judgement must reflect what has been called the distinctive purposes, values and conditions of the public domain (Stewart, 1995). The distinctive public service values include equity, fairness, community, citizenship, justice and democracy. The distinctive conditions include the democratic process, public accountability and openness of decision making. This presents an extremely rich and diverse notion of performance and quality in the public domain, one which involves different values over both service outcomes and the process by which they are achieved.

In terms of performance definitions, the existence of multiple stakeholders and conflicting values within the public domain means that the concept of good performance as 'effectiveness' and 'quality' becomes problematic. Effectiveness, as we have seen, is concerned with outcomes and is about producing desired results – doing the right thing. Similarly, quality is most frequently defined as the extent to which a service as specified achieves its intended purpose – 'fitness for purpose' (Juran, 1979). However, the meaning of 'desired results' or 'fitness for purpose' is less clear-cut in the public domain, given the diversity of stakeholders and values. Effectiveness and quality could be defined in terms of achieving the objectives set by the public service organisation itself, essentially a provider or producer view. A broader view of effectiveness and quality is provided when desired results are judged in terms of the service's capacity to satisfy the wants of the multiple stakeholders who have an interest in the services – not just 'customers', professionals and others directly involved in the service, but also citizens. Since all cannot be satisfied simultaneously, performance and quality in the public domain is inevitably a matter of trade-offs and negotiation with a need to 'balance the complex needs, wants and demands of individuals, communities and society as a whole, with the capacity, resources, legal requirements and technical abilities of organisations and individuals responsible for achieving good quality services' (Gaster, 1995: 21). Defining successful performance requires reaching agreement on the overall purposes of the public service organisation, an essentially political task.

There are further complications which compound the difficulties of defining and managing successful performance and quality service delivery in public services. First, whereas in the private sector there are strong incentives to secure quality performance, since poor quality will be reflected in falling sales, declining profits and ultimate market extinction, in the public services such feedback on performance and quality is much less forceful (Pollitt and Bouckaert, 1995). In many public services, particularly where the service is provided free at the point of use, the real problem is often one of rationing demand, as for example in areas of health care. Falling demand may be seen as a relief and rising demand, particularly where budgets are fixed, a real problem since it increases pressure on staff and facilities and leads to queues. Since many public services are monopoly providers, there is little the dissatisfied customer can do as there are few or no alternative services, particularly for low-income groups. Customer satisfaction as expressed by repeat business, as in the private sector, is not necessarily a measure of success (Flynn, 1997).

Second, there is the nature of public services themselves. A number of public services are different from private ones in that, for example, they involve coercive relationships (policing), dependency (social security), and are non-rejectable (arrest). Such services raise interesting issues concerning the definition and management of performance and quality, since the immediate customer's preferences (for example, the arrested criminal) may be seen as less significant than those of the wider society-citizenry. A further complication results from the fact that a number of public services, such as education, only provide their benefits a long time after their immediate consumption. Moreover, most public activities involve a service relationship rather than the production and delivery of goods. Since services cannot be stored, easily measured nor investigated prior to 'purchase' but can only be assessed in the process of use, it is sometimes difficult to distinguish between activities and the output of a service, since output is also the very process of being served (Morgan and Murgatroyd, 1994). In many services, then, it is the interchange between provider and recipient which is vital to an assessment of quality performance, an interchange which cannot be 'designed in' prior to the event (Gaster, 1995; Pollitt and Bouchaert, 1995).

There is also the complex socio-political environment in which public services are delivered. Considerable uncertainty often surrounds the causal relationships between inputs, outputs and outcomes in the value chain and, in particular, the extent to which performance is influenced by external factors rather than organisational activity itself. Outcomes, moreover, may be produced jointly by a number of public and other agencies, as well as being influenced by external events beyond agency control, with the result that the ownership of performance is hard to establish. For example, the level of criminal activity is influenced by the police service, probation service, prison service and courts, as well as external factors such as the level of economic prosperity. Recent market reforms in the public services sector have exacerbated this complexity, since multi-purpose elected agencies have been replaced by a fragmenting structure of single purpose, non-elected, semi-autonomous 'quangos'. In the differentiated polity, as Rhodes (1997) calls it, performance management becomes an increasingly difficult challenge. Defining and managing performance and quality is both complex and challenging. It must remain an exercise in values, discourse and politics rather than simply a technocratic management exercise (Ranson and Stewart, 1995; Jackson, 1994).

Successful Performance Management and Quality Services

Successful performance management depends upon having both appropriate technical and procedural practice *and* supportive cultural and attitudinal characteristics within an organisation (Rouse, 1997: 87). Jackson and Palmer (1993) stress the need to adopt a strategic management perspective (see chapter 4). A strategic focus fully integrated into the working practices of the organisation enables a systematic performance framework to be developed which encourages and facilitates organisational learning and a problem-solving approach to maximise value added. The systematic performance framework should include:

- a clear organisational mission, with derived objectives expressed as precisely and unambiguously as possible;
- emphasis upon outputs and outcomes in terms of specified objectives;
- a set of targets or 'measurable' performance indicators, related to objectives, for performance monitoring;
- clear expectations, such that each person knows they are responsible for specific results, with these being achievable but stretching;
- supportive performance architecture and organisational culture.

Kay (1993) defines architecture as a distinctive collection of relational contracts. It incorporates relations with employees, suppliers, customers and other organisations. It is about developing organisational structures fit for their purpose, about appropriate staffing and skills levels, information systems and incentive systems and appropriate management style and culture (Jackson, 1998). It is generally agreed that a commitment culture, which is non-threatening and celebrates the learning philosophy of continuous improvement, leads to greater acceptance and ownership of performance and, therefore, a real chance of its achievement. Responsiveness to clients and service users is also essential, with emphasis upon searching for and discovering new solutions to problems, and innovation over time.

One approach which is meant to embrace all of these characteristics is that of Total Quality Management (TQM). Whereas quality assurance is an approach to performance and quality which emphasises the importance of ensuring all the processes and activities involved in producing a service are working properly TQM is far more ambitious. It is concerned to involve everyone in the organisation in a programme of continuous improvement to meet expectations of quality, attempting to 'synchronise strategy, vision and operations' (Morgan and Murgatroyd, 1994: 3). However, TQM has in recent years become sloganised and the label may now be unhelpful, particularly in the public services context. An approach essentially developed for manufacturing industry may be less applicable in the public domain where the key concerns and concepts are very different (Pollitt and Bouckaert, 1995).

The Changing Performance Management Movement

Prior to the managerial revolution of the 1980s and 1990s, performance and quality management within the public services was dominated by the public administration paradigm, premised on the post-war social-democratic consensus. The political model of representative democracy, with service deliverers responsible to elected representatives at both national and local levels, themselves responsible to elected assemblies, was supplemented by an administrative model. In the latter 'emphasis was upon the bureaucratic ideal of efficient and impartial administration characterised by hierarchical structure, clearly defined duties and rule-based procedures, in which tasks which could not easily be controlled by rules were carried out by professionally qualified staff who were given "bounded discretion"' (Butcher, 1995: 2). Hence, political accountability was bolstered by bureaucratic administration and professional accountability, and public services were produced within and delivered by the public sector. Government, to use Osborne and Gaebler (1992) metaphor, both steered (directed) and rowed (provided). Within the democratic political framework, emphasis was upon administrative processes which would secure performance in terms of legal, financial, budgetary and managerial accountability.

The focus of financial performance and accountability was probity. This involves the provision of financial information to demonstrate legality and accuracy of financial statements. Ensuring that the taxpayers' resources entrusted to the organisation are used legally and that there are verifiable statements of income and expenditure remains vitally important in public service organisations. However, though necessary, it is not sufficient to ensure quality performance. Indeed, requirements for probity may be used to justify inflexible financial controls, thereby inhibiting potential performance improvements. Similar comments apply to the other traditional performance standard, budgetary performance. A budget is a plan of operation expressed in financial terms indicating where money is to come from and how it is to be spent in the coming year. Adherence by the organisation to its annual budget is the performance measure. However, the nature of the traditional budgetary process in many public service organisa-

informal mechanisms of bureaucratic and hierarchical control. The purchaser-provider split can be within the same public service organisation (the internal market) or involve outside agencies, including private sector and quasi-autonomous ones ('externalisation' or contracting out).

Reforms in central and local government, health, education, housing and social services in the late 1980s and 1990s introduced increasing elements of contract management and quasi-market operations, with most of it continuing to this day. For example, reforms in the civil service introduced Next Step agencies to undertake responsibilities (act as providers) within the framework laid down for them by the responsible government departments (the purchasers) which set their objectives and performance criteria. Agencies are responsible for implementation, not policy. In 1991 market testing, which required all departments to submit their activities to comparison with the private sector firms, was introduced (see Chapter 9). The internal market in health, education, housing and social services went even further, introducing an element of competition among purchasers and providers and funding based on activities and outcomes. For example, the National Health Service and Community Care Act 1990 established internal markets in health. Semi-autonomous hospital trusts, in competition with each other, community services and private hospitals, bid for contracts to supply health care as demanded by Local Health Authorities and GP fund-holders acting as purchasers on behalf of the public. Within tight strategic guidelines provided by central government, purchasers write annual contract specifications which set down prices and the service standards required (see Chapter 11). Similar policies were introduced in community care and housing.

In education, the Education Reform Act 1988 removed power from LEAs by devolving financial responsibility to school governors, introduced open school enrolments to give parents and pupils greater choice (albeit within a new national curriculum and a framework of school inspection), to stimulate competition between schools, and provide the opportunity for schools to opt out of local authority control altogether and become grant maintained. In local government, the NHS and large parts of the public services sector, the requirements for competitive tendering extended contractual relationships. Compulsory competitive tendering (CCT) was introduced by the Local Government Planning and Land Act 1980 into a limited number of services but extended by the Local Government Acts 1988 and 1992 to cover almost all manual and professional services. CCT aimed to ensure that local and other public authorities undertake activities in-house only if they do so competitively. Even where work was retained in-house through competitive bidding, separate Direct Service Organisation units had to be created within the authority. These have their own trading accounts and the requirement to meet financial and other performance criteria as specified in the contract.

The markets that have emerged from the reforms are essentially administratively designed 'quasi-markets': the market mechanism is combined with government control (LeGrand, 1991). Such markets were expected to challenge traditional bureaucratic and professional delivery and provide incentives for managers to deliver higher standards of performance at lower costs. The need for purchasers to specify more explicitly their service requirements in a contract, and for providers to gain the contract through competitive bidding and demonstrated contract compliance, are supposed to lead to greater efficiency and cost savings, more innovation and greater responsiveness to customer requirements. Even where the in-house provider wins the contract, and this has mostly been the case, the fact that they have to compete with other potential suppliers is sufficient to force them into efficiency savings, both initially and through time. Contracting, it is argued, clarifies roles and responsibilities, leads to stronger financial control, more market orientation, greater managerial control over work leading to more flexible working practices at lower costs, encouragement to invest in new technologies and rationalise or reduce assets which are no longer required (Flynn, 1997).

Criticisms of the quasi-market approach to performance management cast doubt on both the efficiency and legitimacy of their resulting outcomes. The first concern is that commercial criteria tend to force contracting into securing a narrow form of efficiency, one dominated by cost savings to the detriment of quality service delivery. Moreover, since in most quasi-markets the actual user (for example, the patient) is rarely involved in making direct choices but is represented by an agent (GP or care manager), performance outcomes often remain producer-led rather than customer-led. The fact that contracts have been short term and based on clear separation of purchaser from provider within a cost and control approach to management has further narrowed the definition of performance and quality. The 'adversarial contractual relationship', based on low trust and the expectation that each side wishes to gain at the expense of the other, has tended to dominate quasi-markets in Britain, particularly with CCT. Excessive formalisation and the distancing of service providers from service users can lead to inflexibility. Since deviation from the contract specification requires the approval of the purchasers, customers have little impact on services (Flynn, 1997: 150). By contrast, 'collaborative' or 'obligational' contracting, more the norm in the private sector, emphasises trust, longer-term relationships and working together for mutual benefit, sharing risk and going beyond the detail of the contract. Such contracts can be more flexible and innovative and incorporate the contribution of service users to service development and quality service delivery (Davis and Walker, 1998). Though, as Flynn emphasises, different parts of the public sector have adopted different sorts of contract, collaborative ones have not been the norm.

A major problem with markets is the administrative and transaction costs of creating and maintaining them. As the internal market reforms in health in particular have shown, there are considerable costs in managing the contracting process itself, both in writing contracts and monitoring their compliance. As demonstrated by the new institutional economics (Williamson, 1975), such transaction costs are especially high where defining measurable outcomes is problematic, as is the case in many public services, and in uncertain environments when it is very costly to write complete contracts able to deal with all possible contingencies. Without such specification, particularly where contracts are adversarial, opportunistic behaviour is likely on the part of the provider who has an incentive to manipulate information and shape service delivery, perhaps to the detriment of quality performance. Williamson has shown that where such transaction costs are high they may swamp the potential efficiency savings from market transactions, justifying hierarchy and direct provision through organisational bureaucracy. Government by contract, therefore, may not achieve even the restricted notion of performance its adherents claim.

A key outcome of the restructuring associated with quasi-market reforms has been formal decentralisation, a more devolved form of management and fragmentation in the public services. Formerly unified bureaucracies have been divided into discrete parts, each operating a contract, and new players quasi-autonomous public agencies (quangos) as well as private firms – now deliver public services, blurring the boundaries between public and private domains. This raises a number of performance and legitimacy issues. Stewart and Walsh (1994) argue that fragmentation reduces the scope for flexibility, organisational learning and adaptability because information required for learning is contained in separate units with a reduced capacity for integration, thereby compromising the system's overall performance. Jervis and Richards (1997) refer to this as the 'design deficit' in public management which prevents society tackling the 'wicked problems' which are multi-faceted and cross over boundaries, requiring a more co-ordinated approach.

There is a danger too that contractual relationships exclude more traditional public service values of equity, citizenship, community and democracy, which are less easy to incorporate in a contract (Ranson and Stewart, 1994). This is because there is a tendency in the formalised contractual approach to focus on the quantifiable elements of performance and quality 'inhibiting the exercise of judgement which is based on dialogue rather than measurement', thereby invalidating those aspects of work which are invisible and non-measurable (Deakin and Walsh, 1996: 39). Equity, for example, may have been compromised as incentives have been provided for 'cherry picking' strategies. GP fund-holders may have become more selective in enrolling patients, excluding the more expensive ones. Schools may become more selective in their admissions policies so as to compete in the market. Further, many of the cost savings secured through contracting, particularly where they involve deterioration in the conditions of service of the workforce and job cuts, may come into conflict with wider public service values. In many ways, quasi-market reforms have been designed to do just this, to focus on market values and the 'discourse of enterprise' (Hoggett, 1996), to cut costs and reduce the scope for local politics. Indeed, though there has been operational decentralisation as a plethora of new autonomous agencies, particularly in the local economy, have appeared, this has been accompanied by increasing government centralisation over policy direction. The result has been 'centralised-decentralisation' (Hoggett, 1996: 18), with operations devolved to business units such as trusts, schools or agencies but control over policy kept centrally in Whitehall. Central policy direction is ensured by a regime of performance targeting, performance-based funding and rigorous audit and inspection (Power, 1997). This separation of policy and implementation has reduced the ability of service managers to contribute to policy development and shape policy in the light of service experience, leading to a 'development deficit' (Jervis and Richards, 1997). It has also enabled politicians to distance themselves from decisions which are unpopular with the electorate.

Contracts, then, tend to exclude traditional public service values and narrow performance and quality definitions. Furthermore, contracts have important consequences for accountability and the wider frame in which performance is defined and negotiated. Internal markets and externalisation challenge traditional forms of public accountability through the electoral chain of command, leading to a 'democratic deficit' (Stewart, 1993b). This may well be the case where quasi-autonomous, semi-commercial local organisations have been established and run by non-elected boards subject only to central government performance guidelines. Commercial sensitivity may be used to justify reduced access to information for the public; removal from the rigours of financial control may lead to problems of probity and sleaze; the fact that board members are nominated rather than elected offers opportunities for political and personal patronage. Contract accountability, then, could seriously compromise political accountability and the legitimacy of the resulting performance outcomes.

Evidence to support the superior performance of market outcomes is limited and subject to a number of methodological problems (Pollitt, 1995). Deakin and Walsh (1996) conclude that competition and contracting have focused attention on the way that quality of public services can be assessed, but the attainment of quality of service is significantly influenced by the degree to which outputs can clearly be specified and observed. In simple services, where production technology is well understood and performance can be readily observed – such as refuse collection and street cleaning – standards have improved (Boyne, 1998a). There is less evidence on the operation of contracts for more complex services, such as health, social care and education. Recent evidence by Le Grand, Mays and Mulligan (1998) shows that NHS activity has risen faster than resources and faster than before the reforms, suggesting an overall increase in efficiency. Discrimination against high-cost patients was not observed but neither was an increase in choice by individual patients. Their overall conclusion is how little measurable change there was overall.

Charters and Performance Indicators

Quasi-market policies for performance have been complimented by at least two other policies for enhancing performance: the *Citizen's Charter* initiative and the greater commitment to performance monitoring, particularly through league tables of performance indicators (PIs). The *Citizen's Charter* (Cabinet Office, 1991) was an attempt by John Major to challenge further the provider-professional culture of public service organisations in the quasi-market, emphasising the importance of customer-determined services. Its objective was to raise quality, give more choice, secure better VFM and enhance responsibility. The mechanisms used included assessing performance, publicising information and standards achieved (through PIs) and setting up complaints and redress procedures. The approach, however, has been more about designing new forms of process control – seeking to build quality into inputs, systems and procedures – than about designing quality into the work culture through, for instance, participative methods of employee involvement in processes of continuous service improvement (Hoggett, 1996). Moreover, charters have been 'too steeped in the language of the market while ignoring other important considerations, such as citizens as participants, contributors to public life and members of the community with collective rights and responsibilities' (Isaac-Henry, 1997: 14).

The use of PIs in general and league tables in particular have often reinforced this limited view of successful performance. PIs in the public domain, however, have at least two key roles. Their internal management role is to assist the policy planning and monitoring process within the organisation so as to ensure decisions reflect, for example, VFM and quality service provision. Their public accountability role is to provide those outside the organisation with a basis for judging performance and establishing accountability, for example, via league tables. In both roles, they introduce a form of quasi-competition whereby different units within the same organisation, the same unit at different points in time, or the same unit in different organisations, can be compared. However, shaping the perfect set of PIs is extremely difficult in the public domain, given the multiple values and stakeholders and complex nature of the services and contexts in which they are delivered. Likierman (1993) has provided 20 criteria for successful PIs based on the lessons of experience. A systematic performance framework cascaded and integrated top-to-bottom throughout the organisation to ensure value alignment is vital. A learning, non-threatening, culture where PIs are seen as helping in an exploratory process of enquiry instead of providing exact numbers for defining unambiguous standards of performance is essential. Stressed too is the need to avoid over-concentration on the quantitative, the short term and 'targetology'.

In the past, however, not all these lessons have been learned. Crude indicators of success, mainly those associated with inputs and efficiency rather than effectiveness, have been chosen since they are far easier to quantify. Examination league tables in schools, research ratings in universities, waiting times in hospitals have all influenced the definition of performance and caused managers to adjust their behaviour sometimes to the detriment of, for example, wider educational goals in schools, teaching quality in universities and genuine patient priorities in hospitals. Performance has all too frequently been reduced to meeting centrally determined PIs, with activity manipulated to show these have been met, whilst real priorities have been neglected.

Performance Management under New Labour

The approach to performance and quality management under New Labour shows signs of both continuity and change. During its first 18 months in office, the new government accepted not only the fiscal constraints of its predecessor but also most of the institutional arrangements for delivering public services. The purchaser-provider split remains in central government, the health service and most other public services. Labour's emphasis is upon improved standards rather than new structures. Commitment is to 'economic efficiency with social fairness', to quote Tony Blair, within a framework which focuses not only on individual rights but also on reciprocal social responsibilities and obligations. The path chosen is between bureaucracy and markets – the 'so-called Third Way' (Giddens, 1998).

If anything, the performance management ethos has become even more pronounced by the new government, though the overall context in which it is being implemented is being changed. There are a number of examples of highly centralist and prescriptive policies and a strengthening of the management ethos. Unprecedented powers have been given to the Secretary of State for Education and Employment to intervene in local educational authorities where individual schools are failing. Rewards for performance are being strengthened, as with performance-related pay (PRP) for teachers. A new Commission for Health Improvement is now able to intervene where the health system is seen to be failing locally. A new Housing Inspectorate will have similar powers over local housing authorities. Moreover, additional funds for public services from the Comprehensive Spending Review of July 1998 are conditional on achieving targets and objectives set out in 'public service agreements' each department reaches with the Treasury. Much of the money is earmarked for specific purposes rather than left to the discretion of LEAs and Health Authorities. There remains, then, emphasis upon evidence-based performance, with tight monitoring and evaluation.

Other important new initiatives stress the need for multi-agency working through area-based partnerships to overcome the 'design deficit' resulting from market fragmentation. Health Action Zones encourage local health care collaboration, pushing for more integrated care at community level between health, community and social services to overcome health deprivation . Education Action Zones are local partnership forums involving local government and other agencies – including private ones – that are given much greater freedom to innovate in improving educational standards . The Social Exclusion Unit, located in the Cabinet Office, has the key objective of promoting more holistic, 'joined-up', and preventative approaches to social policy problems which emphasise improving the mechanisms for integrating the work of government departments, local authorities and other agencies, private, voluntary and public. There appears to be an 'emergent partnership' model of government and the approach being advocated throughout the public sector is offering a very different architecture for performance management.

Democratic renewal is an important component of the re-design and re-contexting of the performance management movement. The broader political changes are at the level of constitutional reform with greater decentralisation, nationally and regionally, moving the emphasis from consumerism and centralisation to citizenship and democratic participation. At local level there is a particular emphasis upon democratic renewal, with an increased requirement on local government to use a range of methods to consult and involve their local citizens, including local referenda, focus groups, citizens' juries, local community forums and so on to elicit local voices. More emphasis is being placed, therefore, upon the participation of citizens in the planning and production of services which can be built into a more inclusive definition of quality performance. Performance and quality management is to be seen as a dialogue between stakeholders, essentially political and process driven.

The 'best value' initiative combines several strands of New Labour's approach to performance: an emphasis on what counts is what works, collaboration and networking, inclusivity and participation, and an intolerance of low standards. The requirement that local authorities (plus all authorities with tax-paying or precepting powers) achieve 'best value' in their service delivery will supercede CCT. Best value (BV) places a duty on local authorities to achieve effective services, balancing quality and cost, by the most effective and efficient means available. Councils have greater discretion in choosing the delivery mechanisms, though BV is to apply to a wider range of services than CCT. There is no presumption that private or public provision is superior and encouragement is given to developing multi-agency partnerships and collaborative networks. It is also rooted in the principle of democratic renewal, with councils deciding on their priorities and standards of service in consultation with their communities and other partners. This puts local stakeholders in a stronger position to influence services, moving the focus from cost-effectiveness to community-effectiveness. The BV performance management framework is illustrated in Figure 5.2 (Department of the Environment, 1998b).

FIGURE 5.2 *The best value performance management framework*

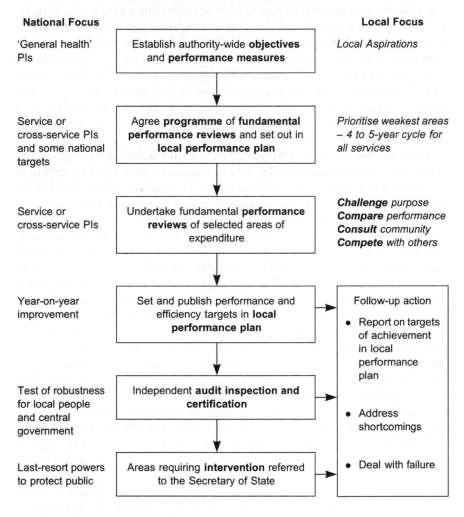

National Focus

'General health' PIs

Service or cross-service PIs and some national targets

Service or cross-service PIs

Year-on-year improvement

Test of robustness for local people and central government

Last-resort powers to protect public

Establish authority-wide **objectives** and **performance measures**

Agree **programme** of **fundamental performance reviews** and set out in **local performance plan**

Undertake fundamental **performance reviews** of selected areas of expenditure

Set and publish performance and efficiency targets in **local performance plan**

Independent **audit inspection and certification**

Areas requiring **intervention** referred to the Secretary of State

Local Focus

Local Aspirations

Prioritise weakest areas – 4 to 5-year cycle for all services

***Challenge** purpose*
***Compare** performance*
***Consult** community*
***Compete** with others*

Follow-up action

- Report on targets of achievement in local performance plan

- Address shortcomings

- Deal with failure

   Fundamental performance reviews of all local authority services are required over a five-year period, starting with the worst performing ones. As such BV is seen as a cultural change designed to achieve a commitment to continuous improvement both in service standards and efficiency. Clear performance targets are to be set and published in Local Performance Plans, which become the basis of audit. Though local consultation and preference is the key to BV, including the determination of relevant performance measures, central government is to continue to set the context for service provision, including a new framework of performance indicators, standards and targets. The Audit Commission and the new Best Value Inspectorate are to be charged with establishing that BV has been achieved. Those achieving excellence will be rewarded with 'beacon' status. Where excellence has not been achieved, there will be central intervention with a range of sanctions. CCT could be re-imposed on the council and, in extreme cases, the service could be removed from the council altogether. This 'naming' and 'shaming', combined with the ultimate sanction of service removal, is replicated in others areas of the public services, including education, health and housing. Indeed, league tables, albeit in a slightly modified form, are being given even more prominence alongside benchmarking, audit and inspection, and incentive structures to reward success with higher investment, more devolved powers and PRP.

Thus, emphasis upon cost effectiveness and achievement of quality standards is as prominent under New Labour as under the Conservatives and there has been no structural upheaval. The essence of the 'Third Way' seems to be around the values and structures of governance rather than the structure of public service organisations as such. What is being sought is a genuine political accountability and an associated notion of performance, one which relates to the distinctive purposes, values and conditions of the public domain, so as to build citizenship as well as responsiveness to customers (Stewart, 1995). The agenda is reinventing democracy rather than government. Constitutional reform, enhanced collaboration through networks of organisational alliances and more participative forms of democracy, particularly at local levels, provide a very different context for performance and quality service definition and management. Collaboration and co-operation are emphasised rather than competition and choice. Another important ingredient of the approach is the campaigning style of the new government. Tony Blair, in particular, sees performance improvement as a crusade, stressing the importance of organisational ownership and empowerment in a new contract between state and citizen. The danger is that the 'harder' performance mechanisms are likely to reinforce central control and may contradict aspects of the democratic renewal agenda which emphasises local dialogue, organisational empowerment and community-based definitions of quality performance. This may be an important source of tension in the very concept of best value and 'Third Way' performance management. There are also doubts as to whether partnership and co-operation can provide an adequate substitute for competition (Boyne, 1998b).

Conclusion

Approaches to performance and quality management range from the technocratic to the developmental. Whereas the latter is concerned with the effective performance of the system as a whole in an essentially political environment, the former concentrates on detailed issues around the delivery of public services, seeing performance as 'unpolitical', a question of good management. Technocratic solutions, particularly those based on competitive markets, have generated the triple deficits of design, democracy and development (Jervis and Richards, 1994). Jervis and Richards, echoing the work of Ranson and Stewart (1995), argue for 'design for effectiveness'. This necessitates the concept of 'control through learning' and 'localness' so that wicked problems can be solved. Control through learning requires organisations to 'invest in improving the quality of thinking, the capacity for reflection and team learning, and the ability to develop shared visions and shared understanding of complex business issues' (ibid.: 12). It requires an organisational culture based on trust and commitment rather than sanctions and fear. It also requires 'localness' – a more pluralistic relationship with the range of stakeholders involved in the production, delivery and evaluation of public services plus networks of collaboration and partnership at many different levels. This is the architecture which can maximise real value added. It is managing performance to empower rather than control and to recognise public sector values. It would seem that New Labour at least aspires to these principles, balancing the constitutional and public management agendas (Painter, 1998). It will be interesting to see whether it can deliver.

6

Marketing in the Public Services

RICHARD CHRISTY and JILL BROWN

This chapter reviews the place of marketing in the management of public services. Growth of interest by managers of public services in the commercial discipline of marketing stems from the period of rapid change in public organisations since the 1980s. These changes placed greater emphasis than ever before on the ideas of business efficiency and customer orientation. Public service organisations were encouraged to recognise service users as customers, understand their needs and preferences and develop services in ways that would maximise customer satisfaction. At this simplistic level, the appeal of marketing for public services managers is clear. If marketing allows private manufacturers to achieve commercial objectives through understanding customer needs and satisfying them more effectively than their competitors, then why should not the same discipline allow public services to achieve their commercial and other objectives? Appealing though this idea may seem, a moment's thought suggests some practical difficulties. For example: are anxious and inexpert patients of a doctor really capable of choosing the particular healthcare service that is best suited to their needs? Is it significant from a marketing point of view that many public services are supplied free at the point of use and may not be paid for directly by the users of those services? Is the relationship between a taxpayer and the Inland Revenue anything like the marketing relationship between a supplier and a customer? What is the appropriate marketing response to very high levels of demand for roads and parking services in the centre of cities? Should households be free to buy or not to buy rubbish collection services, as they see fit? These are some of the issues to be explored in this chapter.

Is Marketing Appropriate for the Public Services?

Public services have special characteristics that differentiate them from private ones. Gaster (1995: 45) argues that not all public services have the provision of satisfaction as their primary aim and there may be inherent danger in 'seeking popularity . . . at the cost of other purposes and values'. The introduction of marketing in the public services has therefore been gradual, with continuing adjustments at all levels. It did, however, become an important aspect of management during the period of Conservative governments between 1979 and 1997. The victory of New Labour, in 1997, appeared to signal a change in emphasis in the provision of public services: during the election campaign, for example, competition between health service organisations in an artificial internal market was portrayed by New Labour as being wasteful of public resources. The preferred model was that of co-operation between public service organisations in providing services to users. This is not to suggest that marketing ideas are now irrelevant in the public services, but rather to point out that some aspects of the reforms of the 1980s and early 1990s are being re-thought, with implications for the role of marketing in these organisations.

At the root of the special problems for marketing are some of the reasons for public sector involvement in service provision in the first place. Walsh (1995) discusses the types of situation in which public service provision may be more effective than the market, including:

- public goods, such as street lighting, which are inherently available to all. To avoid the problem of free riders, who enjoy the benefit but decline to pay, collective decision-making about these services is likely to be superior.
- merit goods, such as education or health care, in which it is beneficial for society for all to take part. There are also demerit goods, such as drugs or alcohol, in which there is a general benefit from restrictions to participation.
- information asymmetries between producers and users, in which expert professionals may over-provide to uninformed consumers and in which the government may play the role of 'honest broker' for service users.

In these and certain other types of situation, a market may not allocate resources efficiently and some form of public sector involvement (for example, as enabler, provider or regulator) may be a solution. This has implications for the way in which marketing is carried out. For example, a public good like street lighting cannot – by definition – be priced and promoted in the same way as a commercial service. However, it need not follow that those who enjoy the benefits of street lighting should have no say in how and where it is provided.

The question of the suitability and value of marketing for public service organisations can be considered at two levels. The first is to ask whether marketing *orientation* can be achieved by an organisation whose circumstances differ so sharply from those of a commercial organisation, while the second is to ask whether the *ideas and techniques* of marketing can have value in their own right, by helping a public service organisation to achieve its objectives. The question of marketing orientation is mainly concerned with the issue of competition. While commercial service providers generally operate in some form of competition with other providers, most public service organisations differ in important ways. For example, public sector comprehensive schools are in competition with each other and with private providers of similar services, but the private alternatives have to be paid for by users. A local office of the Benefits Agency is, in most circumstances, the sole source of the services it provides. And organisations such as the Inland Revenue are not only monopoly providers of the service in question, but also offer very little choice to eligible customers about whether that service should be used.

The ideas and techniques of marketing originated in the highly competitive private markets for fast-moving consumer goods and Foxall (1986) argues that competition is fundamental to true marketing orientation. However, Walsh (1994) claims that the issue of whether marketing is appropriate for public services depends on how the term is understood. If marketing is seen as no more than a set of tools and techniques, then it may well help to improve the efficiency and responsiveness of any service. If, however, marketing is conceived as an integrated set of ideas, based upon assumptions of exchange, profit and competition, then the introduction of marketing into public services may bring difficulties. Public services are characterised not only by the absence of competition, but also by the presence of a distinctive culture and ethos, arising from the fundamental purpose of these organisations. Public service managers should therefore be cautious in introducing commercial marketing into their organisations. According to Walsh (1994), even the unthinking adoption of commercial marketing language by the public services may cause problems because that language may not be able to express the values, tensions and conflicts involved in providing real-life public services.

However, at the second level – the value of individual marketing techniques – the question seems to be much less problematic. Butler and Collins (1995) review the differences between public sector and commercial organisations and suggest that the broad principles of marketing are applicable in the public sector, but the ideas need to be carefully adapted, just as they have needed to be adapted to the service sector and other contexts in the past. Similarly, Chapman and Cowdell (1998) argue that if the concept of public benefit is to be maintained as a basic mission of the public services, then marketing must be seen as fundamental to their operations. Significantly, both of the categories 'commercial' and 'public service' contain a very wide range of types of organisation. Some public services – for example, local authority leisure centres, or subsidised theatres – are very much in competition, with both direct and substitute competitors, for their customers. It is also misleading to portray all commercial organisations as being in a state of unfettered competition. Again, the range is very wide, from those in highly competitive markets to those taking part in some form of regulated competition, for example, privatised utility businesses. The distinction between the two categories is tending to become less clear-cut as the process of commercialisation unfolds in most parts of the public sector.

The Central Ideas of Marketing

Marketing originated in the fast-moving consumer goods (fmcg) markets of the United States and the appeal of marketing in this context is clear: those companies which more successfully understand and find ways of responding to the needs of their customers will be more effective in their chosen markets and will thus be more likely to achieve commercial success. From fmcg markets, marketing has spread to consumer durables, services, business-to-business markets and also a wide variety of 'not-for-profit' organisations. Marketing can be defined as an organisational process designed to understand the needs of customers and then to satisfy them, usually in competition with other suppliers and whilst achieving the goals of the organisation. In a commercial organisation, the goals are usually related to profits, while a public service organisation's goals may be expressed in other terms. In either case, the marketing process has to operate within constraints. A subsidised bus service, for example, may have to operate within strict financial limits, which may in practice constrain managers in much the same way as a profit target in a non-subsidised business.

Nature of the Product

Berry (1980: 24) memorably captured a key element which differentiates products and services when he described a product as 'an object, a device, a thing' in contrast to a service which is 'a deed, a performance, an effort'. Although public services often include tangible elements – such as road works, wheelie bins and flower beds – the service performance is essentially intangible and like all performances is timebound and experiential. Product needs to be understood as comprising not just the physical object, but also all of the added-value features that may be supplied with it, such as training or after-sales service. Marketing the services of a job centre, for example, has more in common with marketing an accountancy practice than it does with marketing physical objects such as work wear. Users of the service are interested in the quality of advice and service provided by staff, including courtesy, confidentiality and professionalism. They are concerned too with opening hours, length of queues and ease of parking, as well as the prospect of meaningful employment. Booms and Bitner (1981) proposed that a marketing mix for services should include a further three 'Ps', in addition to product, promotion, price and place, namely those of the people involved in providing the service, the process through which the service is delivered and the physical evidence of the delivery environment and facilities used by customers in making judgements about the service.

Customer Involvement in the Production Process

Customers are rarely invited to participate in the production of physical products but this is frequently the case with services. Customer co-operation is clearly essential for the effective provision of medical and many welfare services which Lovelock (1996) calls high-contact, people-processing services. Transport and housing services, however, require a lower degree of involvement from customers (medium-contact services), whilst the Inland Revenue can provide its services 'at arm's length' through electronic or physical distribution channels and is therefore categorised as a low-contact service. The greater the degree of customer involvement, the greater the need for customer-contact skills and the higher the risk of customer dissatisfaction with the process of service delivery.

It is inevitable in high-contact services that customers come into contact with one another, for example, queuing in a benefits office. It follows, therefore, that the type of customers who patronise a particular service helps to define the service experience and therefore other customers become 'part of the product'. Managing customer involvement in service organisations is an important task for marketing. Service users also interact with service provider personnel. In many cases the person delivering the service, whether it be a school chemistry class or chiropody is barely separable, in the customer's mind, from the service itself. The challenge from a marketing perspective is that no matter how good the service being offered (the quality of instruction or treatment), if the standard of service delivery is poor for example, the chiropodists attitude is patronising – then customer satisfaction will be adversely affected.

Quality Control Problems

Whilst manufactured goods can be checked for compliance with quality standards long before they reach the customer, services are often produced by service personnel in the presence of the customer and so consistent quality is much harder to achieve. The experiences of two customers visiting a local authority leisure centre, for example, can differ widely according to the behaviour of staff including the receptionist, swimming instructor, cleaner and life saver. Defining 'quality' may itself be more difficult in public services than in an industrial context, as there are fewer external objective benchmarks (Morgan and Murgatroyd, 1994).

Since services are intangible, their quality cannot be properly determined prior to consumption. There are few clues in terms of colour, shape, texture or size to help evaluation. Until a school-leaver actually visits the careers office, for example, it is only the experience of other users which can provide any indication of quality and this may not be reliable information anyway. Public services, in common with other services, therefore tend to be higher in *experience* qualities than *search* qualities and some, such as surgery, are difficult to evaluate even after consumption. One important implication of this for marketing public services is an appreciation of user risk, which is clearly higher where search qualities are lacking. It may be useful to consider strategies which help to reduce user risk, such as the provision of information, incentives for first-time users to encourage trial, and so on.

Absence of Inventories

Most goods can be stored for later sale, although this varies according to the degree of perishability, but a service organisation can only store its 'productive capability' – its equipment, staff, premises and so on – as there is no tangible product. This creates demand management problems for service organisations. If demand does not exactly match supply then one of two unwelcome outcomes occur, either demand exceeds supply and customers are sent away disappointed because there is no 'stock' available as back up, or demand is low and so service capacity is unused and therefore wasted. A key challenge, therefore, for managers of service organisations is to find ways of smoothing demand so that it accords, as far as possible, with supply. A commonly used technique is to adjust pricing to encourage service usage at times of low demand, for example, off-peak telephone rates and rail fares.

For public services, such as health and social security, demand continually exceeds supply but some important differences mean that the demand management methods commonly used by commercial organisations are not always appropriate. First, many public services are free at the point of delivery and therefore the option of using differential pricing to smooth demand is not available. However, by charging for services such as dentistry and spectacles, some customers may be effectively 'removed' from the system. Second, the drive for efficiency needs to be balanced against providing for unseen increases in demand. The effective provision of medical accident and emergency services, for example, requires continuing spare capacity. In reality, demand for health services is controlled by queuing and rationing in the form of charges, waiting lists and excluded treatments. Wiltshire Health Authority, for example, recently asked its doctors to reduce the number of births by Caesarean section because they are too expensive (Murray, 1998). Mark (1994) argues for a more transparent approach to the rationing debate and proposes 'demarketing' , which aims to reduce demand either temporarily or permanently, as an ethical framework for understanding the consequences of such decisions.

The Time Factor and Distribution Channels

Many services are delivered in 'real time' and customers have to be physically present to receive the service which means that waiting times and waiting facilities have to be considered; these are aspects which can have a major impact on customer satisfaction. Service organisations do not need to concern themselves with storage depots, lorries and other elements of physical transportation; rather they can use electronic channels (broadcasting, distance learning) or, alternatively, combine the factory, retail outlet and point of consumption into one, such as with banks or dry cleaning. Public services which are essentially information-based, such as careers guidance and the Inland Revenue, have the potential to be delivered electronically but many others fall into the second category, where effective management of the customer/service provider interface and the customer/customer interface is necessary to ensure customer satisfaction.

Marketing and the Customer

For marketing people, customers are the focus of everything the organisation does. On the way towards that ideal, the process of change from an inward-looking production orientation to a genuine outward-looking customer orientation can take a long time and involve a great deal of anguish. However, the identity of the customer in commercial organisations is rarely in doubt. In the public services, in contrast, the identity of the customer may be more difficult to define. Who, for example, are the customers of the prison service? The end-users of prison services might be thought to be prisoners, but it is the nature of the prison service not to respond to certain of this group's needs. The Home Office might be a closer analogy to a customer but this body may have more in common with a Board of Directors or major shareholder, in that it sets objectives and provides resources. Maybe the public at large should be seen as customers of the prison service, in that they, indirectly through their taxes, pay for the service and benefit from the output of the service in containing crime. How, though, might such a broad definition help managers of the prison service to develop their activities such that the prison service provided more effectively for customer needs?

The categories of public goods and merit goods discussed in the introduction often bring similar difficulties. The customer of a public service like refuse collection seems easy to define: it is the household from whom the refuse is being collected. However, it is also true that the community in general benefits from efficient universal refuse collection, implying that the needs of this customer must be considered alongside those of individual households or businesses and a balance struck where necessary. These basic difficulties in defining the customer are reflected in most other parts of the public service: having to deal with multiple publics and multiple objectives, often under intense public scrutiny, is routine for these organisations (Lovelock and Weinberg, 1978). Although customer definition can be complex, by improving their understanding of users and other beneficiaries, public service managers are more likely to ensure that the service achieves its objectives as efficiently as possible. The decisions that have to be made in using limited resources as effectively as possible can be complex and genuinely difficult. The views of service users are not the only factor to be taken into account, but resource-allocation decisions can only benefit from a clearer understanding of what those views are. Hadley and Young (1990) propose a responsive model of public service, suggesting that organisations should resist the tendency to define service users needs for them, but rather set up a dialogue through the democratic process and through direct contacts. Ham (1998) agrees, arguing that when making difficult decisions about the allocation of healthcare resources, the experts can 'inform' but not 'resolve' the issue and the public should be enabled to contribute to the process of deciding health service priorities.

The resolution of the question 'Who is the customer?' can clarify the development of a public service. Pike (1994) describes the South Thames Blood Transfusion Service, whose quality of service was greatly improved, partly as a consequence of the clarification of the organisation's mission. Staff had been confused about whether the service's customers were the donors who provided the blood or the patients who received it. By putting patients clearly at the centre of the service's efforts, operational changes such as modifying the scheduling of blood processing could be designed to improve quality of service and reduce wastage.

One sign of the growing interest in customer orientation in the public services has been the use of professional marketing research by service managers. The 1997 Annual Report of AMSO, the Association of Market Survey Organisations, showed expenditure on market research of £35m by clients in the Public Services/Utilities sector (up 9 per cent on the previous year) and of £20.8m by clients in the Government/Public Bodies sector (up 13 per cent on the previous year).

Marketing Management and Strategy

Development of a marketing strategy is intended to provide a systematic and rigorous way of answering the fundamental questions: what business(es) are we in, which do we wish to remain in and which new ones should we enter? Who are our customers and what are their needs? Taking account of customer needs and competitor characteristics, how are we going to compete? Clearly, allowance needs to be made in adopting this approach, as not all public services have competitors and most public service organisations have less than complete freedom to select their own markets. But the process of considering these questions can inject new life into monolithic public institutions.

As part of its efforts to revitalise and reform local government, New Labour appears determined to challenge the entrenched provider-led culture by addressing these fundamental issues. According to Pike (1998), local council pilot projects, undertaken with the support of Warwick University Business School, are developing the 'best value' approach to public services, which is planned to replace compulsory competitive tendering. This approach starts from an analysis of the needs of local people, rather than from the services of the local authority. The concept of providing 'best value' services has the potential to shake up the long-established departmental management structures which currently control local services provision. By recognising that user needs cross departmental boundaries and are probably not best served by highly autonomous departments such as social services and education (and asking other fundamental questions about organisational capabilities and customer needs), the way in which local services are managed and delivered could be radically improved.

Anecdotal evidence suggests that the creation of competing GP fundholders in the NHS has also resulted in a clearer focus on these issues. In parts of Hampshire, for example, GPs demanded that Hospital Trusts improve services to patients. Eager to attract the maximum amount of custom, some Trusts responded by establishing 'one stop clinics' which undertake tests and supply the results, all in one appointment. Under the old, non-competitive system, this process involved the patient making five or six visits over an extended period, and an anxious wait for news. In the areas where fundholding has not been introduced, there may be less of an incentive to make these changes. [We are grateful to Jackie Nelson for providing us with this example.] Thus the introduction of marketing orientation into public service organisations may help to improve the relationship between the service provider and service users, but complex issues about the true role and future direction of the organisation may be raised. This complexity arises in part from the fact that public services usually have multiple audiences to satisfy, as discussed earlier. However, difficulties in developing marketing strategy may also result from resistance in some parts of the organisation to the marketing culture, compounded by an initial lack of information about what service users actually want. Similarly profound questions arise when considering the applicability to the public services of some of the other ideas in marketing.

Segmentation, Targeting and Positioning

The ideas of segmentation and targeting in commercial marketing stem from a realisation that there are usually competitive opportunities in seeking to understand the special needs of sub-groups, or segments of a market, with a view to providing for those needs more effectively than any other supplier and thus building a stronger market position. To what extent can the same approach help a public service organisation to achieve its objectives? The enhanced understanding of customers that results from a segmentation study is likely to be of great value to any public service. An agency seeking suitable foster homes for children, for example, is not selling a service, but the segmentation process can yield valuable insights into both the different types of foster-home provider and also into how best to access and communicate with them.

However, whereas commercial organisations are usually free to choose which parts of the market they will aim to serve ('target') and those they wish to withdraw from, many parts of the public service are obliged to provide universal coverage of those parts of the public that they are established to serve. Moreover, the criteria used for targeting segments by public service providers are much more likely to be controversial than in a commercial organisation, and public services managers may have significantly less freedom to target their efforts as a result. Examples of this include the recent controversies surrounding the treatment of infertile couples or people suffering from smoking-related diseases. Similarly, care needs to be taken in the application of positioning techniques to public services. In commercial marketing, an organisation's positioning refers to the way in which it would like to be seen by customers in the target segment(s). In the public services, managers may not always have full freedom to position or reposition their services, for the same reasons that constrain the use of targeting. These services, however, are constantly developing in response to changes in their political, social and technological environments and marketing ideas of positioning can be expected to play a role in helping the services to communicate the changes to their publics.

Analysis of Buyer Behaviour

Understanding how customers go about making purchases is of great interest to marketers and models of buyer behaviour have been developed for both private consumer buying and organisational buying. For providers of public services, useful insights may be gained by thinking about service users as if they were buyers and trying to understand the process through which they come to be users of this service, rather than any other solution that might be available. In more commercial public services, such as leisure services, the service users actually are buyers, with plenty of other possible ways of spending their money. However, many public service transactions are unlike consumer purchasing in one or more of the following ways.

First, the service may be one that is the only available solution to the individual concerned, for example many social security services. Second, in some public services there may be no direct parallel with the marketing idea of exchange, that is, the exchange of the customer's money for one of the supplier's products. The service may be made available without charge to those whose circumstances entitle them to claim it and the costs of doing so are met from the public purse. Third, it will often be the case that customers for a public service in the course of partial commercialisation do not have the experience or the information to make the choices that are becoming available for the first time. What, for example, are the evident characteristics of a good school? To what extent do published exam results provide a reliable proxy? Fourth, some public service organisations, such as the Health Education Authority, do not seek to provide a service to individuals, rather they seek to inform or change attitudes in pursuit of social goals.

However, as Walsh (1994) points out, consumerism has been at the centre of management changes in the public services in recent years, typified by the launch in the early 1990s of the *Citizen's Charter* (Cabinet Office, 1991), which leads service users to expect responsive services of high quality, whether or not they are paid for directly. The special consumer behaviour features of some public services listed above should not be taken to mean that marketing techniques have nothing to offer these services, but rather as defining the context within which a more responsive and consumer-friendly service can be developed.

Relationship Marketing

The concept of relationship marketing (Grønroos, 1994), may well have particular significance for some public service activities. Relationship marketing emphasises the benefits of building up long-term relationships with both customers and other stakeholders in the business, founded upon trust and commitment, from which all parties can benefit. Traditional marketing, by contrast, has an implicit transactions bias, in which the organisation's marketing activities are designed to create large numbers of commercial encounters with individuals, who then disappear into the 'mass market' until the next transaction takes place. In many of the public services, such as health care, education or social security, long-term relationships with service users have been central to providing the services: there seems to be potential for a fruitful exchange of ideas in this area. In commercial marketing, a service provider who builds up a deeper understanding of a long-term customer's priorities and preferences is able to serve that customer both more effectively and more efficiently, in that resources can be concentrated on those services that are most likely to meet customer needs. Business can thus be built up in a mutually satisfactory relationship. In a public service relationship the same applies, with the potential for more effective use of public resources.

Conclusion

This chapter has examined the ways in which marketing is starting to be applied in different parts of the public services. The examples reviewed have provided only a glimpse of a diverse and fast-changing picture, but a common theme of growing customer orientation is clear. There can be little doubt that marketing ideas have provided many valuable insights into how to develop those services towards the needs of service users. Even a sceptic would probably acknowledge the difference that a successfully introduced customer-care programme can make to the experience of contacting and using a public service, however carefully the notion of 'customer' has to be qualified for the service in question. A cynic might dismiss any such changes as trivial and cosmetic. Many, however, would value the difference and would be reluctant to return to the more unresponsive, bureaucratic and sometimes insensitive behaviour of the past.

Beyond the immediate benefits at the point of contact, it also seems reasonable to expect that service users who feel that they have been treated with courtesy and respect may respond in a more constructive way towards the organisation. Dental patients, for example, may feel more strongly motivated to look after their teeth if they are satisfied with the dental care they have received and may also be less likely to put off visits to the dentist for routine checks. Over the longer term, the deliberate development of a closer relationship between the service provider and the users of the service can provide an invaluable stream of information about how the service should be refined and developed in order to meet user needs more closely. Budgets are often very tight for public service managers, of course, which may restrict the short-term scope for improvements; arguably, however, tight budgets make it even more important to understand customer needs, in order that limited funds can be properly allocated.

The potential contribution that a marketing perspective can make to the strategic development of a public services organisation is not always fully appreciated by those who dismiss 'marketing' as an expensive and unnecessary add-on to their organisation's true purpose. If that potential contribution is to be realised, however, it is necessary for marketing to play a full part at the strategic level of the organisation. Increasingly this is being found in public services where marketing departments, with professionally qualified staff, are led by marketing directors who sit on Executive or Management Boards. These developments have resulted from the changes that have been taking place over the past two decades in Britain. The change towards a customer orientation in the public services is likely to be strengthened in the foreseeable future as the New Labour government, in seeking a Third Way between 'old Labour' state control and neo-liberal market capitalism, is committed to more user-friendly public services and more accountability of service providers.

Another recurrent theme in this chapter has been the need to adapt marketing ideas both to the special circumstances of the public sector environment in general and to individual public services in particular. Butler and Collins (1995) provide a clear and useful framework for considering the characteristics of public sector marketing, pointing out how special features of the product, the organisation, the market and the process of provision are common to many public services, posing similar challenges for those in charge of delivering and developing the services. Perhaps, then, managers of public services should not spend too much time worrying about whether or not they are being truly marketing-oriented in the way they use marketing. Certainly, the disjointed tactical use of individual marketing techniques can sometimes be counter-productive, such as moving headlong into mass advertising before the service is ready to deliver the quality that appears to be promised. If, however, the managers of a service have a clear strategic determination to understand the needs of their service users and to improve the way in which the service meets those needs, then a pragmatic approach may well make sense. If an idea or technique from marketing appears to provide valuable insights or new opportunities to develop the service, then managers should make use of it. If a technique appears not to be applicable, then it should be set aside for the time being.

Given the evident diversity of activity under the heading of public services, it may not be appropriate to think in terms of general prescriptions for how marketing should be applied within them. Some parts of the public services can be expected to benefit greatly from the adoption of a wide range of marketing techniques; other parts of the public services may find some ideas in marketing more difficult to apply at present. The examples reviewed in this chapter suggest that marketing is growing at different rates and in different ways in individual public services; this evolution can be expected to continue as each service grows closer to its users and their needs.

7

Human Resources Management and Employment Relations

DAVID FARNHAM

Since the late 1970s, the public services have experienced substantial reforms, in terms of their structure, organisation, administration and management – not least in the ways in which people and employment relations are managed within them. In essence, the reforms are rooted in the underlying beliefs, articulated initially by Conservative governments from 1979 to 1997, and largely accepted by the Blair administration since then, that enhanced quality, effectiveness and value for money (VFM) in the public services depend upon the injection of competition, commercialism and private-sector management ideas and personnel practices into them. Over this long period, public services have been exposed to a variety of initiatives, including privatisation, centralisation and decentralisation, deregulation, market testing and contractualisation. These processes have been primarily aimed at: cutting public expenditure; curbing the power of public sector trade unions and professional workers; strengthening management prerogative; improving performance standards within the public services; and making the public services more responsive to the needs of their 'customers' and 'clients'. This chapter outlines the changing nature of human resources management and employment relations practices in the public services and explores the impact of these developments on how people are managed and pay is determined in this sector of the economy. It seeks to demonstrate, first, that there has been a move away from a predominantly 'soft', welfare-centred, paternalist approach to personnel management to a 'harder', performance-oriented, human resources management (HRM) approach. Second, there has been a shift away from national collective bargaining, to a more flexible, fragmented and partially decentralised system. Third, there has been a weakening of collectivist approaches to managing people and the employer–employee relationship, to a dualist one, where some collective elements remain but many individualistic initiatives have been adopted. These innovations have fostered greater diversity in employment practices and created wider disparities in the terms and conditions of staff employed in public services. Although the changes must not be exaggerated, they provide evidence that HRM and employment relations are following new pathways of claimed 'good practice' throughout the public services.

Employment in the Public Services

In 1997, employment in the public sector stood at approximately five million, representing 19 per cent of the total labour force of some 26.5 million. Between 1984 and 1997 it had fallen by almost two million or over 25 per cent. This substantial change in the size of public sector employment is accounted for by three main factors. First, there were absolute reductions in some areas of the sector (such as the industrial civil service). Second, a number of core services (such as gas, water, telecommunications, and the former polytechnic sector of higher education) had been privatised, resulting in transfers of former public employees into the private sector. And third, some activities (such as catering and cleaning services) had been contracted out to the private sector. Table 7.1 shows that the largest area of public employment in 1997 was local authorities, which had over 2.6 million employees, or just over 51 per cent, of those employed in the public sector. This group included those working in education, social services, fire services and police services. The next largest group of public sector staff was employed in public corporations, which accounted for some 1.5 million staff, or about 30 per cent of the total. These people worked mainly in NHS trusts and the last major remaining nationalised industry, the Post Office. Another 900,000, representing 19 per cent of the total, worked in central

TABLE 7.1   *UK employment by sector, 1961–97: selected years, by headcount (thousands)*

| Mid-year | Central government | | | | Local authorities | | |
	HMF	NHS	Other	Total	Education	Social Services	Police
1961	474	575	741	1790	785	170	108
1971	368	785	813	1966	1297	276	152
1979	314	1152	921	2387	1539	344	156
1981	334	1207	878	2419	1454	350	1886
1984	326	1223	810	2359	1430	368	187
1992	290	916	800	2006	1390	410	204
1994	250	205	760	1215	1176	408	207
1997	210	78	653	941	1187	400	207

government. This is defined as all those bodies for whose activities a minister of the Crown is accountable to Parliament. Central government consists of HM forces and the 'rump' of NHS administration at regional and local levels but the largest category is 'other central government'. This includes the civil service, those employed in executive agencies and a number of non-departmental public bodies (NDPBs) including research councils, the Equal Opportunities Commission and the British Council.

The public sector has experienced considerable changes in its structure, size and distribution of employment since 1979, as shown in Table 7.1. Public employment, by headcount, peaked at some 7.5 million in 1979, falling to just over five million in 1997. The decline has been most gradual in local government, where employment remained fairly static at around three million until the mid-1980s but then fell by 12 per cent between 1984 and 1997. In contrast public corporations experienced a dramatic fall of some 45 per cent between 1984 and 1992, due largely to the privatising of the former nationalised industries. However, after 1992, and the creation of NHS Trusts as public corporations, the number employed within them increased by over 250 per cent up to 1997. This was, of course, only a shift from one category of public employment to another and did not affect overall numbers. There has been a consistent decline in the civil service where government has, arguably, the most direct control over employment. This was achieved by: natural wastage, redundancy and reduced recruitment; privatisation of the Royal Ordinance Factories and the Naval Dockyards; hiving off staff into NDPBs; selling off services such as HMSO and parts of the Property Services Agency; and contracting out of other services to the private sector. Overall, between 1979 and 1997, civil service employment declined by over 30 per cent.

			Public corporation					
Construction	Other	Total	Nationalised Bodies	NHS	Other	Total	Total Public Sector	(Civil Service)
103	703	1869	2152	0	48	2200	5859	672
124	803	2652	1856	0	153	2009	6627	727
176	782	2997	1849	0	216	2065	7449	738
143	766	2899	1657	0	210	1867	7185	698
126	831	2942	1410	0	189	1599	6900	630
97	796	2897	459	314	106	879	5782	591
87	764	2642	385	966	82	1433	5290	555
65	736	2595	316	1121	84	1521	5057	493

Source: Derived from the CSO (1998).

TABLE 7.2 Employment in the main UK public services, 1979–97: full-time equivalents (thousands)

Mid-year	Civil Service	NHS	Education	Police	Social Services	Other local authority	Total public services	(NHS Trust)[1]
1979	724	977	1110	172	235	701	3919	—
1980	700	1001	1087	176	235	699	3898	—
1981	684	1038	1058	180	240	692	3892	—
1982	659	1047	1041	180	241	681	3849	—
1983	643	1047	1034	182	246	686	3838	—
1984	619	1036	1027	182	251	689	3804	—
1985	596	1030	1021	182	256	689	3774	—
1986	597	1018	1029	184	263	675	3766	—
1987	584	1016	1043	186	271	677	3777	—
1988	577	1017	1046	190	277	674	3781	—
1989	567	1013	992[2]	191	282	681	3726	—
1990	559	1008	990	194	288	692	3731	—
1991	558	904	982	197	287	720	3750	102
1992	567	750	970	199	285	706	3753	256
1993	551	424	838[3]	201	279	697	3530	540
1994	529	163	818	201	288	662	3444	788
1995	512	69	806	201	295	678	3937	876
1996	492	70	817	202	288	632	3385	884
1997	472	65	813	202	283	627	3365	903

Note:
1. Since 1994, 96 per cent of all major hospitals have trust status and have been reclassified as public corporations.
2. From 1989 polytechnics, HE colleges and grant-maintained schools were transferred from local authority control to the private sector.
3. FE colleges and 6th form colleges were transferred to the private sector from April 1993.

Source: Derived from the CSO (1998) Economic Trends.

Table 7.2 shows that total employment fell from just under four million full-time equivalents (FTEs) in 1979 to just over three million in 1997 but that change was variable. Again the greatest fall was in the civil service, whilst between 1979 and 1997 the police and social services increased their FTEs by 17 and 20 per cent respectively. This reflected successive governments' priorities on law and order and their commitment to increasing police resources and the law and order budget. Expansion of social services, in contrast, has been a necessary response to increasing demands for social support arising from an ageing population and rising unemployment.

FTE employment in the NHS was fairly steady over the period although there was a small overall decline. Following increases of 7 per cent in the early 1980s, there was a fall of 4 per cent in the late 1980s and a further fall of 4 per cent between 1991 and 1997. The composition of NHS staffing has changed, however, with increases in managerial staff and nursing support workers and declines in manual, medical and nursing staff. Numbers employed in education have decreased more significantly, by about 26 per cent between 1979 and 1997. Part of this change can be explained by transfers from the public to the private sector, rather than absolute decline. In 1989, the former polytechnics, colleges of higher education and grant-maintained schools were transferred from local authority control to the private sector and these were joined, in 1993, by further education and sixth-form colleges. All these are now classified as non-profit, private-sector organisations.

Reclassifications and transfers of employment from the public to the private sector only provide a partial explanation of the overall decline in public employment in the NHS and education. Much is attributable to other policies, such as compulsory competitive tendering (CCT) and market testing. These processes, which required public bodies to tender for services they traditionally provided directly or 'in-house', resulted in substantial staffing reductions. These policies impacted most conspicuously on ancillary staff doing cleaning, catering and laundry services. In the NHS, for example, according to Department of Health (1993) statistics, the numbers of ancillary workers fell by 50 per cent between 1981 and 1991. The effects of market testing and CCT introduced to professional services in 1994 caused reductions in administrative and clerical staff too. The New Labour government is committed to replacing the rules on CCT with a new statutory regime to provide 'best value'. This seeks to link price to quality and encourage the public and private sectors to work together to improve service standards (see Chapter 5). It is too soon yet to assess the impact this is likely to have on employees.

Another important characteristic of public sector employment is the numerical dominance of women workers, who comprised some 67 per cent of the total workforce in 1997. Amongst these, however, only 51 per cent were full-time, whilst 48 per cent were part-timers. In contrast, some 75 per cent of male employees were full-time and 16 per cent were part-timers.

Overall 25 per cent of all public employment in mid-1997 was male full-time employment, 36 per cent female full-time employment, 34 per cent female part-time employment and 5 per cent male part-time employment.

There were also wide variations in the structure of employment amongst specific services. In health, education and the caring services female part-time and full-time workers predominate, although not in higher managerial posts. Similarly, female full-time and part-time workers represent the largest proportion of the public administration workforce at 35 per cent and 15 per cent respectively. There is an increasing trend in all these services to employ more female part-time workers. The situation differs in the police where, in 1997, some 80 per cent of those employed were male full-timers, 13 per cent female full-timers, 4 per cent female part-timers and 3 per cent male part-timers.

In summary, there have been considerable changes in the composition and structure of public employment since 1979. Whilst aggregate employment has fallen, the police and social services have demonstrated moderate expansion. Further, although females dominate the public services, there are distinctive gender distributions within specific services. There are also relatively high proportions of part-time workers in education, social services and the NHS. This trend seems to be increasing as greater emphasis is being placed on flexible workforces (Farnham and Horton, 1997). Although the majority of public employees are on permanent contracts there is a trend towards fixed-term contracts. This is particularly at senior management levels but occurs more generally where public employers are employing contract workers to provide specific skills, meet high seasonal demand, control costs or ease change.

Traditional Personnel Management in the Public Services

Traditional personnel management practices and the institutions of employment relations in the public services had distinctive features and were broadly universalistic, across the sector. These traditional practices contrasted with the relative heterogeneity of the private sector and were largely influenced by the bureaucratic characteristics of the British state and government's role as a 'model' and 'good practice' employer. The concept of the model and good practice employer was defined by the Priestley Commission (1956: 39), which stated:

> The 'good employer' is not necessarily the one who offers the highest rates of pay. He seeks rather to provide stability and continuity of employment, and consults with representatives of his employees upon changes that affect both their remuneration and their conditions of work. He provides adequate facilities for training and advancement and carries on a range of practices which today constitute good management, whether they are formalised in joint consultation along civil service lines or not. Such employers are likely to be among the more progressive in all aspects of management policy.

This role originated from the state's need to: harmonise and improve the effectiveness of public service provision nationally; enhance political accountability; and contain public expenditure as the public services expanded.

But as a model and good practice employer, government also set an example for other employers to follow and sought to develop the best employment practices in line with those of leading private-sector businesses. The state's objectives were to: provide terms and conditions necessary to attract, retain and motivate the most skilled and professional staff; ensure harmonious and equitable employment practices across the public sector; and promote stable employment relations.

Traditionally, personnel management was administrative, centralised and bureaucratic. Overall personnel policy was determined at national level by ministers and top civil servants and then administered and monitored through civil service departments and health, municipal and police authorities locally. Local managers had limited discretion in the interpretation and application of standardised policies and national collective agreements. In the civil service, for instance, recruitment and selection of senior staff was not a line management concern but was carried out by a separate civil service commission. Pay and conditions of employment were standardised nationally, to ensure fairness and equality of treatment for given grades of staff, whilst industrial relations procedures were applied consistently and uniformly within each part of the service. Traditional establishments/ personnel departments, therefore, largely assumed a policing and advisory role, monitoring policy and maintaining stable staffing arrangements. They also acted as a 'buffer' between management and employees and sought, as far as possible, to satisfy both parties in the employment relationship.

Employment relations in the old public services were essentially collectivist and pluralist. Whitleyism, introduced after the First World War, was a system of centralised joint councils and, in some cases, district-level council and workplace consultative committees, through which issues of pay and terms and conditions of employment were negotiated jointly. The central aim of Whitleyism was to foster 'joint co-operation' between employers and unions, through their representative organisations, which played equal parts in regulating the employment relationship. Decisions were normally taken by the majority of each side voting separately and, where agreement was impossible, independent arbitration was used. Union membership was actively encouraged in the public sector and high membership density persisted throughout the 1980s and 1990s.

An Industrial Relations Survey (WIRS 3), conducted in 1990, showed that almost 90 per cent of public sector establishments recognised at least one union, compared with just over a third in the private services and 44 per cent in private manufacturing (Millward *et al.*, 1992). This was corroborated by later Labour Force Survey statistics (1994), with reported levels of recognition at 88 per cent in education and 94 per cent in 'hospital activities', whilst the private sector as a whole stood at only 34 per cent. These figures confirmed that public sector employers were far more likely than private sector ones to recognise unions. In 1990, 78 per cent of employees in all public sector establishments were covered by collective bargaining, compared with only 33 per cent in private services and 51 per cent in manufacturing.

WIRS 3 also showed that public services were more likely to agree joint procedures with trade unions for resolving disputes over pay and discipline and for consultation than was the private sector. It was also evident that bargaining took place over a wider range of issues than in the private sector. For both manual and non-manual workers, higher proportions of public service establishments were involved in negotiating on recruitment, physical working conditions, redeployment, staffing levels and reorganisation of working hours than were private sector establishments.

Other features of model and good employment practices in the public services have been positive commitments to equality of opportunity. Many public services, such as the civil service and NHS, had equal opportunities policies long before most private sector organisations. These covered: recruitment, selection and promotion procedures; equal pay for work of equal value; and career development. Traditional paternalist employment practices in the public services have also included: stability and security of employment; pay awards on the basis of 'pay comparability' with comparators in other sectors; incremental pay systems; career structures; generous holiday entitlements with pay, often based on seniority rights and length of service; sick pay benefits; occupational pensions; and opportunities for training and development for career advancement. Recently, these practices have been substantially modified.

Developments in Human Resources Management

Following the election of the Conservative party to power in 1979, major new developments occurred in personnel management, now sometimes called HRM, in the public services (Farnham and Horton, 1996b). Successive Conservative governments effectively rejected the 'old' public sector traditions of earlier post-war administrations outlined above, as they pursued neo-liberal and managerialist policy objectives. These were to reduce the size of the public sector and public expenditure, create high quality, efficient, cost-effective, 'customer-driven' services, inject market forces, commercial criteria and competition and strengthen management's right to manage. The efficient and orderly management of resources – including 'human resources' – was seen to be the key to achieving efficiency savings, structural reforms and more customer-focused public service organisations. The measures used included: creating tight financial management systems to control spending; introducing performance management techniques to set targets and quantify and measure achievements; and, in the 1990s, systematically developing a quality culture designed further to enhance organisational performance. From the outset, government also urged a more assertive and forceful management to curb the authority of public sector unions and professional workers which, traditionally, were believed to have 'used their privileged position to extort excessive pay rises out of hapless governments' (Winchester and Bach, 1995: 305).

Strengthening the Right to Manage

Strengthening the right to manage in the public services was a central plank of governmental policy during the 1980s and 1990s. It was achieved by asserting greater political and managerial control over public enterprises and importing private sector practices and techniques into the public services. Initially government called upon the expertise of prominent business people to conduct investigations and write reports for public service organisations; appointed senior business people on secondment to senior public service posts; recruited individuals, with private sector backgrounds, into public services; introduced new management practices inspired by 'management gurus' and multinational management consultants; and organised conferences and management development programmes for public service managers (Farnham and Horton, 1996b).

Further major elements in the managerial reforms were devolution of management authority and responsibilities to semi-autonomous business units in the civil service, NHS and education (see Chapters 9, 10 and 11). Public service organisations were all expected to adopt rational management systems, based upon new planning and information systems and accountancy procedures, incorporating financial and performance targets. Such systems were intended to increase managerial accountability, measure and enhance organisational performance, control costs and eliminate waste. In addition, public managers were required to deliver quality and organisational responsiveness to public consumers. Public service managers, therefore, are becoming increasingly affected by the financial and performance parameters within which they operate, whilst organisational concerns for employees are increasingly giving way to 'corporate' concerns for 'consumers' and 'customers'.

The main HRM and employment relations implications of strengthening the right to manage are that public managers have assumed greater discretion, albeit within centrally determined frameworks, in the ways in which they deal with staffing matters. They are less restrained in implementing their own preferred (unilateral) employment practices than in the past; formerly they were more tightly constrained by national collective agreements and local joint consultative arrangements involving union and staff representatives. Now unions have to collaborate and be co-operative with management or they are marginalised, at national and local levels. As managers increasingly adapt employment policies to meet their labour market needs, budgetary pressures and performance targets, a diversity in the ways in which people are managed and employment relations issues are handled emerges.

The introduction of CCT, market testing and internal markets have served to extend this process further. Unlike in traditional systems of personnel management in the public services, contract managers, in securing tenders to do work, have far more flexibility and discretion in the employment practices which they adopt to manage staff than in the past. They do not have to adhere to the traditional 'model' employment practices of that authority. Consequently, policies relating to pay and equal opportunities have been considerably weakened (Colling and Ferner, 1995) in local authorities. Whilst the New Labour government is pledged to abolishing CCT, and replacing it with 'best value', most local councils, apart from a minority piloting best value, are continuing to abide by CCT legislation until it is abolished. Whilst CCT is essentially about getting the lowest contract price, 'best value' attempts to link price with quality, as well as encouraging partnerships between the public and private sectors. This is in response to the highly legalistic and competitive structure of CCT, which has often led to soured relations between councils and private contractors.

In their attempts to create a new managerialist culture in the public services, governments have not only facilitated renewed confidence by managers in their right to manage but also created a new 'culture of management'. This has aimed at getting public service managers committed to organisational change and greater efficiency within the limits set by given resources, especially in higher echelons of management. Governments have sought to do this by: emphasising management's key role in achieving efficiency; individualising the contracts of service of top managers; providing them with reward packages incorporating private-sector 'fringe benefits'; and initiating PRP arrangements. Individualised (or personal) contracts of employment are now provided for a range of public service managers, including chief executives in civil service agencies, general managers in the NHS, senior managers in local government, university vice-chancellors and top police officers. Many of these employment contracts are for fixed-term periods. Some senior managers, such as those in local government, also have fringe benefits, including private medical care, life insurance, 'company', leased cars and pension options.

One of the most widely copied private sector practices being used to get the personal commitment of top public managers is PRP. PRP provides for periodic increases in pay which are incorporated into salaries resulting from assessments of individual performance and personal value to the organisation. Supporters of PRP argue that where scope for increasing salary budgets is severely limited, PRP enables the money available to be distributed in the most cost-effective way. It is also claimed that it enables employers to reward excellence and retain key staff. Critics of PRP, on the other hand, argue there is no evidence that it motivates people unless large sums are involved There is also criticism of appraisals as employees sometimes regard them as unfair and divisive in the ways in which they are applied (Pilbeam, 1998). PRP was introduced into the civil service in 1985 for more senior ranks. Despite the mixed reception given to the scheme, PRP has since been extended to other management and non-management grades and now covers the whole of the service. In local government, chief officers' pay scales are now sufficiently flexible to provide performance rewards and PRP appears to have been especially supported by Conservative-controlled authorities, which use variations of discretionary increments in existing scales, merit bonuses or awards for exceptional performance. In the NHS, the Griffiths Report (1983) required action on PRP and, in autumn 1986, PRP was introduced for the service's then 800 general managers.

Innovations in Human Resources Management

Since 1979, public service managers have been under increasing pressure to adopt new, arguably, more sophisticated, HRM approaches to managing people. Throughout the 1980s and 1990s there has been a lively academic debate about what HRM actually means and the differences between HRM and traditional personnel management (Legge, 1989; 1995; Storey, 1989, 1992, 1997; Turnbull and Blyton, 1992; Beardwell and Holden, 1995). In its ideal form, HRM is claimed to have four main features. First, it is concerned with employees as 'human resources' and the ways in which they are proactively managed. Its direction stems from corporate and managerial strategies within organisations and presupposes an integrated approach to managing people. Consequently, HRM activities such as recruitment, selection, appraisal, rewards, communication and training are being more aligned and integrated with one another than is the case with traditional, more paternalist personnel management practices. Second, HRM seeks to elicit the commitment of employees to organisational goals, not merely compliance with them. Third, HRM is owned by line managers rather than by personnel specialists. Fourth, managerial attention is shifted away from relying exclusively on collective forms of accommodation with their workforces to a more individual 'human resources' approach (Storey, 1989). In practice, two similar yet extreme versions of HRM have been identified, giving HRM a so-called 'Jekyll and Hyde' quality (Sisson, 1994). These have been described as 'soft' and 'hard' HRM (Storey, 1995). Soft HRM values human resources, regarding them as a vital investment, and focuses on altruistic, people-centred policies, such as employee development, training, communication, motivation and leadership. In contrast, hard HRM is rational, calculative, business-centred and rooted in managerial concerns for efficiency and economy. Staff, therefore, become a cost to be minimised and controlled rather than an asset to be valued.

There is growing evidence that public service managers are experimenting with so-called HRM techniques. These techniques are focusing increasingly on individuals and this is creating an effective challenge to trade unions and traditional collectivist employment processes. One set of innovations in public personnel management practices during the 1980s and 1990s was associated with a shift to more flexible employment arrangements. A variety of factors was driving these changes. These included: pressures from government; constraints on public spending; the search for increased labour productivity; demands by some staff for atypical forms of work; equal opportunities legislation; a rejection of the rigidity of Whitleyism; and a desire by some more forceful managements to control their workforces and enhance organisational performance. Although flexibility can take a number of forms (Farnham and Horton, 1997), one is in relation to pay.

In the civil service in 1985, for example, standard pay levels were abandoned and special pay additions introduced in order to address recruitment and retention difficulties and skill shortages in particular localities. During the 1990s new pay determination arrangements, incorporating the introduction of flexible pay, were introduced and, under the Civil Service (Management Functions) Act 1992, individual departments and agencies assumed responsibility for developing their own pay and conditions policies to suit local 'business' needs. By 1996, responsibility for pay and grading of all staff below senior levels had been delegated to departments and agencies, thus replacing national pay agreements. A survey of 135 chief executives of Next Steps agencies in 1995 indicated that they thought pay delegation would result in 'greater flexibility, increased efficiency, improved performance and new working practices' (Farnham and McNeill, 1997: 41). There is also evidence of government support for greater working-time flexibility in the civil service. The Mueller Report (1987) resulted in the extension of part-time working, fixed-term contracts and home-working within the service. The service has also introduced more variable contracts including temporary and annual hours contracts and term-time arrangements. These moves towards more flexible working arrangements are intended to modernise the way the civil service operates, reduce its costs, allow technological change, attract the 'best' staff into the service and facilitate its equal opportunities policies.

In education the introduction of LMS and GMS schools has resulted in the devolving of management responsibilities from LEAs to individual schools. These arrangements have given school governing bodies greater discretion and flexibility over expenditure on staffing and employment matters. These include: staffing levels; recruitment; promotion; and elements of pay. Although teachers have contractual entitlements conferring entitlements to sick pay, periods of notice and maternity rights, except those under GMS, schools now have wide discretion on payment to teachers, promotion and allocation of allowances.

Employment flexibilities are being adopted throughout the public services (Fowler, 1993). These include fixed-term and temporary contracts, especially for senior managers and in areas where levels of public funding are unpredictable. This is particularly the case in education, where budgets are increasingly allocated to schools, colleges and universities on the basis of student numbers or pupils recruited each year. Educational institutions are finding it difficult to plan ahead and support long-term staffing commitments and cope with such uncertainties. Thus institutions are turning to fixed-term contracts, where employment can be terminated after a period of time (Ironside and Seifert, 1995). The government's Research Assessment Exercise (RAE) in the university sector is, arguably, extending this process in higher education. The RAE provides additional funding to universities based on peer assessment of the extent and quality of research being undertaken. This varies from one assessment to another and funds are often exhausted before the end of the assessment period. A corollary of RAE is an increase in employment of researchers on fixed-term contracts, which are terminated when funds are exhausted. A major problem associated with these contracts is that individuals are frequently offered more limited employment conditions than their lecturing counterparts and sign away rights to, for example, redundancy pay and unfair dismissal claims.

Recruitment has also been reformed in parts of the public services to produce more open and speedier processes to attract the 'best' employees from the private sector. Public employers have begun to use a wider range of methods, such as psychometric testing, biodata sifting and assessment centres. In addition, they have sought to increase the volume and range of candidates by removing unjustified age limits and unnecessarily high qualifications and targeting populations or locations to meet skill shortages or equal opportunity requirements (Farnham and Horton, 1992, 1996b).

Staff appraisal is now commonplace throughout the public services although the most developed systems are, arguably, within the civil service. Borrowing heavily from private sector practice, public services are using annual staff appraisal systems, which principally assess staff performance in current jobs, in many cases related to targets and objectives set in advance. Such systems place considerably more emphasis on assessment of individual performance than on personal promotability and underpin performance management and PRP systems. A main concern, especially of unions and professional workers, about the process is that by linking appraisal to job performance and, in turn, rewards, appraisal becomes a tool of managerial control. With problems in setting objective performance targets in areas such as teaching and medicine, there is a fear that appraisal may become judgemental, divisive and inequitable and that its more developmental side may be neglected. For this reason, some public service unions and staff remain sceptical about these 'new' appraisal systems.

There have also been innovations in training. The public services have always trained their staff, although their traditions have varied across the services. A significant growth in training stems, in part, from the substantial structural and managerial reforms introduced into public services after 1979. Training has been employed to: provide employees with skills to adapt to new management systems; influence employee attitudes; facilitate change; and inject new values emphasising quality, customer responsiveness, cost-consciousness and value for money into public service organisations. With the introduction of National Vocational Qualifications (NVQs), the Management Charter Initiative (MCI), British Training Standards, Investors in People and, from the early 1990s, national training targets, the public services are increasingly developing training initiatives to meet national developments. These training innovations have been particularly important in management development.

Management development seeks to integrate the training needs of employers with those of individual managers or potential managers. It has three main purposes: to develop, consolidate and use the skills and experience of managerial staff effectively; to identify future managerial talent and develop those who have it; and to help managers develop their potential. Management development programmes have been running in local government and the NHS for many years. They have been extended into the civil service and education more recently, including a national qualification scheme, introduced by New Labour, to train potential and current head-teachers. Many programmes are focusing on developing new skills and competencies, so that public service managers can act more effectively as 'agents of change', as well as enhancing their own self-development and continuous professional development.

A New Employment Relations?

Accompanying these innovations in HRM have been new patterns of industrial relations, or what are now more often described as 'employment relations'. This is signified primarily by the removal of pay bargaining rights for some staff in the public services and the introduction of pay review bodies (PRBs) for others. These developments mark a more employer-centred approach to pay determination and a general shift away from the primacy of collective bargaining – particularly in the NHS, school teaching and the civil service – as a method of pay determination.

PRBs, long established for the armed services, senior civil servants, doctors and dentists, the judiciary and Members of Parliament, were extended to school teachers, nurses, midwives, health visitors and the professions allied to medicine (PAMs) during the 1980s. The reasons why government adopted this approach varied. In the case of NHS staff, government wanted to avoid industrial action by the nurses in particular, as it sought to push through its reforms. Government brought nurses and other groups into a pay review system in return for them agreeing not to get involved in industrial action. Although the pay of qualified nursing and midwifery staff has generally improved under the PRB, this has been at the expense of nursing auxiliaries. In addition, government reforms have resulted in work intensification, cutbacks in staff and a mass exodus from the profession. In 1995, following governmental attempts to impose a maximum pay increase of 1 per cent nationally upon midwives, nurses and related staff, with a maximum of 3 per cent (the PRB recommendation) to be allocated at the discretion of local line managers, these groups of staff changed the rules of their professional body, which now allow them to take industrial action. Staff had become particularly concerned that government's encouragement of decentralised pay bargaining would enhance regional wage inequalities, widen differentials and worsen terms and conditions of employment.

The rationale for removing pay bargaining rights for school teachers in England and Wales grew out of an increasing disillusionment by government with the deterioration of relations between the employers and teaching unions, and by the prolonged industrial dispute with teachers in 1985–6. As a result, the Burnham Committee, which determined teachers' pay under the Remuneration and Teachers Act 1965, was abolished. A temporary teachers' review body, the Interim Advisory Committee, was set up but replaced in 1991 with the permanent School Teachers Review Body (STRB). This offered benefits to government and local authority employers. These included: reducing industrial unrest; allowing government to control education funding; and providing a limited voice for unions in pay determination (Farnham and Giles, 1996).

Collective bargaining rights were also removed within part of the civil service in 1984, because the then-Foreign Secretary believed the existence of independent unions threatened national security at GCHQ in Cheltenham. As a result of a sustained campaign by civil service management, most of the 5000 staff at GCHQ left their unions. Staff who stayed incurred financial penalties, were denied pay rises and allowances, and failed to obtain promotion and training. Despite governmental statements that dismissal would not be an appropriate penalty, 14 union members refusing to give up their union membership were dismissed between November 1988 and March 1989 (Farnham and Pimlott, 1995). It was only 13 years later, following the election to power of the Blair administration, that the newly elected government restored the freedom for GCHQ staff to join independent trade unions.

National collective bargaining has been further undermined by government's attempts to develop decentralised pay bargaining in parts of the public services, including NHS trusts and larger executive agencies in the civil service. Local bargaining also became more important in 34 local authorities which opted out of national agreements for non-manual employees in the late 1980s and early 1990s (Bryson *et al.*, 1993), and for local authority employees affected by CCT. For the Thatcher and Major governments, strongly committed to free market ideas and the enterprise culture, national pay bargaining was regarded as an interference with the workings of the market mechanism. Decentralised bargaining, in contrast, seemed to offer the prospects of facilitating flexible employer responses to local labour-market conditions, lowering labour costs and dissipating trade union bargaining power. Although these developments must not be overstated, and some of these measures have been reversed, there is now more willingness by some public bodies, such as large Next Steps executive agencies, to adopt local employment relations initiatives.

In these cases, the right to manage and employment flexibility take priority over traditional model employer and good employer practices, with employers having more discretion and autonomy in how they implement their new employment policies. However, the extent of the changes associated with moves to decentralisation should not be overstated. Although collective bargaining reforms are apparent, there are still wide areas in the civil service, NHS, local government and further and higher education where more traditional patterns of collective bargaining persist. Various factors have impeded full decentralisation, including the inconsistent and incrementalist nature of government policy. Although governments have supported decentralisation in principle, they have frequently restricted management discretion in practice, by imposing expenditure limits and pay-bill targets centrally. Trade unions have generally resisted decentralisation to protect jobs and have sought to harmonise terms and conditions through national agreements. Moves to decentralisation have also been impeded by local managers, who have not fully exercised their new-found powers of local autonomy. This is because they do not have the necessary expertise to negotiate pay locally, particularly with experienced union representatives. They find it difficult to override union and staff resistance and can achieve flexibility within reformed national pay structures. They also want to avoid pressures of pay 'leap-frogging' locally and/or they are frustrated by successive governments' variable expenditure restrictions (Lilley and Wilson, 1994; Winchester and Bach, 1995). In the NHS, for example, although many trust managers have negotiated procedural reforms for decentralised pay, they have been discouraged from using them 'by government caution prior to the 1992 general election, and . . . pay restraint policies' (Winchester and Bach, 1995: 325). In large agencies in the civil service, such as the Employment Service, where union resistance is substantial, managers have been unable to implement as many innovative and varied employment policies as smaller agencies, where unions are weaker (Corby, 1993, 1997).

Changes in national collective bargaining have impacted considerably on public sector trade unions. Although union density has remained higher than in the private sector, there has been a significant decline since 1979. This is partly due to overall reductions in the size of the public services and transfers of employment to the private sector but it is also because union membership is no longer actively encouraged by some public employers. In addition, some groups of managerial staff, in NHS trusts and new universities for example, have been effectively de-recognised, after employer initiatives to promote individualised pay determination and remove these groups from national-pay bargaining arrangements. Many of these staff, now employed on personal contracts, negotiate pay individually with their employers (Farnham and Giles, 1995b).

New patterns of employment relations are also signified by the adoption of 'softer' pluralist practices by employers and unions. In the NHS and 'opt-out' local authorities, for example, employers are merging traditionally separate negotiating machinery to form single-table bargaining for all employee groups. This typically involves non-union and union staff representatives from trade unions, staff organisations and professional associations sitting around the local bargaining table together. This process has been facilitated by increased flexibility in working arrangements, the blurring of job boundaries and the harmonising of manual and non-manual workers' terms and conditions of employment (Colling and Ferner, 1995). Some managers are also by-passing traditional collective forms of staff communication, preferring more direct individualised channels of employee voice, such as newsletters, briefing groups, in-house journals and staff attitude surveys.

One of the most profound changes in industrial relations stemmed from CCT and subcontracting under Conservative governments in the 1980s and 1990s. The requirement to put services out to tender in central and local government had significant impacts on both collective bargaining and union members. Under CCT regulations, contracts for services could only be awarded on the basis of commercial criteria and were ordinarily awarded to the lowest tender. Although quality was scrutinised, it was difficult to refuse or terminate a tender on the basis of quality alone or, indeed, employment matters. Under CCT, managers of contracted services were given more discretion over issues previously determined centrally, such as service strategy, purchase of materials and personnel management. To meet competition and enhance tendering success they aimed to make services more commercial and efficient, achieve greater flexibility and productivity, and enhance service quality. These were largely sought through restructuring, labour force reductions, changes in terms and conditions, and technological improvements.

In the NHS, civil service and local government, contracting out, originally confined to low-pay areas, initially had a damaging impact on pay and conditions. Where flexible working patterns were sought to cut costs, many employees, particularly manual workers, experienced increases in working hours, work intensification, task inter-changeability, loss of employment security and deterioration in pay and benefits (Bach, 1989; Sinclair *et al.*, 1994; Ironside and Seifert, 1995). For example, holiday entitlements, overtime pay, sick pay and sick leave were often reduced. CCT in manual services significantly increased the role of market forces in influencing locally determined employment conditions and also provided opportunities for increased managerial control over pay and work, as well as encouraging moves from national to local bargaining (Sheaff, 1987; White and Hutchinson, 1996).

Decentralised bargaining, under CCT, challenged traditional bases of union power and solidarity, particularly where managers were assertive and unions weak. Forceful managers generally imposed CCT with little employee consultation. However, some local managers, under increasing pressure to enhance efficiency and performance, actively sought employee and union participation in the process. This was particularly the case in some Labour-controlled local authorities, where managers were inexperienced, where there was a history of co-operation between management and the workforce, or where union representation was strong and inclusive (Geary, 1993).

Early developments, however, were undermined by the European Court of Justice (ECJ) and its interpretation of the Transfer of Undertakings (Protection of Employment) Regulations 1981 (TUPE). TUPE Regulations protect the terms and conditions of employees who transfer employers. The UK government always insisted TUPE did not apply to public sector contracting, because transfers to the private sector were not 'commercial ventures'. The ECJ, however, rejected this interpretation and since 1993 TUPE has been recognised as applying to the public sector too. Under TUPE, employers transferring employees under CCT have to protect employees' previous contractual rights, recognise existing unions and collective agreements, and consult with employees about the transfer (Fowler, 1995). Unions have seized upon these developments to influence employers, protect their members and resist unilateral change. As a result, local authorities and civil service agencies are now closely adhering to TUPE regulations (White and Hutchinson, 1996).

Conclusion

Clearly, there has been a significant shift in the styles and content of personnel and employment relations practices in the public services since 1979. These changes are epitomised in increased use of the terms 'HRM', 'employee relations' and the 'new industrial relations' in describing how staff are managed, all of which originated in the private sector. Public services can no longer claim to be traditional 'model' or 'good practice' employers, setting an example for other employers to follow and providing terms and conditions more favourable than those of private employers. They, like their private sector counterparts, are now more likely to be concerned with effective employee performance, flexible working arrangements and widening pay differentials amongst employees and employee groups. Again, like leading private employers, some public service employers appear to be adopting: more sophisticated recruitment practices; staff appraisal procedures; performance related and individualised reward systems; structured management and staff development processes; direct communications between managers and employees; and decentralised negotiating and consultative arrangements.

There are no longer broadly universalistic employment practices across the public services. Extensive reforms, over many years, have transformed traditional, monolithic, public bureaucracies into an array of semi-autonomous business units, with responsibility for their own staffing, personnel and employment practices. There is far more managerial discretion and this is creating greater diversification and flexibility in approaches to managing people and employment relations. The old collectivist, paternalist, bureaucratic and standardised systems are increasingly being replaced or supplemented by more varied, individualistic, novel personnel management or 'New People Management' practices, incorporated from the private sector (Farnham and Horton, 1996b).

The extent of these changes, however, must not be exaggerated, since many traditional features of personnel management have been retained. Although union power has diminished and new employment practices have threatened the unions' negotiating and representative roles, some unions have played an important part in the changes taking place throughout the 1980s and 1990s. In addition, trade union density is still much higher in public services than in the private sector, whilst membership of some professional associations has actually risen over the period (Farnham and Giles, 1995b). As unions begin to reorganise to face the challenges of decentralisation, some have enhanced their involvement locally.

Though organised industrial conflict has declined from 1970s levels, unions have successfully co-ordinated some disputes. In schools, for example, teaching unions, in resisting government's initial proposals on the core curriculum and compulsory testing, successfully secured concessions and policy modifications. Other disputes, such as those in the 1990s involving midwives, nurses and PAMs, and further education staff, provide additional evidence that unions and their members are not prepared to be totally acquiescent in unilateral management change. They demonstrate that staff are willing to resist what they consider to be unacceptable reforms, although not always successfully.

Despite moves to 'employer affordability' as the main criterion in pay determination, and greater emphasis in lining up pay with market forces, pay comparability has not been totally undermined. Increasing use of PRBs has generated a form of 'arms-length bargaining'. As government, employers and unions are allowed to submit evidence to the PRB, arguments from all parties are considered. In addition in their recommendations, PRBs systematically analyse a wide range of employment and pay data. Since PRBs have generally improved the terms of staff overall, they have arguably strengthened traditional comparability (Winchester and Bach, 1995). Employer affordability has also been restricted by inconsistency in government policy. Despite governments' stated commitment to decentralised pay, they have continuously imposed expenditure limits, ceilings on pay and frozen pay-bills, which have limited managerial discretion and frustrated bargaining developments locally. Moves to decentralised bargaining have also been impeded by a number of factors. These include union resistance, variations in managerial forcefulness, and the diversity of some occupational groups. In parts of the NHS, for example, some occupations are represented by a number of different unions and professional bodies, which complicates local bargaining arrangements and retards change.

Public managers are facing an increasingly challenging task. With more decentralisation, they are expected to: develop new employment and business strategies; implement more flexible working practices; lead cultural change; increase customer responsiveness; and, ultimately, enhance efficiency, competitiveness and organisational performance. At the same time, they are having to deal with the uncertainties of frequent legislative and budgetary changes, which continually modify organisational boundaries, resources and structures. In local government, for instance, there have been over 100 pieces of legislation introduced since 1980. Public employers are certain to be affected by New Labour's programme of legislative reform introducing a minimum wage, signing up to the Social Chapter of the Maastricht Treaty, introducing its Fairness at Work White Paper (DTI, 1998) in the Employment Relations Bill (1999)and rescinding CCT legislation. Other areas of change likely to affect public sector employers are government commitment to greater fairness and opportunities for women, ethnic minorities and the disabled. Some of these policy priorities may either reverse or modify the effects of the changes introduced by the Conservatives but there is nothing in government's plans which suggests any major change in the direction of employment policy.

Public managers are faced with having to respond to lower staff morale, as they continue to adjust working practices, implement redundancies and undermine customary terms and conditions. The devolution of managerial authority, the introduction of flexible employment practices and moves to decentralise pay bargaining have resulted in increasing heterogeneity of employment practices, both within and across the public services. The 'New People Management' is more fragmented and balkanised than in the past. Further moves to decentralisation and greater emphasis on employer affordability and flexibility are likely to enhance variation, increase inequalities and widen differentials amongst comparable staff. If reform continues, it seems unlikely that a unified personnel management system will re-emerge. Future practices are more likely to follow developments in the private sector. These will be conditioned by local factors including the financial resources available, managerial styles, workforce structure, union power and organisational performance.

In summary, HRM and employment relations in the public services appear to be shifting away from traditional practices towards a 'New People Management', based on HRM principles, and a 'new employment relations'. These developments in the personnel management process, taken from the private sector, have aimed to make the public services more efficient, as the political and economic demands of the state change and are redefined (Farnham and Horton, 1996b), under both 'old' Conservative and 'new' Labour governments. In this context, five key features of contemporary HRM and employment relations seem to be emerging in the public services. First, the personnel function is attempting to become more strategic than administrative in its tasks, but within resource constraints structured by the state. Second, management styles are tending to shift towards more rationalist, performance-driven ones, away from paternalist, pluralist ones. Third, employment practices are becoming more flexible and less standardised than in the past. Fourth, employment relations are becoming 'dualist', with most non-managerial staff continuing to have their pay and conditions determined through collective bargaining, whilst public managers are increasingly working under personal contracts of employment. Fifth, the state is moving away from being a 'classical' model employer. In its place, it appears to be depending increasingly on HRM ideas and practices taken from leading-edge private organisations, whilst adapting them to the particular contingencies of the public services.

8

Exploiting Information and Communications Technologies

CHRISTINE BELLAMY

One of the most potentially radical aspects of the Blair government's agenda for public services is its proposal to exploit information and communications technologies (ICTs) to 're-engineer' government. New Labour's programme of modernisation is designed for an 'information age'. It is based on the conviction that ICTs can be harnessed in new ways to speed up administrative processes, 'join-up' fragmented services, and provide new, more effective means for government and public to transact and interact. If these aims can be fulfilled, they would indeed amount to a revolution in government. They point to a programme of reforms that, in one important way at least, is quite different from those that have gone before. By exploiting the power of ICT, they offer to square an apparently unsquareable circle: to drive costs out of public services while by the same means enhancing their effectiveness and quality. As we shall see more clearly as this chapter unfolds, the New Labour government is offering not only to reburnish the tarnished promise of government computing, but in harnessing the power of IT to the new telecommunications, it is also attempting a technological fix for the seemingly ineluctable tensions between efficiency, effectiveness, quality and democracy. If, indeed, it can really set this agenda successfully in train, New Labour may also have begun to recast relationships between citizen and state, based around new conceptions of the role, organisation, delivery and transparency of public services.

The purpose of this chapter is to explain the thinking behind this ambitious project, and in so doing to offer a realistic and critical assessment of its implications and challenges. However, before embarking on this task, it is helpful to set this programme in recent historical context, for it is by no means one that the British government has invented for itself. On the contrary, it reflects a widespread, cross-national consensus in the western world about the properties of information-age technologies, the directions in which they are said to be 'driving' organisational change, and their significance for the processes of contemporary government. The building of this consensus has been strongly encouraged by global business in the form of the multinational telecommunication, computing and data services companies, most of which now own divisions dedicated to 're-engineering' government. It has also been well fanned by the professional interests of various occupational groups (CSSA, 1997; FITLOG, 1998; SOCITM, 1998). But its significance has also been flagged up by academics (Bellamy and Taylor, 1998a; Snellen and van de Donk, 1998), independent think-tanks (Byrne, 1997; 6, 1998a), and parliamentary committees (House of Lords, 1996). Readers should also consult the series of reports published by the British Parliamentary Office of Science and Technology, which stand as powerful testament to the excitement surrounding these claims (POST, 1995; 1998).

The agenda which is reported in these documents has been constructed around the widespread assumption that governments have much to learn from corporate business, particularly those sectors which engage heavily in analogous transactions. The financial services sector, for example, has invested heavily in the provision of telephone call centres, supporting the introduction of direct, round-the-clock banking and insurance services. New ways of exploiting ICTs have not only allowed such businesses to shed layers of bureaucracy, they have also permitted them to offer dramatic improvements in customer service. At the same time, the wealth of information which can now be harvested from electronic transactions enables companies to construct detailed customer profiles with which they can identify new markets and open up new business opportunities. Information-age businesses also make increasingly rich use of electronic data exchange with suppliers and customers, constructing flexible supply-chains to meet their changing needs. The lesson appears to be that governments, too, could reap important improvements in productivity, quality, flexibility and customer service by adopting similar ICT-led business strategies.

Implementing such strategies is, however, much easier said than done, especially in a 'business' so vast, complex and sensitive as government. At the very least, this is an agenda whose trajectory is probably better measured in decades rather than years. Pursuing it to fruition would require not only a major 'rewiring' of government – in the sense of huge investments in telecommunications and information systems – but also demands a paradigm shift in the way in which governments conceive of and exploit ICTs. Most fundamental of all, it points to a reformulation of the principles on which government is conducted. In other words, this is an agenda that assumes that government is capable of large-scale institutional change. In order to elucidate this crucial point, we look initially at the history of computing in government and explore its close relationship to the ways in which public services have been organised and managed.

The Technological Trajectory in Public Administration

British government has for long been a heavy user of computing technology. The first computers to be used for administrative, rather than military, purposes were installed in central government in the late 1950s. By the mid-1960s there were some 59 computers in central government, supporting data-heavy 'housekeeping' functions such as payroll, storekeeping, purchasing, accounts and statistics (Fulton, 1968). By the 1970s, automatic data processing (ADP) was spreading to service-delivery functions, such as the administration of social security and the processing of local authority welfare benefits. Indeed, the automation of a wide range of operational functions was critical to the rapid expansion of the welfare state, especially the growth of the personal and corporate taxation systems. If the 'new managerialism' of the Thatcher period was a political reaction to the 'nanny state', then it was the increasing availability of ADP which, for perhaps too many years, masked many problems endemic in big government.

The growing use of ADP was also important in forming attitudes to new technology in government. ADP is typically concentrated within specific, labour-intensive elements of information handling, where it is used to drive out costs by shedding staff. Large-scale computer systems are used to process pre-existing data into highly structured information, often in ways that seem remote to customers and front-line staff. At the same time, the capture, validation, transmission and input of that data continues to be undertaken manually, usually by means of a huge number of different forms which are still routinely issued by government departments. The consequence is that computer-supported administration is no more reliable and timely than the weakest data-handling process in what is often a prolonged and cumbrous information-handling chain. More importantly still, ADP presents a static, piecemeal approach to managing information in government: it provides no incentives for conceiving how flows of information connect different administrative processes, even when those processes relate to the same groups of clients or geographical locations. The upshot is that computerised information systems have too often become 'islands of automation' within ever-more complicated bureaucracies, and have done little to make public services more speedy, convenient or friendly to use. Indeed, many large-scale computerisation projects, both in government and elsewhere, have proved to be serious disappointments (Willcocks, 1994). For example, the well-documented history of the Department of Social Security's Operational Strategy (Bellamy, 1996) shows that this massive computerisation programme substantially reduced staffing levels in the DSS but did so by wiring old ways of transacting with claimants into new computer systems, so that the DSS continued to collect personal data on paper forms to pay out cash by means of giros and order books. The upshot was that the computerisation did little to increase the accuracy with which benefits were calculated or to reduce benefit frauds. As a result, the Operational Strategy has raised rather than lowered the technological barriers to 're-engineering' social security administration in a customer-oriented direction.

The Synergy of Information and Communications Technologies

The last 15 years or so have witnessed two related trends which are combining to challenge the automation approach to government computing. First, computing technology has been 'democratised' and demystified, in that direct access to and personal control over computers have become part of everyday working life. By the late 1980s, for example, there had been a 'progressive diffusion' of computer usage in British local authorities from specialist IT departments to front-line professional and administrative staff (Taylor and Williams, 1989). Direct access to computerised information has also been made available to the general public through such innovations as on-line library catalogues and public information videotext systems. The second, closely-related change, has been the digitalisation of telecommunications, allowing computers and other office equipment to become fully inter-operable. It is this increasing synergy of information and communications technologies that has made possible such innovations as the Internet, electronic mail, video-conferencing, electronic data interchange, computer-supported co-operative work and teleworking. Indeed, the long-term importance of this synergy can hardly be overstated because this is what makes possible the widespread introduction of electronic networks, the defining technologies of the so-called 'information age' (Castells, 1996).

The term 'informatisation' is often deployed to capture the combined significance of these changes for the organisational structures in which they are deployed (Nora and Minc, 1980). Its significance derives from the unique property of IT. IT, that is, is capable of acting not only as a *production* technology – by automating processes previously undertaken by human beings or other machines – but also as an *informating* technology, by harvesting data from those processes. However, information produced by computers inevitably changes perceptions of its social context (Zuboff, 1988). 'Informating' may be an unintended or informal by-product of the automation process – causing information workers themselves to see their situation in a new light – or it may be exploited consciously as a management or service-delivery tool. For example, information generated from computerised library issue systems can be used to match stock to customer demand; data used for financial transactions may yield information for management accounts; or data entered into social security benefits systems can optimise advice to clients about their claiming strategies. Informating takes on yet more significance, however, when we grasp that information can become a dynamic factor in organisations, by virtue of being made to move around networks. Electronic networks make possible the automatic, instantaneous flow of data from the point where it is captured to the point where it is used, rendering the exploitation of information and knowledge potentially independent of constraints such as time, geographical distance, organisational boundaries or even national frontiers. It follows that by drastically reducing the significance of such factors, ICTs should be able to facilitate fundamental major changes in organisational life.

The potential of informatisation can be illustrated by identifying five closely-related ways in which electronic networks change the way in which information is exploited:

- Networks permit the integration of data from a number of sources, thus permitting the organisational memory to be vastly enlarged in size and scope.
- They also permit an equally vast increase in organisational intelligence, by enabling new kinds of knowledge to be created and applied. For example, commercial organisations match credit card records to postal codes or analyse the data yielded by loyalty cards to pinpoint the spending habits of specific groups. In turn, this information permits the stocking of shops, the targeting of marketing campaigns, or the vetting of credit applications to a high degree of precision. Under an Act of 1996, the Department of Social Security (DSS) now uses similar techniques to match social security data against records in other government departments, in order to detect fraud.
- Networks also permit the linking of data from different parts of an organisation, permitting the integration or co-management of client records located in different parts of government. For example, the British government is experimenting with 'intelligent forms', which will allow personal or corporate information needed by different government departments to be collected through a single form (COI, 1997).
- They also permit greater flexibility of access to information resources needed to support service delivery. Electronic networks can allow street-level staff and their customers to access customer records, consult expert advice or transact business over the wires. For example, by wiring up different parts of the NHS, the new NHSnet will enable GPs or patients themselves to book appointments on line or to receive test results over the wires. The White Paper on 'The New NHS' also aims to provide patients with a 24-hour telephone care and advice line, staffed by nurses (Department of Health, 1997a). The use of such technology could give customers greater choice about how and where they conduct transactions with public services, and could help to make a full range of services and advice widely available, even in remote geographical areas.
- Networks also permit interactive communications and, in contrast to the mass media, offer more discriminating, user-controlled access to

information resources. For example, networks such as the Internet permit individuals to search actively and selectively for information, conduct business transactions over the wires, or to put themselves in touch with people with similar interests or needs. Indeed, such facilities are enabling the emergence of new electronic information services, new kinds of business relations, including electronic retailing, new on-line electronic communities, and new kinds of political alliances.

Networking Information in British Government: the Thatcher and Major Years

Although most of these kinds of innovations were becoming technically feasible by the late 1980s, their exploitation in British government has been patchy at best. Innovation was constrained by the legacies of the large-scale, mainframe systems that were installed in the 1970s and 1980s, as well as by the orientations of the technical expertise and commercial supply networks that grew up to support these systems. Throughout most of the 1980s, moreover, the Thatcher government's efficiency drive also locked government into an automation approach to new technology in which the main criterion applied to technical investment was its capacity to shed jobs. In consequence, as the Director-General of the Inland Revenue noted, public sector computing projects were driven 'by the efficiency aspect rather than anything else' (quoted in Dyerson and Roper, 1991: 305).

This situation began to change, albeit very slowly, in the late 1980s when the realisation slowly dawned that there are powerful limits to shedding costs through automation. As we saw above, most large-scale computerisation projects of the 1970s and early 1980s were either laid over unreconstructed, bureaucratic arrangements or simply bolted on to those arrangements. The problem is that this process exacerbated the complexity and fragmentation of government bureaucracy. Not only did it do little to reduce burdens falling on the public, it also kept government's own administrative costs unacceptably high, as huge volumes of paper continued to flow between the islands of automation as well as between public services and their clients. The result was a growing interest in building bridges between the islands. For example, the publication in 1992 of a *national* information technology strategy for the NHS was a direct response to the enormous administrative costs generated by the increasing volume of paper flows between health agencies in the internal market, as well as to long-standing problems in generating commensurate statistics from the enormous variety of information systems (Keen, 1994). The same sorts of problems led to the development of a project known as 'The Co-ordination of Computerisation in the Criminal Justice System', now known as 'Integrating Business and Information Systems' (IBIS), which aims to rationalise data-flows between the Home Office, the Lord Chancellor's Department, the

Crown Prosecution System, the Prisons Service, probation service and police service (Bellamy and Taylor, 1996). IBIS is a response to chronic problems in securing robust crime statistics, which have become a major political problem for recent governments. Even more importantly, IBIS will yield important operational enhancements. It aims significantly to speed up the huge flows of paper files which act as a serious barrier to the speedy and effective prosecution of criminal cases. It is no overstatement to say that it is ICT-led administrative reforms, such as these, that appear to hold the key to securing the fast-track justice on which the New Labour government sets considerable store (HM Treasury, 1998).

Networking computing systems would also yield important economies of scope, while offering customers greater convenience and choice. For example, in the early 1990s DSS developed proposals for one-stop benefits shops, specifically as a way of breaking down the functional domains that were the legacies of its earlier computerisation projects (Bellamy, 1996). One-stop shops could make more efficient use of staff and office resources, whilst offering customers a more holistic approach to service delivery. There is no reason, moreover, why one-stop shops should be created only in a physical sense. Once customer records can be accessed on-line, the public can be offered facilities for direct on-line transactions with public services. The Inland Revenue, for example, has not only shifted around 10 million taxpayers on to the self-assessment system but also provides facilities for direct electronic lodgement of tax assessment forms (Inland Revenue, 1994). Similarly, the DSS's Pathway project will shift the distribution of benefits payments away from giro cheques and order books on to cash transactions in post offices through swipe machines. These departmental initiatives are being challenged, however, by an alternative view which argues that government would be better advised to develop smart cards capable of providing a flexible gateway into a wide range of public services. In other words, ICTs could support the introduction of *virtual* 'one-stop shops'.

Re-engineering Public Services: Better Government as Electronic Government

This brief outline of government computing shows that many key elements of this agenda emerged in a piecemeal, bottom-up way, within such data-heavy sectors as tax administration, social security, the health service and the criminal justice system. The main stimuli for this interest were undoubtedly the high costs and severe difficulties associated with attempting to shed costs and enhance these politically sensitive services in the context of an inflexible and fragmented government machine. This, indeed, has been a long standing, but largely hidden, agenda, with roots in problems that were becoming obvious by the late 1980s. What raised its profile substantially in the 1990s, and caused it to cohere, was the hype associated with the so-called information superhighway.

In 1993, the American Federal government published its 'reinventing government' prospectus (Gore, 1993), linking it directly with plans to build a National Information Infrastructure (NII). In the two or three years that followed, several other national governments in the developed world rushed to join the USA on this information superhighway (Bellamy and Taylor, 1998a). Their plans typically envisage a strong role for governments, not only in promoting, but also as model participants in, what was by now being referred to as the Information Society. These plans were taken up in a joint European Union–G7 summit in 1994, which launched the Information Society Initiative, including a project known as Government Online (European Commission, 1995). Within British government, the cause of electronic government was promoted in a series of reports published by the Government Centre for Information Systems (usually known as CCTA) (CCTA, 1994; 1995). The most tangible outcome of this interest in Britain was the establishment of a Government Information System (http://www.open.gov.uk), which offers access to government information through a single gateway on the World Wide Web.

It was not until the autumn of 1995 that the British government created CITU, the Central IT Unit. CITU was established in the Office of Public Service, with a brief to co-ordinate the strategic exploitation of ICTs *across* government. This initiative was followed in February 1996 by the creation of a high-level ministerial group (GEN 37) specially charged with taking forward inter-departmental projects. The result was the publication in November 1996 of *government.direct*, a Green Paper billed as a 'prospectus for the electronic delivery of public services' (Cabinet Office, 1996). The aim of *government.direct* was to seek public reaction to new forms of electronic service delivery (ESD), based on four sets of innovations in the use of ICTs. First, it proposed that an increasing amount of the business passing between government and the public should be transacted by means of direct electronic links. Second, it suggested that public services should collaborate to offer a single 'one-stop' gateway to government, to be available 24 hours a day. Third, a new information infrastructure should be created, capable of linking (but not merging) the various information systems in government. And fourth, information handling in government would be rationalised by reducing duplications in datahandling, for example by establishing common databases of basic personal information held by different public services. Following extensive public consultation, the principles of *government.direct* were accepted by the outgoing Conservative government in March 1997, when a series of pilot projects were launched (Cabinet Office, 1997b).

The Blair government has broadly accepted the proposals of *government.direct*, but has located them more firmly within a wider programme for modernising government, including constitutional reform. Within a few months of coming into power, it published its own prospectus for the information age and issued a brave, some say foolhardy, pledge to make 25 per cent of government services available electronically by 2002 (COI, 1997).

Its 'programme of action' towards electronic government included the publication of the NHS White Paper (Department of Health, 1997a) and a Green Paper on Welfare Reform (Department of Social Security, 1998a) which set out plans to improve customer services with ICTs. It also flagged up the launch of the Government Secure Intranet, as secure means of exchanging data, documents and messages in government. However, the flagship of New Labour's vision of information-age government is the *Better Government* White Paper, which was to 'lay out our approach to re-engineering government services in the information age' (COI, 1997: 31).

Publication of *Better Government*, in October 1998, had already been delayed for several months. Nevertheless, its main thrust had become clear. The big theme is 'joined-up government' which is to be brought about in three different ways. First, more public services are to be offered on-line, thus fulfilling Blair's pledge to use ESD to 'join up' government directly to the public. Second, government itself is to be 'joined-up' through the establishment of information-sharing partnerships – between departments, between tiers of government and perhaps between public and private sectors – aimed at supporting holistic service provision for groups of clients, such as the unemployed, who have previously been obliged to deal with multifarious agencies. And third, operational levels of government are to be 'joined-up' to policy-making levels – for example, by rethinking relations between core departments and Next Steps agencies – so that issues relating to *effectiveness* can be made to feature more prominently in public management.

Re-engineering Government with ICTs?

So what are we to make of this agenda, and what sort of issues does it raise? The main point is that the delays in bringing out the *Better Government* White Paper bear witness to the fact that this is a highly complex and sensitive agenda. As we have seen, contemporary prospectuses for electronic government draw heavily on ideas associated with business process re-engineering (BPR). At its most radical and hard-edged, BPR envisages no less than a fundamental structural transformation of business organisations (Hammer and Champy, 1993; Davenport, 1993). It aims to shift organisations decisively away from the producer-oriented functional principle, which still dominates complex bureaucracies, by re-configuring business processes along a customer-focused chain, integrating suppliers, producers and consumers. Thus BPR is intended to reverse the functional division of labour: 'it is to the next [industrial] revolution what specialisation was to the last' (Hammer and Champy, 1993: 5). In line with many 'soft' BPR projects, however, the agenda that has taken shape since *government.-direct* draws back from such a brutal confrontation with the established structures of government. As *government.direct* made clear, the strategy envisaged for government is that the functional domains of government, and the information systems which have been mapped on to them, will be left more or less intact, at least at first, but that government will be joined up electronically in two main ways: first by providing secure electronic linkages between government information systems, so that data can be connected in a logical, if not in a physical, sense and second, by providing common electronic gateways into government, so that services *appear* to be seamless to their customers. In other words, the hope is that technology can be used to manage complexity and mask fragmentation. Although much of the proposed re-engineering of government will initially take place only in this virtual sense, the scale of this agenda should not be underestimated, involving, as it does, a massive re-configuration of information flows and business relationships.

Re-wiring Public Services

The commitment to joined-up government implies that there will eventually be significant re-wiring of the information systems and telecommunications of government. In planning these investments, important choices must be made, For example, what kinds of equipment will the public be prepared to use? Should government assume, for example, that digital TV and top-set boxes will come into widespread use, or should efforts be devoted to the development of public access information kiosks? How many public service customers will have access to personal computers and the Internet? Should government develop its own electronic networks or, as seems more probable, should it try to piggy-back on commercial private networks, such as those developed to support High-Street banking, retailing or the National Lottery? What kinds of arrangements need to be put in place to safeguard the security and integrity of government infrastructure, including protecting it from terrorist attack?

These questions also expose continuing problems about financing and managing technological development. ICT formed the largest single sector for both the market-testing and the Private Finance Initiatives (PFI). Extensive outsourcing has, however, brought two major problems in its wake. It is well recognised that the use of PFIs in this sector has not been nearly as profitable as was hoped, and several major projects, including the DSS Pathway project, have been subject to considerable delays. There are growing concerns about procurement and contract monitoring procedures in government (for example, POST, 1998). There are concerns, too, that, mainly as a result of the sheer scale of its ICT contracts, UK government has become highly dependent for delivering and refreshing its information systems on a few multinational companies that can cope with projects on this scale. These uncomfortable facts raise important questions about the British government's ability to act as an 'intelligent customer', one that is able to shape as well as to respond to its own ICT agendas.

Sharing and Exchanging Information

The second set of issues relates to the management of information. The use and protection of personal data is, of course, one of the most sensitive political questions raised by 'joined-up government' and featured prominently in the responses to *government.direct*. If government is to rely heavily on ESD then individuals and businesses must be able to trust government with their data (Raab, 1998; 6, 1998b). Among the many problems that must be solved, then, is how to verify personal identity and authenticate documents on-line, a problem that has led to worries about the legal acceptability of digital signatures, electronic 'locks' for plastic cards, and biometric gateways such as fingerprints tests. Next there are issues about protecting personal data held in the government's computer systems. Problems here range from deciding the principles on which personal data should be exchanged, and constructing adequate 'fire-walls' between computer systems, to protecting on-line transactions with encryption. Then there are questions about the extent to which government agencies should use third-party 'data donors': to take one example, government could save enormous sums of money and increase MoT test compliance rates if applications for motor vehicle tax disks were to be automatically cross-checked with MoT test records.

As well as being a heavy user of personal data, government is an increasingly important supplier of information. In this role, government is extending its use of such media as the World Wide Web, but this process is also pointing up important policy issues. In particular, there is a difficult balance to be struck between reaping commercial value from public information and New Labour's commitment to Open Government. In turn, this issue has raised questions about the future of crown copyright, which will be severely challenged by the ease with which documents can now be copied and distributed (House of Commons, 1995–6).

The Organisational Politics of Information

Research suggests that even if these technical and policy issues can be sorted out, there are major internal problems in re-engineering government which may yet derail, divert or substantially delay it (Bellamy and Taylor, 1998a; 1998b). By definition, the prospectus set out in *government.direct* and *Better Government* involves new kinds of partnerships, leading to horizontal integration between organisational domains, each of which has its own mission statement, business aims, business systems and budgetary constraints. One problem lies in securing finance for projects which may have demonstrable benefits for government as a whole, but uneven or even negative benefits for individual departments. This problem has, of course, been exacerbated by the New Public Management, which has placed more emphasis on the bottom line of public sector accounts. It reflects, too, a pervasive issue in capital investment appraisal in UK government, under which each project is required to pay for itself, regardless of its contribution to long-term strategy.

A second problem is perhaps less obvious but probably more difficult to manage. As every systems analyst knows, organisations evolve a variety of information systems, holding more or less incompatible data. Some incompatibilities arise, for example, from the semantic sensibilities of different occupational groups and some from the differing information logic of departments' business needs. Whatever the reason for this huge variety of systems, however, it remains the case that every part of government has already set in place a complex set of business processes, information systems and data sets designed to supply information for its own operational, management, policy and performance-measurement requirements. In turn, the inflexibilities these processes impose become important barriers to major network redesign. As the BPR agenda develops, moreover, researchers are becoming strongly aware of the important symbolic role that information systems play in organisational cultures and power structures. By acting as the tangible manifestation of organisational routines, IS embed 'the way we do things here' into organisational life: 'information systems become interwoven within organisational practices, within the culture of the organisation, and . . . mediate and reinforce the meaning of those practices' (Bloomfield and Coombs, 1992: 468). Unsurprisingly then, BPR-type projects become strongly imbued with organisational politics. As one of the gurus of BPR has acknowledged, a high proportion of BPR-type initiatives fail: 'the primary reason is that the companies did not manage the politics of information' (Davenport *et al.*, 1992: 3).

The Social and Political Consequences of Electronic Government

This discussion would be far from complete without identifying what are perhaps the most fundamental issues raised by electronic government: its social and political implications. We concentrate here on some of the most important. The first concerns the effects of re-engineering on public sector employment. Comparable changes in the banking and retailing sectors have resulted in major downsizing and loss of jobs: these sectors lost some 17 per cent of middle management and front-line staff between 1989 and 1995 (POST, 1998). Furthermore, the high reliance on outsourcing government computing to the global IT industry has already led to a significant transfer of public sector jobs to the private sector and could lead to further transfers away from the UK. Many jobs that remain are likely to change, especially those in the front line of public services. The heavy focus on economies of scope will place more emphasis on the development of flexible skills, as the old divisions of labour are broken down. There is likely, too, to be growing importance attached to knowledge-workers with high IT and communication skills, especially those workers capable of operating across organisational boundaries.

Second, re-engineering government through ICTs may also have important implications for citizens. One prominent issue raised by the information society is whether it will lead to major social cleavages between the information rich and those who by virtue of lack of skill, lack of confidence or lack of access are likely to remain information poor. On the one hand, the government's response to the public consultations on *government.direct* show that CITU is trying hard to develop accessible and user-friendly means of electronic services. Indeed, if they are introduced in appropriate ways, ICTs could in principle widen access to public services, for example by supporting a greater range of outlets, sustaining public service provision in sparsely populated areas and adapting service delivery to the needs of the physically disabled or other minority groups. On the other hand, in a country where, in several inner-city pockets, the penetration of ordinary telephony remains surprisingly low, we cannot assume that the commercial market will provide universal access to the information superhighway, even in its most basic form. One comfort is that both these issues have been widely noticed, not least in the public responses to *government.direct*.

In contrast, there is a third issue which has been less well remarked, but which is nevertheless deeply implicated in the re-engineering project as it has been described in this chapter. This concerns the implications for public service values of re-orienting government from the functional principle to a customer focus (Bellamy and Taylor, 1998a). At first sight, perhaps, this re-orientation is to be welcomed, implying as it does a desire to treat individuals in a holistic and responsive way. On the other hand, it erects as a principle of government the doctrine that customers should be more transparent to government, just as government should be more transparent to customers. In an age whose defining technological capabilities are associated with a shift from Fordist to post-Fordist forms – with a reorientation from producing standardised services which are indifferent to individual wants to the targeting of highly differentiated products to specific customer needs – perhaps we should be more apprehensive about their application to public services. How much information, for example, should governments be able to assemble on individual citizens, and how far should public services be sensitive to personal circumstances and social difference? At what point does providing customised advice and targeting services slide into policing lifestyles and disciplining non-conforming behaviour? 'Targeting', 'selectivity' and 'customisation' are the buzz words of BPR, but their down side may lie in their potential for directing the power of new technology towards the creation of new capabilities for pinpointing, discrimination and surveillance.

Conclusion

The issues discussed above raise critical points of principle for information-age government. They therefore serve to reinforce the importance of a final issue which must also be seriously addressed. This is the issue of public accountability. As we have seen, the fundamental aim of re-engineering government is to provide an apparently seamless public service. If this aim can really be fulfilled – and it has been the purpose of this chapter to cast some doubt on how quickly and consistently this can be done – it will inevitably obfuscate the underlying structures of government and the way they relate both to formal lines of accountability and responsibility for resources. If new forms of electronic government are not to deepen still further the democratic deficit in modern states, they must be accompanied by equally innovative thinking about democratic structures for the information age. The most important point to make, by way of conclusion, is that the 're-engineering' agenda which is now coming to the fore in British government is by no means to be regarded simply as an instrumental tool, one that will amount to no more than the revamping of the technological infrastructure of government. Rather it should be recognised as a vision of electronic government, one that goes to the heart of what values and practices are appropriate for public services in an information age.

PART III

Cases

9

The Civil Service

SYLVIA HORTON

During the 1980s and 1990s the civil service moved from an administered to a managed bureaucracy and from a system of public administration to one of new public management (NPM). The transformation was carried through by reforming Conservative governments under Margaret Thatcher and John Major and is being continued by the New Labour government, led by Tony Blair. Since the 1960s the civil service has been the subject of much criticism and debate, with the Fulton Report (1968) challenging its ability to carry out its contemporary functions efficiently or effectively, primarily because it was poorly managed. The legacy of Fulton can be found in an earlier version of this book (Horton, 1993). The main attack came, in the late 1970s, from the 'New Right' wing of the Conservative party which was committed to changing radically the role of the state, shifting the boundaries between the public and private sectors and reducing the size and *modus operandi* of the remaining public organisations. Since 1979, and the election of Margaret Thatcher as Prime Minister, the civil service has experienced unremitting, continuous change. The outcome is that it is smaller, its structure has radically altered, its methods of delivering services have been transformed and it is now staffed by a new cadre of public managers. The rapidity of the changes and their permanent impact are undoubtedly due to the fact that reforming Conservative governments were in office for an uninterrupted period of 18 years, which enabled effective and strong political steering.

Although there are differences of opinion as to whether the Conservative governments between 1979 and 1997 had a clear strategy for the civil service which they implemented (Fry, 1984;) or whether it was a case of pragmatic incrementalism (Barberis, 1995), there is general consensus that a revolution occurred (Butler, 1994; Cabinet Office, 1997a). This chapter chronicles and evaluates the structural, cultural and managerial changes associated with that 'quiet' revolution and explores their effect on civil servants, the public they serve and the political system of which they are a part. Finally, it considers the impact of the Blair government and assesses its plans for better government and modernising the civil service.

The Quiet Revolution

Armed with beliefs that public services, especially the civil service, were wasteful, inefficient and poor value for money, and that the better-managed private sector should be the model for the public sector, Conservative governments post-1979 embarked upon their programme of reform. In retrospect, a number of stages or initiatives are evident. The first was the efficiency initiative directed at reducing public expenditure, making civil servants cost conscious, implanting managerial ideas and practices and providing an infrastructure within which managerialism could develop. The second initiative involved restructuring the civil service to increase its flexibility, facilitate performance management (PM) and introduce a new people management. The third stage, post-1991, marked a new public-service orientation in which responsiveness to service users, combined with setting down quality standards, would increase public accountability to the 'market' and curb service-provider power and control. Throughout the 1990s, markets and contracts increasingly became mechanisms for achieving greater accountability, transparency, precision and challengeability (Mather, 1994). Government took stock of its achievements in the mid-1990s and opted for a period of 'continuity and change'. This was not so much a fourth initiative as a reaffirmation of government's determination to press ahead with promoting greater efficiency through competition, markets and ever-closer links with the private sector.

The Efficiency Initiative

In 1979 Margaret Thatcher took responsibility for driving through reform of the civil service and the Cabinet Office became the powerhouse. She appointed Derek Rayner, from Marks and Spencer, as her Efficiency Adviser to head a small unit in the Cabinet Office, briefed to bring about immediate efficiency savings and change the administrative culture of the service. Every department had to examine areas of work which might yield savings and produce a report in 90 days. This bottom-up approach yielded claimed savings of £350 million from more than 300 scrutinies undertaken up to 1983. Although the real savings were disputed the scrutinies, combined with government's other policies of forced staffing cuts and cash limits, created a climate for management change and sowed the seeds of a 'value for money' (VFM) culture.

In 1982 government announced an extension of the efficiency drive in the form of the Financial Management Initiative (FMI) (Cmnd 8616, 1982). FMI introduced devolved management systems with managers at all levels responsible for clarifying objectives, accounting for budgets and improving performance, and committed to VFM. Though departments were left to formulate their own approach to FMI, they all introduced top management information systems for ministers and senior officials which informed them of what was going on in their departments and who was responsible for what. Common accounting systems and systems for monitoring and controlling expenditure were also developed, thus ensuring that financial information was available on costs, expenditure patterns and budget profiles and providing a much clearer picture of how resources were being used and how much programmes cost. These elements of FMI, combined with other statistical returns on work in progress and out-turn, provided the building blocks for PM.

PM is essentially a rational approach to management in which goals and objectives for the organisation overall, and for each constituent element within it, are clearly identified and set down in a strategy document. Performance measures are specified and targets are set, against which performance can be assessed. This applies also to staff, who are set individual goals, objectives and targets and whose performance is assessed through regular appraisals and reviews (Williams, 1997). By 1987 some 1800 performance indicators (PIs) were in use as tools for measuring VFM and increased efficiency whilst a new staff appraisal system and performance related pay (PRP) were also being introduced. Most PIs, however, concentrated on input measurements and were being used primarily as instruments of management control and cost cutting (Pollitt, 1986). The House of Commons Public Accounts Committee (House of Commons, 1987) found evidence of PM throughout the civil service but commented on the relative failure of FMI because of continued intervention by the Treasury over budgets and spending.

Next Steps

An internal report of the Efficiency Unit in the Cabinet Office (Cabinet Office, 1988) pointed to barriers to further management change and stated that devolved management could only be achieved by separating responsibility for policy from service delivery. This led to the second major stage of reform of the civil service, namely the restructuring of departments and creation of Next Steps Agencies (NSAs). Service delivery was gradually transferred to NSAs, headed by chief executives (CEs) responsible for day-to-day operations and management of clearly defined areas of administration. Agencies operate within a framework of policy objectives and resources set down by a parent department and the Treasury. The centre, in theory, has arms-length control, leaving agency CEs with freedom and flexibility to manage. Each agency responds to its own market, clients and users in an appropriate way, so as to increase service efficiency and performance.

Since 1988 over 150 agencies have been created and nearly 80 per cent of civil servants now work within them. Agencies vary greatly in function, size and how they are managed. Although the stated aim of Next Steps was to create administrative structures more relevant to the needs of NPM, and its guiding principle was that 'the structure should fit the job to be done', there was clearly another government agenda reflected in the process of deciding upon agency status. This process, known as 'prior options', required all agency candidates to be subjected to the following tests. Did the activity need to be done at all? If yes, could it be transferred to the private sector? If not, could it be contracted out on grounds of efficiency or must it remain within the department? If all these options were ruled out, then agency status was considered. Prior options were revisited when agencies came up for review (at first after three and then, from 1995, after five years) and so agency status was always seen as a possible interim stage to the next step of transfer out of the civil service (Jordan, 1993). By 1998 there were 11 NSAs which had been privatised, three wholly contracted out, 11 merged or amalgamated, one abolished, one transferred to a non-departmental status and one transferred back to a central department. Further privatisations were in the pipeline (Cabinet Office, 1998b).

Creating NSAs provided an opportunity to rethink the recruitment of agency CEs and draw up new job descriptions. Although the first appointments were of civil servants *in situ*, all appointments are now openly advertised and set for fixed periods, subject to reappointment. The majority of CEs still come from within the civil service or the armed forces but a significant minority are recruited from the private sector and other public sector organisations, such as the NHS and local government (Horton and Jones, 1996). All CEs are required to behave increasingly like their private sector counterparts. Although there are still some significant differences between being in charge of a public service and running a private commercial company, the evidence suggests that the differences are becoming less, as public sector managers are required to operate in quasi markets, are exposed to competition, and have to achieve performance targets such as efficiency savings and increased productivity.

In 1991 government pursued its policy of devolved management further by enabling CEs of NSAs to exercise discretion and flexibility in 40 areas of personnel management (HM Treasury and Cabinet Office, 1991) including recruitment, flexible working time and training. In 1994 the 32 largest agencies were allowed to develop their own policies on grading and pay structures and in 1996 all agencies were given these further flexibilities. Many smaller agencies, however, chose to remain within the framework of their parent department. Research shows that agencies now have a lot of autonomy in day-to-day management and variations in policy are emerging as agencies exercise their delegated powers (Horton, 1996b). But there are still areas where controls remain and the Treasury and Cabinet Office continue to impose very strong steering from the centre (Talbot, 1997).

Quality and Re-engineering

By 1990 a sea change was taking place in government's thinking about the management of public services, which was confirmed in the launching of the *Citizen's Charter* (Cm 1599, 1991). The main theme of the Charter was commitment to responsive and high-quality public services, and privatisation and competition were seen as means of achieving this. Following quickly on the *Citizen's Charter* was the White Paper *Competing for Quality* (Cm 1730, 1991). These two documents marked the start of government's third initiative in steering public management further towards the market through re-engineering and raising the quality and responsiveness of public services through charters. Charter standards were to be set down for each part of the public sector and publicised so that external bodies and individual consumers, patients or users could judge performance against these expectations. Charters and contracts were to be means of increasing the accountability of public services and making them more transparent.

Competing for Quality set out three aims for departments: to concentrate on their core activities; to introduce more competition and choice into the provision of services, in particular their non-core activities; and to improve standards of quality provision to the citizen. The Cabinet Office took responsibility for market testing from the Treasury, issued *The Government's Guide to Market Testing* (Cabinet Office, 1991) and imposed market testing targets upon departments and agencies. Most departments and large agencies set up their own Market Testing Units and proceeded to market-test selected activities. The *Second Report of the Citizen's Charter Unit* (Cm 2540, 1994) indicated that some 389 market tests had resulted in 195 contracts being awarded externally and 147 internally. Restructuring was clearly taking place and in 1996 government decided to abandon setting targets for market testing. Instead all departments and NSAs had to produce annual Efficiency Plans. These were to explain how they proposed to achieve their efficiency targets and in particular they were required to demonstrate their use of market testing and other management techniques, such as process re-engineering. By 1997 market testing had become a widely accepted management strategy for exposing public services to competition to ensure VFM.

In 1992 government had embarked upon another strategy for involving the private sector and keeping public expenditure down. This was the Private Finance Initiative (PFI). Private companies were invited to invest in public service projects such as roads, bridges and hospitals and then lease them back to government for an agreed period of time. This, it was claimed, would transfer the risks of investment away from government, reduce public expenditure, or at least the Public Sector Borrowing Requirement, and enable the private and public sectors to work more closely together (Flynn, 1997).

The *Citizen's Charter*, adopting the language of the market, signalled a new emphasis on consumers and users of public services. The aim was to shift the accountability of the producers of services away from political institutions and traditional hierarchies to the 'market'. Government originally laid down six principles of public service that all 'citizens' should expect. These were: explicit standards; information on the purpose, costs, and performance of the service; provision of choice wherever possible; consultation with users; courtesy at all times plus effective remedies if things go wrong; and all public services were to demonstrate VFM. In April 1997, six more standards were added, requiring targets to be set for answering letters, keeping appointments, operating a help-line, consulting users, operating a redress system and catering for the needs of all people, including those with 'special needs' (Cm, 3370, 1996). The White Paper, *Citizen's Charter – Five Years On*: reiterated that the *Citizen's Charter* was intended to act in lieu of a market: 'In short, it applies wherever there is no effective competition or choice for the individual consumer' (Cm 3370, 1996: 2). Many agencies, particularly those providing services to the public, produced their own charters while others received charter awards such as ISO 9000, an international quality mark.

A survey of NSA annual reports indicates that agencies are being innovative in measures adopted to improve quality (Horton, 1997). The Benefits Agency claim their satisfaction levels have increased continuously since they started their user surveys in 1992 and the Employment Service points to constant improvement in the time taken to sign people on. Whilst criticisms can be levelled at customer-satisfaction surveys, PIs and league tables, they do serve as an alternative to competition and act as benchmarks. They can also alert policy makers to areas of concern. A fall in satisfaction levels at the Child Support Agency between 1994 (61 per cent) and 1996 (46 per cent) led to changes in policy and removal of the CE. Complaints are also used as a proxy for quality of service and an important PI requiring remedial action. Published service standards give users 'rights' to those standards and serve as sources of redress. In a survey of CEs of NSAs (Horton, 1999, forthcoming) 75 per cent rated accountability to customers as very important and paid close attention to PIs of consumer satisfaction.

Continuity and Change

In the mid-1990s government set out its thoughts and plans for the future in *The Civil Service: Continuity and Change* (Cm 2627, 1994). Its contents confirmed the radical nature of the changes since 1979 but stated there was still room for improvement in quality and efficiency. Further agencification, managerial delegation and resort to commercial accounting methods were to be introduced. Efficiency Plans were to replace market-testing targets, but all parts of the service were expected to demonstrate strategies involving the private sector as a means of improving VFM. They were also expected to adopt private sector techniques, such as business process re-engineering (BPR) and benchmarking, as means of making continual improvements in their performance. Although there was a commitment to 'sustaining the key principles on which the British Civil Service is based – integrity, political impartiality, objectivity, selection and promotion on merit and account-ability through Ministers to Parliament' (ibid.: 1) government acknowledged that continuing reforms could only be carried through by a well-trained and highly professional group of senior advisers and managers working closely in support of ministers, both in the development of policy and in the management of services. This resulted in the creation of a new Senior Civil Service (SCS) of around 3000 people brought into a new pay and contrac-tual arrangement. All members of the SCS, including CEs of NSAs, are now on individual employment contracts and PRP and recruitment is by open competition.

A report of the Select Committee on the Treasury and Civil Service (TCSC), *The Role of the Civil Service* (House of Commons, 1995), was almost totally supportive of the changes in the service over the previous decade. It emphasised however the need to protect the traditional values of integrity, political impartiality, objectivity, selection and promotion on merit and accountability as unifying features of the service. Government responded in *Taking Forward Continuity and Change* (Cm 2748, 1995) by introducing a Civil Service Code and extending the powers of the Civil Service Commissioners to ensure unbiased recruitment. It also fleshed out plans for further increasing civil service efficiency. These included: contain-ing running costs up to 1997, implying a 10 per cent cut in real terms; requiring all departments to undertake fundamental expenditure reviews; and rigorous application of the prior options techniques. This meant that they had to look for possibilities of privatisation, contracting out, PFIs and BPE in order further to improve performance and VFM.

The last innovation of the Major government, launched in April 1996, was the Benchmarking Exercise. Anxious to keep up pressure for continuing improvement in service delivery, government required agencies to identify and adapt, for their own use, best practice in management, not just amongst agencies but across the wider public sector, the private sector and inter-nationally. A pilot study was undertaken to benchmark 30 agencies against a standard of generic organisation performance – the Business Excellence Model. The claimed success of the pilot resulted in Phase 2, from April 1997 to January 1998, which involved over 100 public sector bodies covering 360,000 staff, or half the civil service (Cabinet Office, 1998c). This was underway when Labour won the election in May 1997.

The New People Management

The effect of the transformation of the civil service on the people working within it has been profound. First, there have been significant changes in the composition of the civil service. These include a reduction of industrial staff, due to privatisation and contracting out of services and increases in the flexible workforce, namely temporary and part-time staff. The service is now some 35 per cent smaller than it was in 1979, as numbers have fallen from 742,000 (1979) to 480,000 (1998). The greatest fall has been in the industrial civil service, from 180,000 (1976) to 32,800 (1998). Whilst the overall number of permanent staff has been falling, part-time staff as well as temporary staff have increased. In April 1998 there were 430,500 non-industrial permanent staff, of whom 56,800 were part-time and there were also 17,700 temporary staff (Civil Service Statistics, 1998) (see Table 9.1 for comparative statistics).

A second major change has occurred in the approach to people management. The Cassels Report on Personnel Management (1983) identified key differences between the civil service and private organisations in their approaches to managing people and recommended major changes, including delegation to line managers for all personnel decisions and a more strategic role for the professional personnel function both in departments and at the centre. This was consistent with changes occurring in the financial field and reinforced and facilitated the move towards PM. By the early 1990s departments and agencies were responsible for 95 per cent of all recruitment.

TABLE 9.1   *Civil Service statistics, 1979–98*

Year	Permanent staff		Casual staff	Total
	Non-ind.	*Ind.*		
1979	567,770	167,660	7,560	742,990
1980	549,410	158,520	6,000	713,930
1981	541,790	150,940	6,160	698,880
1982	529,790	139,190	6,920	675,900
1983	520,220	131,010	9,090	660,320
1984	505,940	120,250	7,450	633,640
1985	499,790	101,520	10,670	611,990
1986	500,430	95,950	10,790	607,160
1987	510,090	90,730	11,850	612,670
1988	509,530	73,390	10,310	593,230
1989	503,190	69,710	11,100	584,000
1990	499,100	67,480	13,120	597,700
1991	494,660	64,150	13,610	572,420
1992	509,450	61,390	16,960	587,700
1993	508,760	51,680	18,260	578,700
1994	494,140	46,150	21,110	561,410
1995	474,880	42,020	18,240	535,140
1996	458,660	35,920	20,010	514,580
1997	439,630	36,028	19,610	494,600
1998	430,500	32,800	17,700	481,000

Source: Civil Service Statistics (1998).

They had developed new staff-appraisal systems linked to performance, development and rewards, with performance evaluated against pre-determined targets and objectives set at the previous appraisal. Highly rated performance entitled individuals to PRP, first introduced in 1986 for senior staff but covering all civil servants by 1992. Poor performance is normally accompanied by training, closer monitoring or transfer, but continuing poor performance can result in dismissal (Office of Public Service, 1996).

Training was given high priority throughout the 1980s, both to provide the service with the new managerial and IT skills required in a more business-oriented environment and to act as a conduit for the new managerialism and enterprise culture. Departments carry out most training but the Civil Service College (CSC) provides about 6 per cent of it and offers advice on training interventions. It has developed a comprehensive menu of management training programmes, based upon the development of core competencies identified for first line, operational and strategic managers by the Management Charter Group of private leading-edge business people. Over 6000 civil servants a year attend the college, whilst some courses are delivered on site to many more.

One of the major programmes is for top managers drawn from both the public and private sectors. It is designed to facilitate a sharing of experience and good practice and a cross-fertilisation of ideas amongst those responsible for developing strategy in their respective organisations. This, combined with the employment of private sector consultants and the use of visiting speakers, ensures that civil servants are infused with private sector ideas and transmit them into their departments. Since the late 1990s, all departments and agencies are committed to Investors in People (IiP), which is an award signifying an excellent human resources development strategy.

The traditional approach to managing people in the civil service has given way to a new people management (Farnham and Horton, 1996b). This is based on ideas imported from the private sector and associated with human resources management (HRM), where people are seen as the key resource in organisations and as assets rather than costs. Recruitment, development, performance and reward are all part of the HRM cycle, designed to ensure that people are fully committed to organisational goals and objectives and are used in the optimum way (Storey, 1989). Civil servants are now more obviously managed, with the personal review acting as an instrument of control, although it is more often presented as an instrument of consultation and individual empowerment. The performance criteria set down in appraisals enable the managerial emphasis on costs, output, performance and quality to be internalised throughout the service. The introduction of PRP was also designed to reinforce the move towards PM and HRM.

Linked to developments in HRM have been changes in industrial or employment relations. Throughout the period of the postwar settlement, industrial relations in the civil service were stable. The Whitley system, established after the First World War, provided the framework within which widespread collective bargaining took place. Union membership was high, reaching over 80 per cent density in most areas, and penetrating to top management level, where most senior officials were members of the First Division Association. Pay was determined for top officials through a pay review body and for other civil servants by national collective bargaining. Government sought to set an example as a model employer and operated on the principle of fair wages and comparability with the private sector (see Chapter 7).

Industrial relations began to change after 1979, when a series of Trade Union Acts gradually removed both the legal immunities of trade unions and challenged their collective power (Farnham, 1997). This was bound to impact on the civil service because of its high levels of unionionisation. Government, determined to deprivilegise the civil service, no longer sought to be the model employer but followed private sector practice (Farnham and Horton, 1992). Relationships between government and civil service trade unions became very confrontational when in 1981 government abolished the Civil Service Pay Unit and the Standing Commission on Pay Comparability, which formed the basis of the pay system. In 1982, the Civil Service Department, seen as defending trade union action, was abolished and its functions divided between the Cabinet Office and Treasury. The long-standing Priestley Principle of pay comparability was replaced by 'what the government could afford' or 'what it had to pay to get the staff it needed' (Megaw, 1982). This opened the way for a more market-oriented approach to pay determination.

Because of the entrenched position of civil service unions, it was not easy for government to reduce union influence amongst employees but it flexed its muscle by unilaterally derecognising unions in the General Communications Headquarters at Cheltenham in 1983 (see Chapter 7). The main attack of Conservative governments, however, was on the system of national collective bargaining which it saw as costly and no longer in tune with government policies on PM. Government sought to undermine national bargaining by encouraging NSAs to develop their own pay and grading structures, and by 1996 all departments and NSAs had delegated powers to determine their own systems of industrial relations. A diverse pattern is beginning to emerge (Corby, 1997; Farnham and McNeill, 1997). Although most agencies continue to recognise trade unions, the scope for collective bargaining has begun to narrow and throughout the civil service new and alternative channels of communication between management and employees are being developed. Industrial relations is now much more individualised, with the use of personal contracts and PRP; more fragmented, as the service has become balkanised into hundreds of agencies; and less collective, as trade union membership has fallen and trade unions have a less prominent role in the decision-making process.

There is evidence, in spite of government's commitment to being a good employer (Cm 2748, 1995), that the old 'welfare' orientation of industrial relations has given way to a more instrumental managerialist one. The growing use of personal contracts, PRP, lateral recruitment from the private sector and the performance culture of the reformed service has changed attitudes amongst staff. Preoccupation with cost-cutting and market testing means the civil service is no longer perceived to offer a career for life, whilst job insecurity, linked to market testing, has produced low morale. The civil service is clearly being managed along HRM lines, with a new culture cementing new structures and processes, and a more entrepreneurial and service orientation. By the late 1990s, a hybrid or dualist system of industrial relations had emerged which shows some elements of the past collectivist tradition but is increasingly fragmented, diverse and more individualised, with managerial prerogative in the ascendancy. This was the Conservative legacy to the new government.

The Way Forward to Better Government?

In Opposition New Labour, led by Tony Blair, supported the changes taking place in the civil service, particularly those linked to increasing efficiency and effectiveness, ensuring VFM and improving quality. It had its own agenda, however, and was committed to achieving 'Better Government'. This meant, first, constitutional reform to take government closer to the people; second, more democracy to involve people in decision-making processes; third, 'joined-up government' to ensure co-operation and co-ordination between government bodies and voluntary and private sector organisations in delivering services Finally, it meant modernising public services and creating learning organisations committed to continually seeking ways of improving performance, achieving best value and meeting the needs of the public. Its ideas on the civil service were spelt out in more detail on the publication of the White Paper *Modern Public Services for Britain: Investing in Reform* (Cabinet Office, 1998g).

Taking Charge and Steering from the Centre

The changeover of government was smooth, largely because of John Major's decision to allow Labour shadow ministers to have meetings and discussions with civil servants during the year preceding the 1997 election. This partly diffused the suspicion that after 18 years of serving the Conservatives, it would be difficult for senior civil servants to give impartial advice to the new Labour Government (Hennessy *et al.*,1997). Although a small number of permanent secretaries chose to take early retirement there was no cull of senior officials. The new government, however, appointed over 60 special advisers (twice the number in the Major administration) and many of these filled posts which would normally be held by civil servants.

Accusations that this amounted to politicisation of the civil service and political patronage met with the rejoinder that it was intended to protect the political neutrality of the civil service and 'establish and maintain clear boundaries between official and political advice and advisers' (Theakston, 1998: 18). This was difficult to sustain when, during the government's first year in office, 20 out of 40 departmental press secretaries were replaced by people who were prepared to 'put a political spin' on their presentation of information (Butcher, 1998).

Sir Robin Butler, who oversaw the 'quiet revolution' of the service from 1983 to 1997, was replaced as head of the civil service in early 1998 by Sir Richard Wilson, previously Permanent Secretary at the Ministry of Defence. His first task, at the request of the Prime Minister, was to undertake a review of the centre of government. His report identified a number of major weaknesses including poor linkage between policy formulation and implementation; a lack of co-ordination of policy and service delivery across departments; an underdeveloped strategic management process with too little strategic analysis; failure to generate strategic choices; and failure to evaluate policy outcomes. Wilson made a series of recommendations for improving performance at the centre of government, moving towards best practice and innovation in government and strengthening corporate management of personnel, IT, government communication and science advice. These he argued could only be achieved if there was better training and development of top staff. The Prime Minister endorsed Wilson's recommendations and proceeded to strengthen the Cabinet Office so that it could spearhead and monitor the implementation of the government's policies of modernisation.

The Cabinet Office has been restructured to reflect government's priorities and to strengthen its strategic role in pushing forward government policies and ensuring close monitoring of their implementation. A Social Exclusion Unit, created in 1997, is the model for an integrated, cross-departmental, joined-up government approach to tackling social deprivation, unemployment and crime. Upon re-launching the Citizen's Charter in 1998, under the new name of *Service First*, the former Citizen's Charter Unit became the Service First Unit. It is involved not only in encouraging increased participation of service users and the public in public services but also in underpinning the move towards more joined-up government. Two new units, the Performance and Innovation Unit (PIU) and the Centre for Management and Policy Studies (CMPS), were added in October 1998. The PIU has two major responsibilities: to conduct a rolling programme of policy reviews in areas that cross departmental boundaries, and select for review areas of government policy, involving more than one agency, which require better co-ordination and practical delivery of policy and services. The unit calls upon civil servants and outsiders to work in project teams which disband at the end of each scrutiny. The CMPS, which includes the Civil Service College (CSC), is intended to be the centre for corporate training and development of future leaders of the civil service. Other new units include the Womens Unit, transferred to the Cabinet Office from the Department of Social Security, the Better Regulation Unit, responsible for implementing and monitoring government's new regulation policy, and the Government Information and Communications Unit.

The internal management of the Cabinet Office has also been reformed and reflects the new integrative approach. The former Office of Public Service has been abolished and its work absorbed into the mainstream of the Cabinet Office. A new second permanent secretary and accounting officer (Brian Bender) now has overall responsibility for all aspects of management and deployment of resources in the department. A new Cabinet Office Management Board assists him. The previous fragmentation of the Office has been partly removed with the creation of a Central Secretariat supporting the Head of the Civil Service (Sir Richard Wilson) on all matters relating to machinery of government issues, relations with Parliament and proprietary and personnel questions.

The separate European Secretariat, a small group of about 24, continues to play a key role, along with the Foreign and Commonwealth Office and the UK Representatives (Co-Reper) in Brussels, in co-ordinating EU policy in Whitehall. (The EU is one of four secretariats – the others are responsible respectively for Home and Economic Affairs, Defence and Overseas Policy and the Constitution and Machinery of Government Issues). The role of the European Secretariat, apart from servicing the relevant cabinet committees, is to: survey developments within Whitehall and insure that all interested or affected departments are informed, co-ordinate inter-departmental action and act as a consultant to Whitehall departments. It also plays an important link role and is in close touch with all UK civil servants and representatives to ensure it knows what is going on and is involved in strategic thinking on Europe. This unit has grown in importance in recent years as the link between Whitehall and the Prime Ministers Private Office.

These changes are designed to provide a powerful strategic centre, co-ordinating government policies, steering and monitoring major policy initiatives and, at the same time, integrating strategic human resources policies and planning to ensure that the civil service has the leadership and skills needed to carry those services out. Jack Cunningham replaced Labour's first Minister for the Civil Service, David Clark, in September 1998, to take control of this strengthened central department.

Modernising the Civil Service

New Labour's idea of 'Better Government' as securing more efficiency, 'best value' for money, better quality and greater responsiveness to the public is not new, since these were the aims of their Conservative predecessors. Government departments and agencies are still expected to make efficiency savings of between 3 and 10 per cent per year (Cabinet Office: 1998a). Emphasis also continues to be placed on competition and market testing as means of ensuring 'best value'. The publication of *Better Quality Services* (Cabinet Office, 1998d) provides new guidelines for departments and agencies on reviewing services and creating partnerships through contracting out. Furthermore, government is continuing with the PFI and encouraging public bodies to seek partnerships with private organisations. Privatisation is still very much on the Labour government's agenda too, as it continues to approve the transfer of NSAs to the private sector and sells public assets. The Treasury published a *National Assets Register* in December 1997 (HM Treasury, 1997) listing the land, buildings and equipment owned by government departments and agencies which they are encouraged to sell if 'surplus to requirements', and they can keep part of the proceeds as an incentive.

Another example of continuity and change is government's relaunching of the Citizen's Charter under the title of *Service First – The New Charter Programme* (Cabinet Office, 1998e). Again Labour has built upon the previous government's policy, reiterating the same commitment to promoting quality, efficiency and responsiveness, although there is a greater emphasis on citizen participation and accountability to service users. During the relaunch there was a large-scale consultation exercise involving a wide range of organisations and individuals on all aspects of the charter programme. *Service First* offers extensive guidance to public services on how to draw up national and local charters, how to conduct participation exercises and how to deal with complaints. A major innovation is the creation of a national focus group, 'The People's Panel', of some 5000 members which is being used by government, departments, agencies and other public organisations to find out people's views on a wide range of service-delivery issues. Democratic participation is certainly a major thrust in the government's policy changes.

The relationship of ministers, CEs of NSAs and parliament had become blurred under the Conservatives, as a result of the development of agency framework agreements. The dismissals of two CEs, Derek Lewis of the Prison Service and Ros Hepplewhite of the Child Support Agency, for what were clearly policy issues, had exposed the accountability gap which existed (Polidano, 1999; Barker, 1998). Whilst reaffirming support for NSAs and the principles on which they are based, government's new direction has been to strengthen political control and reaffirm full ministerial responsibility. Ministers are now required to report annually to Parliament on the performance of their NSAs and ensure that the targets set are rigorous. Changes in the organisation of the Next Steps Report (Cabinet Office, 1997a) highlights ministerial responsibility. At the same time, it emphasises 'improving co-operation between NSAs and other organisations, notably local government, the voluntary sector and private businesses, in order to provide seamless delivery of services to the end user' (ibid.: iii).

As stated above, the Labour government inherited the second stage of the benchmarking exercise begun by the Conservatives in 1996. An evaluation of the first two years of the project (Cabinet Office, 1998c) stated that agencies in Phase One of the programme on average scored better in customer satisfaction, and almost as well in business results, policy and strategy, and the management of financial resources, as the private sector. The only two areas where agencies were behind the private sector was in leadership and use of non-financial resources such as information technology and fixed assets. The verdict of the report was that the best public sector organisations are now within striking distance of world-class performance in many areas but most notably customer satisfaction and people satisfaction. Spurred on by these findings New Labour has embarked on Stage Three of the programme, which covers over 100 public organisations. Other Conservative policies which New Labour are pursuing include IiP (with a commitment to have all departments and NSAs holding or registered for IiP status by 2000); adoption of resource accounting, currently being introduced throughout the service, and the networking of all government organisations (see Chapter 8).

During the last Conservative government there was much concern about standards of public service conduct (Nolan, 1996) and the pressure put upon civil servants to aid ministers in withholding information from Parliament and the public, which had been exposed by the Scott Report (1997). These concerns were reflected in the Labour government's first Queen's Speech (*http://www.coi.gov.uk/coi/qs_97/speech.html*). This promised more open and transparent government, a White Paper on proposals for a Freedom of Information Act (FIA) and enhancing peoples' aspirations for better, more accessible and accountable public services using IT to the full. Government published a White Paper *Your Right to Know* (Cm. 3818, 1997) which proposes a FIA to include a general statutory right of access to official papers and information held by public authorities and a duty laid on all public bodies to release information as a matter of course. This excludes policy advice, however, which, it is argued, must be protected to ensure that civil servants are not inhibited from speaking frankly to ministers. To date there is no enactment and none was included in the legislative programme for 1999.

Restructuring

During its first two years in office the New Labour government carried out or activated many of its manifesto commitments including devolution for Scotland and Wales, reform of Parliament, open government, incorporation into law of the European Convention on Human Rights, the Council of Europe Convention on Local Self Government and local government reform. There were, however, no major machinery-of-government changes, apart from the extended brief of the new Department for the Environment,

Transport and the Regions and the changes referred to above in the Cabinet Office. The impact of devolution is likely to be considerable although it is difficult at this stage to assess. Legislation providing for devolution to Scotland and Wales was passed and ratified by referenda in 1998 and elections to the new legislative assemblies take place in May 1999. Large numbers of civil servants, currently employed in the Scottish and Welsh Offices and Scottish and Welsh NSAs, will be affected, as the changes will fragment the civil service still more. Although government has stated that it is committed to maintaining a single, unified civil service, it is likely that separate civil services for Scotland and Wales will eventually be created along the lines of the Northern Ireland model.

Although, excluding devolution, no major architectural changes have taken place, New Labour's commitment to partnership and co-operation, in place of competition, is producing a 'new corporatism'. From the outset, government has sought to adopt an open system of consultation and participation in all areas of policy. This has definitely slowed down the process of decision-making but is ensuring that all stakeholders have an opportunity to influence policy and is creating new networks and policy communities encompassing some previously excluded groups. The civil service is consequently more open, especially at the top, and is once again having to take the views of a much wider public into consideration when advising government.

Another major difference in the priorities of the Labour government, which is impacting on the civil service, is its commitment to 'joined-up government'. Recognising the dysfunctional aspects of the vertical and horizontal fragmentation of government that characterised the Conservative era, Labour is strong on co-ordination. One initiative, spearheaded by the Cabinet Office, is *Better Government for Older People* (Cabinet Office, 1998f). This aims to improve services for older people by promoting more integrated service delivery from across different sectors and tiers of government. The Service First Unit is currently co-ordinating 28 pilot studies throughout the country and steering the direction from the centre. Similarly, the work of the Social Exclusion Unit and Women's Unit are centralising and co-ordinating the work of departments and agencies to bring about more effective policy and more user-oriented delivery of services. Co-ordination, rather than decentralisation, is the hallmark of government's strategy for modernising and achieving better government.

Conclusion

Though change has been a continuing feature of the civil service throughout this century, the period from 1979 has witnessed a radical transformation. Successive Conservative governments made an ideological attack on the state and the administrative culture of the civil service and succeeded in changing the welfare state into an enabling, contract state and the civil service into a managed bureaucracy. The policy-making and service-delivery roles of the service were separated, with the latter dispersed amongst a large number of public and private bodies. The role of the core of government, it was claimed, was to steer rather than row society and the economy (Osborne and Gaebler, 1992). By 1997 the major part of the civil service had become a fragmented collection of business machines which deliver services and are close to the private sector organisations with which they are increasingly in competition. Whilst the SCS still performs its traditional policy role, it has also taken on a strategic management function. However, as the internal Wilson report suggests, it still has a long way to go before it performs that well.

New Labour has not sought to change these roles of government and the civil service but it is committed to modernising them. Tony Blair, addressing a civil service conference on Modernising Central Government in October 1998, described the civil service as 'a priceless asset' but one still in need of reform. 'The civil service is good at preparing legislation and managing policy. It is less good at focusing on outcome or ensuring effective implementation. . . Many parts of the civil service culture are still too hierarchical and inward looking and it is too short-termist. Above all the civil service is too risk averse' (*http://www.open.gov.uk//co/scsg/conference/ pm*). Government is seeking to remedy these faults in part through its reinventing government policies. It is committed to more democracy, participation and 'joined-up' government. Although internal and external contracts remain in place, government is promoting more partnership and co-operation between state, voluntary and private organisations in place of competition. It is also revisiting the organisational dilemmas of centralisation, decentralisation, devolution, specialisation, co-ordination and control. It is seeking to remedy the effects of fragmentation and decentralisation, which it inherited from the Conservatives, and place much more importance on co-ordinating policies and implementation. This is to avoid a waste of resources, conflict and a failure to achieve government objectives and intended outcomes and to ensure that services are delivered in ways which are simple and convenient for individual citizens. It is also placing greater importance on regulation and democratic participation than its predecessors and, in place of disengagement, it sees a role for the state in easing the social costs of economic change and facilitating social inclusion. It will require great skill and resourcefulness on the part of the civil service to carry these policies through. Reorganisation of the Cabinet Office at the centre of government is aimed at ensuring that a supply of strategic public managers with leadership skills and imagination will emerge to carry through the government's Modernising Government programme (Cm 4310, 1999).

10

Managing Local Public Services

CHRIS PAINTER and KESTER ISAAC-HENRY

This chapter examines the principal changes in the management of public services in local authorities during the 1980s and 1990s, including the increasing role of strategy and the call for greater leadership. A particular contention is that local government must now be seen in the broader context of local governance, given the restructuring of local public services under the Conservatives, prior to the election of Labour to national office in 1997. The chapter considers the tensions in management reform objectives generated by this restructuring process, threatening as it did to accentuate fragmentation at the expense of co-ordination by entrenching new institutional barriers. These developments led in turn to the growing importance of inter-organisational management, bringing issues to do with partnership, network management and network leadership very much to the fore. As we make the transition to the new millennium, it will be argued, a fundamental change in the role of local authorities is taking place, a move from their traditional service-providing role to one encapsulated in the phrase 'community leadership'. The momentum behind this development is accelerating under New Labour.

Local Government Management: the Thatcher–Major Conservative Years

Whatever facet of local government is being discussed, management effectiveness, style and process is never far below the surface. Concerns were expressed about such management issues in the 1960s and 1970s with the reports of the Maud Committee (1967) and the Bains (1972) and Paterson (1973) working parties. In the 1980s that concern was again highlighted by the Widdicombe Report (1986) and by the Audit Commission (1988; 1989a). Now, with a Labour administration breathing new life into local government by suggesting that it potentially has a key role to play in the quality of life experienced by local people (DETR, 1998a), management is once again firmly on the agenda. But local government is not immune from wider environmental influences nor from the fads and fashions of management theories. Hence, changes in its internal management structures and processes come not only from central government initiatives and European directives and regulations but also from local authorities themselves responding to this wider public service environment.

Local government was a veritable test bed for many developments in the New Public Management (NPM). The Conservative Party, which up to the 1970s could be regarded as a defender of local government, appeared to regard that institution in a different light after taking office in 1979. By the middle of the 1980s local government was being viewed in a most unfavourable light, as shown in Table 10.1. Radical action was considered necessary to improve value for money (VFM) and the quality of services to users.

During the 1980s a raft of legislation erected a formidable system of restraint on local government finance, resulting in tight control on capital spending, real reductions in grant, rate-capping and the community charge (poll tax), which was 'intended to sharpen the relationship between local taxation and local spending' (Audit Commission, 1988: 7). This tax, which led to riots in certain towns and cities, was repealed in 1993. While it could be argued that its replacement, the council tax, brought some sanity back to local government finance, by the 1990s the financial corset had been pulled so tightly around the local government frame some feared that it might take its breath away! The relationship between central and local government had moved from one of consultation and discussion in the 1960s and 1970s to one of confrontation in the 1980s, through to central dominance in the 1990s. At present less than 20 per cent of expenditure is determined by local government.

Compulsory competitive tendering (CCT) has been a major influence on all aspects of local government. Introduced in the early 1980s to force local authorities to tender out manual services, by the 1990s its tentacles had extended deeply into white-collar services as well. It was leading to a

TABLE 10.1 *Conservative critique of local government*

Conservative view of local government	Action to be taken
Inherently inefficient	Financial safeguards Efficiency measures Performance indicators
Badly managed	Competition Market ethos
Unconcerned with the user	Customer orientation
Suffered from too much political interference and professional dominance	Loss of powers and responsibilities to reduce political influence

purchaser–provider split and establishing a contract culture in local government. Although most contracts were won 'in-house', contractors still had to display an arms-length approach to the rest of the authority and ensure adequate returns on capital. At the same time CCT was encouraging the formation of internal trading markets. Local authorities were also encouraged to display entrepreneurship in an endeavour to increase their resources. They were expected to market themselves so as to attract development into their areas. Contacts with the private sector were to be cultivated to benefit the local authority. For example, the Conservative government launched the Private Finance Initiative (PFI) as a means of helping the public sector (including local government) to alleviate the chronic capital famine it was experiencing. PFI therefore allows public authorities to make contracts with private sector bodies for the provision of public service infrastructure.

Alongside the development of CCT and the contract culture was the movement towards consumerism. Even stout defenders of local government recognised that it needed to be more responsive to the wishes of individual service users as well as to the general public. Local government existed to provide services 'for' and not 'to' the public (Stewart and Clarke, 1987). The term 'customer' was used to indicate a move towards the private-sector market ethos. Although strongly criticised at the beginning as inappropriate for public services, this ethos – which lay at the heart of the *Citizen's Charter* (Prime Ministers Office, 1991) and was launched in the early 1990s – had an important influence on the way local government was managed. Now 'the consumer of a public service is seen less as the generic citizen and more the specific client or (increasingly) paying customer' (Gray, 1998: 10). Service quality was therefore increasingly equated with customer satisfaction.

The changes related to competition, customers and quality were bolstered by the growing importance of performance measures. Measuring performance was not new to local government. The Bains Report had recommended the setting up of sub-committees to review performance, although very few authorities made effective arrangements for this to be done (Kerley, 1994). With reduced financial resources under the NPM and with authorities expected to do more with less, performance measurement and control became a logical development. Although the government was constantly emphasising its importance, for example when in 1992 it required the Audit Commission to publish performance indicators for local authorities, this was pushing at an open door. As Kerley observed, 'assessing performance has now become so entrenched in commonsense practice as to be almost value free and not for political debate and argument' (ibid.: 140). However, the movement towards performance measurement and performance indicators did generate controversy. There was conflict over which indicators should be used and opposition to the number of indicators proposed by the Audit Commission as criteria for measurement. After extensive consultation a compromise was reached and performance measures are now an integral part of the management of local government services.

TABLE 10.2 *Local government trends by mid-1990s*

Old certainties	New trends
Organisational self sufficiency	Multi-agency approaches
Service uniformity	Customer focus and service quality
Direct local authority control	Plurality of local public service provision
Service professionalism	Development of generic and strategic management
Bureaucratic culture and hierarchical responsibility	Entrepreneurial culture and management through contracts
Process rather than results	Pursuit of performance management

Source: Adapted from J. Stewart (1995) *Local Government Today: An Observers View*, LGMB.

So the 1980s and early 1990s witnessed the move towards a market ethos, with the competitive council allied to a customer and performance culture. At the same time powers were being taken away and given to other agencies (see Table 10.2). By the middle of the 1990s local government's attempt to manage effectively therefore confronted the difficulty of a fragmented, sometimes disjointed system, perpetrated not least in the name of competition.

Nonetheless local government has proved to be resilient. John Stewart, a long-time observer of management in local government, was moved to say that at 'no period during the . . . years in which I have been associated with local government has there been such innovation and initiative' (1995: 7). Notwithstanding the then – unwelcome changes that were being forced on them by Conservative governments in the name of NPM and incessant criticisms concerning outdated bureaucratic structures and lack of strategies, a number of local authorities viewed these changes not so much as threats but as opportunities. They began to develop new management styles, processes and structures. By the middle of the 1990s old certainties were giving way to new trends.

Such changes were in large measure responsible for pushing local government into innovative ways of managing which now seem to be bearing fruit. But local government had suffered increased fragmentation of services, loss of power and flexibility, lack of resources for proper implementation of policies from the adversarial approach encouraged by the competitive agenda. However, looking back from the vantage point of the late 1990s local government could be said to have made substantial gains by the introduction of such changes. Efficiency and value for money have become part of the culture of a much more businesslike local government. The individual service user, as well as the group, has become important in the eyes of most local authorities. Increasingly local government is working with private business and other partners in the community to decide what and how services are to be provided. There is an awareness that both management practices and culture have to change to deal with the cross-sectoral and 'wicked issues'.

More fundamentally, perhaps, such changes challenged the very existence of local government and pushed local authorities into re-examining their role and posing the question 'what business are we in?'. In so doing answers such as 'civic leadership' and 'community government' are suggesting themselves. The latter development has profound implications for management thinking and practices in local government, forming the basis for much of the new Labour administration's strategy on the role and management of local government. Of course changing practices and cultures will disadvantage certain groups while advantaging others. The extremely tight financial regimes that they were forced to run pushed many local authorities into becoming 'flexible' employers. For some, this was a euphemism for introducing less favourable terms and conditions for employees. The threat of CCT meant that in some cases, regardless of whether the contract was won in-house, staff faced the prospect of competing for their jobs with precisely the above effect (Wilson and Game, 1998). The changing culture and practice also meant that some of the once-cherished ideas of local government being 'model employers' or 'equal opportunities authorities' had to be sacrificed on the altar of winning contracts and saving jobs.

It has often been suggested that middle managers in local government have been greatly empowered by the NPM. Devolved management, greater responsibility and flexibility to take risks, as well as the opportunity to manage people, finance and projects, are said to have enriched their role. Like their top-tier counterparts many have to operate outside their professional boundaries since other management skills are now required. On the flip side, however, it is generally agreed that the work of middle managers has become more intense and pressured, their role having expanded not only qualitatively but also quantitatively. They are fulfilling both their 'professional' and 'managerial' functions. A source of dissatisfaction is the perception of many that there is a decline in job security, that there are fewer promotions and career opportunities and that there is the persistent threat of downsizing (Rigg and Trehan, 1997). So, while top management may be promising to give greater importance to human resource management and emphasising the need to value employees, they are often simultaneously contemplating staff reductions.

There is ample evidence demonstrating that New Labour has no intention of turning the clock back. It has acknowledged the improvement in efficiency of local authorities in recent years as a result of central government measures and also as a result of the intelligent response to wider environmental pressures. It has also, however, acknowledged that some measures under the previous government at one and the same time improved efficiency, services and management in some areas whilst having a deleterious effect in other areas. CCT is such an example. It persuaded reluctant local authorities to address difficult management issues that needed to be tackled. But CCT often proved inflexible in practice and has been contrary to the requirements for healthy partnerships (DETR, 1998b).

Strategy and Management

If local government organisational change had in the past often focused on concerns about structure, by the 1990s consideration had moved towards strategy. Isaac-Henry and Painter (1991), in a survey of chief executives carried out at the beginning of the 1990s, found that while some chief executives were relying on a change of structure as an effective response to a rapidly changing environment, others considered management styles and processes more important and were taking a strategic approach to managing their authorities. The paradox is that as government policies and legislation fragmented local services the greater was the appeal of strategic management. With the scarcity of financial resources and reduction of powers and functions many local authorities were forced to prioritise objectives and identify key strategic issues. For example, Leach, Stewart and Walsh (1994) noted how local authorities in the 1990s were making strategic decisions about whether to play a residual role as provider of last resort, give primacy to the market, or be a community enabler based on the premise that the authority exists to meet the varied needs of the local population.

Stewart (1995) observed that over 60 per cent of authorities prepared strategic or corporate plans and were concerning themselves with missions, visions, core values and the culture of the organisation. This was an attempt to focus on a more holistic approach and move away from the traditional hierarchical model of management, by restricting the power of departments to act individually. An impetus towards such a change included the new roles that some local authorities were seeking to develop in terms of community government. The New Labour administration has given much emphasis to this role of community leadership, encouraging local authorities to provide a vision and a focus not only for themselves but for the local area as a whole (DETR, 1998b).

It is of course one thing to produce a strategic document replete with its mission, visions and values. It is another to ensure that these core values and missions are really those of the authority as a whole. If strategic management means anything it is about the process of changing the organisational culture to reflect these core values. For many local authorities the culture has not changed sufficiently to reflect the new concept of management. Visions and missions created on paper by top managers do not descend far enough down the hierarchy to influence the thinking and practice of the organisation (Leach, 1996). Thus the attempt to manage strategically does not always succeed. Many local authorities still lack what Collinge and Leach (1995) term the organisational 'capacity' (the structures, processes and support) effectively to undertake the holistic approach that strategic management demands. In a case study of Birmingham City Council, it was found that, despite attempts to develop a strategic approach since the latter part of the 1980s, the culture and structure of that authority still reflected the values of a disaggregated, segmented or even at times federal type of management (Isaac-Henry, 1999).

This is not to belittle the accomplishments of local government in this area in recent years, especially given the difficulties it has faced. But there is still more to be done, notably in convincing politicians of the need to change to a more integrated, corporatist approach. Management theorists tend to argue that too much emphasis should not be put on structure when management of change is being considered. However, structure has its place. Certainly the present government, which is in favour of instilling a more strategic approach in local government, is hoping that its proposed reform of political management structures, in separating executive responsibility from the representational one, will facilitate such a change, especially if this helps to develop stronger leadership (DETR, 1998b).

Management and Leadership in Local Government

Over the last decade or so management theorists have been arguing that in a turbulent environment organisational effectiveness can no longer be dependent on (traditional) management alone. Much will depend on leadership. Defining management as coping with complexity by planning, organising, budgeting and staffing, leadership is concerned more with managing strategic change, which involves articulating a vision and deciding the direction in which the organisation should be heading. Often leaders were visualised in the heroic mould, as someone possessing the power and charisma to transform organisations by creating, expressing and communicating a vision, and through these personal characteristics able to change the values and assumptions of organisations (Terry, 1995). In 1972 Bains had argued that, for a local authority to be effective, there must be leadership on both the political and the managerial side. At the end of the 1990s that concern for (the lack of) effective leadership still remains, centred on the dearth of high-profile leaders and the role that politicians play in the decision-making process.

Much has been made of the way that local government works through the committee system. It is a system which, it is said, not only wastes councillors' time and opportunity to play a more representative role, but also stifles transparency and accountability since it is not clear who is making the decisions (DETR, 1998b). At the same time it encourages fragmentation as strong committee chairpersons, dominating their departments, often act as individual barons. That the present government shares this view of lack of clear leadership in local government is demonstrated in its July 1998 White Paper: 'Councils need new structures which create a clear and well-known focus for local leadership. Local people should know who takes decisions, who to hold to account, and who to complain to when things go wrong' (DETR, 1998b: 24). For this to happen the government suggests a separation of the executive from the (backbench) representative role and proposes a choice from three types of executive structure, two based on a variant of the elected mayor model while the other follows the cabinet model. Whatever option is chosen will profoundly influence local government management. The government earlier had proposed an elected Mayor for London visualised in the truly 'heroic' mould: 'We expect the Mayor to become a high-profile figure who will speak out on London's behalf and be listened to. This will change the face of London politics' (DETR, 1998c: 9). The hope is that such a powerful figure will excite public interest, help to raise turnout at elections and rekindle enthusiasm for local leadership, which raises questions concerning the role of chief executives in local government.

It is difficult to evaluate the role of the local authority chief executive in a period of rapid change, since that role has not been nationally defined and is determined by a number of variables (Clarke and Stewart, 1991). There have been suggestions that the role ought to be enhanced, clarified and formalised (Widdicombe) and that the chief executive should be the crucial figure in the development of organisational culture, the creation of a vision and in the setting of the direction in which the authority should go. In short, chief executives ought to be leaders of their authorities. Thus the Audit Commission (1989a) saw them as both the source of continuity and an agent of change.

Although distinctions can be made between types of chief executives (Asquith, 1997), in general the effectiveness of managerial leadership is highly dependent on political leadership:

> the real transformers are the politicians who have had the vision of where the authority should be going and the power to see that it goes in the desired direction. They quite often bring the managerial side into line by appointing officers who are skilled in communicating the vision and have the ability to implement the process. (Isaac-Henry, 1999, forthcoming)

In the mid-1980s, for example, it was the new Conservative leader of Kent County Council who initially embarked on a programme of radical managerial reform and who chose a chief executive of similar mind to implement the programme (Holliday, 1991). In the celebrated case of Kirklees, John Harman, the Labour leader, was seen as the inspiration for the transformational approach taken in that authority. He too appointed a chief executive to help translate his vision into reality. Hence the relationship with the leader of the council is crucial to chief executive's effectiveness (Stoney, 1997).

The push for separate political executives signified in the July 1998 White Paper is likely to have repercussions for such officers. But they will remain key figures in the world of local government. In many ways chief executives will be doing what they have done so well up to the 1990s, adapt and adjust to suit their political masters, but above all they will hope to work harmoniously with them. The move towards local governance and networking will also be an influence on their role. In a recent survey it was found that a 'number of chief executives, most notably in metropolitan districts . . . [were] spending half or more of their time in meeting with community partners and, more generally, in networking with local institutions'(Travers, Jones and Burnham, 1997: 39). Given the new Labour government's keenness to encourage local partnerships and inter-organisational solutions to problems, the proportion of time spent on networking will no doubt increase.

From Service Management to Community Government

The July 1998 White Paper contended: 'Community leadership is at the heart of the role of modern local government' (DETR, 1998b: 79). Viewed as the centre of local public services and local action, and ideally placed to tackle the difficult cross-cutting issues, the community government role has thus been endorsed by the present government. Not only are they to be thought of as community leaders, 'beacon' local authorities are to be given enhanced powers to pursue that role. Such endorsement is a vindication of those authorities that at the end of the 1980s and the beginning of the 1990s, facing a reduction of powers and functions as well as competition from unelected agencies and private sector organisations, began to develop the concept of community government. This section therefore examines the move of local authorities away from their traditional position as direct service providers, one of the most momentous developments in local government in recent years.

A striking phenomenon during the Thatcher–Major era had been the rise of the local unelected state and the 'new wave' quangos or local public spending bodies (LPSBs) (Painter, 1997). The institutional map of local government was transformed post-1979 by the growth of these non-elected agencies, a development itself partly a reflection of the managerialist/consumerist bias during the Conservative years: 'The overall effect . . . can be summarised as a shift from a system of local government to a system of local governance. Local authorities now share to a greater extent than before 1979 service provision and . . . decision-making responsibilities with other agencies' (Stoker, 1997: 53). Local authorities had tended to view themselves as pre-eminent: 'Now their position is under challenge as they find themselves sharing the local "turf" with a whole range of bodies also exercising governmental powers at the local level' (Davis, 1996a: 1). The general tendency was toward an increase in the use and relative importance of single-purpose agencies as opposed to multi-purpose bodies such as local councils (Davis and Hall, 1996). Indeed, numerically representation on appointed (and self-appointed) bodies eventually exceeded representation on elected councils!

One distinct advantage of single as opposed to multi-purpose bodies is that as dedicated agencies they can bring focus to their task and be organised over optimal territorial areas – especially where the activity concerned is relatively self-contained (Davis and Hall, 1996). However, many deleterious consequences follow. The safeguards in place to regulate the conduct of non-elected agencies have been less stringent than in the case of local authorities, a procedural reform issue addressed in the Second Report of the Nolan Committee on Standards in Public Life (1996). Their appointed (or self appointed) status has created a local 'democratic deficit' – with a narrow stakeholder base often acting to the detriment of the community at large and wider concepts of public accountability (Painter *et al.*, 1996). Significantly, a more open consultative style of decision-making and new forms of participation have been developed by some of these agencies to strengthen their community links (Painter *et al.*, 1994).

However, LPSBs' autonomy is often more apparent than real, given that lines of accountability in many cases lead directly or indirectly to Whitehall. The reality was thus often one of centralised control (Greer and Hoggett, 1996). There is a related weakness particularly relevant to this chapter. Whatever the arguments for organisational specialisation, the downside is a reduced capacity for institutional integration: 'Yet many of the problems faced by local communities demand co-ordinated action from many services, which is hard to achieve in a fragmented structure' (Davis, 1996b: 19). The new-wave local quangos were intended to nurture managerial accountability, emphasising results rather than the due process that characterised the traditional public administrative culture. Nonetheless, enhanced 'technical' efficiency may be at the expense of 'allocative' or 'system' efficiency because of the way in which costs are 'externalised' to other organisations (Painter *et al.*, 1996).

To handle the 'integration deficit' emerging in these fragmented structures local authorities needed to develop new forms of relationship – networks, partnerships and joint working (Davis, 1996a). They hinge more on co-operation than the competition dominating market exchanges, or the principle of hierarchical control at the heart of the management structures typically found in traditional public service bureaucracies. Loose informal networks can provide a foundation for more formalised partnership arrangements. Indeed, it has been argued that it is important to maintain a conceptual distinction between partnership as an organisational structure and networks as a form of social co-ordination in contrast to markets and hierarchies (Lowndes and Skelcher, 1998). Involving a range of stakeholders, partnerships were becoming a notable feature of urban regeneration and local economic development programmes under the Conservatives (Skelcher *et al.*, 1996). Here, it was not just a matter of local authorities relating to other local public bodies but also to the private, community and voluntary sectors. Multi-agency and multi-sector approaches to complex urban and social problems were increasingly imperative in a cash-starved public sector as well as being a logical corollary of local institutional fragmentation, increasing the resource dependence (in the broadest sense) of local authorities. What was now required was a capability to manage across organisational boundaries. It has become one of the key strategic management issues facing local authorities (Painter, 1997). The implied greater organisational flexibility has profound implications for their internal decision-making and management structures.

Focusing specifically upon relations between local authorities and other (non-elected) LPSBs, the pattern to be discerned is 'one of variety and complexity . . . a continuum between co-existence and conflict' (Greer and Hoggett, 1996: 165). Relationships were particularly difficult during the Conservative years where responsibilities had been taken away from local government. Conversely, close co-operation between local social services and local health authorities (for instance in the context of community care) was becoming more the norm – including joint commissioning of services. Generally, however, the trend was towards greater pragmatism in relationships, given that 'the effective local authority of the future will need to be imaginative in its approach to inter-agency working' (Hambleton *et al.*, 1995: 2). The evidence suggests that working with other organisations and hence the ethos of the 'collaborative council' is becoming a higher priority for most local authorities. This is not to underestimate the obstacles to managing across institutional boundaries, which is 'a different and more difficult type of management (by influence) than the direct management ethos of traditional local government' (Painter *et al.*, 1997: 239). Internally, such an approach requires new skills, making heavy demands on the time of local authority officers/members and requiring appropriate organisational support for them. Externally, the differences in organisational culture that any form of joint working inevitably confronts have to be bridged.

The challenges facing local authorities in the changing structures of local governance are even more far-reaching than so far suggested. In ascending order of complexity those challenges can be summarised as follows:

- Devising strategic approaches to relations with other agencies;
- Providing the 'network management' for which arguably their attributes uniquely qualify them;
- Abandoning the traditional service delivery culture and, in the language of strategic management, repositioning the organisation to assume the broader 'community leadership' role referred to above.

There have been marked differences in the approaches of local authorities to the growth of the local unelected state – from the purely passive (those authorities at a loss to know what to do in response) to the highly strategic. The latter have adopted a corporate view of the form relationships with outside agencies should take and the priorities to be pursued. In particular, there is strategic targeting of agencies in the light of organisational priorities, and corresponding mobilisation of those resources of influence at the disposal of the local authority that have not always been skilfully deployed in the past (Painter, 1997). Such proactive strategies have been adopted by local authorities at the 'leading edge' of policy innovation.

Local authorities also have opportunities as 'network managers' when problems are not susceptible to single-agency solutions, given the broader perspective that only they as multi-purpose bodies can bring to bear. Network management relates to improving the conditions for collective action in complex organisational environments – initiating and facilitating interaction between multiple actors. The skilful network manager can operate effectively in such a complex domain, creating the prospect of results that would be unattainable through 'go-alone' single-agency approaches. The democratic legitimacy of local authorities as elected bodies also means they have an important part to play as vehicles for public accountability and articulating the interests of the unrepresented or under-represented in a networking environment (Kickert, Klijn and Koppenjan, 1997).

This strengthens the case for redefining the local authoritys role as one of responsibility for the overall well-being of the locality (Prior, 1996). They need to take on board a new vision, as indicated earlier in the chapter, making strategic choices accordingly. Instead of the traditional ethos of direct service provision, a more wide-ranging governmental role encapsulated in the phrase 'community leadership' indeed now seems more appropriate (Leach, 1996). It is, of course, important to be realistic about what is feasible. The structure of local governance and the incentives woven into that framework is largely the prerogative of central government, given the subordinate position constitutionally of local government (Painter *et al.*, 1997). Nor have many of the LPSBs, in practice, had much autonomy from the centre. Hence the danger for local government 'in believing oneself to be the conductor when in reality one is simply a minor player' (Greer and Hoggett, 1996: 166).

Nonetheless, a number of councils are 're-engineering' their processes so as to pursue more effectively this broader community-leadership vision (Painter, 1996). They particularly need to reform management structures so that internally they are more flexible and externally their boundaries become more permeable (Painter *et al.*, 1997). Both have been impeded by the organisational barriers traditionally erected by departmental and committee structures. However, even now, not all councils have grasped the magnitude of the organisational and management challenges they face. The new agenda fits

> uneasily within organisational structures and culture that were created to serve the needs of local authorities operating in a far less interdependent institutional environment . . . whether local authorities can respond by transforming their internal . . . relationships to support their changing role in the external environment may be a critical factor in determining whether they can consolidate and enhance their positions as the leaders of local networks. (Prior, 1996: 102–3)

This applies even more so following the outcome of the 1997 general election.

Local Government and the European Network

In looking at networks the relationship between local authorities and the European Union should not be forgotten. Indeed the European Union (EU) and its institutions figure largely in both the strategic and operational thinking of many local authorities. The reason for this is obvious. As Bennington (1994) points out, the EU is having an increasingly important economic, political and social impact not only on the UK central government but also on local government. The tentative approach to Europe exhibited by local government in the 1980s and early 1990s is tending to give way to a more positive attitude to influencing EU policies and procedures and to taking advantage of what that institution has to offer. Clarke (1998) argues that 'all across the European Union local governments [including that of the UK) are simply getting on and doing day-to-day business in the implementation of EU policy and legislation' (p.16). But local authorities in the UK are doing more than this. Some of them are attempting to take a strategic view of their relations with the EU in order to ensure co-ordination and awareness across the whole authority and to endeavour not to compartmentalise European issues in one department (Terry, 1997: 278).

That there is an increasing number of local authorities setting up offices in Brussels, where the European Commission is located, indicates the importance of the EU to local government. The Commission is regarded as the engine of the EU where policies and regulations are generated. Local authorities, by having their offices and representatives close to such a power base and being in close contact with the Commission, hope to

- be forewarned of initiation of regulations and policies so as to prepare their responses to them;
- act as pressure groups and themselves attempt to initiate, influence and at times prevent, the development of policies and regulations;
- boost the chances of obtaining the EU funds.

The Maastricht Treaty of 1992 enhanced the opportunity for local government to influence EU policy by the creation of the Committee of the Regions. Representing regional and local authorities within the EU, the Committee has to be consulted as of right on issues relating to education, culture, trans-European communication networks, certain aspects of economic and social cohesion and on the structural i.e. regional and social funds. However, as pointed out by Bennington this is only the beginning and, since its inception, its members have been working hard to widen those issues on which it should be consulted and to increase its influence in EU policy-making.

One of the main reasons for local government's sustained interest in the EU, is that the latter can be an important source of funding for local authority and regional projects. Birmingham City Council, for example, was able to transform part of its area by developing high profile projects from funds (reputed to be about £400 millions) from the EU. However there are other considerations. An increasingly important feature of UK's local government relationship with Europe is the myriad of trans-European networks being spawned as the EU becomes more integrated. Bennington points to three major categories of such networks namely:

a) Sectoral interest – relating to regional and local authorities affected by economic restructuring and the demise of important industries such as coal, motor car and aerospace;
b) Spatial interests – relating to those authorities or areas wanting to promote a common shared interest such as the network for large cities (EuroCities), middle sized cities and sea side towns;
c) Policy interests – relating to social and policy areas such as poverty and women's issues.

In recent years, up to 1997, when the relations between local and central government were at a low ebb, local government employees and local government itself attempted to use the EU as a stick with which to beat central government. For example, local authorities attempted to use the European Community directives concerning the Transfer of Undertakings and Protection of Employment (TUPE) to restrict the spread of privatisation and contracting out in local government. Central government, in its turn, refused to endorse the *Council of Europe Charter of Local Self-Government*. Indeed up to 1997, it often appeared that local and central government were failing to act in concert where the EU was concerned, to the detriment of both. The coming to office of the Labour Government may be of crucial importance in the development of EU/Local Government relations. First, it appears that New Labour is more favourably disposed towards Europe than its predecessor which might encourage even more local government activity within the EU. Second, the improved relations between local government and the Centre may well result in a more co-ordinated response to EU policies and regulation from the UK. The signing of the *Council of Europe Charter of Local Self-Government* by the present Administration and the acceptance of the Social Chapter in the Amsterdam Treaty may be taken as an endorsement of local government in the UK, of the EU and of local government's relationship with the EU.

Blair and New Labour: Managing Across Institutional Service Boundaries

The Prime Minister's own words on the future position of local authorities are revealing: 'There can be no monopoly of service delivery by councils; the 1970s will not be revisited. Delivering quality services means that councils must forge partnerships with communities, agencies and the private sector' (Blair, 1997). It is hardly surprising in the light of such sentiments that networking and partnership are part of this Governments 'best value' orthodoxy. If for the first 30 years after the Second World War the bureaucratic (monopolistic) model of public service management predominated, then superseded by the New Right public service market paradigm, the partnership model seems to be very much in the ascendant following the election of New Labour. Hence, for example, the Social Exclusion Unit was formally launched in December 1997 as a task force under the personal guidance of the Prime Minister, with the objective of promoting more holistic (and preventative) approaches to social policy problems. Indeed, one of the Unit's initial priorities is to improve mechanisms for integrating the work of central departments, local authorities and other agencies.

It is easy to distort reality by equating particular eras exclusively with an archetypal model of public services management. Life is more complex and ambiguous than this implies. Despite the association of the Thatcher–Major governments with (quasi-competitive) public service markets, some of the infrastructure necessary for multi-agency collaboration had already been put in place – notably in the local economic development/urban regeneration context (Skelcher *et al.*, 1996). However, partnership and networking were often ad hoc responses to the dysfunctional consequences of local institutional fragmentation. The striking development under New Labour is the extent to which collaboration is becoming an intentional strategy (Painter and Clarence, 1998). The challenge for local authorities to change their internal management structures and processes to make them more flexible and appropriate to an interdependent institutional environment is therefore even more pressing.

Significantly, the area-based partnerships that had become such a feature of local economic development are being used as a prototype for other policy initiatives, especially in addressing the problems of disadvantaged communities. Nowhere is this more apparent than in the action zone programmes. Health action zones (HAZs) are pilots for greater health care collaboration. The first 11 successful bids for such status were announced in March 1998, with a remit to experiment with new ideas in the way health care is delivered and to show what can be done to promote better health in areas of high need. Although HAZs are health authority led because of accountability structures, it was a precondition for bids that there should be evidence of a sound basis for joint working with local government – to be reflected in the composition of the non-statutory HAZ partnership boards. Similar principles apply to the 25 pilot education action zones (EAZs) announced in June 1998. Consortia usually involving the local education authority bid for these EAZs, which will be overseen by partnership forums and targeted at deprived areas containing under-performing schools. They will pioneer innovative approaches to improving educational standards, and will be allowed to dispense with the national curriculum and national agreements on pay and conditions.

These examples demonstrate that partnership is seen by New Labour as crucial to delivering quality local services and to handling complex (cross-cutting) policy issues that defy conventional organisational and functional boundaries. Tony Blairs' own words are once more worth citing: 'The days of the all-purpose authority that planned and delivered everything are gone. . . It is in partnership with others – public agencies, private companies, community groups and voluntary organisations – that local governments future lies. Local authorities will still deliver some services but their distinctive leadership role will be to weave and knit together the contribution of the various local stakeholders' (Blair, 1998: 13). Such a role requires not only the new forms of executive political leadership in local government promoted in the July 1998 White Paper, but also determination on the part of senior managers to challenge and break down professional/departmental barriers. Yet, many local authorities have discovered over the years just how great can be the resistance to working across such frontiers. Implying a shift in emphasis to lateral rather than traditional hierarchical communication, these managers needed progressively to change their priorities from internal organisational control to external agency networking. Evidence of this happening in some local authorities has already been cited.

The price of failure by local authorities to reform their traditional practices could be high. The Blair government has made it abundantly clear that in such circumstances they would have no compunction in looking for other 'partners' to achieve key policy and service goals. Hence the shock waves because of the acceptance that EAZs, though generally to be run by partnerships involving local authorities, might in certain instances be business-led, reflecting a belief in government circles that private companies are sometimes best-equipped to manage change and innovation, even in public services. There are clearly positive opportunities for local government under New Labour – but also potential threats!

Conclusion

Given the long-standing search for greater organisational cohesion in local government, many of the developments in the period 1979–97 under Conservative stewardship seemed to be retrograde, leading as they did to both internal and external fragmentation in the delivery and management of local public services. And yet, some of these developments have been instrumental in pushing local authorities to re-examine their values, mode of managing and, importantly, their roles. New Labour has no intention of revisiting the pre-1979 world of local government. The government seems generally comfortable with the plural structures of local governance it inherited. Nonetheless, building on some established local partnership institutional infrastructure, the emphasis is markedly shifting towards multi-agency approaches. The challenge for local government is, in some respects, even more formidable than that hitherto. In a changed institutional environment, holistic policy and service delivery now coming into favour demand more effective external agency linkages and enhanced capability to manage across organisational boundaries. The 'partnership authority' or 'collaborative council' – with corresponding management (as well as political) skills and strong leadership – is the model in the ascendant, underpinned as it must be by informal networking processes.

These demands relate in the final analysis to a fundamental reappraisal of local government's role for the new millennium – in the language of strategic management, to the need for local authorities to reposition themselves as community leaders. The enormity of the challenges should not be underestimated. Constraints on local authorities' room for manoeuvre are all too apparent. A community leadership role is hard to sustain given the established legal framework. To some extent the government has recognised this by arguing that the 'current statutory framework for councils can inhibit local innovation and diversity by setting out too rigidly the way in which particular functions must be discharged. It can get in the way of closer integration of council functions . . . It can also limit the scope for working with other organisations' (DETR, 1998a: 83). The government has promised to simplify this framework, but only for councils who can satisfy it that they have the ability and capacity to manage greater freedom and wider powers – the so-called 'beacon' councils. This might be considered too controlling on the part of central government. There are those who think that that framework must be comprehensively reviewed if local government 'is to build the capacity for integration within an increasingly fragmented system' (Kitchen, 1997: 5). Moreover, it is all too easy to raise unrealistic expectations about the prospects for achieving change of the magnitude envisaged, given the complexities involved in managing such processes.

Nonetheless, local government has the opportunity for revival, given the low ebb to which it had sunk in the years up to 1997. The rhetoric of New Labour is that local government is essential to the management and conduct of modern British government. But Labour is not about to release local government from all the shackles placed on it during the Thatcher–Major years, and the legacy of the low-trust mindset fostered by the competitive ethic in public service markets remains. The performance ethos integral to the Conservative management reforms is, if anything, becoming more pronounced under New Labour. This translates not only into performance monitoring but also central intervention in the event of 'poorly performing' councils. Hence the unprecedented powers for the Education Secretary to intervene where local education authorities (or individual schools) are deemed to be failing. The trust needed to sustain the multi-agency working necessary for holistic – as opposed to fragmented – service delivery has still fully to recover from recent adversarial agency relationships and central–local tensions!

11

The National Health Service

SUSAN CORBY

The National Health Service (NHS) celebrated its fiftieth birthday in July 1998. It was established to deliver healthcare according to clinical need and is free at the point of use. Essentially it is funded by central government out of general taxation, receiving £45 billion in 1996–7 of which over 70 per cent was spent on the costs of its one million staff. Throughout its 50 years the NHS has been beset by tensions. There is a tension between the government's wish to constrain public expenditure and its desire to provide a free service to its citizens. This tension is exacerbated on the one hand by an unwillingness of governments to raise taxes and on the other hand by growing public expectations, medical advances and the rising proportion of elderly people in the population. There is also a tension between managers, who generally focus mainly on financial targets and efficiency measures, and clinicians, who focus on professional autonomy; between the requirements of central accountability and discretion for local managers; and between the interests of the professionals/staff who work in the NHS and those who use its services. This chapter sets out to show how the Conservative governments from 1979 to 1997 sought to resolve these tensions, the problems caused and the impact on stakeholders. It then considers the impact of the Blair government and assesses its plans for further reform highlighting the potential difficulties with these proposals. It argues that the tensions inherent in the NHS remain and that the circle is unlikely to be squared.

Background

1948–1979

In 1948 the NHS was established as a tripartite structure. One part comprised self-employed contractors to the NHS: general practitioners, dentists, pharmacists and opticians. Another part comprised local government: councils remained responsible for preventative services, ambulances, health visiting and child welfare. The third and largest part comprised hospitals. Great Britain was divided into 19 (later 20) regions, each controlled by a regional hospital board responsible to the Health Minister under which there were groups of hospitals (occasionally a single large hospital) presided over by a hospital management committee of part-time appointees with doctors heavily represented (Harrison, 1988). Each hospital was run by a triumvirate of hospital secretary, medical superintendent and matron, but from the outset doctors 'were the most powerful group in the Service' (Harrison *et al.*, 1992: 32). Not only did consultants have a key role in the NHS, they were employed by regional hospital boards, rather than by hospital management committees like other staff, and were allowed to use NHS facilities and part of their working time for private practice. Moreover, a committee of eminent consultants gave distinction awards to almost a third of its peers (NHS Executive, 1994).

A new organisational structure was introduced in 1974 which removed the local government limb of the NHS and created 14 regions in England, subdivided into 90 areas. (The structure and terminology varied slightly in other parts of the UK.) Rather more than half the areas in England were divided into two or more districts, each based on a district general hospital. Regional health authorities (RHAs) and area health authorities (AHAs) were established as statutory corporate bodies, whereas the district level was an administrative creation, but at each of these three levels there were multidisciplinary management teams whose mode of decision-making was by consensus (Harrison, 1988). GPs and other independent contractors, although preserving their self-employed status, were brought under family practitioner committees which were accountable to the AHA. Finally community health councils were established in each district, charged with representing the views of the local population.

This new semi-unified structure coincided with a period of relative public expenditure restraint: in 1976 the Treasury introduced the 'cash limits' system of financial allocation to the public sector. This meant that the NHS was given an annual budget rather than being demand led. It also coincided with a struggle between the then Labour government and the medical profession over private beds in NHS hospitals, which resulted in their reduction but not extinction. Otherwise, the position of the doctors was essentially unchanged.

The 1970s were a period of union growth in the NHS, partly fuelled by the introduction of bonus schemes for ancillary staff and by the requirements of the 1971 Industrial Relations Act, under which the professional associations, such as the British Medical Association (BMA), the Royal College of Nursing (RCN) and the Chartered Society of Physiotherapists (CSP), registered as trade unions and adopted some of the organisational features of unions, such as stewards (Mailly *et al.*, 1989). In addition, the 1970s were a period of union militancy throughout the public sector, including the NHS (Winchester and Bach, 1995), culminating in 1978–9 in the so-called winter of discontent, which played a large part in the election of the Conservatives in May 1979.

1979–1990

The Conservative government considered that the NHS, like other public services, could and should be made more efficient. This would enable it to satisfy the public's demand for healthcare while limiting public expenditure. Influenced by public choice theories which claim that public servants' prime concern is to run a service that meets their interests rather than those of the public, it also aimed to reduce the power of the professionals. Accordingly during the 1980s it sought to put managers in the driving seat and to place managerial priorities ahead of clinical priorities.

First, it reorganised the NHS in 1982, retaining the 14 regions in England but abolishing the area level and creating 190 district health authorities and eight special health authorities. Second, the government introduced performance indicators in 1983, allowing health authorities to be compared on the basis of value for money. Third, in an attempt to get more for less, in 1983 the Conservative government set manpower targets for all staff, a policy that it continued intermittently, for instance requiring RHAs in 1993 to limit their staff to 200. Fourth, Rayner scrutinies, involving intensive study of a particular area aimed at improving efficiency, pioneered in the civil service, were introduced into the NHS. Fifth, health authorities were instructed to engage in competitive tendering for laundry, domestic and catering services (Mailly *et al.*, 1989). In part this reflected the Conservative government's ideological belief in the superiority of the private sector over the public sector and in part it was a pragmatic attempt to curtail the power of public sector trade unions and to reduce NHS expenditure.

Most important of all, in the 1980s, was the implementation of the recommendations of the NHS Management Inquiry report (Griffiths, 1983). The report diagnosed a lack of management. It said: 'if Florence Nightingale were carrying her lamp through the corridors of the NHS today she would almost certainly be searching for the people in charge' (Griffiths, 1983: 12). Accordingly, it recommended the ending of consensus decision-making and the vesting of the general management function in one person at each level – hospital, district and region – with a chief executive at the centre. In addition, on the assumption that policy and management could be separated, a part-time supervisory board was established, chaired by the Health Secretary, to determine strategy, with a full-time, multi-professional management board to oversee the implementation of strategy. Roughly one-third of the members of the management board had a commercial background, with the remainder from the NHS and the civil service. The chief executive, the first two of whom came from outside the NHS, and the general managers were employed on fixed-term contracts with a performance-related pay element, then a novelty in the NHS (Harrison *et al.*, 1992). In short, the Griffiths and related reforms set out to challenge the professional domination of the NHS but they did not dent clinical freedom.

Moreover, the supervisory board rarely met and the management board did not manage. It advised ministers (Day and Klein, 1997).

During this time, the industrial relations arrangements partly changed. As before, there was a multiplicity of staff organisations and Whitley machinery at national level, that is, joint management/trade union committees to determine terms and conditions of employment. Industrial action, however, in 1982 resulted in the withdrawal of collective bargaining for nurses, midwives, health visitors and the professions allied to medicine, and the introduction of a pay review body, which makes recommendations to government, which is the ultimate decision-maker. Doctors and dentists had had a pay review body since 1962, but this second pay review body resulted in less than half of NHS staff having their pay determined by collective bargaining.

The Internal Market

In 1990 the government set in train more fundamental changes to the structure of the NHS, under the National Health Service and Community Care Act. As before, the rationale was both ideological and pragmatic: the government considered that markets and the private sector led to more efficiency and thus could provide more with less. Allied to this, in an attempt to control NHS costs, the government wanted to assert managerial priorities over clinical ones and make managers operators, rather than administrators.

Accordingly, the Act created a proxy market with quasi-contracts. It separated the purchasing of health care from its provision, with purchasing carried out by district health authorities (health boards in Scotland) and general practitioner fundholders. Purchasers make annual quasi-contracts (non-legally binding agreements) with providers: NHS trusts (that is, NHS hospitals) and private hospitals. There are three types of such contracts: block contracts, cost and volume contracts and cost per case contracts. The first type, which initially predominated largely because of a lack of information on costs, gives patients access to a range of facilities and services. The second type, defined in terms of a given number of treatments or cases, is more sophisticated. The third type is used where the purchaser does not already have a contract with the provider, so-called extra-contractual referrals (House of Commons, 1990).

The 1990 Act not only adopted market mechanisms, it also brought in people from the private sector. For instance, both health authorities and trusts had to have non-executive directors who were mainly drawn from the private sector. In addition, the 1990 Act decentralised the NHS, introducing a looser, multi-divisional (M-form) structure found in many large private sector companies in place of a unitary (U-form) one (Williamson 1975).

Before the Act hospitals were part of district health authorities (DHAs) (health boards in Scotland) which reported to regional health authorities (RHAs) (except in Scotland) and ultimately through the management board to the Secretary of State. The Act, however, gave considerable powers to DHAs as they could choose with whom and on what basis to contract, setting not only prices for treatments or services but also standards of quality. As to NHS trusts, they were given considerable freedom on financial matters (for example, they owned their estates) but they had three duties: to break even, to earn a 6 per cent return on capital and to live within the external financing limit set by the Secretary of State. They were given considerable freedom on employment matters too. For instance they became the employers, whereas before 1990 most hospital staff were employed by DHAs with consultants employed by RHAs. Also trusts were empowered to set their own terms and conditions of employment irrespective of the national arrangements (NHS Management Executive, 1990).

In carrying out this restructuring, the government considered that decentralised units would be able to respond more flexibly to local circumstances but such a structure is not unproblematic. First, it sits uneasily with the political realities of ministerial accountability to parliament and government funding of the NHS. Second, the decentralised structure sits uneasily with legislation, particularly the Transfer of Undertakings (Protection of Employment) Regulations (TUPE)1981, which limits trusts' autonomy in setting terms and conditions of employment. Under its provisions staff previously working in a unit which became a trust can continue to receive nationally determined terms and conditions for as long as they choose to do so, provided they stay in the same job. Third, as Day and Klein (1997) point out, this decentralised structure sits uneasily with the strengthening of the centre. In 1995, the NHS Executive became responsible for both management and policy. Before then there was a separation, a policy board (formerly a supervisory board) and an NHS management executive (formerly a management board). Also eight regional offices replaced 14 RHAs. The offices are part of the centre, staffed by civil servants, instead of being at arms length as were the RHAs, which were staffed by NHS employees.

Finance

One of the tensions in the NHS, as mentioned above, is between managers and clinicians. The former essentially give primacy to financial imperatives and the latter essentially to medical imperatives. The internal market was opposed by the BMA on the grounds that it might constrain doctors' autonomy and undoubtedly the introduction of quasi-contracts negotiated by managers gave the latter an enhanced role and led to a growth in their numbers (Corby, 1996). Quasi-contracts made clinicians aware of the cost of their treatments and to tie clinicians further into the contracting process, many trusts devolved their activities into clinical directorates, headed by a clinician aided by a business manager. Then trust managers centrally used the information provided by the clinical directorates in the contracting process.

The internal market also sought to assuage the tension between the need to constrain public expenditure and the need to provide universal, free healthcare. To this end, the Act introduced a new system of capital accounting, which included depreciation and interest charges. The government argued that this would encourage hospital managers to make the most efficient use of their physical resources as contracts were to be agreed on a full-cost basis (that is, including the cost of capital) and cross subsidisation of services would not be permitted. It would also enable purchasers to make comparisons of cost and performance between different parts of the NHS and the private sector. Managers in trusts with higher-than-average capital costs could avoid losing contracts by disposing of surplus assets to reduce their capital costs and/or increase throughput to reduce the average capital cost per unit (Shaoul, 1998).

Although managers have done this, the circle has not been squared for two main reasons. First, labour is the main cost, not capital. Over 70 per cent of a trust's costs are labour. Second, there is a political commitment, in principle at least, to a full service, so managers of NHS trusts, unlike private hospitals, cannot vary their activity mix and concentrate on high-flow, relatively uncomplicated treatments. In short, although the Conservative government's reforms resulted in putting managers in the driving seat, it did not obviate debate about the level of state funding of the NHS.

Employment

The NHS is labour intensive, so any restructuring is likely to affect employees. The reforms of 1990 affected employees in a number of ways. First, although numbers in employment: did not alter greatly – the total non-medical labour force declined by 6 per cent over the period September 1986–96 – the numbers in certain occupational groups changed dramatically (Department of Health, 1997c). The decline in the numbers of nursing and midwifery staff in England, by 13 per cent, was mainly the result of the fact that from 1990 the figures have not included student nurses. The numbers of general and senior managers in England rose dramatically until 1995 when the basis of the statistics changed. Accordingly comparisons can only be made in the number of administration staff which includes all grades from clerical staff to senior managers. The numbers rose by 44 per cent in the 10 years from 1986.

The numbers in the professions allied to medicine (PAMs) rose by 34 per cent in the period September 1986–96 but the numbers of whole-time equivalent ancillaries fell substantially, by 49 per cent over the same period, reflecting competitive tendering for laundry, cleaning and catering services. Although the majority of contracts remained in-house, competitive tendering enabled managers to alter working practices, to cut jobs/hours and to change shift patterns, undermining the unions and at the same time constraining costs (Kelliher, 1996).

In a drive to substitute cheaper labour for more expensive labour, a new grade of health care assistant (HCA) was introduced in 1990. Official figures differentiate between those who support nurses and those who 'mainly' work in hotel services, but trusts often do not make this differentiation and adopt a host of titles for this grade. Nevertheless, even though the official figures may not accurately reflect the position, this is now clearly a major new employment category (Thornley, 1998).

Numbers apart, the volatility engendered by the annual contracting process between purchasers and providers has had a significant effect on the type of employment contract offered by trusts. Previously most staff were employed on indefinite contracts with job security being a feature of NHS employment. According to a survey by Seccombe and Smith (1996) the number of nurses on short-term contracts has risen. They found that 5 per cent (seven per cent in community trusts) of all nurses and a quarter of those nurses who joined or returned to the NHS in the year 1995–6 were employed on short-term contracts in 1996. They also found that short-term contracts were being renewed: almost half of those on short-term contracts had been employed in the same trust for more than a year, despite the fact that most contracts were for less than a year. A survey in 1996 by Incomes Data Services (1997) also found that the use of temporary and short-term contracts had risen and that the average proportion of temporary staff (that is, not just nurses) was 7 per cent of the NHS workforce. It said (Incomes Data Services, 1997: 164):

> The main reason cited by organisations for a rise in the proportion of temporary workers was uncertainty in funding due to the short term nature of the contracting process.

The volatility of the annual contracting process and cost constraints have also led to an increase in the number of casual staff in the NHS. Casuals are used to cover for absent staff, to match peaks in workload and to reduce paybill costs, as they usually do not receive pension and leave entitlements and are placed on the lowest increment. Statistics are collected on the number of so-called bank nurses and midwives. 'Banks' are internal, that is, trust run, employment agencies and thus cheaper than employment agencies outside the NHS. 'Bank' staff signal to the trust their availability for work in principle and when the trust is short-staffed it contacts a person on the bank to see if that person can come into work. Looking at whole time equivalent (WTE) figures, in 1990 there were 6580 bank nurses and midwives in 1990 and 15,610 in 1996 (Department of Health, 1997c). During that period the number of agency staff was fairly stable: just over 6700 WTEs in both 1990 and 1996. According to Seccombe and Smith (1996) one in four NHS nurses reported undertaking other paid work in addition to their main job. Half were doing bank work and a further fifth were doing agency nursing. Also some trusts have established 'banks' for professions allied to medicine and for junior doctors. For instance Salford Mental Health Services Trust had 10 doctors of various grades in its 'bank' in 1997. Paradoxically, at the same time as seeking to cut employment costs and treating at least some staff as easily disposable, many trusts are seeking the Investors in People (IiP) standard, which entails making a public commitment to develop all employees to achieve business objectives, principally through training. IiP, however, has barely affected doctors, who have remained a privileged occupational group: GPs remained self employed, while consultants retained the right to work both in the NHS and privately, to use private beds in NHS hospitals and to obtain distinction awards, albeit managers became involved in a minor way in their distribution (NHS Executive, 1994).

As to pay, traditionally those employed in the NHS had their terms and conditions determined nationally, either by collective bargaining or by pay review bodies (see above). The 1990 changes, however, gave trusts power not only to employ staff but to remunerate them on trust terms rather than on national terms, though because of TUPE existing staff could choose whether to opt for the former or the latter. The Conservative government promoted local pay, for instance giving some trusts, such as Derby City General Hospital, money to develop a new, job-evaluated structure. It considered that local pay arrangements would enable trusts to react to their local labour market and to reward such objectives as flexibility. Importantly also, local pay arrangements could reinforce loyalty to the trust and help in the development of a new organisational culture, whereas national arrangements, with pay determined according to functional group, served to reinforce inter-professional differences and loyalty to the profession.

By 1996 nearly a third (31 per cent) of staff were on trust contracts (Incomes Data Services, 1997), mainly those recruited since the hospital had become a trust and those who had changed jobs. The proportion, however, varied from trust to trust. Trust employment contracts are of two kinds: those which mirror the national arrangements in most respects and those which are radically different. The latter category were common in ambulance trusts, and for healthcare assistants, a category of staff for whom there have never been nationally determined terms and conditions. According to Thornley (1998) nearly a quarter of HCAs were worse off than nursing auxiliaries on the national arrangements.

Also, as part of its drive to encourage local pay determination, the NHS chief executive in 1994 asked trusts to establish machinery for determining local pay (Langlands, 1994). As a result trusts set up collective bargaining machinery, often on a 'prime union', single-table basis, whereby all the staff organisations are recognised but a smaller number have seats on the negotiating executive, that is, the main bargaining table (Corby, 1992; Corby and Higham, 1996). With government encouragement, the pay review bodies for nurses and paramedicals in 1995 recommended a national pay rise to be supplemented locally by top up pay. However, this led to a major industrial dispute, with the moderate RCN and Royal College of Midwives (RCM) repealing their rules prohibiting industrial action. The dispute was resolved through a complex agreement for 'local pay in a national framework' applying to all those covered by national arrangements, except doctors. In brief, this provided for national pay rates to be maintained at the same time as allowing local bargaining over part of the annual pay rise, but with an uprating mechanism through which national pay rates would be adjusted annually to reflect the outcome of the previous years local negotiations. In fact, these complex provisions for local pay, having been used in 1995 and 1996, were abandoned in 1997, just before the general election (Incomes Data Services, 1998).

Quality

Performance indicators (PIs) were introduced into the NHS in 1983. The Conservative government, however, decided to develop performance measures, the so-called *Citizen's Charter* (Prime Minister's Office, 1991), across the public sector including the NHS, and this spawned patients' charters in England, Scotland and Wales. The government saw these charters as a means by which the needs of customers could be given priority over the interests of the professions and they included, for instance, specific times for out-patient appointments and to be seen within 30 minutes of that time; the use of day-case surgery; time spent on a waiting list; ambulance service emergency response times; and a named nurse or midwife to be responsible for each patient's care. In addition, to aid the contracting process, the government introduced a purchaser efficiency index, essentially centred around 'bottom line' measures. The NHS Executive has monitored performance against the objectives set by government, while trusts normally have denoted a board member to be ultimately responsible for quality, often the Director of Nursing, and have established quality units.

Labour's 'Third Way'

After the general election of 1997, the Labour government published White Papers on the NHS in England (Department of Health, 1997a), Scotland (Scottish Office, 1997) and Wales (Welsh Office, 1998). The changes are limited as Labour has retained the purchaser/provider split, which it considers is the best way to make health care providers responsive to patient needs (Department of Health, 1997a). Similarly, it has retained decentralised management in semi-autonomous NHS trusts. Nevertheless the language has changed: the purchaser/provider split is no longer called an internal market and quasi-contracts are now called funding agreements, not contracts.

Also, Labour is adopting and adapting GP commissioning, a practice introduced by the Conservatives under the so-called fundholding scheme but which had problems. Because fundholding operated outside a strategic plan, it led to fragmentation and gave advantages to some patients (whose GPs were fundholders) at the expense of others. Accordingly the government is requiring health authorities to provide strategic leadership by developing local health improvement programmes and it is introducing what it calls primary care groups for *all* GPs. As well as commissioning health care, primary care groups will have to work closely with social services and contribute to the health authority's local health improvement programme. Each group, which typically will serve 100,000 patients, is to be accountable to the health authority and will have a governing body which includes representatives of other professions such as community nurses and social workers, as well as GPs, so limiting the power of doctors, and its meetings are to be open to the public, so empowering patients – in theory at least. Furthermore, groups can take one of four forms. They can:

- act in an advisory capacity to the health authority;
- take devolved responsibility for managing the budget for health care in their area, acting as part of the health authority;
- become established as a freestanding body accountable to the health authority for commissioning care;
- become established as a freestanding body accountable to the health authority for commissioning care (as above) but with added responsibility for the provision of community services for their population, excluding mental health or learning disability services.

Primary care groups could start at any one of the four options but the government would expect groups over time to move to the last two forms, to be termed Primary Care Trusts, which may include some or all of the services previously provided by NHS Community Trusts. The White Paper (Department of Health 1997a: 27–8) says:

> Such an approach provides a 'third way' between stifling top-down command and control on the one hand, and a random and wasteful grass roots free-for-all on the other. . . . It harnesses the strategic abilities of health authorities and the innovative energies of primary care commissioners for the benefit of patients.

The changes to the NHS in Scotland mirror those in England with some exceptions (Scottish Office, 1997). Scotland has never had a regional and district health authority structure. Instead it has had health boards which combine the functions of the English regions and districts. Under Labour it is to have primary care trusts, typically comprising community hospitals and mental health services as well as networks of general practices in local health care co-operatives, and acute hospital trusts, with health boards monitoring and drawing up local strategy. In Wales there will be health authorities, NHS trusts and local health groups. The latter will be groups of practitioners commissioning healthcare initially on an indicative basis (Welsh Office, 1998). Both in Scotland and Wales, the Scottish Parliament and the Welsh Assembly respectively are to assume responsibility for health functions exercised by the Secretary of State at the time of writing.

Finance

In many respects the financial regime instituted by the Conservatives has been untouched by Labour's reforms. Thus NHS trusts still have three financial duties: to break even, to make a 6 per cent return on capital and to stay within the external financing limit set by the Secretary of State. Moreover, the system of accrual accounting has been retained. Labour, however, aims further to contain NHS expenditure in a number of ways. First it is expanding the private finance initiative (PFI), started by the previous government, whereby private sector consortia (usually a construction company, a bank and a facilities management contractor) design, build, own and operate hospitals for the NHS. The NHS trust pays the consortium a regular fee for a given period (typically 20–30 years) to cover construction costs, the rent of the building, the costs of support services and the risks transferred to the private sector. PFI obviates the need for capital expenditure by the government and by mid-1998 the Labour government had approved PFI schemes for 15 acute hospitals in England and three in Scotland (Socialist Health Association, 1998).

Second, it aims to reduce NHS expenditure by cutting the number of contracts for the purchase of health care. Thus individual cost-per-case contracts are to be abolished and annual contracts are to be replaced by longer-term three-year, or in some cases five-year funding agreements. In addition, with the replacement of GP fundholding by primary care groups, the number of commissioning bodies will be reduced from around 3600 to 500. The government maintains that its 'changes will reduce costs by £1 billion over the lifetime of the current Parliament' (1997 to 2002) and the money saved can be invested in patient services (Department of Health, 1997a: 8). It admits that primary care groups will incur management costs but believes that essentially such costs can be met by a redeployment of the GP Fundholding Practice Fund Management Allowance. Third, the Government is seeking to contain costs by shifting the financial responsibility on to GPs and other primary care professionals. This is because primary care groups will have a single cash limited 'envelope'.

Employment

The pay of NHS employees remains a central problem, given that the NHS is labour intensive and employs over one million people. This problem has been exacerbated by a tighter labour market in a stronger economy: the general election of 1997 coincided with shortages of staff nurses, especially in certain specialities (Brindle, 1998a). This was fuelled by the extra cash given by the government in 1998 to the NHS to bring down waiting lists, which has increased trusts' staffing requirements, by the falling intakes to pre-registration nurse education in the first half of the 1990s, and by the fact that more than a fifth of those on the nursing register were 50 or over in 1996 and thus coming within the scope of early or normal retirement (Seccombe and Smith, 1996). According to the RCN, there were at least 8000 nursing vacancies nationwide in November 1998 (Peston, 1998).

Second, there are equal value problems. The government has settled out of court some of the speech therapists equal value claims, including *Enderby v Frenchay Health Authority* after a decision by the European Court of Justice in 1993, as it is now clear that comparisons can be drawn across different bargaining groups. They can also be drawn across a service, for example, nurses in different trusts, as a result of the decision by the Employment Appeal Tribunal in 1996 in the case of *Scullard v Knowles*. Equal value claims are unlikely to be obviated by the Health Secretary's proposal for 'a system which combines national pay determination with appropriate local flexibility' or by the review body proposal in 1998, accepted by the government, for some discretionary increments on top of some of the scales for senior nurses, midwives and professions allied to medicine or even a single pay spine, as Unison has suggested (Incomes Data Services, 1998).

As to job security, many continue to be employed on short-term contracts and on the 'bank'. The Health Minister asked the NHS Executive to produce plans by October 1998 to cut the routine use of short-term employment contracts for health workers (Brindle, 1998b) but at the time of writing it is not known what these will be. Moreover, under PFI a considerable number of staff – certainly domestic, catering, maintenance, security and portering staff and possibly receptionists, secretaries and laboratory technicians – will be employed by private companies rather than the NHS (Socialist Health Association, 1998).

Nevertheless, it would be inaccurate to conclude that the change of government in 1997 has as yet made no positive change to NHS employment. NHS trust boards are to be required to review regularly whether they are doing enough to involve staff and are enjoined to work imaginatively through staff consultative committees and other local arrangements to improve dialogue about decisions affecting local health services' and to make sure that staff can speak out when necessary, without victimisation (Department of Health, 1997a: 51).

Quality

PIs, as noted above, were extensively used by the Conservative government. The Labour government maintains that under the Conservatives performance was driven by what could be readily measured, which distorted priorities in the NHS and failed to reflect the needs of patients. It does not, however, plan to jettison performance measures in the NHS. On the contrary, it plans to build on them as, like its predecessor, it sees quality improvements as a way of delivering value for money both in terms of cost effectiveness and clinical effectiveness, and thus also a way of assuaging the tension between the need to constrain public expenditure and the needs of patients. It also sees quality measures as a way of shifting the balance both from the autonomy of the professional associations, particularly doctors, to the interests of patients, and from local discretion to central control, as the centre will monitor trusts' performance.

Accordingly, the government is establishing a number of measures to improve quality (Department of Health, 1997a). First, it is setting up a National Institute for Clinical Excellence, whose membership will be drawn not only from the health professions but also from health economists and patient representatives. Second, it is developing a programme of new evidence-based national service frameworks setting out patterns and levels of service which should be provided for patients with certain medical conditions. These frameworks will be drawn up by government after discussions not only with the professions but also with representatives of users of the NHS. Third, it is creating a Commission for Health Improvement. As a statutory body at arms length from government, the new Commission will spot-check local arrangements to monitor and assure clinical quality, will be able to intervene to investigate and identify problems, and will have powers to remove chairs of NHS trusts and/or non-executive directors where there is evidence of systematic failure. Like the Institute, the Commission's membership will not only be drawn from the professions but also from patient representatives. Fourth, the performance of health authorities and trusts will be monitored in England by the centre through its regional offices and, fifth, Labour is developing a new national performance framework to provide an improved basis for the benchmarking of performance.

Finally, the government is instituting 'clinical governance', an initiative 'to assure and improve clinical standards at local level' (Department of Health, 1997a: 82). As a result, chief executives of trusts will not only have financial duties, they will also have a duty for the quality of care, and NHS trust boards will have to publish an annual report on quality assurance and investigate adverse events. Allied to this will be so-called professional self-regulation but as the BMA has said (1998: 7) 'the requirements of professional self-regulation and outcomes, driven performance assessment required by NHS management can be mutually incompatible.

Conclusion

When the NHS was founded in 1948, the distinction between public and private health care was blurred. Consultants could work in both sectors and there were private beds in NHS hospitals. Over 50 years on, the dividing line between the public and the private has become even more indistinct in order to limit the demands on the public purse and boost managerialism. In particular, since 1990 NHS purchasers have been able to buy healthcare for NHS patients from the private sector and PFI schemes are resulting in long-term and major NHS involvement in commercial operations. This insertion of the private sector, however, has not been problem free. NHS staff may lack judgement or expertise and/or take risks with public money. Several examples have been uncovered recently in the NHS in respect of computer projects, with one (the Read codes program) involving a potential conflict of interest according to the National Audit Office (Wighton, 1998). Similarly, the Royal National Orthopaedic Hospital lost £3.5 million in a venture with a private sector firm for an incinerator (Brindle, 1995).

As noted above, there is a tension between the centre and local management discretion. In the last decade the purchaser/provider structure introduced by the Conservatives and only marginally changed by Labour has been partly justified by government on the basis of the need to turn local managers from administrators into operators and there has been much rhetoric about the devolution of responsibility. Local management discretion, however, remains constrained and the centre has increased its powers both as a result of structural changes and its increased role in monitoring the burgeoning quality measures.

There is also a tension between the interests of professionals and the needs of patients, and clinical freedom is increasingly being limited by the expansion of quality measures. Furthermore, there is a tension between the Government's desire to control public expenditure and the public's health care needs. The Conservatives tried to assuage that tension by giving a key role to managers whom it expected to deliver efficiencies. Labour has sought to control public expenditure by reducing the number of managers and making GPs take on a managerial role and act as the gatekeepers for health services. It assumes, however, that GPs will be equal to their managerial tasks and that they will want to act as managers. It also assumes that GPs will be willing to ration health care. According to *GP* magazine, which carried out a survey of 300 GPs in the first half of 1998, the majority of GPs were opposed to Labour's proposals. For instance, it quoted one GP as saying that 'the whole point of the exercise [Labour's planned changes] is to shift the blame for the failings of the NHS on to GPs and mask the true cause – a lack of money', and another as saying 'they will not work . . . and are a complete waste of my time' (*GP*, 1998: 36). At this juncture, it is too early to assess whether these comments are accurate.

12

Education

**DAVID HOLLOWAY, SYLVIA HORTON
and DAVID FARNHAM**

Responsibility for education is highly fragmented in Britain. There is a division between schools, further and higher education and within each sector there is a wide range of institutions delivering the service. Prior to the 1980s, education policy was set down by central government which also largely funded the service. Local education authorities (LEAs) had responsibility for implementing policy, except for the university sector, which consisted of autonomous chartered bodies. Schools and further education (FE) colleges had a great deal of autonomy in delivering the curriculum but LEAs allocated funds and administered them. The teaching professions and national examination boards largely determined the content of the curriculum. This tripartite structure of central government, LEAs and universities, and the teaching professions was accompanied by a largely bipartisan approach to education (McVicar, 1996).

Since 1979, public education has been transformed as successive Conservative governments, and now a New Labour government, introduced policy, structural, financial and managerial changes at all three levels of the service. Initially the changes reflected Conservative beliefs that in order to increase efficiency and effectiveness in schools, colleges and universities, they had to be managed better, held more accountable and exposed to competition and markets. The teaching profession had to be brought under control and directed in what they taught and how they taught it, if the education system was to meet the needs of the economy. Furthermore, parents and students should be given more choice and have more power in running schools and colleges. During the 1990s, the focus turned to issues of quality, standards and funding, especially in higher education (HE). This chapter examines the changes which have transformed the management of education, and their impact upon the teaching professions, over the past 20 years.

The Market for Education

The major thrust of Conservative government policy was the introduction of a greater market orientation into compulsory and post-compulsory education. Ball (1990, 1992) identifies five elements in this market approach: choice, competition, diversity, per capita funding and new organisational styles. Choice was fundamental to Conservative education policy after 1979. They argued that parents should be able to send their children to the schools of their choice and students should be able to choose their courses amongst competing FE and HE institutions. Competition was initially introduced by the Education Act 1980, which required LEAs to publish their examination results and schools to hold compulsory open days for parents. The Education Reform Act (ERA) 1988 introduced open enrolment as a further means of increasing competition. But choice, if it was to be real, required diverse schools. If all schools were comprehensive then there was no choice. The ERA 1988, aimed at undermining state educational monopoly, allowed schools to 'opt out', assuming that this would facilitate the continuation and re-emergence of grammar schools. Government also assumed that increased competition would highlight differences among state schools. Similar pressures of competition were injected into FE and HE. Following the Further and Higher Education Act (FHEA) 1992, FE colleges were given corporate status and they began to compete with one another. The already corporatised polytechnics of England and Wales were designated 'new' (post-1992) universities, in direct competition with 'old' (pre-1992) chartered universities for students, resources (including research funds) and staff.

A cash nexus was established through per-capita funding from 1990, when school funding became based on numbers and types of pupils enrolled. It was envisaged that this arrangement would stimulate competition by rewarding successful schools and penalising unsuccessful ones, with the latters incomes falling if they failed to attract pupils. Similar per capita funding arrangements were later introduced into FE and HE.

The educational market created new organisational styles, which stemmed in schools from the devolution of budgets from LEAs. Under ERA 1988, schools assumed responsibility for most of their expenditure and, as a result, the functions and roles of head teachers were changed from those of senior professionals, leading teams of teachers, to 'managing directors' answerable to school governors, who acted as 'boards of directors'. In short, schools were to become more like private sector commercial organisations. With the legal incorporation of FE colleges, colleges of HE and post-1992 new universities, these institutions were also reorganised on executive management lines. College principals and vice-chancellors of universities became chief executives of institutions, accountable to more business-based governing bodies.

This move towards a market-orientated model of education was driven by central government, with little participation by LEAs or the teaching professions in the policy-making process. There are now centrally determined policy frameworks governing schools, colleges and new universities. There are leaner bureaucracies at LEA level but inflated bureaucracies of new managers and support staff at institutional level, due to devolvement of finance, staffing matters and accountability to schools, colleges and new universities. There is now greater parental choice in selecting schools and more student choice in the post-school sector, although this should not be exaggerated. Finally, education has been managerialised as head teachers, college principals and university vice-chancellors have assumed chief executive roles and adopted managerial practices copied from the private sector.

Local Management of Schools

The ERA 1988 was a radical piece of legislation and transformed the management of schools. Previously, head teachers had limited managerial responsibilities. Buildings were provided and maintained by LEAs, which also employed, appointed and paid all staff and determined staffing levels. Personnel procedures were generally negotiated nationally or locally through collective agreements with the teacher unions and any disputes with staff were usually referred to LEAs to resolve. The introduction of local management of schools (LMS) was designed to achieve a number of objectives. These included more flexibility, reduction of the professional power of teachers, more accountability of schools in how they used resources, and greater managerial efficiency (McVicar, 1996). The ERA 1988 required LEAs to delegate 85 per cent of school budgets to individual schools. Devolvement of funds was according to a published formula, the key element being pupil enrolments based on school numbers and pupils' age. School governors replaced LEAs as responsible for managing school budgets, including determining the number of staff and the appointment and dismissal of teachers and support workers. LEAs, however, remained the legal employers of those working in LEA-maintained schools. The New Labour government's White Paper, *Excellence in Schools* (DfEE, 1997), is continuing this policy of devolvement, stating that whilst the LMS framework would be subject to review, government commitment to devolved school budgets and school management would be maintained.

The role of headteachers has been transformed under LMS and is now clearly a managerial role. The relationship between headteachers and their boards of governors is critical in determining the real locus of power. In some schools, governors have a decisive influence, whilst in others they defer to the headteacher who effectively takes all managerial decisions. In larger schools, managerial hierarchies have emerged with heads, deputy heads, school managers and enlarged support staff making up a managerial team. The headteacher, a title still reflecting a profession rather than an activity, has responsibility for drawing up the school's mission statement, business plan and school budget. Decisions on staffing, maintenance, supplies and all resources are taken on a day-to-day basis. Such managerial responsibilities are often delegated to deputies who may be non-teaching or part-teaching staff. The costs of sustaining these management structures have to be borne by the school budget.

The effect of pupil-led funding of schools is that school budgets are dependent upon the number of children enrolled. Schools are forced to compete for pupils in a market environment, where, since the Greenwich judgement in 1989 (Morris, 1995), parents are no longer required to send their children to their neighbourhood school and LEA boundaries are no longer a barrier to parental choice. Schools have responded to the competitive situation in a variety of ways, including the adoption of appropriate marketing strategies. Since the early 1980s, schools have been required to hold open days, produce a prospectus and provide statistical data relating to attendance rates and performance in public examinations. These data are then used to compare and rank-order the performance of individual schools and are published by the Office for Standards in Education (OFSTED) nationally, and as school league tables locally. Despite widespread criticism from the teacher unions, the Labour government is continuing these policies and has announced its intention to widen the information available to parents, by introducing a 'value-added' element into the statistical tables.

Emphasis on parental choice and a greater market orientation has led to some marginal increase in diversity, as some schools have opted for Grant Maintained Status (GMS) and are funded directly by a government quango, the Funding Agency for Schools. Opting out did not prove as popular as the Conservative government had hoped, despite an extension to the scheme in 1992 when a target of 1500 GMS schools by April 1994 was set. This had not been achieved by the time of the 1997 general election, when the number of schools opting out had virtually dried up (Barber, 1997). New Labour has abandoned opting out but still favours diversity. Labour's policy is to introduce a new framework locating all state schools, including GMS and the 15 City Technology Colleges, into one of three categories: community, aided and foundation schools. Only community schools will be subject to admissions procedures determined by LEAs. The Standards and Framework Act (1998) allows schools opting for the foundation status, as specialist schools, to select 10 per cent of their intakes based on aptitude in a particular specialism. The Labour government has committed itself to increasing the number of specialist schools from the current 330 (1998) to 450 by 2001.

The Role of LEAs

The ERA 1988 and the FHEA 1992 resulted in the role and functions of LEAs being severely curtailed. The Audit Commission sought to redefine their post-ERA role as: leading the education service, supporting schools, planning facilities for the future, disseminating information to the education market, regulating quality and channelling funds to enable institutions to deliver. In reality LEAs have been squeezed between increased centralisation and decentralisation. As the Audit Commission (1996b: 39) pointed out:

> The dispersal of LEA powers encourages central government to take more powers for itself and to use these powers more actively; which in turn limits the scope and incentives for LEAs to act of their own volition; which in turn encourages central government to assume more powers of direction and coordination; which in turn reduces the LEA role still further.

New Labour appears to have retained some of its predecessors' ambivalence towards LEAs. Whilst LEAs retain responsibility for providing a limited number of pupil-specific services, mainly related to special educational needs, they have not regained responsibility for day-to-day management of schools and colleges. However, they have been given a key responsibility for school improvement in order to raise educational standards. This involves developing a strategic overview of schools within their local authority boundaries, setting down a range of targets including pupil performance in public examinations, facilitating (but not directing or imposing) the improvement process in individual schools and assisting schools with OFSTED inspections. These local development plans require DfEE approval and the Secretary of State has a reserve power to secure proper performance of LEA functions, which could involve inviting another LEA or a private company to assume responsibility.

The Audit Commission and OFSTED

The Audit Commission, set up in 1983 as an arm of central government, has had an important impact on schools. It has reported extensively on all aspects of school activity including institutional management and performance indicators (PIs) (Holloway, 1998). Its reports have often been interpreted by schools as guidelines, if not directives, for management restructuring and good practice and, along with OFSTED inspections, have been an effective system of external control. OFSTED, established by the Education (Schools) Act, 1992, introduced a new approach to inspection. All schools are now inspected on a four-year cycle, using a standardised procedure with explicit, published national criteria. Inspection covers all aspects of a school and involves parents and school governors in the process. An evaluative report is published and schools are required to produce action plans to respond to specific issues in the report. OFSTED reports are now so significant in determining the rating of a school that they dominate the time and focus of schools for months before the event.

The 1992 Act also requires publication of performance tables of school work. There is evidence that league tables have met with some success, in that school managers are made acutely aware of their school's position in the tables and can focus on maintaining or improving school performance. However, league tables have been criticised as highlighting academic results at the expense of other indicators, thus favouring schools serving more prosperous catchment areas. The Labour government has, to a limited extent, accepted this criticism and is reformulating tables to take into account a value-added element, but targets are still a central concern. In *Targets for the Future* (DfEE, 1997b), national targets for specific age groups are set, including 80 per cent literacy and 75 per cent numeracy for all 11-year-olds and 95 per cent of all school leavers to have at least one GCSE. These will inevitably become performance targets for low-achieving schools.

The OFSTED regime has come under a battery of criticisms from teachers and researchers with the conclusion that, rather than providing a stimulus for improvement, highly critical OFSTED reports only serve to reinforce a cycle of decline. The Labour government has responded in what might be described as the fourth major education act this century. The Schools Standards and Framework Act (1998) gives the Secretary of State powers to curb 'failing schools' and to close them if they persist in a record of continuing failure . They can then make a Fresh Start under new management. The Act also provides for the creation of Educational Action Zones (EAZs) aimed at increasing involvement of industry, commercial organisations and the voluntary sector with under-performing schools in deprived areas. Initially a sum of £75 million – over three years - was injected into 25 pilot EAZs to increase staff, promote homework, and strengthen the use of information technology. Schools in EAZs have the power to deviate from the national curriculum and to opt out of the teachers Pay and Conditions Act 1991 – so giving head teachers and Boards of Governors more powers. Further policies to create Beacon Schools, which are schools of excellence, and to reward them with additional funding seems likely to perpetuate the divisive impact of the performance-based OFSTED system.

Impact on the Teaching Profession

The reforms within the school sector have had a dramatic impact upon the teaching profession. First, ERA represented a clear attempt to control teachers' professional work. Introduction of a national curriculum closed down many areas of discretion previously available to them (Ball, 1990). Schools and teachers no longer have control over what is taught and both the national curriculum and the OFSTED inspection process have been interpreted by the teaching profession as attacks by central government on an overworked, underpaid and demoralised occupational group. Teacher unions point to such attacks as a major factor in the current recruitment and retention crisis in the profession. Despite national advertising campaigns run by the government quango, the Teacher Training Agency (TTA), recruitment to initial teacher training courses has failed to meet targets.

The teacher trade unions have used poor recruitment to support their campaign for higher pay for the profession, which has fallen well behind that of people working in business and commerce. The Teachers Pay and Conditions Act 1987 took teachers out of the system of national collective bargaining, which had determined their pay and conditions for over 60 years. After an interim period a School Teachers' Review Body (STRB) was appointed in 1992 to advise the government on teachers pay. Changes to the salary scales of teachers in 1991, and the introduction of incentive payments, gave schools more flexibility over rewards but this has led to a widening of differentials between those holding management and responsibility posts and mainstream teachers. Arguably, therefore, the real problem is not initial or basic salaries but the removal of a progressive career structure, unless they take on managerial responsibilities (Farnham and Giles, 1996a).

A further factor in the crisis facing the teaching profession is that until recently continuing professional development (CPD) has had a relatively low priority amongst teachers. Consequently, the profession has been poorly equipped to deal with recent structural, management, curricula and assessment change. There is no mandatory requirement for teachers to update either their subject knowledge or their pedagogic skills, although schools are funded to undertake training days. Since the 1980s, there has been a shift from a *laissez-faire* approach to more systematic control of staff development by central government. The publication of *Teaching Quality* (DES 1983) marked the introduction of specific grants and a more directed approach to in-service training (INSET), as government sought to implement major changes in the curriculum and its delivery. The 1990 Grants for Educational Support and Training (GEST) was introduced to support the implementation of the ERA, particularly introducing the national curriculum. Tomlinson (1993) suggests that this reflected changes in the perception of the professional status of teachers from an autonomous to a more limited functionary one. However, government has continued to encourage personal professional development and has provided funds to support it. The need for management training was acknowledged by the School Management Task Force set up in 1989 to advise on institutional management (DfE, 1993). Its reports emphasised the short-fall in management skills which would impede implementation of governmental policies and emphasised the need for structured management development. In 1994 the DES increased the amount of money available for management training and thousands of teachers took advantage of courses offered at local, regional and national levels.

The Labour government has responded very positively to the problems faced by the teaching profession and its Green Paper, *Teachers Meeting the Challenge of Change* (DfEE, 1998b), proposed a new staffing structure to recognise the different roles of staff in schools, offer incentives for high achievement, introduce new arrangements for managing teacher development and ensure all managerial posts are held by qualified staff. A new scheme for linking pay to performance comes into effect in September 1999 and by 2002 it will be mandatory for all new headteachers to have a National Professional Qualification in School Management. The new structure will consist of first and second-level teachers, (advanced skills teachers) with a performance threshold separating the two and a school-leader structure at the top which constitutes a management level. There will be a single pay spine for all leadership posts (senior management team) with rewards linked to achievement of agreed objectives. A new system of performance management, involving annual appraisals, will be introduced to facilitate this. There is also a proposal to introduce fixed-term contracts for senior management. There will be a fast-track system to attract able graduates, who will receive extra training in return for accepting supplementary contracts with a longer working year and greater mobility. Finally, Labour intends to recruit 2000 non-qualified teaching assistants by 2002.

Teachers' representatives, largely excluded from the policy-making process throughout the 1980s and 1990s, have been invited to respond to the Green Paper. Divisions within the highly unionised teaching profession, with its multi-union structure, have weakened their ability to withstand the onslaught of reforms in the past (Farnham and Giles, 1995b; Seifert and Ironside, 1993). There is little evidence to suggest the present governments determination to push ahead with its reforms will be deflected.

Further Education

Underpinning FE reforms was a set of beliefs that colleges were inflexible and unresponsive to the needs of industry, commerce and their local communities. In addition to their inefficiency in terms of resource utilisation, they were seen as suffering from unacceptably high rates of student wastage and non-completion of courses. There was also a long-standing governmental concern about the low participation rate in post-16 education and what was perceived to be poor performance in the sector (Steedman and Green, 1996; Audit Commission *et al.*, 1993).

The FE sector is characterised by great diversity and, since the ERA and FHEA, by market competition for students and resources. There are 435 institutions (further education corporations – FECs) varying considerably in size, with 27 per cent having under 2000 students and 24 per cent over 10,000. Numbers of students attending FECs have increased by 31 per cent since 1994–5 to 3.9 million in 1997–8. Although FECs recruit school leavers, the majority of students attend on a part-time basis and some colleges are increasingly becoming adult institutions with 63 per cent of students aged over 25 (THES, 1998). Whilst the focus of the ERA 1988 was on schools, it also legislated for the post-16 sector, requiring LEAs to delegate financial responsibility to colleges of FE, the then-polytechnics and other colleges of HE, according to a government formula. Under FHEA, the constitutions of college governing bodies have been reformed with at least 50 per cent of their members being drawn from local industry and commerce. Although sixth form colleges were part of the school sector, they were subject to FE financial delegation requirements. Thus the changes affecting colleges were congruent with those in the schools sector.

The FHEA 1992 completed the process of removing post-16-sector institutions from LEA control, and responsibility for funding moved to a new Further Education Funding Council (FEFC). The latter is required to ensure that there are adequate facilities for FE to meet the needs of students; to contribute to the development of a world-class work-force as envisaged in the National Education Training Targets; to promote improvements in quality; and to promote access to FE (DfE, 1993). Colleges, like schools, have been placed in a market environment responsible for their own strategic planning and day-to-day management, within a financial and quality framework determined by the FEFC.

Managing Colleges

From 1 April 1993, FE colleges and sixth form colleges became independent corporations with charitable status. Each college took on responsibility for staffing, finance, estates and marketing, which had previously been the responsibility of LEAs, although some larger colleges had exercised de-volved powers. These functions were in addition to curriculum development and administration, for which colleges had always been responsible. The result of incorporation was a substantial increase in the number of managers and the creation of new managerial structures. From the outset, central government sought to influence the new managerial systems and withheld funds until colleges had set in place formal staff-appraisal systems, a necessary underpinning for performance management (Warner and Crosthwaite, 1995). Although FE had been moving in the direction of NPM, with an emphasis on cost cutting, performance and tight managerial control, it was post-incorporation that the move to managerialism really took root.

All FECs are characterised by performance management systems. Each college has a mission statement and strategic and business plans. These are translated into departmental plans and budgets with PIs (set both nationally and internally) providing the targets by which the college and its depart-ments are evaluated. Internal management information systems, personnel systems and quality control systems are still being developed to enable colleges to be managed more efficiently. Marketing has also emerged as a new and important activity as colleges compete for students, contracts and money.

Funding Colleges

Changes in funding, along with government's commitment to expanding student numbers, forced the management changes outlined above. The FEFC has the duty of providing a coherent national funding regime for FE, striking a balance between securing maximum access to the widest range of opportunities in FE and avoiding a disproportionate charge on public funds (FEFC, 1992). In 1997–8 the FE budget was £2942 million. The FEFC developed a scheme intended to reduce student wastage, with financial penalties for colleges if the stages or funding elements are not successfully completed. In addition to improving student retention and course completion rates, the funding methodology also seeks to encourage colleges to widen access. The FEFC agrees an annual funding contract with each of the 435 institutions for which it has responsibility. Until 1998, funding was based on 'core funding' for meeting specific enrolment targets and a 'demand-led element' which enabled colleges to earn more money by taking additional students at a cheaper rate. Failure to meet recruitment and retention targets set resulted in the FEFC reclaiming funding in the next financial year.

The Labour government has promised to review the funding system. The outcome of the Comprehensive Spending Review (1998) is, first, a commitment to provide an extra 700,000 students in FE in 2001–2, compared with 1997–8 and, second, to provide an extra £255 million in 1999–2000, rising to an extra £470 million in 2000–1. Government has also introduced downward pressure on costs, by reducing efficiency savings to 1 per cent and at the same time planning to reward colleges showing improvements in quality and results.

Also involved in college funding are Training and Enterprise Councils (TECs), which were established in 1989 as a major policy innovation in vocational education and training. There are currently 72 TECs in England and Wales and 20 Local Enterprise Councils in Scotland, membership of which is composed mainly of local business interests. TECs fund as much as a third of some college vocational programmes but in many areas the relationship between colleges and local TECs has been one of mutual suspicion (Cantor *et al.*, 1995; Ainley and Bailey, 1997).

Since the expansion of student numbers has not been accompanied by a proportionate increase in funding, the unit of resource paid to colleges has fallen. This is on top of a fall by 30 per cent between 1989 and 1995. Colleges were expected to finance expansion out of increased productivity, supplemented by additional sources of funds. Some larger colleges are able to attract overseas students, sell consultancy, provide full-cost courses to industry and utilise their estates fully. In the main, however, FECs have relied upon increases in staff productivity and elimination of waste. Responses by colleges to the funding regime have affected virtually every area of college activity. There has been expansion in the use of sophisticated

MISs, although Cantor *et al.* (1995) report that few FECs make best use of their systems. Institutions have designed student tracking systems and record-training credits. There has been an impact on marketing, as colleges have responded to a greater market orientation and enterprise culture driven by the funding regime. They have attempted to identify symptoms of poor marketing, including high wastage rates, shortfalls in enrolments, non-viable classes and wasteful duplication of resources. Good marketing practices have been developed, including attempts to establish stronger linkages between marketing, strategy, the curriculum and the management of resources, including personnel.

Quality Control

Since publication of a critical Audit Commission/Ofsted report (1993) on the efficiency of the FECs, there have been steadily increasing demands for systematic quality controls. By the late 1990s there were pressures from FEFC and DfEE for quality control systems to assist auditing and inspection. The Audit Commission recommended that all colleges should record pre-course data about students, rates of completion and non-completion and remedy unsuccessful course outcomes, so reducing waste. FEFC established new funding structures to discourage indiscriminate student recruitment and colleges responded by developing induction, advice and guidance provision. This led some to implement systems drawn directly from the industrial and commercial world, such as BS 5750 and Total Quality Management (TQM). Until the 1992 Act, colleges were inspected, albeit infrequently, by HM Inspectors and LEAs. These have been replaced by an FEFC procedure, akin to OFSTED, with inspections of all aspects of college activity every four years. Inspection visits focus on curriculum areas and college management, resulting in activities being graded. Those grades are taken into account by the FEFC when determining institutional funding.

The Impact on Staff

The real costs of the managerial changes and centrally directed funding regimes have been borne by the sector's labour force. With corporate status, college principals became chief executives (CEs), with wide-ranging responsibilities for finance, staffing, estates, educational planning and student discipline. Well-publicised salary increases for CEs accompanied the new roles but many principals found the pressures hard to cope with. Only one third, who were in post on 1 April 1993, were still there in 1998 (*FE Now*, 1998). Driven by a need to reduce costs, college managements embarked on reorganisations and restructuring involving delayering, staff flexibility and changes in employee terms and conditions of service. New contracts of employment were imposed after staff took industrial action against their employers in 1995. The new contracts are generally less generous in terms of work content, hours and conditions. People brought in on new contracts often have hybrid roles, neither conventional lecturing posts nor support staff, but ones created to manage the introduction of guidance services, curriculum support and the development of learning resources. In addition, new support-staff roles have appeared, including 'para-professional' posts on non-teaching salary grades. Whether such developments are indicative of de-professionalisation of FE teachers is debatable, as the impact of recent changes on core professional practice remains unclear. However, they have resulted in work intensification and removed a lot of custom and practice flexibility, which had characterised FE earlier. College managements, driven by FEFC funding regimes, have introduced employment practices associated with NPM, including staff appraisal, performance-related pay for senior staff, short-term contracts and part-time employment. What have impacted most on professional practice in FE are demands of quality assurance.

The impact of New Labour is being felt most through its policies on *New Deal* (DSS, 1998c) and *The Learning Age* (DfEE, 1998a). The former is requiring an expansion of student numbers and funding for unemployed people choosing to take the education option as a means to employment. The latter is intended to change the composition of boards of governors, increase college links with the community and strengthen the links with TECs. The imposition of student fees, abolition of maintenance grants and transfer of funding from the state to students will inevitably have an effect in the medium to longer term. But the additional funding and massive expansion of adult student members have yet to be assessed.

Higher Education

HE, like the schools and FE, has undergone radical restructuring and a series of intrusive governmental innovations impacting on its provision, funding and management in the last decade. These interventions have resulted in major institutional changes, expanded student numbers, more student choice of courses, competition within and amongst institutions for students and resources, per capita funding and new forms of institutional management. Except for the independent (private) University of Buckingham (founded in 1973), HE is a largely state-funded, centrally driven system, governed by common rules and regulations set down by central government but managed locally. These central rules relate to finance, assessment of teaching quality, assessment of research, and quality assurance. Institutions exhibit some variety in their systems of management but central control is resulting in more standardisation, uniformity and bureaucracy than characterised HE in the 1980s.

Structural Reorganisation

Before 1992 there were 43 independent, chartered universities classified according to the period in which they were created (Farnham, 1999). Relations between these old universities and successive governments were largely consensual, with the Universities Grants Committee (UGC), founded in 1917, playing a key role. The UGC monitored university activities, advised government on university needs and national needs, and had executive responsibility for allocating funds to institutions. In the early 1980s the new Conservative administration scaled down university funding and the UGC responded to government policy by becoming increasingly intrusive in university affairs. In 1989 a new funding body – the University Funding Council (UFC) – was set up as successor to the UGC.

Outside the 'old' university sector, HE took place in a variety of institutions including colleges of HE, FE colleges and polytechnics created post-1966, after the Secretary of State proposed a binary system of 'separate but equal' institutions to the universities. There were 30 polytechnics complemented by some 60 smaller colleges and institutes of higher education (CIHE). All these institutions were under the control of LEAs but after 1979 their funding was transferred to national funding bodies which enabled closer national control. With the establishment of the first national funding body, the National Advisory Board, in 1982 and the Polytechnics and Colleges Funding Council (PCFC) in 1988, government could direct institutions towards particular types of provision and increase their 'efficiency' (Turner and Pratt, 1990). The FHEA 1992 created a new system of HE with the old polytechnics becoming 'new' universities. There is now a unitary hierarchy of over 100 universities, replacing the former status hierarchies. An interim Higher Education Funding Council (HEFC) replaced the UFC and PCFC, but three national HE funding councils, for England, Scotland and Wales subsequently supplanted this. Although there appears to be a single university sector, Trow (1995) suggests that the diversity, which existed prior to 1992, made the emergence of status groupings within the single hierarchy almost inevitable. These status groupings are major research universities, research and teaching universities and teaching universities, with most of the 'old' universities in the first two and the 'new' universities in the latter two groups. Contemporary HE, therefore, is best described as a single system, with institutional and organisational diversity (Farnham and Jones, 1998).

Expansion, Diversity and Choice

HE has been expanding continuously since the 1960s. In 1961–2, there were 203,000 full and part-time students, rising to 1.6 million in 1997, an increase of almost 800 per cent. The participation rate is now about a third of school leavers (NCIHE, 1997) but there is also an increasing number of adults entering at all ages. The reasons for the expansion are a complex mixture of social, economic and political factors, but one key is the widening choice given to students in terms of institutional provision, subject disciplines and geographical spread of courses.

Funding

Universities and HE colleges now receive funding from a variety of public and private sources. The largest proportion of funding comes from the three HEFCs, with another major source being tuition fees. The mission of the HEFC in England is 'to promote high quality, cost-effective teaching and research within a financially healthy education sector, having regard to national needs' (HEFCE, 1996). Funding councils are charged with encouraging institutions to support these aims and ensure effective and efficient use of their funds and assets, deliver VFM, strengthen their managerial capabilities and formulate well-developed strategic plans. In 1996–7, total government funding for teaching and research in England and Wales was £3.1 billion. Of this 70.7 per cent was allocated for teaching, 20.3 per cent for research and 9 per cent for 'other related funding' (HEFC, 1996). Similar proportions underpinned funding in Scotland.

Each year HEFCs advise government on the funding needs of HE but it is the funding councils which are responsible for distributing monies to HE institutions, mainly universities but also to FECs providing HE. As independent, corporate or chartered bodies, universities are free to raise money from other sources – such as research councils, contract research and consultancy services – to add to their revenues. The distributive methodology used by the HEFCs is to allocate funds to each university or college to support teaching, research and related activities as a 'block' grant. HE institutions are free to distribute this grant internally at their discretion, providing funds are used for the purposes for which they are designated. This requires very strict internal accounting and auditing procedures to demonstrate that this has been done.

Between 1988 and 1996, funding the polytechnics/new universities was the same as that described above for the old funding of FECs, namely 'core' and 'demand-led' funding based on capitation fees. McVicar (1996) explains the effect that this had on effectively reducing the unit of resource and forcing colleges into expansion to retain their income. This system was abandoned in 1996 and funding is now based largely on a formula which includes a teaching element (student numbers, linked to price bands) and a research element. Significant funds have been allocated to support special initiatives such as the Poor Estates Initiative, which funds capital works, and grants which are available for IT infrastructure and research laboratories' refurbishment. Efficiency savings, set down at 4 per cent per annum by the Major government, have since been reduced to 2 or 3 per cent. However, higher efficiency saving rates have been imposed on those universities receiving above-average funding per student in particular subjects, whilst lower efficiency savings are sought from universities with low levels of funding per student. In this way the intention is to close the historic gap between high and low levels of funding received by universities for what is seen as broadly the same activity.

Research funding is based upon the Research Assessment Exercise (RAE), which takes place every four years and rates university units of assessment on a scale of one to five, with five attracting the highest funding. The Labour government, anxious to enter into partnership with private research bodies, has set up two new sources of funding. These are the University Challenge Fund (part-funded by government and the Gatsby Foundation) and the Joint Infrastructure Fund (involving government and the Wellcome Foundation). Universities can bid for these funds but only those with four- or five-star rating are likely to succeed. The result of this new competition is likely to reinforce the tendency for a small number of centres of research excellence to emerge.

In England and Wales, with similar arrangements in Scotland, tuition fees from the Department of Education and Science and Welsh Office traditionally funded full-time undergraduates. They were paid to LEAs, which in turn passed them on to universities. Similarly, maintenance grants were channelled via LEAs and paid directly to individual students. These were known collectively as 'mandatory awards' provided out of general taxation. Under the New Labour government, undergraduates are now required to contribute up to £1000 per year towards their own tuition fees on a means-tested basis and, from 1999, all means-tested maintenance awards for students' living expenses will be covered by student loans. HE institutions are having to adapt to this and devise financial procedures for determining what contributions students are required to make and how to collect payments. This is likely to result in shortfalls of cash flow in the transitional period. It also means that HE is being transformed from a collective service and merit good, funded out of general taxation, to a commodity bought by those with independent means or provided selectively to those who have been means-tested.

Internal Management of Universities

The new universities have in some respects found it easier to adapt to NPM and to increased centralisation within HE, because LEAs formerly administered them. On the other hand, the transition to independence has been difficult, because they lacked experience of personnel management, marketing, and estate management. Further, 'independence [meant] providing a range of financial services, previously provided by the LEA, including payroll, debt collection, internal and external audit, and banking' (McVicar, 1996: 235). Rapid growth of student numbers has also posed problems of providing buildings, equipment, staff and student accommodation. Furthermore, institutions were under external pressure from central government to develop management systems and techniques imported from the private sector, including new strategic, financial, accounting and performance systems, alongside quality assurance procedures and human resources initiatives. The latter include performance pay for 'middle managers' and staff appraisal. Although diversity exists in the internal governance and management of universities, reflecting their different histories, traditions and practices (Jarrett, 1985; Collins, 1994), some convergence is emerging.

Both 'old' and 'new' universities have spawned management structures reflecting traditional management functions such as finance, marketing, personnel, estates and 'production' (or academic affairs), and new functions such as quality assurance. Increasingly universities also have separate international and research departments and business units dealing with contracting and consultancy work, which is a growing source of income. There are major differences, however, at top management level. Old universities generally have a vice-chancellor supported by two or three pro-vice-chancellors, appointed for limited periods. Administrative support reports through a secretary or secretary and registrar, who in consequence is a major figure in university management. New universities, recognising the need for stability in service management, have generally opted for a vice-chancellor and two or three pro-vice-chancellors, each of whom has a line management responsibility for a part of the university's activities and associated support functions. Each functional department is headed by a manager and staffed by administrative and technical personnel. Most management practices have been copied from private businesses, as universities are expected to demonstrate increased efficiency, VFM and meeting student demands. Externally imposed PIs and the requirements of the Audit Commission have also driven the introduction of management information systems, which facilitate increased centralisation and control.

Below top management, structures vary but one pattern is for academic departments or schools to be grouped together into faculties headed by deans and faculty offices. In some universities, departments or schools, in turn, are run by heads, responsible for budgets and staffing, with deputies responsible for research and programmes of study. These may be appointed posts, either permanent or fixed-term, and attract head-of-department salaries. Where there is extensive delegation to faculties, they replicate the centre and have their own registrars, personnel, finance officers and marketing units. This has resulted in a major growth in managerial and administrative staff, which now often exceed numbers of academics per institution.

In new universities, there has been a reduction of the power of academics in decision-making. Although institutions still have academic councils and representation of academic staff on boards of governors and faculty executives, their role is limited. Academic councils, restricted to 40 in size, cannot take decisions on resources, only on academic policy. Since academic development and resources cannot be easily separated, academic decisions are severely constrained. At best academics are consulted but in many cases simply informed of decisions already taken. Old universities have more powerful academic senates, with a veto over resource and academic initiatives. However their large size, sometimes in hundreds, makes them unwieldy and their power is dispersed through committees.

Throughout HE, mass education is resulting in the replacement of relatively flexible, decentralised systems of delivery by highly bureaucratic, standardised systems, characterised by modularisation, unitisation and a loss of control by academics in favour of managers and administrators. The latest emphasis is on quality assurance, with all universities moving to standard systems for demonstrating internal monitoring of quality and providing the basis for PIs of student satisfaction and accountability to the market, as league tables of universities provide potential consumers with powerful information.

Impact on Staff

All universities and CHEs are employers of their academic staff. Pre-1988, LEA-controlled HE institutions were dominated by bureaucratic rules and procedures emanating from central government decisions and national collective bargaining (NCB). Old universities had more autonomy but were also involved in NCB. Staff in each sector were highly diverse, consisting of academic and research staff, administrative, clerical and support staffs, manual workers and a wide range of technical staffs. As in school teaching and FE, union membership was high, with different unions representing staff in the two sectors, but the major ones were the Association of University Teachers (AUT) and the National Association of Teachers in Further and Higher Education (NATFHE) for academics, and UNISON, MSF and TGWU for non-academics. In both sectors pay and grading structures were determined through collective bargaining and there was little freedom for employers to deviate from the national schemes.

Since 1988 there have been significant changes. New employment contracts in new universities released employers from earlier rigid, collective agreements, as almost all staff accepted the financial incentives offered to sign the new contracts. Part of the new contract involves the commitment of staff to participate in staff appraisal and development, which provide a basis for performance management. Both old and new universities have also sought some pay and numerical flexibility, through employing more temporary staff on short-term contracts and part-time hourly paid staff. Although these forms of flexibility have mainly affected academic and research staff, support staff have not been exempt (Farnham, 1999). CCT is extensively used in catering, maintenance, printing and other support services, with the result that staff conditions of service and pay deteriorate. Senior academic and managerial staff have been taken out of NCB and are on individual contracts and PRP (Farnham and Giles, 1995b).

One major improvement has been in training and staff development. Almost all universities now have staff development officers and educational development units. Development encompasses teaching, research, IT and management skills, with particular emphasis on the latter (Whitchurch, 1994). New systems of staff appraisal are linked to staff development, although there are still wide variations amongst universities as to how rigorously these are implemented and monitored (Farnham and Giles, 1996a).

Finally, there have been determined attempts at implementing equal opportunities policies to redress the imbalance in representation of women and ethnic minorities in academic and managerial hierarchies. Although there is some evidence of improvement, women and ethnic minorities are still the exception at the top of institutional structures.

Conclusion

The past decade has witnessed fundamental changes in the provision, funding and management of education in all sectors in the UK. Schools have had to adapt to the needs of the National Curriculum, LMS and inspections by OFSTED. The FE sector is currently in transition and still experiencing considerable change, with a new funding regime, the shift to market provision and new systems of institutional management. In universities too, the traditional autonomy of the teaching profession is being penetrated by ever-higher staff–student ratios, continued financial stringencies and endemic managerialism within institutions. The era of massification, which policy makers believe needs to be 'managed' better and more efficiently, has resulted in what Trow (1995) calls the adoption and adaption of American elements in the system. Many of the features of HE in the United States (Horton, 1999) are certainly evident now in the UK. Semesterisation, modularisation, credit accumulation, interrupted study patterns, self-funding, cafeteria-option choices, flexible academic workforces and limited tenure are all present. There is a clear trend towards an educational marketplace and growing partnerships between private business, educational foundations and universities.

Throughout the 1980s and 1990s educators were not really trusted by their political masters. Consequently, politicians and others argued that they (teachers and educators) and the institutions in which they work, need managing by professional accountable managers to make sure that staff carry out their specialist roles efficiently and effectively, within the parameters established by institutional management. Rear (1994: 151), for example, argues that the new managerialism in the universities has been prompted by their past reluctance to change and serve the economy, as well as by their reluctance in the past to give an account of their stewardship of vast sums of taxpayers money. He concludes that: 'the economic viability of universities and the retention of their institutional autonomy depends upon effective management.'

The high profile given to education by New Labour, and the spate of recent legislation and policy documents, promises further change. However, there does not appear to be any sea change in direction. On the one hand, it is putting more money into schooling and is committed to reforming the teaching profession and creating a partnership between major education stakeholders. There is a slight reinstatement of the LEAs, which are intended to be lead agencies in developing partnerships within local communities. On the other hand, there is increased centralisation, reinforcement of performance management, PRP to reward super teachers, increased emphasis on training managers and heads, retention of PIs and an enhanced role for OFSTED. Labour is also continuing with many of the policies of their predecessors in FE and HE, including shifting the cost towards the market and, at the same time, tightening central control over funding and quality. Although *The Learning Age* green paper and substantial increases in funding for FE indicate that New Labour has more of a commitment to the sector than earlier administrations, there is a danger of strategic drift, as the sector accommodates to massive expansion of diverse students.

HE has not, as yet, received the same attention as schools and FE, apart from the introduction of fees, already in the pipeline. There has been a slight relaxation on pressure to reduce the unit of resource, although efficiency savings are still built into funding each year. Government is likely to accept the anticipated recommendations of the Betts Review on pay in HE. One possibility is to take teaching staff out of NCB and appoint a pay review body, as the Conservatives did with school teachers. If that happens FE might follow. There seems, therefore, to be no going back, and the legacy of 18 years of Conservative government is safe in Labours hands, even though there are more students and more money in the system.

13

Managing the Police

BARRY LOVEDAY

For the police service, the period 1979 to1987 was one of mixed blessings. Lauded by Mrs Thatcher as a central plank in her government's 'law and order' strategy in the early years, the service was to be ultimately castigated by senior Conservative ministers for letting them down on the crime problem (Baker, 1992). The period demonstrated how difficult it is to take policing out of politics, particularly with a government which moved away from mainstream consensus policy. The increasingly radical programmes adopted by the Conservative government were ultimately to lead to a direct confrontation with the police service upon which it had earlier depended so heavily. But if the Conservative government's political programme inevitably engulfed the police service, it was also the case that management reforms encouraged across the public sector would also impact upon the police. Management reforms, initiated as early as 1983, have now comprehensively embraced the police service. This is because Audit Commission reports, along with statutory reform, have required the police to respond positively to new managerial imperatives. The application of performance measures is now accepted as commonplace in the police service, while senior officers now grapple with costing outputs and outcomes of police activity. If in the past the police service was 'administered' rather than managed, this has changed and it is increasingly appropriate to refer to police management as a meaningful activity.

The Legacy of Conservative Reforms

The move away from administration to resource management was sustained by the Conservative government's commitment to devolved budgeting, which gives chief officers immediate responsibility for resource allocation, and is considered in more detail later. It is the case, however, that the Police and Magistrates Courts Act (PMCA) 1994 has, perhaps more than any other police legislation, served to emphasise the new 'chief executive' role, which the Conservative government was determined to give chief officers of police. A number of police reforms can also be traced back to the Sheehy Inquiry into *Police Rewards and Responsibilities* (Sheehy, 1993). Although the reaction of police associations to the Sheehy report proved to be swift and effective (Savage and Leishman, 1994) it remains the case that many recommendations of that report continue to 'drip feed' into current policing arrangements. Almost all officers of ACPO (Association of Chief Police Officers) rank are now subject to fixed-term contracts of employment. Management structures are, at least in some police forces, in the process of adjustment to reduce costs by slimming down often top-heavy management bureaucracies (West Midlands, 1997). The influential Home Affairs Report (House of Commons, 1997) on police discipline and complaints has led to significant reform of the labyrinthine protections offered to errant police officers. Effective dismissal procedures for officers who break their trust will be given to chief officers, which will for the very first time enable them to act as real managers in the service (see below).

Nor has Sheehy's interest in performance proved to be a temporary phenomenon. While performance related pay (PRP) was ultimately abandoned, the movement toward individual performance review has been sustained and remains a matter of continuing interest for chief officers. Regular use of activity analysis (considered as recently as 1984 by many police forces as an unnecessary waste) continues to provide current chief officers with a better picture of police activity than their immediate predecessors ever enjoyed. Absence of effective oversight along with paper supervision of officers had traditionally meant that policing on the ground was as much a mystery to chief officers as it was to anyone else. Traditionally, use of comparative police force data by reference to 'families of forces' (that is, those which exhibit similar socio-economic and demographic features) provides opportunities for identifying good practice. Since annual performance data, produced by the Audit Commission, is publicly available, it is now possible for police authorities to assess the relative efficiency of their police forces (Audit Commission, 1997).

Although the Conservative inheritance was to be significant in terms of managerialism in the police service, it was also the case that spending on the police had reached new heights. The White Paper *Protecting the Public* (Home Office, 1996a) stated that over a 17-year period spending on police had increased by 98 per cent in real terms (see Figure 13.1) The increase in spending had provided 15,000 more police officers and 17,000 more civilian support staff. In 1996–7 £6.6 billion was made available for policing in England and Wales. It seemed that in spite of the government's commitment to reducing public expenditure, and requiring all parts of the public sector to find economies, the police were the exception to the rule. Although Kenneth Clarke as Home Secretary in 1992 was committed to greater efficiency, his successor, Michael Howard, is claimed to have almost automatically accepted all police requests regarding equipment, new powers and increased

FIGURE 13.1 *Expenditure on the police service in England and Wales, 1978–9 to 1996–7*

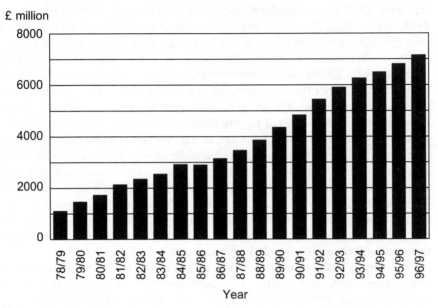

Notes:
(1) Includes current, capital and central government expenditure on the police.
(2) 1995/96 and 1996/97 figures are estimates.

establishments. Prior to the 1997 General Election the then Prime Minister, John Major, committed government to increasing police numbers further by recruiting an additional 5000 police officers. Clearly the demands of national politics, particularly at election times, placed the earlier emphases on efficiency gains on a much lower pedestal. Certainly Michael Howard as Home Secretary appeared to defer to police requests for increased resources in pursuit of what became an overt crime-control policy based on arrest and incarceration of offenders.

Policing Structures

The development of policing strategies has continued to be influenced by successive Audit Commission reports. These 'Police Papers', directed at a range of police activities, have embraced management structures, the role of the police in dealing with crime, and improving police effectiveness. One long-term trend within all police forces following Audit Commission re-commendations has been a commitment to de-tiering in order to reduce bureaucratic hierarchies, whilst also establishing boundaries which are coterminous with those of local authorities. Divisional and sub-divisional structures have now been universally replaced by basic or basic command units (BCUs) to which officers of superintendent rank have been appointed, replacing chief superintendents, a rank itself eliminated by legislation in 1994. More streamlined policing units, it is expected, will facilitate better internal communication while also rationalising internal police organisation.

The earlier commitment to hierarchy, where seven ranks exercised responsibilities above that of the operational constable, had in the recent past generated an expensive 'on-cost' which the Audit Commission considered could pay for an additional 1200 operational police officers (Audit Commission, 1989b). De-tiering has therefore involved many police forces, particularly larger metropolitan ones, in management 'downsizing' as fewer and larger police units have superseded older divisional and sub-divisional structures. This, together with flattening management hierarchies, has reduced the number of officers required at middle and senior management level. As the Chief Constable (CC) of West Midlands Police reported (West Midlands, 1997:5): 'Continuing devolution of decision-making and the recognition that local policing should be locally delivered has reduced the need for superintendents and chief inspectors.'

De-layering has been identified as a means of increasing policing outputs with limited additional inputs. This, taken together with decentralisation of decision-making and devolved budgets, is intended to ensure that decision-making takes place much closer to the community policed than in the past. It is also a further recognition that the large and anonymous police bureaucracies created by successive police force amalgamations in the 1960s and 1970s only served to remove the police from the community, while reducing overall police effectiveness (Loveday, 1998). Speculation continues, however, as to whether continuing decentralisation of police provision may allow for further amalgamations to create regional police forces.

As originally planned the BCUs, which replaced divisions and sub-divisions, were seen by the Home Office as building blocks, which could be effectively managed by a much-reduced number of police headquarters staff. Certainly in his original plans for police re-organisation, Kenneth Clarke was to indicate that his plans included reduction in the number of police forces from 43 to around 20. Any plans for further police amalgamations would, however, have to assimilate the lessons recently learned from the debacle of the Crown Prosecution Service (CPS). As the Glidewell report (1998) was to note, reduction of CPS areas from 34 to 11 regions, along with the centralisation encouraged by this development, had undermined the effectiveness of the service by fatally weakening local associations and accountability. One consequence of this has been the public commitment by New Labour to establishing a new regionalised CPS, where its boundaries are made coterminous with those of local police forces. This commitment may only reflect a current interest in 'joined-up government' which seeks to establish coterminous boundaries for most criminal justice agencies across the country. The drive to establish coterminous boundaries will also be reinforced by recent legislation, particularly the Crime and Disorder Act (1998), which encourages development of partnership and effective inter-agency agreements between services.

The Impact of Police Reform

The PMCA 1994 radically altered the role and function of police authorities (PAs), whilst also giving both the Home Secretary and CCs new responsibilities. Under the Act, it could be argued, managerial accountability effectively replaced electoral accountability as a means of improving police effectiveness and performance. Total membership of the new PAs was reduced to 17, which since 1994 have included five independent members and also three magistrates, with elected members now contributing just half of the total membership of each PA. These are indirectly elected to the local PA, being selected from constituent districts or the county councils. Inevitably, therefore, even for elected members, PA business may be seen as only incidental to their interests, which will be much more locally focused. In justifying this reform, the Conservative government claimed that smaller PAs would be much more 'businesslike' and better able to identify policing strategies and monitor performance. The local PA has responsibility for developing local policing plans and for identifying local objectives and targets. Identification of local objectives results, at least in part, from a further responsibility given to the PA, which is to sustain and develop community liaison bodies to channel local views and opinions concerning police priorities to the PA and thus into the police planning process.

Community consultation was a new required element in the managerial and planning process within police forces. It was intended to compensate for the greatly reduced representativeness of the new PAs by engaging wide sections of the community in the policy and decision-making process. The decision to reduce the size of the new PAs was defended by reference to the high salience that would be given to identifying community priorities and interests through community consultation. Established police community liaison arrangements were expected to provide an effective source of information to assist PAs in identifying local police objectives for the policing plan. Some commentators, supporting the development, argued that every police authority would be obliged to produce annual prospective policing plans which must, *inter alia*, consider any views obtained from the police community consultative committees, established under Section 106 of the Police and Criminal Evidence Act. As Morgan and Newburn (1997:148) argue:

> These new responsibilities may. . . serve to stimulate greater commitment on the part of the police authorities to the process of formulating local policing policies than their predecessors ever demonstrated.

The optimism exhibited by those supporting the statutory reform of PAs may, however, have proved to be misplaced. Evidence suggests that police community consultative committees, as a mechanism for identifying community views, have proved to be highly problematic and have failed to match up to expectations (HMIC, 1997a, 1997b, 1997c).

Nevertheless PAs have an immediate responsibility for channelling community views into PA deliberations by way of police community liaison committees. Thereafter, having agreed the policing plan, the primary function of the PA has become one of monitoring performance of the police force. If the strategic function of the PA has been enhanced, this has been achieved at some cost, however. PAs are no longer responsible for civilian staff, buildings, equipment or maintenance. While in theory they are responsible for resource management issues, day-to-day responsibility for the budget now resides with the CC. In what has proved to be an interesting example of devolved budgeting arrangements, the CC is now the effective budget holder, not the PA. CCs are also statutorily responsible for the immediate drafting of the local policing plan, not the PA. Additionally, identification of objectives for the plan now encompass national policing objectives set by the Home Secretary.

Early concern that the new powers given to the Home Secretary would inevitably centralise the policing function may have been misplaced (Loveday, 1994; Newburn and Jones, 1997). To date, the national objectives set for the police prove to be of such a general nature as to be easily assimilated into the local policing plan. Determination of targets for both local and national objectives have, however, become highly performance-orientated. In what has proved to be an interesting if unforeseen development, the 'new configuration of accountability' has emphasised the CC's role by making that officer, as budget-holder, the effective purchaser and provider of police services. While the CC must account for overall resource allocation to the PA, day-to-day finance decision-making falls almost entirely to that officer. Following the requirement of PAs to devolve budgets, most police forces now employ their own civilian accountants and/or finance managers. These officers are of course directly responsible to the CC, not the PA. As Loveday (1998) identifies, delegation of responsibility for finance has now led to the accumulation of powers to the CC which are collectively highly significant. The CC is now responsible for the operational control of the force, for all police and civilian personnel, buildings, vehicles and estates, in addition to being budget-holder for the police force.

Strategy and Planning

The development of managerialism within police forces has encouraged the creation of new executive bodies made responsible for planning and performance issues. In Merseyside the CC's team is identified as the 'Board of Directors' and consists of five chief and assistant chief officers and two civilian counterparts. Each director takes functional responsibility for key strategic areas of the force (HMIC, 1997c). In Warwickshire the director's team is made up of three chief officers, a director of finance and the CC who, as strategic director, is made immediately responsible for the public relations team (HMIC, 1997f). Elsewhere, the planning process is overseen by the Force Executive which consists of assistant chief officers and also the director of finance (HMIC, 1998h).

The introduction of Strategic Directors' teams or Force Executives reflects the high salience now given by senior police officers to strategic planning. Forces now develop corporate plans which, by encapsulating all force plans, provide the 'unifying statement' of force objectives. Interestingly, the strategic plan can usually be expected to encompass the local policing plan by identifying the overall aims and direction of force policy. The emphasis placed on strategic planning demonstrates the importance of internal police planning as opposed to PA planning. One consistent feature of the new managerial planning process, encouraged by HMIC, is the emphasis placed on self-generated strategies initiated internally and formulated by police managers for annual planning purposes. Police-initiated and police-led, the annual planning cycle is heavily dependent on information provided by the police force. This is perhaps inevitable, as the PA has no independent source of information and consists of part-time members. As the CC retains statutory responsibility for drafting the police plan, it is certain to be subsumed within the strategic plans generated by his/her officers. Given the significant resource advantages enjoyed by the CC, it was predictable that planning processes would be monopolised by the police, and generated internally. The CC's budgetary control only further emphasises the degree to which these officers constitute the primary group in police planning processes. While the PA may officially set the budget, thereafter devolved budgeting removes from the authority any effective responsibility for resource allocation.

The central role of the police in managing the planning process is illustrated by the following description of the planning process (HMIC, 1998h: 7):

> The planning process commences in July of each year when divisional commanders and departmental heads prepare their contributions to the senior management seminar held in September each year. Following the seminar each division and department will be notified of the goals for the forthcoming year and will convene unit/shift workshops to take place in February when planning activity will be initiated. The process is closely linked to the budgetary process.

In Northumbria, a qualified accountant has been appointed as director of finance. He reports to the monthly chief officers' policy group and is able to 'exert influence on decision-making' (HMIC, 1997e), whilst the PA treasurer only attends the same meetings 'on a quarterly basis'.

A continuing problem remains the degree to which the PA and the public are involved in the development of the annual policing plan and planning processes generally. HMIC recommended that the planning process should ensure that members of the PA, external focus groups and members of the force are actively involved (HMIC, 1998g). Absence of communication, along with the content of the plans, may also explain HMIC's discovery that there was little evidence that plans were being read by operational constables, even though the objectives were 'well understood by their supervisors' (HMIC, 1998g: 5). HMIC also found that there was little evidence of 'junior staff' being actively consulted in the police planning process (HMIC, 1998e). The issue of internal consultation in the development of policing plans may indeed assume a greater salience than that of external consultation. As reports from HMIC regularly demonstrate, the organisational culture based on clear hierarchic relationships continues to exert a singular influence over managerial initiatives in some forces. While HMIC noted in North Yorkshire that 'front line officers' were aware of the service plan, he considered that its impact on their operational activities 'was somewhat limited' (HMIC, 1997d). Elsewhere, HMIC has found that failure in internal communications meant that staff 'particularly those on the front line could have been better informed about major force issues' (HMIC, 1997f). In South Wales, HMIC 'found very little perception of having been consulted amongst those spoken to at the level of service delivery' and was of the view, in relation to internal consultation, that there had to be 'a major change in managerial attitude to service deliverers' (HMIC, 1997f: 8). In Kent Constabulary, HMIC noted that a decision had been made not to introduce a staff suggestion scheme on the grounds that 'the value of the suggestions made would be unlikely to justify the expense' (HMIC, 1998e).

Evidence collected by HMIC suggests that junior officers, as immediate service deliverers, may only rarely be involved in developing policing plans and only rarely consulted in their preparation. Their exclusion from this management process is reinforced by the frequent failure by senior management to communicate to them thereafter. This is surprising, since senior management depend entirely on those officers for successful implementation of their strategies. In the absence of effective communication, the planning process might become little more than an elaborate bureaucratic exercise that fails to influence policing on the ground. The introduction of managerialism, therefore, appears in a number of police forces to be a top-down process reflecting a strong hierarchic, organisational culture. This is perhaps best summed up by HMIC's reference to a planning process which 'illustrated an historic culture instilling compliance at a junior level rather than active participation' (HMIC, 1998c).

Devolved Budgeting

One critical test of the application of new management processes within police forces is the extent to which budgets have been devolved. As noted earlier, commitment to devolved budgeting, making the CC the budget holder, was planned to correspond with further devolution to service deliverers. The principle that decision-making on finance was best made closest to the public, by those immediately responsible for delivery of service, meant that CCs could be expected to relinquish immediate responsibility for budgets, which would be devolved to heads of department and BCUs. The degree to which devolution of budgets has been achieved presents a mixed picture. In some forces there is clear evidence of a movement towards devolution. In West Mercia, for example, of the £106 million budget, £84 million had been devolved and was divided between its six operational divisions and two central departments (HMIC, 1998h). In others however, such as the West Midlands, in 1997 officers were not permitted to spend more than £50 on any service or item without going through the central purchasing department. This has since been raised to £500 (HMIC, 1997g). Although there are some examples of good practice many forces have failed to implement devolution as requested.

In Greater Manchester, where 'Local Financial Management' (LFM) has been introduced, staffing levels and salary budgets are still established by central decisions. As HMIC have argued, areas of expenditure which are actually devolved to divisions by LFM are small, given that neither police nor civilian staff salaries are included (HMIC, 1997b). In Warwickshire, whilst the budget is 'fully devolved to areas and support teams, it excludes police officers' pay and allowances and certain elements of the vehicle fleet budget' (HMIC, 1997f: 13). In Dorset, 'with the significant exception of police pay', most of the budget is devolved to divisions and departments (HMIC, 1998a: 21). In South Wales LFM is restricted to costs for overtime, support staff, premises, repairs and decorations, and does not include police or civilian pay (HMIC, 1998 :13). In Hampshire, HMIC found a very cautious approach to the devolution of budgeting control and management to divisional and departmental heads 'with only small areas of finance released to local control'. There was limited enthusiasm amongst middle managers for LFM, which may have arisen from the perceived inadequacy of support systems, training and staffing (HMIC, 1998d: 34).

Internal devolution of budgets provides a distinct contrast to the devolved budget arrangements between PAs and CCs. While delegation of budget holding has been universally implemented at chief officer level, devolution within police forces has proved to be problematical. The 'power of the purse' in most police forces now effectively lies with the CC rather than the PA service deliverers. As Oliver (1996: 618) states:

> After 1994 a greater emphasis was placed on giving the Chief Constable more control of the budget so that it would be possible to unite operational priorities to the capacity to spend money in a way that appears to be more appropriate to the management of the force.

The significance of the change in responsibility for the budget is immediately apparent. As one former CC was to argue in relation to his own PA (Alderson, 1984: 111):

> The Chief Constable held most of the cards and only the budget control prevented this power becoming autonomous. At least in my own experience. The budget was the only issue upon which I was seriously challenged.

The power position of the CC has become more salient, therefore, where devolved budgeting fails to percolate down to service-delivery level. Even where such devolution is achieved, the position of the CC, already independently responsible for all operational policing matters, must be enhanced as statutory responsibilities and planning policies remain centrally driven and centrally controlled.

Where LFM has occurred, it would appear that the benefits of decision-making made by those who deliver police services are clear. Devolved budgeting, other than providing a useful VFM initiative, establishes greater sensitivity in terms of service provision to local need and may be more responsive to local requirements than a central bureaucracy is ever likely to be. A strong residual resistance to surrendering the budget suggests that organisational cultures and traditional hierarchical concepts continue to exercise a major influence within a number of police forces.

Performance Review

Every police force now operates within a clearly defined system of PIs designed to measure individual police performance and provide comparative performance data. The police service now works to a set of PIs which provide a comprehensive cover of police activities. These are devised by HMIC, the Audit Commission and ACPO, and enable senior managers to assess individual performance, whilst also providing a means of assessing police efficiency and overall effectiveness. With the absolute decline in electoral accountability, occasioned by the PMCA 1994, performance evaluation is now seen as a primary method of delivering managerial accountability for police services. A matrix of PIs, devised by HMIC and first used in 1986, enables both the Inspectorate and CCs to make comparisons between families of forces (Carter *et al.*,1992). The matrix, consisting of 435 PIs, relates to a number of functional categories and includes manpower deployment, organisational structures, crime detection, community relations, crime prevention and complaints. HMIC reports provide detailed evaluations of individual police performance and offer a valuable insight into policing activity at force level. Most reports range in terms of performance analysis from core management to management of financial and human resources, operational deployment, performance review and information technology and communications.

A detailed analysis of performance review cannot be attempted here, but one interesting example pertains to crime management. Here, HMIC (and the Audit Commission) have demonstrated commitment to improving detections by primary means. Primary detections are those which generally follow some significant police investigation and are distinguished from secondary detections, which are usually achieved by way of admissions by convicted prisoners during the course of prison visits conducted by police officers. Secondary detection, achieved traditionally by Criminal Investigation Departments, has been one way of artificially boosting crime clearance but may have achieved next to nothing in terms of effective crime fighting. HMIC have continued to pursue those forces which have a propensity to use secondary clearance.

In its 1997 report on West Midlands Police, HMIC noted that the percentage of detections achieved through post-sentence visits by police officers in 1995–6 was 45.7 per cent, which was 'significantly higher than the provincial average'. HMIC also expressed concern about standards of post-sentence visit files generated by secondary clearance (HMIC, 1997g: 41). HMIC noted that the apparently good overall clear-up rate in South Wales was also due to the high proportion of secondary clear-ups, 'the second highest reliance on secondary clear-up rates through prison visits in England and Wales (HMIC, 1998g: 29). The Inspectorate also expressed concern over post-sentence visits made by police, the quality of interviews, their lack of focus on intelligence-gathering and the high overall level of resources applied to this activity. Their concern was reinforced because local intelligence officers, to whom the Inspectorate spoke, stated that they rarely received useful intelligence as a result of prison visits. HMIC urged:

> Stricter supervision to ensure the primary purpose of interviews with convicted prisoners is intelligence-gathering rather than clearing up old crimes, in a way that distorts overall performance against crime. (HMIC, 1997f : 30)

One consequence of measuring performance in relation to national PIs is the pressure which this may induce artificially to boost statistics by use of secondary clearance. Commitment to ethical recording of crime may also be compromised, as police forces seek to achieve the targets set for them by central government. Incorrect classification of recorded crime can be one means of achieving crime-reduction targets. As HMIC found in one force, while systems were in place to ensure crime was recorded accurately and consistently, 'a recent audit found a significant number of incorrect classifications' (HMIC, 1997f : 31). In another force HMIC recommended that the force ensure 'accurate recording of crime and the proper conduct of post-sentence visits by urgently introducing new procedures with rigorous supervision and audit processes' (HMIC, 1997g: 41). In response to this, CCs have been encouraged to target primary detections. Unfortunately, such a change in emphasis is likely to lead to a fall in detection rates as the relatively easily gained clearance from prison visits is replaced by the more difficult strategy of investigating and detecting crime as it occurs. Yet one CC has argued, increasing the 'more-difficult-to-achieve primary detections' whilst reducing secondary detections has demonstrated that 'targeted effort can lift levels of genuine performance' (West Midlands, 1997: 6).

Performance Culture

Underlying the approach encouraged by the Audit Commission, HMIC and the Home Office is a strong commitment to a performance culture within police forces which is expected to improve police-service efficiency and effectiveness. There is an implicit assumption that a culture of performance can itself be identified, encouraged and measured. A commitment to performance culture, for example, has been identified by HMIC as an explanation for the fall in recorded crime and rise in detections (HMIC, 1998h: 2):

> Performance culture is having an impact. Recorded crime has fallen again by 2.4% following a significant reduction the year before. The detection rate is a very creditable 34.6% and of some encouragement is a more direct focus on primary detections.

HMIC has applauded the impact of performance culture on crime detection, commenting for example on Dyfed Powys's exceptional performance in the detection of crime. The Inspectorate noted that a number of factors contributed towards this, including 'geographical location, pride in the results achieved and a "performance culture at all levels"' (HMIC, 1998b). The eulogy accorded to performance culture unfortunately appeared to ignore the national trend in recorded crime, which in 1997 fell by 9 per cent across England and Wales and appeared to have more to do with the business cycle than individual police performance (Travis, 1998).

If performance culture remains problematic, quality assurance issues have become more important within the police service. Most police forces are now engaged in the use of customer-satisfaction and public-attitude surveys across a range of activities. These seek to identify the views of members of the public who have been in contact with the police. Quality assurance has become a significant factor in contemporary police management and police forces are increasingly involved in providing local surveys carried out periodically to assess the value of specific policing projects. Although community consultation has proved difficult to sustain, many police force commanders have found that public meetings held to address specific issues can yield useful outcomes (HMIC, 1997f).

In addition to quality assurance, police forces are also committed to regular application of activity analysis, whose value is becoming more apparent with devolved budgets and the need to link financial and operational decision-making. Activity analysis is also now 'recognised as having a key role to play in the development of a sound performance culture by better informing managers about which outcomes are attributable to certain activities' (HMIC, 1998a). Information gained by activity analysis has increasingly been used to determine resource allocation and identification of priorities within the local policing plan. It may also form a major element in the allocation of personnel. This relatively sophisticated approach to any future allocation of resources by police managers is linked to the increasing pressure placed on police forces to 'cost' policing activity and identify, where possible, the cost of both outputs and outcomes. HMIC has predicted that 'the next step is to develop accountabilities for results, i.e. outputs and outcomes, as it is only by holding managers and supervisors to account for performance that real ownership and improvement will occur' (HMIC, 1998a: 20). Increasingly, processes holding divisional and departmental commanders accountable to CCs for the performance of their staff will involve the application of activity-analysis reports. These developments represent a significant change from earlier police service provision and supervision. Where local commanders have control of the budget and are made accountable for local policing by costing activities, high levels of local accountability can be expected.

Partnership

One major development which will increasingly engage police managers is the Crime and Disorder Act 1998. Under the Act, a new emphasis in crime fighting will be placed on partnership arrangements with other agencies engaged in reducing crime. The legislation effectively implements the recommendations of the Morgan Report on Safer Communities (Morgan, 1991) and reflects the view that the police service can only control crime by working effectively with other agencies. Inter-agency arrangements will be a major element of this initiative, particularly in relation to youth crime, where new Youth Offender Teams, comprised of youth justice workers, probation, education, health and police officers, will target young offenders with the aim of changing their behaviour rather than processing them through the criminal justice system.

Although much of the Act pertains to youth justice, the new statutory responsibility given to local authorities for crime reduction programmes has led to the creation of Chief Officer teams consisting of Chief Executives and CCs based on local authority boundaries. These are jointly responsible for developing crime prevention strategies. Joint police and local authority responsibility for crime audits (conducted triennially) will allow local communities to help determine local priorities, which are expected to feed into the local policing plan. Already in many forces community safety partnerships have been developed between the police and local authorities as it is recognised that joint local authority and police strategies may prove to be more successful in crime reduction than any unilateral action taken by the police alone. The Act represents one facet of the Labour government's commitment to 'joined-up government' in requiring local agencies to work together to achieve crime reduction targets. It is also exerting further pressure to establish coterminous boundaries between agencies. As the partnership arrangements develop, it will become increasingly necessary to develop joint PIs as the police work in close conjunction with other agencies. Joint performance measures have, of course, already been established with the Joint Performance Management initiative for police forces and the CPS (Home Office, 1996b). Nevertheless, the Crime and Disorder Act marks a new departure for the police service as it is now statutorily tied to local authorities in terms of crime reduction and crime prevention strategies. For the first time all local agencies and not just the police, are required to develop and monitor crime reduction programmes which are likely to be subject to new and national performance measurement.

Managing People

The traditional system of people management within the police service slowly changed during the late 1980s and 1990s as it was subject to the same NPM pressures as other public services (Horton, 1996a). There was resistance, however, and in the late 1990s the service still bears some hallmarks of the traditional hierarchical rank structure, with a rule-bound and male-dominated culture. The high priority given to law and order by Conservative governments ensured there was no contraction of staffing, and numbers of police officers and civilian staff increased throughout the period (see above). Pay also rose consistently above the national average, although there were lower increases in the latter years. Furthermore, police authorities were not subjected to the same rigorous VFM regimes as other services. Although New Labour has not reversed this trend it is clearly committed to improving performance, and required the police to achieve two per cent efficiency savings over the year 1998–9. This may send a signal to police of what is to come.

Attempts by the Sheehy report (1993) to introduce quite dramatic changes in personnel policy were met with strong opposition from the police staff associations and government backed down. However, the proposals are slowly being adopted. A major change in personnel management came with the PMCA 1994 when the roles of the Home Office, PAs and CCs changed. The Home Office no longer sets down establishment figures for each police force and although responsible for overall police efficiency and effectiveness, its role is now more strategic and less interventionist. PAs are responsible for securing the maintenance of efficient and effective police forces but their most important personnel/human resources role is appointing the CC, who is now the professional manager and leader of the police force. The CC has overall responsibility for the deployment, direction and control of all staff and is the *de facto* employer of uniformed police officers.

Personnel departments, within individual forces, have expanded and are staffed increasingly by civilians with professional qualifications. The head of personnel is in most cases a member of the top management team, whether a uniformed rank or a civilian. In many police forces people management responsibilities have been devolved to divisions or BCUs, each of which has its own personnel section staffed primarily by civilians. Headquarters has a strategic role and develops people management systems, provides guidance and advice and monitors and evaluates outputs with local units implementing policies. Devolved personnel responsibilities are constrained, however, by the extent of devolved budgeting (see above).

There is a growing convergence between police officers and civilian staff, who are now in the ratio of 2:1, and police forces are seeking to harmonise terms and conditions. There are moves to encourage PAs to adopt local bargaining structures for both and to narrow differentials between civilian and police pay, especially at senior levels. Pay is still centrally determined through the Police Joint Negotiating Board and a Whitley council for white-collar staff (Horton, 1996a). Although civilianisation has transformed the composition of personnel within police forces and is likely to continue, the practice of outsourcing may deplete the numbers of civilian employees. This practice is already well advanced in the Metropolitan Police, which has contracted out the management of payroll and pensions.

Training has continued to receive priority throughout the 1990s after the appointment of a National Director of Training in 1993 (Home Office, 1993). Over 70 per cent of training is set down nationally and 30 per cent is determined locally. Training is provided by the National Police College at Bramshill, eight regional centres and 43 local force training units. Many forces have market-tested their training and there is condiderable outsourcing to private training consultants and training centres. Some of the more progressive forces are registered for Investors in People status, for example Nottinghamshire. There has been much criticism of the insular nature of police training, however, especially for senior ACPO, management ranks (Charman *et al.*, 1999 forthcoming). A strategic review of National Police Training is currently underway 'and is looking at the constitution and organisation of police training with a view to making it increasingly independent of the Home Office and more responsive to the needs of the users without sacrificing its accountability' (Home Office, 1998: 19). Labour has already approved revised programmes of training for new recruits and inspectors, based upon the competency framework found in other public services. There are two emerging trends which are likely to be reinforced by the review; these are strengthening national standards for training, on the one hand, and encouragement of flexibility, linked to local needs and priorities, on the other.

Two major areas of change planned by New Labour relate to police sickness and pensions. Both are motivated by cost considerations. Police sickness absence has been an escalating problem for some years. As police are entitled to unlimited sick leave on full pay, it is very expensive to manage. Government is approaching this problem from two fronts. It is acting upon the previous government's Police Health and Safety Act (1997) by bringing the police in line with other occupations, thus aiming to reduce the costs of sickness as well as civilian claims for damages. On the other hand, it is examining closely cases of long-term sickness and seeking to reduce the numbers taking early retirement on health grounds. Government is also anxious to reform the police pension scheme, which cost £821 million in 1997–8. The Home Office (1998) proposes to raise the retirement age of all new recruits from 50 to 55 and reduce the full pension from two-thirds of final salary to one half. This will be accompanied by reducing contributions from 11 per cent of salary to 6 per cent as for other public employees.

As stated above, Sheehy was very critical of the privileged terms and conditions of employment enjoyed by the police and rejected the 'jobs for life' and security of tenure tradition in favour of fixed-term contracts after ten years in the service. It also advocated that all police officers should come under normal employment law and managers should have the power to make police redundant and dismiss them for incompetence or other disciplinary offences. Although fixed contracts have only been introduced for top ACPO posts, Labour has replaced the Police (Discipline) Regulations by a non-statutory code of standards, operational from April 1999. This transforms discipline from a criminal to a civil offence and brings the police closer to civilian employment practice. Police officers facing disciplinary hearings will also be judged on the basis of the 'balance of probabilities' rather than the more stringent test of 'beyond reasonable doubt'. From now on CCs will be able to dismiss officers caught committing crimes or disciplinary offences, subject to following correct ACAS-recommended procedures. They will also be able to dismiss officers who are lazy or incompetent, unless they improve their performance within six months. All police forces have introduced staff appraisal, which is consistent with this general move to performance management, and both officers and police managers have been trained to operate the new system. There is, however, widespread scepticism amongst the lower ranks about the way in which it will operate.

The Labour government has responded very positively to the demands for an independent complaints procedure to handle cases brought against the police by members of the public. The adverse publicity following recent cases, such as the Stephen Lawrence case, and the dramatic rise in complaints against the police have led government to commit itself to a greater openness and accountability for the police. The Home Secretary has welcomed an HMIC Review into Integrity of the Police Service, which will report in 1999. Both the Review and the proposal for an independent complaints procedure, once strongly resisted by the police federations, now have their support but they are opposed to the new powers given to managers to deal with internal discipline.

The police service has traditionally been dominated by men and characterised by a strong male culture. Equal opportunities legislation made little impact on the police until the 1980s, when internal and external pressures brought about change (Home Office, 1989). There are now two women CCs and women are slowly increasing their presence amongst ACPO ranks. Recruitment of ethnic minorities has been more difficult, however, and they remain very under-represented . Despite some *causes célèbres* (Alison Halford and Cydena Fleming), most police forces are committed to equal opportunities policies in terms of gender and ethnic origin. A large number of forces have introduced equal opportunity strategies which encompass part-time working, job sharing, career breaks, flexitime and term-time working. Police forces are also engaged in regular monitoring of recruitment, selection and promotion statistics. Many police forces now employ full-time equal opportunities officers who have an immediate responsibility for this increasingly high-profile area.

All forces have sexism and racism awareness training, aimed at both internal and external relationships. Police forces do differ, though, in their approach to implementing equal opportunities. In West Mercia there is no dedicated equal opportunities unit as equal opportunities is seen by management as the responsibility of all staff, rather than a single unit. In other forces investment in equal opportunity professional support has taken place. In Lancashire, the equal opportunities unit takes an active role in assessing the impact of new policies and projects in terms of equal opportunities. The same unit also inputs into all divisional plans. Within the force, policies and projects cannot come to completion without first having been 'signed off' by the equal opportunities unit, and regular scanning takes place which monitors female representation in specialist departments (HMIC, 1998f). While problems remain, police forces clearly demonstrate an increasing commitment to the provision of equal opportunity for their officers. Once so clearly male-dominated, these kinds of initiative break new ground in terms of an earlier organisational culture although HMIC Reports (1998i) do call into question the effect of policy on practice in some forces.

The impact of the Macpherson Report (Home Office, 1999), which highlighted institutional racism in the Metropolitan Police, is likely to reverberate throughout all police forces. Amongst its 70 recommendations for reform, it calls for an immediate review and revision of racism awareness training and targets to be set for recruitment, progression and retention of minority ethnic staff. The management of cultural diversity is likely to have a very high profile over the next few years.

Conclusion

It is evident that over the last 15 years the organisation and management of the police service has changed but it still remains very much in the control of the police. Unlike some public services, professional police officers have not been overlaid by a new managerial elite. The elite remains a police elite, although its role may be different. NPM came later to the police but HMIC and Audit Commission reports suggest that most forces are grappling with new management initiatives which emphasise restructuring, performance measurement and managerial accountability. Whilst the picture remains mixed, it is clear that police forces have embarked on a process of change which provides a remarkable contrast to the administrative procedures which characterised their work in the late 1980s.

New systems of financial and performance management are well entrenched and new systems of human resources management are also taking hold with the introduction of staff appraisals, performance reviews and training and development, although performance related pay has not yet reared its head. Where CCs, as budget holders, have actively sought to devolve budgets, evidence suggests that financial and operational decision-making made by service providers is more sensitive, and better able to reflect local need. As police forces have been made increasingly financially accountable for what they do, demands placed on police managers has grown. Managing the police service has become an increasingly complex activity and clearly reflects the demands for greater managerial accountability identified by both the Audit Commission and the Police Acts 1994 and 1996. There is no doubt that the HMIC has been a major agent of change, and close monitoring of the police continues to ensure that good practice is disseminated and is the basis for bench marking. Current developments in training are establishing high standards and ensuring police officers are adequately prepared for their management role.

Although the ideas of internal markets and competition have had less impact on the police than on other public services, the requirement to look for opportunities of contracting out and VFM are reflected in the extensive use of private companies in catering, IT services, vehicle maintenance, training and other non-core activities (Horton, 1996a; Savage and Leishman, 1996). Police are currently being encouraged to pursue Private Finance Initiatives and to look for partnerships with private business. Further, police have been encouraged to use their estates fully and to earn a return on their assets. Hence police property is either being sold off or made available for hire to outside organisations.

While some organisational rigidities remain, it is evident that NPM strategies have been embraced and this is reflected in a greater internal commitment to strategic planning, activity analysis, identification of outputs and the costing of police activity. If , therefore, managerial accountability has become central to police service provision, it is equally important, as argued recently by the Home Secretary (Police Foundation, 1998), that the process of improving efficiency and performance remains a 'continuous one'. New Labour's interest in performance management appears to be as strong as that of previous Conservative governments and pressure for more effective police management is challenging any residual resistance within the organisational culture to managerial change. The Crime and Disorder Act will, however, place new demands on police managers. The partnership arrangements required by the Act, particularly those giving a statutory responsibility to local authorities for crime prevention, will assume a high profile for police forces which, together with local authorities, will be made responsible for crime reduction strategies locally. Another aspect of policing which will assume greater importance in the future is the European dimension. Under the Maastricht Treaty of 1992 and the Amsterdam Treaty of 1997 member states, including Britain, agreed to pursue inter-governmental co-operation on border controls, combating drug trafficking, international fraud and terrorism. Police are already collaborating and working together in Europol and at major ports of entry and exit, including the Euro-tunnel. Police officers will increasingly require training in languages and European legal, police and justice systems. International co-operation will also call for further changes in culture.

Joint performance management, both locally and internationally, will increasingly characterise the management and measurement of police activity. One consequence of all these developments could mean the identification of a new paradigm in the management of the police, a development which few either inside or outside of the police can be expected to object.

14

Social Services and Community Care

MARGARET MAY and EDWARD BRUNSDON

Driven by the desire to reform what were seen as bureaucratic, inefficient and ineffective local care services, Conservative governments in the late 1980s and early 1990s, initiated unprecedented changes in local government Social Services Departments (SSDs). Through the introduction of market mechanisms and commercial management practices, these governments saw an opportunity to increase the quantity and quality of independent provision whilst simultaneously increasing choice for users and securing better value for money in continuing statutory services. Inter-organisationally, SSDs were required to promote markets of non-statutory care providers and develop the commercial practices necessary for purchasing services from them. Intra-organisationally they were expected to restructure and re-shape their service profiles. This chapter explores the challenges SSDs faced in managing the transformation of social care services for adults in England and Wales.

The Context: a Vulnerable Service

A coherent structure for personal social services did not emerge until the Local Authority Social Services Act 1970 when, following the recommendations of the Seebohm Report (1968), welfare, mental health and children's departments were merged. The new SSDs became responsible for children and families and adult services. The latter included institutional and community care for the elderly, services for adults with mental health care needs, sensory, physical or learning disabilities, and alcohol or drugs problems. In line with Seebohm, unification also signalled a shift from specialist to generic social work and a more universalist approach to provision. In administrative terms, the new departments generally adopted hierarchical, gendered, 'bureau-professional' practices common to local government. Status divisions ensured the continued separation of residential from fieldwork, direct care from social work, finance and administration from delivery. Social workers, the one professional grouping, had considerable autonomy; otherwise services were typically centrally administered with a heavy emphasis on standardised provision and institutional care.

From the outset this structure and the service pattern it sustained were subject to several waves of criticism. Initially, this focused on the Seebohm Committee's equivocation about the balance between institutional and other forms of care, the absence of a clear philosophy for the new SSDs and its failure to confront resource, distributional and consumer issues (Townsend *et al.*, 1970). A second wave of criticism developed in the mid-1970s with the emergence of user groups objecting to the paternalist, producer-dominated nature of provision and the over-reliance on institutional care (Clarke, 1993). This fed into a more extensive critique of SSDs' failure to develop community care programmes and collaborative links with health authorities, despite the exhortations of successive governments (Jones, 1989).

The Conservative Party drew on a number of these criticisms when it returned to power in 1979, incorporating them into its broader assault on state welfare. Throughout the 1980s SSDs were subject to a series of inquiries that substantiated earlier concerns and proffered solutions in terms of neo-liberal conceptions of the market and American 'new management' thinking. This amalgam saw answers to many of the public services' problems in the adoption of commercial values and practices. For SSDs, a key proponent of this view was the Audit Commission (Kelly, 1991; Henkel, 1991).

Established in 1982, the Commission was charged with ensuring that local authorities made economic, efficient and effective use of resources. Its preliminary assessment of local governance revealed a general management malaise (Audit Commission, 1984). It was particularly disturbed by the low level of strategic management in SSDs – a concern reinforced by further more specialist studies that presented a powerful case for 'new management' style restructuring. Whilst recognising examples of innovative practice, the Commission endorsed previous accounts of the under-development of community-oriented care. Provision was generally seen as expensive, inflexible, impervious to user views and institutionally based. Services varied widely between and within SSDs and co-ordination with health and other agencies remained fragmented. These failings, it maintained, stemmed not from inadequate resources, as many local authorities claimed, but from their neglect of basic business principles. Few SSDs had a clear understanding of local needs or unit costs. Budgets were allocated on an historic-service – rather than needs-led basis, whilst provision reflected professional discretion rather than systematic objectives and eligibility criteria. In sum, SSDs were seen to offer a poor return on public money.

The Commission also drew attention to what it termed the 'perverse effects' of social security payments that had fuelled a dramatic growth in private institutional provision, undermining both the government's community care policy and its commitment to reduced expenditure. Department of Social Security (DSS) spending on continuing care had rocketed from £10 million in 1979 to over £1000 million in 1989 (Department of Health, 1989). Faced with the need to curb spiralling costs and secure a community care programme commensurate with its spending plans, the government established a higher-level inquiry. Headed by Sir Roy Griffiths, the inquiry centred on the optimal use of public funds as a contribution to community care and it was this financially driven imperative that ultimately shaped the new social service agenda.

The New Framework

Griffiths' (1988) solution to the fiscal and management problems revealed by the Audit Commission lay in clearly articulating the notion of 'care by' rather than 'care in' the community, and welding it to a market-based approach to public services. Rather than abolishing SSDs, as many feared, he proposed re-designating them as lead agencies responsible for co-ordinating and promoting a mixed economy of care. Central government was to provide a clear steer by setting general objectives, allocating earmarked funds and monitoring progress. Social security payments were to be transferred to SSDs on a 'targeted' basis, but future financial support was to be based on assessments of the need for institutional care and of applicants' ability to pay. Griffiths suggested that financial support should be confined to low-income groups and individuals should be encouraged to self-provide through forward financial planning.

His proposals were initially stalled by Thatcherite antipathy to local government. However, mounting concern over the size of the DHSS care budget and the failure to find an alternative to local authority leadership forced the release of a White Paper (DoH, 1989) followed by legislation in 1990. Together, these established a new national framework for adult social services based on a clear set of policy objectives. The over-arching principle was a re-statement of the commitment to community care. Wherever possible individuals were to be supported in their own homes through packages of domiciliary, day and respite services. Aligned to this was a new commitment to users in the form of increased choice, tailored provision and involvement in service planning and design. Carers' needs were also to be given greater recognition.

Within these broad objectives SSDs were vested with the strategic role of securing high quality, cost-effective services that enabled client choice. Rather than functioning Seebohm-style as monopolistic providers, they were to operate as service 'arrangers and purchasers' with a mandate to promote the development of a flourishing independent sector. Concomitantly, they were also expected to re-shape their own services in the light of assessments of local need and annual community care plans. New care management programmes and quality assurance procedures were to be introduced involving both the monitoring of services that SSDs provided and those they purchased. These were to function through contracts with suppliers, clear 'in-house' customer care and complaints procedures, and the establishment of 'arms-length' inspection.

Change Management: the Central Steer

Implementation was initially scheduled for April 1991. However, government's growing awareness of the need to manage the change process, combined with pre-electoral pressures, led it to delay this until April 1993. Whilst recognising SSDs' autonomy in determining local services, it aspired to a national pattern of service quality and performance. To this end, government sought to steer the transformation of provision through changes in finance and a series of policy directives and practice guidelines. In terms of funding, it orchestrated a phased transfer of the DSS' social care budget to local authorities. Signalling its intention to develop non-statutory provision, the government required them to spend 85 per cent of this special transitional grant (STG) on 'independent sector' services. This was within a context of relentless downward pressure on local government spending, despite rising demand from an ageing population.

The government's broader legislative aims were conveyed in a stream of guidance material, regulations and implementation targets. Much of this emanated from and was overseen by national agencies such as the Social Services Inspectorate (SSI) and the Audit Commission working with specialist teams in the DoH. Having been instrumental in initiating the new framework, the Commission continued to monitor progress and dispense advice on the managerial reforms necessary to secure the community care 'revolution' (Audit Commission, 1992a). Its recommendations were paralleled by those of the SSI. Traditionally operating as an advisory and educational service, the Inspectorate had been re-designated in 1985 and given the remit of assisting local authorities 'to obtain value for money through the efficient and effective use of resources'. Central to this, as its 1987 mission statement made clear, was a shift to performance-based evaluation aimed at improving SSDs' managerial competence and the quality of service delivery. Together with the Audit Commission the SSI played a central role in steering the transformation of SSDs.

Change Management: Local Shaping

As the Audit Commission observed (1992b: 19), implementing central government guidelines entailed: 'turning organisations upside down'. Not only did the reforms imply new divisional structures and redeployment of staff, they also involved the establishment of new responsibilities in finance, personnel and resource management, the reconceptualisation of service delivery in terms of performance standards and user involvement, and the simultaneous task of developing local care markets. To add to these pressures, government also expected SSDs to implement the 1989 Children Act and, in many instances, participate in the broader reorganisation following the development of unitary local authorities. The response of senior managers and social service committees to these demands should therefore be understood in this broader context, along with the recognition that SSDs differed in size, resources and political environments. Thus while the tasks set by government were common, the scale of the challenges facing departments varied markedly, as did the resource base available with which to respond.

The Creation of Markets

One of the leading tasks for SSDs involved the creation of local markets. For many departments this constituted an immense challenge. They were expected to develop market-making and service-procurement skills in very demanding circumstances. Independent provision was unevenly developed and concentrated in institutional care. Managers lacked data on user needs and potential suppliers and an appropriate information technology infrastructure. Several studies have also pointed to a wariness of non-statutory suppliers. There was a distrust of commercial enterprises and doubts about the capacity of voluntary agencies (Wistow *et al.*, 1996; Means and Smith, 1998). Nevertheless, government pressure to spend STG money on independent providers forced even the most reluctant authorities into a market-making role.

The initial focus of market creation was on residential care for the elderly, the service where independent provision was most developed. Here managers typically utilised an 'historic grounds' approach, relying on known suppliers, particularly voluntary agencies and housing associations whose value-base was seen as more attuned to that of SSDs. Providers were also encouraged to widen their services remit and diversify into day and respite care. More generally, care markets were fostered through commissioning, tendering, start-up grants and advisory services. The development of domiciliary care however proved problematic. Supply consisted largely of individuals working part-time on the fringes of the formal economy and was characterised by high turnover and uneven quality. Faced with these conditions, many local authorities sought to develop a more stable and consistent form of provision. They encouraged voluntary agencies to enter this market and sought to oversee suppliers through registration and accreditation procedures, often supported by preferred contract arrangements.

SSDs added to these forms of market creation by winding down and 'outsourcing' their own services. Again this was undertaken at varying rates across the country, but most authorities began by disposing of residential units. They tended to opt for voluntary agency or management 'buy-outs', less frequently they sold their assets and provision to commercial enterprises. By the late 1990s, they were adopting similar mechanisms and outlets for 'externalising' home-care. Previous doubts about care markets had generally given way to a more informed, if pragmatic, acceptance of the new enabling role and a clear growth in the volume of non-statutory provision. Between 1993 and 1997 the numbers of people placed in independent residential provision rose from 20 per cent to 66 per cent, whilst publicly funded independent provision of home care rose from 2 per cent in 1992 to 44 per cent in 1997 (SSI, 1998a).

Managing Demand: the Purchaser–Provider Split

In tandem with promoting markets, SSDs were expected to revise their own activities. This was not simply a question of providing less and buying more, it was also a matter of developing a new form of service allocation (care management) and reorganising along purchaser–provider lines. The DoH felt that these activities had to be differentiated in order to ensure that 'the respective interests of user and provider [were] separately represented' (Price Waterhouse and DoH, 1991: 15). The policy guidance on how this might be undertaken was very general. Price Waterhouse suggested three possible approaches: separation at strategic level only; at local level, operating through a series of purchaser and provider teams; or at senior management level. Most authorities adopted or are moving towards the last of these options, with assistant directors taking overall responsibility for each function and dedicated line management structures at area or district level. The implementation of this division however was not easy. SSDs were confronted by two main challenges: the transition in terms of personnel and the development of financial and purchasing strategies in a climate of increasing fiscal and revenue support constraints.

In many ways reorganisation was a step into the unknown for SSD staff at all levels. For providers there were questions about their future viability in the face of anticipated competition from independent suppliers with lower overheads. There was also concern about their status within departments in relation to purchasers. For purchasers, there was the issue for senior managers of developing a financial strategy and budgeting structure, while, at a lower level, care managers were confronted with the new needs-assessment practices and the purchasing of individualised packages of care. Both purchasers and providers faced relational tensions of how to work with ex-colleagues. In many ways these difficulties proved to be transitional: they dissipated with experience of the new arrangements or through the reallocation of tasks, particularly the involvement of providers in aspects of user assessment.

The difficulties that staff had adapting to the new regime formed an important backcloth to understanding the challenges faced in developing purchasing. In the words of Lewis and Glennerster (1996: 69) '[p]urchasers . . . had a steep learning curve and little history or experience to fall back on.' The DoH had visualised SSDs devolving their budgets to care-manager level, generating a conception of 'multiple purchasers close to the clients', and thereby enabling purchasing to flow from assessments of client need. This, however, only happened in a minority of cases. Most authorities chose instead to separate 'macro-' from 'micro-' purchasing. Macro-purchasing was typically undertaken by a central commissioning and purchasing body that negotiated block contracts with suppliers. SSD committees and senior managers maintained that this was necessary to retain financial control, minimise transaction costs and secure best value. Micro-purchasing was devolved to care managers who were given the twin responsibilities of assessing individual needs and constructing tailored care packages. Whilst there was space for individual negotiation and 'creative purchasing' (Leat and Perkins, 1998), care managers had to operate within centrally deter-mined budgets, contractual arrangements and assessment procedures.

At both levels, government-imposed financial constraints led SSDs to develop techniques for managing the demand for services through the stratification and prioritisation of different categories of need. These included: new eligibility criteria, raising thresholds, restricting the total cost of care packages and introducing new forms of targeting and priority setting. Assessments increasingly emphasised risk rather than need and the ability of individuals and their support networks to contribute to provision. Variations in fees and means-testing schemes meant that there were major differences between authorities in the revenue raised and the costs met by different consumer groups but, by the middle of the decade, users were contributing £1 billion to SSD budgets (DoH, 1998a). The overall effects were both to increase the revenues of SSDs and make provision more selective.

Empowering the Consumer

For government, care management was not only central to its drive to re-cast social care services on market-based lines, it was also a means of meeting the related goal of empowering users and carers. This latter aim was promoted through two mechanisms, community care planning, and SSI and Audit Commission guidance designed to facilitate the development of 'management systems powered by the voice of the user' (Waldegrave in Philpot, 1994). The government stipulated that consumers as well as relevant agencies should be involved in community care planning. They were also to participate in individual care plans, a process reinforced by two privately sponsored measures in 1996: the Carers (Recognition of Services) Act and the Community Care (Direct Payments) Act. The former gave carers a right to separate assessment as part of care programming; the latter granted under 65s with physical or learning disabilities the possibility of receiving payments to organise their own care.

Community care planning initially relied more on consultations with other agencies than user groups or the wider constituency of potential users (Henwood, 1995). But, as managers acclimatised to the new planning cycle, procedures became more open and extensive and by the mid-1990s SSDs were undertaking 'market research' and 'customer satisfaction' surveys. In spite of such developments, many commentators still felt there was room for major improvement. User groups in particular felt planning was still more reliant on 'consultation' than on participation. Furthermore, structures to facilitate such inputs, particularly for the least organised and ethnic minority groups, were also underdeveloped (Barnes, 1997; SSI, 1998b).

Similar unevenness characterised efforts to institute more user-centred modes of service delivery. The SSI and Audit Commission guidance operated with an uneasy combination of business-based practices and the more participative models advocated by user-groups and traditional social work. Drawing on the former, SSDs invested considerable effort in the development of promotional literature disseminated to potential service users (often in several languages) through a wide network of outlets. Reception services too gained a new priority as managers imported various customer-care and charter-style schemes. User participation in individual care planning, however, progressed at a much slower rate, as did the implementation of carers assessments and self-managed care schemes. While reporting high levels of user satisfaction, a number of studies also revealed the continuance of practitioner-dominated services (Ellis, 1993; Croft and Beresford, 1996) and constraints on effective quality assurance.

Quality Assurance, Regulation and Inspection

Quality management, as promulgated in the guidance literature, drew heavily on business models. SSDs were expected to replicate the practices of contract specification, standard setting, quality assurance and complaints procedures central to the commercial conception of good customer care. Many departments introduced service-level agreements with in-house providers but their primary concern was securing quality services from external suppliers. In terms of contracting, most developed templates or *pro forma* contracts specifying the service standards required. They also stipulated that providers operate their own quality controls including user/carer involvement and complaints procedures. These arrangements were often backed up by general codes of practice and guidelines for purchasing staff as well as committing suppliers to user-sensitive provision through attaching 'value statements' to contracts.

Compliance monitoring and review, particularly of spot and domiciliary care contracts, proved expensive and difficult to implement (Walsh *et al.*, 1997). SSDs therefore increasingly relied on other forms of user protection and quality control. Of these potentially the most powerful was their duty under the 1990 Act to establish arms-length inspection units. These units were responsible for registering non-statutory residential homes and inspecting all homes, including those provided by the authority. Homes were to be inspected twice a year, reports published and the process monitored by the authority's chief executive and an advisory committee of councillors, lay and provider representatives.

There were pronounced differences in the pace at which departments were able to establish this new inspection system. Operationally, there were also considerable variations in the size and resources available to these units as well as contrasting regulatory regimes (Klein and Redmayne, 1996). Within such differences, however, there was a detectable pattern in which both business-style and user-centred forms of review employed more consultative approaches geared to 'building quality in' through provider self-evaluation (Gostick *et al.*, 1997). In some local authorities inspection was also extended on a voluntary basis to in-house domiciliary care providers and external suppliers.

By the late 1990s the SSI reported rising standards, particularly in residential care, as inspection combined with tighter contracting forced suppliers to improve their facilities. The arms-length system nonetheless had its critics. Some, particularly providers, sought de-regulation or at minimum the allocation of inspection to an independent body. Others maintained that it should remain a local authority unit but have more power over both statutory and independent suppliers to deal with complaints.

Complaints procedures had been seen as a critical feature of the new quality-assurance system. Under the 1990 legislation, SSDs were obliged to establish a three-stage system enabling users to dispute the fairness of their treatment. Central guidance presented this new scheme as a key management tool for gauging user satisfaction and assessing service performance. Rather than adopting a damage limitation approach, SSDs were actively to encourage complaints as a means of securing continuous improvement. They were also to develop pre-emptive customer-care practices and encourage staff to engage in a regular process of self- and service evaluation. SSDs responded to these injunctions by publishing information on the availability of redress and ensuring that complaints procedures were built into contract specifications. Research on the implementation of these procedures is somewhat limited, but the available data again points to inconsistencies in application (Dean, 1996) and the poor circulation of information. Nonetheless, the existence of complaints procedures was indicative of the broader changes in the working environment of SSDs.

Human Resources Management

Empowering users in 'new management's' conception of customer-focused services was mirrored by the empowerment of staff. This embraced both investment in employees and devolution of decision-making powers and responsibilities to those closest to consumers. For SSDs, the scope for such change was inhibited by two factors: the pressures of engineering large-scale change within time and financial constraints and the pressures of local political accountability. In these circumstances, the creation of the purchaser–provider divide necessarily took precedence over other human resources strategies. It was a restructuring that had an impact on all levels of staffing, entailing a substantial redistribution of personnel and, in many instances, delayering and reductions in the number of full-time staff. Many SSD employees, including senior managers, were forced to reapply for jobs, to compete for reduced numbers of posts or to opt for early retirement. Employment in the new order typically increased the range of responsibilities and thus the workload of each member of staff within what remained a top-down system of management. Senior managers continued to hold a tight rein on financial matters. Middle managers gained more operational tasks but were denied the autonomy that might be associated with their level of responsibility in commercial enterprises. A similar dissonance between responsibilities and power also took place in social work.

With the profession under immense pressure from both government and a hostile press, many thought that the 1990 Act was intended to reduce the autonomy of social workers but the outcome has proved more complex. Whilst professional social workers continued to dominate recruitment into senior, middle and care management, the practitioner role was itself transformed by the new framework. Care management demanded broader skills than those of traditional social work, particularly in relation to resource and demand management. SSD providers in the new system were also required to take on more extensive responsibilities as needs-led assessment and targeting processes produced heavier caseloads with higher-dependency client groups.

Administrative and front-line care workers faced additional pressures as competition from independent suppliers forced changes in skill mixes and employment conditions. The presence of outside providers strengthened managers' negotiating powers, enabling them to introduce more flexible work rosters, cut traditional out-of-hours payments and utilise more short-term contracts. They also made greater use of agency, sessional and part-time staff, thereby increasing SSDs' reliance on a low-paid, predominantly female careforce. By 1995, 57 per cent of staff working in English SSDs were part-time employees (DoH, 1995). Though benefiting marginally from the introduction of 'single-status' arrangements in local government, such staff faced demands for efficiency gains and rising insecurity as SSDs reduced or out-sourced services.

In this climate, many local authorities were unable to sustain their traditional 'model employer' stance. This was most evident in the loss of momentum in equal opportunities programmes and training. In terms of the former, departmental restructuring at management level appeared to advantage white males (Newman, 1997; Douglas and Philpot, 1998). This pattern has been replicated at other levels, with the same group occupying the major roles in purchasing, whilst women and members of ethnic minorities are concentrated in the less powerful provider units (Brown and Smith, 1993). With regard to training, the initial phasing-in of the legislation was accompanied by a flurry of initiatives. Most effort went into preparing senior, middle and care managers for their new tasks with only short induction sessions for other staff. Follow-up training was limited, with few authorities undertaking skill audits or workforce planning. On-going staff development was geared to managers and professional staff, thus accentuating past patterns of differential provision and reliance on a largely unqualified workforce (Balloch, 1997).

Performance Management

By the mid-1990s, SSD managers and social service committees were coming under increased government pressure to improve training and establish a performance culture. Whilst the landscape of care had changed dramatically, the SSI and Audit Commission reports revealed substantial gaps in a number of management processes (SSI/Audit Commission, 1997). They were particulary critical of the piecemeal development of services, the continuing lack of a strategic vision and the general failure to link the costs of services to performance. Few authorities could project future spending or detail 'how many people receive what service, at what standard and at what cost', nor did they 'know whether assessments are carried out promptly or [if] services deliver the outcomes users require'. These deficiencies partly stemmed from the failure fully to disaggregate in-house budgets from SSDs' other activities, and low investment in information systems (Bovell *et al.*, 1997). More fundamentally, however, they reflected the lack of clear target setting and appraisal systems for staff and services.

Equally critically for the Conservative agenda, provision still varied across the country and collaboration with health authorities remained patchy. The government had anticipated that the creation of care markets would not only increase independent provision but also encourage joint commissioning by health and social care authorities, and thus achieve the ideal of a 'seamless' service for users. Pressure along these lines however did little to counter long-standing professional, financial and organisational barriers or secure more than piecemeal progress.

In an attempt to boost joint working and inculcate a stronger performance culture the Major government tightened central regulation. From

1996 the Audit Commission (focusing on efficiency and value for money) and the SSI (concentrating on effectiveness, professional practice and service delivery) became responsible for more stringent joint reviews of English SSDs. This was paralleled in the build up to regional government in Wales by the production of SSDs' planning arrangements. The first joint review reports on England were generally favourable, but by 1997, as the review teams refined their assessment methodology, SSDs' overall performance was again being questioned, particularly in the areas of mental health and child care, where the SSI reported substantial service shortfalls (Laming, 1997). The slow progress made by departments in bringing about change (combined with broader electoral concerns) led the government to propose yet further reductions in their provider role through a mandatory expansion of non-statutory services (DoH, 1997b).

Labour's Vision of Adult Social Care

What Labour inherited in May 1997 was an adult care system that still showed marked variations in service quality, care patterns, and managerial effectiveness. With persistent erosion of the revenue support grant, many authorities also had problems with funding their services and securing effective collaboration with health and housing authorities. Labour's election brought little immediate change. Its manifesto provided few detailed proposals on social care beyond the promises to set up a mental health review, a Royal Commission on long-term care funding and introduce a community care charter. In its first few months in office it established the review and commission but the difficulties posed by adult social service reform delayed publication of its Social Care White Paper. Nevertheless, it has become increasingly clear that, while there are strong affinities with Conservative social care programmes, Labour's vision heralds a significant change of approach.

Like its predecessors, Blair's government seems to have accepted that social care services should be selective and will only function to support 'the most vulnerable in society' (DSS, 1998a). Equally it recognises that demand for social care can only be met by the combined efforts of independent and statutory providers. Where it appears to differ is in its approach to service allocation, regulation and performance management.

While the Conservatives advocated market-based forms of allocation and competition between public and independent providers, Labour favours allocating services through partnerships involving both statutory and non-statutory organisations. This is particularly apparent in a range of 'best-value' and 'intelligent commissioning' initiatives designed to ensure that local authorities invest in the most effective service provider. Gauging effective performance for the Conservatives was primarily a question of efficiency in the form of cost reductions; for the current government it is essentially a matter of service quality and accountability to users and the local electorate.

Again, in contrast to the Thatcher and Major administrations, Labour openly advocates the use of regulation to protect users and secure high-quality services. This is already evident in Labour's response to the SSI's concerns over childcare (the Quality Projects Initiative) and ministerial pledges to end the 'community care lottery'. The government looks set to introduce a national framework for community care charges and, more fundamentally, a new quality assurance system for assessing SSD provision. Tighter quality control is likely to flow from the Joint Reviews assessments, the establishment of a new 'social care and training council', the strengthening of social care registration and regulation procedures, and the allocation of further powers to the SSI.

The government's responses to the long-standing problems of social care funding and collaboration with health authorities seem likely to follow a similar performance-related path. As the Comprehensive Spending Review and new pooled-funding arrangements indicate, SSD finances will increasingly be linked to effectiveness including the extent of collaboration with health authorities. The government's expectations have been spelt out in the first joint guidance, setting priorities for the NHS and social services and subjecting both to a raft of detailed targets (DoH, 1998b). Unlike Conservative initiatives on collaboration, the government is imposing national standards for local authorities for the first time. Moreover, it not only promises stable funding for those who 'meet the grade', but penalties for failure.

Conclusion

For SSD managers, then, the return of a Labour government presages further changes in their responsibilities and working environment and, above all, greater external scrutiny. Over the last ten years they have both experienced and implemented major structural and operational change, contributing to a more diverse mixed economy of care. In the next decade, they face the operational challenge of setting and meeting more rigorous targets, closer management of costs and service activities and creating more effective forms of staff development and appraisal. At a strategic level, senior managers have the tasks of creating a more integrated approach to service delivery, more effective partnerships with other agencies, and direct user participation. For Labour, such changes are part of a process of renewal in which departments will provide more effective service outcomes; for SSD managers and staff it is a matter of acclimatising to further change in an ethos of continuous 'self-improvement'.

PART IV

Conclusion

15

New Labour and the Management of Public Services: Legacies, Impact and Prospects

SYLVIA HORTON and DAVID FARNHAM

One of the legacies of 18 years of reforming Conservative governments from 1979 to 1997 was a well-entrenched system of 'new public management' (NPM) in the public services. First, the Thatcher and Major governments wanted to transfer services from the public to the private sector in the belief that the private sector was more efficient and responsive to consumer needs than was the public sector. Other objectives were to reduce public expenditure and create a property-owning democracy, in which the public would become wedded to the virtues of private ownership and an enterprise culture. Second, the Conservatives intended to destroy the power base of the public sector professions and trade unions, by breaking up public monopolies, promoting competition and choice and restricting traditional trade union freedoms. Third, they aimed to managerialise the public services and create performance management and quality management cultures, aimed at achieving greater efficiency and effectiveness in the provision of public services.

The whole public sector was reconstructed during the Conservative administrations and its architecture changed. Services were privatised or contracted out and pseudo-markets were introduced into the remaining public services to facilitate the use of contracts, instead of traditional rule-bound hierarchies, to regulate relationships between 'purchasers' and 'providers'. The impact of markets on public service organisations was profound, as they gradually replaced political decision-making in operational areas of public service and the boundaries between the public and private sectors were redrawn. A wide range of mechanisms was used to effect the reconstruction of the state, with privatisation and marketisation taking many forms. First, there was the sale of public assets to the private sector. This primarily involved public utilities and nationalised industries, such as gas, electricity, water, railways and telecommunications. But smaller public assets such as public bus companies, nursing homes and public housing, owned by local authorities, were also transferred into private ownership.- Second, there was the process of' 'contracting out'. This was a consequence, in part, of government's imposition of compulsory competitive tendering (CCT) on local authorities and the NHS, and its policy of market testing in other parts of the public sector, including the civil service and police. By the mid-1990s, however, general acceptance of private sector involvement in public service provision ensured that all activities of government were potentially open for contracting out.

In the early 1990s, a third strategy of introducing internal markets took hold. Educational reforms had introduced forms of market choice and business units in local government were providing services to internal purchasing departments but it was reforms of the NHS in 1990 that instituted the strongest examples of internal markets. Here a regulated system of contracts between providers (NHS trusts and GPs) and purchasers (health authorities and GP fund-holders) operated to meet local health needs (Flynn and Williams, 1997).

Within these reconstructed public services, NPM took root and grew. Indeed, some would argue that 'public management' has now superseded 'NPM' and is the dominant orthodoxy of public service organisation. Many writers have discussed the principal features of NPM and public management (Dunleavy and Hood, 1995a; Hood, 1991, 1995; Hughes, 1994; Massey, 1993) and there is much debate about its doctrinal coherence. Its main characteristics include new structural forms, managerial rationalism, measurement of organisational effectiveness and efficiency, innovations in human resources management (HRM), cultural change and the creation of flexible, responsive, learning organisations (Farnham and Horton, 1996b). In essence, public management is associated with the importing of private-sector management structures and techniques into the public services. These include delayered hierarchies, separation of policy and implementation and delegation of responsibility to line managers for managing performance, quality and people. A more rational approach to management is reflected in the high profile given to strategic planning, performance and quality management and use of performance indicators to measure efficiency and facilitate greater managerial control over resources. These have been accompanied by new systems of HRM aimed at weakening traditional collectivist approaches to employer–employee relations and developing more individualised relationships between the parties to the wage–work bargain. The aim is to replace staff compliance with staff commitment to organisational goals and objectives and satisfy 'customer' needs. Above all, public management is underpinned by a business-oriented culture in which people at work are driven to accept a continual search for greater efficiency and effectiveness and are expected to cope flexibly with continuous change, so that organisational learning becomes a norm of public service working life.

The ideology of managerialism has been used to justify a central role for managers and management within the 'new' public services. It has challenged both the independence of public service professionals and the implicit syndicalism that characterised the old system of administrative bureaucracy. In some services, the professions have fought a rearguard action to stem the take-over of organisational power by public managers but they have done this only by becoming managers themselves. Most heads of clinical directorates in the NHS are doctors, academics continue to fill top management posts throughout all sectors of education and qualified social workers and police officers dominate top jobs in social service departments and police forces respectively. They all operate within new management systems, however, and are constrained by externally imposed budgets and audits. Many have undergone customised management training and have adopted a common managerialist language and frame of reference. All this produces similar thinking and shared managerial practices across public services. Such developments reduce differences in the ways in which public managers perceive and act out their roles within and across public services, despite their diverse personal backgrounds, qualifications and professional experiences.

Changes in public service cultures have been engineered in a number of ways. First, they have been led from the top. Governments have used all the instruments at their disposal to bring about organisational and managerial change including legislation, administrative direction, financial controls and external inspectorates. Anglo-American 'management-speak' has created new images of organisations and the nature of management. It has also projected new 'corporate' values, symbols, logos, ceremonies and 'folk heroes', with whom members of public organisations are expected to identify. Second, rewards have been structured to act as incentives for those conforming with the new business culture incorporated within the public services, especially those in top positions. Conversely, penalties have been imposed upon those who do not 'move with the times', including promotion blockages, early retirements and redundancy packages. Third, training and development programmes have been major vehicles for transmitting this new business-oriented culture within public organisations, as well as developing the skills required to manage reformed public organisations.

The orientation of the public services has changed, therefore, from one founded on the old principles of public administration to one founded on the new principles of public management. The old system placed great emphasis on rigid hierarchies, prescribed roles, formal procedures, financial rectitude and equity and fairness when dealing with the public. The dominant culture was one of mistake avoidance, caution and systematic rule application. Public management in contrast lays emphasis on the tasks to be done and the customers, consumers or users being served. The focus is on ensuring that efficient use is made of all resources to ensure value for money for taxpayers and the state. Under classical public administration, units of resource were standardised and standards of public service were assumed to be common amongst providing organisations. Under public management, in contrast, organisations compete for resources and status hierarchies of organisational competence emerge, with some players becoming 'winners' and others 'losers'. Innovation and enterprise are encouraged to ensure that public organisations compete with one another to keep ahead in the 'league table' in their sector. Each is then able to benchmark itself against the best in their field. Staff are more likely to be rewarded for their individual efforts and there are more open career structures, encouraging movement into and out of each service. Competition is inherent in the managerialist culture and contracts largely replace rules and regulations in disciplining and controlling relationships between internal and external purchasers or providers.

In practice, the extent to which public services approximate to the public management model varies, although the studies in this book show that it is found to greater or lesser extents in them all. The complexity and heterogeneity of modern public organisations defies standardisation either between or within each service, although this was true of the old system of public administration too. Ferlie and his colleagues (1996) point to a substantial transfer of private-sector models of management and managerial concepts into the public sector to make them more like firms. In particular 'maintenance management' has given way to a self-proclaimed 'management of change'. They identify four models of NPM: the efficiency drive model, the downsizing and decentralisation model, the 'In Search of Excellence' model and the 'public service' model which signify the stages of development and refinement of NPM throughout the 1980s and 1990s. Their observations are that these variants of NPM illustrate both convergence and divergence between public and private management. How organisations actually operate in practice, is contingent upon their dominant values, size, function, staff, technology and, not least, their history. Diversity, even within cultural frameworks, is likely to be the norm. Clarke (1998) and Walsh *et al.* (1997), for example, have illustrated the wide variations found in forms of contracting across different public services, while Farnham and Horton (1996b) have shown the different approaches to human resources management and employment relations within the major services.

There are many claims made for public management, although there is only limited research on which to base definitive conclusions about its impact or its outcomes. This is in part because of the rapidity with which changes have taken place but also because previous governments placed little importance on evaluation. Much of what was done was based on faith. Some of the claimed benefits of public management include: increases in productivity and efficiency; more cost-effective and rational approaches to organisational decision making; greater responsiveness to customer needs and service users; greater financial accountability by public officials; some decentralisation: and better adaptation of national policies and activities to local needs. There are counter claims that while public management has brought some of these benefits there are also negative consequences associated with it. These include the: high transaction costs involved in introducing and operating many of the new management systems; de-professionalisation of groups of public service workers; the non-consultative management styles of some public managers; work intensification experienced by many public sector employees; low morale amongst public workers such as nurses and teachers; the adverse impact of managerialism on the public service ethic; and the so-called 'democratic deficit', arising from the creation of appointed management boards.

A major objective of public management has been to replace traditional bureaucracies with flexible, responsive organisational structures. Paradoxically the only way that the radical reforms associated with public management could be implemented was through increasing centralisation and installing control systems to direct behaviour. As Painter (1999: 95f) states:

> Some elements of UK public management reform had the consequence, if anything, of making bureaucratic characteristics more pronounced. This manifested itself in the powerful centralising tendencies unleashed under the Conservatives and new kinds of formalisation arising from a performance management ethos that was to prove highly mechanistic in its approach to performance measurement and monitoring.

Further, as Hoggett (1996: 28) points out, in many public services, excessive formalisation has proved to be dysfunctional by:

> creating new layers of bureaucracy engaged in contract specification and monitoring, quality control, inspection, audit and review, and diverting the energies of professional staff away from service delivery into a regime of form-filling, report writing and procedure-following which is arguably even more extensive than that which existed during the former 'bureaucratic era'.

Performance management, which is intended to increase managerial control to ensure greater efficiency and effectiveness, appears in some instances to make managerial control an end in itself. Furthermore, external audits and inspectorates divert attention away from the normal work of schools, colleges, police forces and local authorities. They also structure the priorities of public services towards what is externally required rather than what is necessarily in the interests of service users, whether pupils, students or the general public.

Another unintended consequence of public management reforms has been the difficulties faced by governments in trying to integrate the highly fragmented institutional structures created in the name of decentralisation and functional relevance. As Painter (1999) points out, a 'differentiated polity' can undermine the ability of governments to govern and can prevent effective co-ordination of public services. It is the public who are the 'losers' in this case. Finally, there is the claim that the culture of public management, with its emphasis on performance, value for money, competition and entrepreneurialism, is undermining the public service ethic. The new contract state is more exposed to possible fraud and corruption and the traditional values of honesty, probity and integrity are being sidelined (Doig, 1997; Chapman and O'Toole, 1995). The public is no longer being treated equally or equitably but according to market criteria or local managerial discretion.

These, then, are some of the legacies of the Thatcher–Major administrations in developing and institutionalising public management in Britain. The debate has now moved on to consider what impact the New Labour government is having on the public services and how these are to be managed over the next few years. With the New Right hegemony in politics ended, has there been an irreversible paradigm shift in the public services or is Labour looking for a 'Third Way' in managing them? The evidence to date is that public management is safe in Labour's hands. New Labour seeks to be a government of economic competence and the record indicates that it is continuing to look to the market and private sector to provide the nation's wealth, as the basis of raising living standards. In turn, New Labour expects public sector managers to continue delivering efficient and effective public services, in customer-centred ways. With its ambitious plans for significant economic, political, institutional and social reforms, and its commitment to not increasing basic or top rates of income tax over its first five years' of office (Labour Party, 1997), New Labour wants both value for money and quality public services which satisfy public demand. 'Good' management practices are continuing to be encouraged throughout the public services. As Tony Blair (1998: 17) argues in his project for a Third Way in British politics: 'We must equip government with new capacity and skills'. In the revitalisation of the public service ethic, 'public servants must do more than administer services; *their job is to generate greater public value from our stock of public assets*' [editors' emphasis].

New Labour thus appears to be building on the New Right legacy and has no wish to return to former systems of traditional public administration or high public spending. Indeed, in its election manifesto (Labour Party, 1997: 12), Labour stated that it gives:

> high priority to seeing how public money can be better used . . . New Labour will be wise spenders, not big spenders. We will work in partnership with the private sector to achieve our goals. . . And because efficiency and value for money are central, ministers will be required to save before they can spend. Save to invest is our approach, not tax and spend.

After the election, the new government committed itself to the inherited public expenditure plans of the Conservatives for its first two years in office and pledged no increases in income tax during the lifetime of that Parliament. It also targeted for low inflation and delegated the setting of interest rates to the Bank of England, to ensure that monetary policy was free of short-term political intervention. Finally, Labour spelt out its 'golden rule' of public spending, which was to borrow to invest, not to fund current expenditure. This economic conservatism was reflected in conservatism on other fronts. Labour moved cautiously in its first years in office in terms of structural and managerial reform, with the exception of political devolution. It set up task forces and policy review groups, embarking on a series of pilot studies before introducing full-scale reforms. There was no 'big bang' of change but rather cautious incrementalism and a pragmatic approach to introducing change.

However, there are some indications of the directions in which Labour is moving. First, it is laying far more emphasis on political reforms than market reforms to bring about greater democracy and citizen participation. Its focus is on how Britain is governed, hoping that devolution for Scotland and Wales will bring government closer to the people and open the way for more coherence in both policy and service implementation in those parts of Britain. In England, nine new development agencies came into existence in April 1999 and may well prove to be a test bed for full-blown regionalism sometime in the future. It also appears that Labour is anxious to establish a new relationship with a strengthened local government. Thus, in addition to giving local authorities new financial powers, it also plans to acknowledge excellence by awarding the best councils with 'Beacon' status. Government is clearly committed to making local government more democratic, with its plans to create a new authority for London, with an elected Mayor – a model which may well be extended to other metropolitan areas. It is also encouraging the use of referenda, surveys and forums to extend local democracy. The objective is 're-inventing democracy' rather than re-inventing government. However, there is no evidence that Labour is prepared to relinquish general control over local government expenditure. In fact, it has increased centralisation by giving the Secretary of State powers to impose a management team upon any local authority found, by the Audit Commission, to be under-performing, to close individual 'failing' schools and to assume housing and health responsibilities too. Reforms of local government executive structures are also likely to be mandatory.

Second great emphasis is being placed on co-operation, collaboration and partnerships. In response to criticisms of the fragmented administrative structures created by the Conservatives, Labour is promoting both vertical and horizontal co-operation between governmental bodies, the voluntary sector and private businesses. One of its first actions was to create the Social Exclusion Unit (SEU) in the Cabinet Office which is promoting a multi-departmental, multi-agency approach to environmental, social and economic deprivation. The first problems which it tackled were run-down housing estates, truancy and school exclusion, and the needs of older people. Of equal importance are area-based partnerships, based on the model of the SEU. These include Education, Employment and Health Action Zones. The first 25 Education Action Zones established in 1998 are designed to be test beds of action in areas of low educational achievement. Local education authorities, voluntary organisations, businesses and schools are working together to get results. Schools are free to experiment with the national curriculum and deviate from national pay structures, while businesses, which provide half the funding, are expected to play a full part in bringing skills and expertise into schools.

A smaller number of Employment Zones, involving a wide range of partners are concentrated in areas of high, long-term unemployment. Health Action Zones are based on a consortium of local bodies, including NHS organisations, local authorities, voluntary bodies and businesses. They are intended to spearhead actions in areas of high need, with the aim of reducing health inequalities. Under Labour, collaboration is an intentional strategy and a new architecture of multi-agency, joined-up government is replacing the fragmented, disjoined structures under the Conservatives. Collaboration and co-operation are replacing competition and choice.

Changes in the centre of government, in both the Prime Minister's Office and Cabinet Office (Burch and Holliday, 1999), provide further evidence of government's determination to overcome the co-ordination deficit and the strong culture of departmentalism, which still exists. The Prime Minister's Office has been enlarged and now has a Chief of Staff and four sub-units, the Political Office, Press Office, Policy Unit and the Strategic Communication Unit. Ministers are expected to clear policy issues with the Policy Unit, while the Prime Minister's Press Officer keeps close control of media communication. Nevertheless, tensions still exist, particularly between departmental press officers and Number 10. Major changes in the Cabinet Office, have strengthened its policy co-ordination and strategic management role and provide a focus for a corporate approach to human resources management and strengthening the managerial competencies of the senior civil service.

Government's policy of 'joined-up government' is reflected in its commitment to using ICT to improve communications between all levels of government and to make much greater use of the Internet. The Prime Minister has set a target for 25 per cent of all government transactions to be available electronically by 2002. This is designed to meet the needs of the public for more convenient and coherent delivery of services. It also has potential for making information available to all parts of government and the public, thus breaking down the power bases of individual units, departments and groups as well as meeting the promise of more 'open government'. This strengthening at the centre is enhancing the steering capability of government. If the Conservative's mantra was competition, New Labour's is partnership. These include partnerships between: different types and levels of public organisations; public, private and voluntary bodies; and purchasers and providers in the NHS. Partnership is the preferred model of government, not bureaucracy or the market. Indeed, the Prime Minister, Tony Blair, has argued that 'excellent public provision for the next generation' must be 'built on partnership and driven by performance' (Blair, 1998: 15f).

These represent the major areas of difference between New Labour and the Thatcher–Major approach. More significant, perhaps, are the areas of similarity. Labour continues to promote performance management, which it advocates even more zealously than its predecessors, and seeks value for money in the public services, although it has chosen to adopt the term 'best value'. Whilst it promises to abolish CCT, and permit government bodies to choose who should provide public services, the expectation is that there will be more, not less, partnerships with the private sector. Government is not opposed to bringing in private organisations to run public activities, believing that they are sometimes better equipped to manage and innovate, even in public services. The first private company contracted to manage a maintained school was in Guildford in February 1999. New Labour is placing great emphasis on the Private Finance Initiative and projected that some £3 billion of contracts would be agreed during 1999–2000.

After its first year in office, government undertook a comprehensive spending review in which there was a root-and-branch examination of all aspects of public expenditure. The outcome was a three-year programme of expenditure set out in *Modern Public Services for Britain: investing in reform* (Cm 4011, 1998). Government defined its overall objectives for the remaining years of office as: to increase sustainable growth and employment: promote fairness and opportunity; and deliver efficient and modern public services. These are reflected in every area of central government activity, but especially in the policy priority fields of education, health, welfare to work and criminal justice which were identified in the 1997 manifesto.

A second white paper, *Public Services for the Future* (Cm 4181, 1998: 5), published in December 1998, explained the introduction of Public Service Agreements (PSAs) which 'bring together in a single document important information on aims and objectives, resources, performance and efficiency targets and related policy issues'. In *Public Services for the Future*, it is clear that Labour has retained the public quality systems set up under the Conservatives and strengthened its attachment to performance management. Labour is determined to use targets and performance indicators (PIs) as means of increasing not only productivity and performance but also accountability of ministers for their departments. Departments have very stringent PIs set for them and are expected to make efficiency savings ranging from one to 10 per cent per year. In fact, government has stated that all departments have to 'save to spend'. This is designed to encourage increased productivity and sift out unnecessary expenditure, so that savings can be spent on new initiatives. Paralleling this idea is 'invest to save'. Here spending is intended to reap economies in the longer term. In areas receiving extra money, like education and health, there is an expectation that they will deliver good results. Even experiments with inter-agency co-operation have PSAs. One example is 'Sure Start', where several central government departments work with local community groups, local education authorities, social services, health services and statutory, voluntary and private-sector bodies to improve support for disadvantaged families and children to ensure those children get the best start in life. A PSA sets down its objectives, aims, targets and PIs and allocates money to the participating departments, although there is a lead department to account for the expenditure and the performance. In this case it is the DfEE.

Other examples of continuity include government's commitment to public quality assurance systems and its strengthening of that commitment in *Service First* (Cabinet Office, 1998e). All public and private bodies involved in public service provision are expected to develop 'service first' standards or charters, to carry out consumer and user surveys and to have effective complaints and appeals procedures. New Labour is also enthusiastic for continued privatisation and disposal of public assets, as means of raising funds and ensuring higher rates of return on fixed assets. Treasury compilation of a list of public assets and its requirement that all departments and agencies justify the use of their assets goes far beyond the Conservative government's general encouragement to sell public assets 'surplus to requirements'. Although government has stated that it plans to abandon the internal market for health care, there is very little evidence supporting that statement. The fact that it is retaining the purchaser–provider divide and continuing to use contracts, albeit longer-term ones and renamed 'service agreements', suggests the health care market is 'safe in their hands'. In fact, Labour is no less enthusiastic about contracts than the Conservatives, although it has taken on board some of the criticisms about transaction costs and short termism. Longer-term contracts, based upon continuing relationships between purchasers and suppliers, are likely to reduce costs and remove some of the uncertainty that makes any form of long-term planning difficult but this implies simply doing the same thing better.

These plans and projections indicate that there is likely to be a period of consolidation in the practices of public management during the next few years. This implies that the tasks and competencies expected and required of top public managers are unlikely to change significantly over this period. But the strategic management skills of top civil servants need to be developed, along with the 'reticulist' skills of all senior managers working in new partnerships at international, national and local levels (Elcock, 1996). The sorts of competencies needed by all managers include:

- having the leadership and vision to take their organisations forward, within the resource constrains imposed by central government
- having the necessary financial and budgetary skills to ensure the financial survival of their organisations
- being able to apply relevant strategic and marketing skills to maintain their organisational share in the market place
- maintaining appropriate performance and quality management systems, to avoid direct government intervention in their activities
- developing effective human resources policies, enabling them to carry their staff with them in conditions of change, competition and challenge
- keeping up with ICTs to facilitate communication exchange and the sharing of information internally and externally

In addition, managers involved with inter-agency activities need to have political skills, to enable them to build coalitions, facilitate communication, negotiate agreements and achieve consensus decisions. These are the skills already required of those civil servants working within the context of the European Union and other public officials involved with international bodies. Such a 'shopping list' of requisite skills implies, in turn, continued need for appropriate management training and development programmes to facilitate these competencies. Labour has placed education and training at the top of their political priorities both for the country at large and the public services.

For those subscribing to the determinist view that public management is an international phenomenon, caused by developments in international capitalism and globalisation, public management has a momentum of its own and no government can do more than move with the times and make marginal adjustments. This view, initially very popular amongst early writers on the subject, is no longer widely supported. Studies of public management indicate that countries exposed to the same international trends respond differently and, as a result, public management can and does take very different forms (Farnham *et al.*, 1996). The Anglo-Saxon countries, which include Canada, Australia, New Zealand, Britain and the US, appear to have restructured and transformed their systems of public administration in very different ways from mainland European countries. What seems to be a key factor in explaining the nature of public management in these countries is exposure to American ideas. They have been greatly influenced by American neo-liberal theorists, management gurus and the practices of top American companies and US government. Certainly that has been the case in Britain, where public choice theories and neo-liberal economic ideas informed the thinking of the Thatcher and Major governments and where the close relationship between Margaret Thatcher and Ronald Reagan meant that the US was looked to for good practice. A similar special relationship exists between Tony Blair and Bill Clinton.

Many policies and strategies for reinventing government have crossed the Atlantic (Massey, 1995: Pollitt, 1990) and there is some similarity between 'the new deal' of the Clinton Administration and Labour's claimed 'Third Way' (Reich, 1998). Unless New Labour is more successful in creating the broad alliances amongst diverse stakeholders that it needs to achieve its political objectives, and in particular finds the revenue to fund it, the Third Way may go the way of Clinton's new deal.

Most of the critics of New Labour (Crick, 1997; Mather, 1998) point to a philosophical deficit and lack of ideology in its political project, which makes it difficult to predict what direction it is likely to take. New Labour claims to eschew ideology, embrace pragmatism and be committed to change only where it is necessary. In the absence of an ideology of market socialism, or of a new social democracy, Labour is ideologically rudderless. There is extensive evidence provided in this book that the Blair government has in fact embraced many of the values of the Thatcher–Major governments, including much of their neo-liberal thinking and views on the state; there is little evidence of a clear vision of a different future. This is despite the fact that its rhetoric is emphatic that the 'Third Way' is distinctive. In practice, New Labour's 'inclusive populism' looks remarkably like 'One Nation Conservatism'. Although planned constitutional changes are likely to transform the British state, it seems unlikely that it will be managed in a fundamentally different way. Another managerial revolution is not waiting to happen. It is more likely that a 'hard' form of managerialism will persist in the public services under New Labour, underpinned by a softer ethic based on co-operation, partnership and greater democratic participation, where there will be some displacement of the 'customer' by the 'citizen' in holding public managers to account.

The long awaited *Modernising Government* White Paper (Cm 4310, 1999) was published in March 1999. It sets out a long-term programme of change with a vision of a future with better government 'to make life better for people and business'. The emphasis is on change in the way government makes policy, delivers services, uses information technology and 'in the way the public service is valued' (ibid: 63). There are all the hallmarks of 'inclusive populism', 'open government', 'joined-up government' and 'quality public services', which have been identified as distinctively 'New Labour' throughout this book. The White Paper is essentially a restatement of what has been said before in earlier documents, although it clarifies the vision, aims and objectives against which government's achievements can be assessed. There is nothing in it to cause the editors of this book to revise their view that public management is now the accepted orthodoxy in British public services but, under New Labour, it is likely to be 'better' management than under the Conservatives. There is a clear rejection of the legacy that denigrated the public services. They are now clearly identifies as key agents of change in forging new partnerships with the private and voluntary sectors.

Bibliography

Ainley, P. and Bayley, B. (1997) *The Business of Learning* (London: Cassell).

Alderson, J. (1984) *Law and Disorder* (London: Hamish Hamilton).

AMSO (1997) *Annual Report* (London: AMSO).

Asquith, A. (1997) 'Achieving Effective Organisational Change in English Local Government' *Local Government Studies*, 23(4).

Audit Commission (1984) *The Impact on Local Authorities' Economy, Efficiency and Effectiveness of the Block Grant Distribution System* (London: HMSO).

Audit Commission (1986) *Performance Review in Local Government: A Handbook for Auditors and Local Authorities* (London: HMSO).

Audit Commission (1988) *The Competitive Council* (London: HMSO).

Audit Commission (1989a) *More Equal Than Others: The Chief Executive in Local Government* (London: HMSO).

Audit Commission (1989b) *Reviewing the Organisation of Provincial Police Forces* (London: HMSO).

Audit Commission (1992a) *The Community Revolution: Personal Social Services and Community Care* (London: HMSO).

Audit Commission (1992b) *Community Care: Managing the Cascade of Change* (London: HMSO).

Audit Commission (1993) *Helping with Inquiries: Tackling Crime Effectively* (London: HMSO).

Audit Commission (1996a) *Streetwise: Effective Police Patrol* (London: HMSO).

Audit Commission (1996b) *Trading Places, The Supply and Allocation of School Places* (London: HMSO).

Audit Commission (1997) *Local Authority Performance Indicators Police Services* (Abingdon: Audit Commission Publications).

Audit Commission/OFSTED (1993) *Unfinished Business: Full-time Educational Courses for 16–19 Year Olds* (London: HMSO).

Bach, S. (1989) 'Too high a price to pay?' *Warwick Papers in Industrial Relations*, 25 (Coventry: Industrial Relations Research Unit).

Bacon, W. and Eltis, W. (1976) *Britain's Economic Problem* (London: Macmillan).

Baggot, R. (1997) 'The NHS Internal Market' *Public Administration*, 75(2).

Bains, M. (Chairman) (1972) *The New Local Authorities: Management and Structure* (London: HMSO).

Baker, K. (1992) *Turbulent Years: My Life in Politics* (London: Faber).

Ball, S. (1990) *Politics and Policy-Making in Education: Explorations in Policy Sociology* (London: Methuen).

Ball, S. and Bowe, R. (1992) *Reforming Education and Changing Schools: Case Studies in Policy Sociology* (London: Routledge).

Balloch, S. (1997) 'Issues facing the social services workforce', in May, M., Brunsdon, E. and Craig, G. (eds) *Social Policy Review 9* (London: Social Policy Association).

Barber, M. (1997) *The Learning Game: Arguments For An Educational Revolution* (London: Indigo/Cassell).

Barberis, P. (1995) 'The Civil Service from Fulton to Next Steps and Beyond; Two Interpretations: Two Epistemologies' *Public Policy and Administration*, 10(2).

Barberis, P. (1998) 'The New Public Management and a new accountability' *Public Administration*, vol. 76, no. 3.

Barker, A. (1996) *Myth versus Management: Individual Ministerial Responsibility in the New Whitehall*. Essex Papers in Politics and Government no. 105).

Barker, A. (1998) 'Political Responsibility for UK Prison Security – Ministers Escape Again' *Public Administration*, vol. 76, no. 1.

Barnes, M. (1997) *Care, Communities and Citizens* (Harlow: Addison, Wesley, Longman).

Beardwell, I. and Holden, L. (1997) *Human Resources Management, A Contemporary Perspective* (London: Pitman).

Bellamy, C. (1996) 'Transforming Social Security Benefits Administration for the Twenty-first Century' *Public Administration*, 74(1).

Bellamy, C. and Taylor, J. A. (1996) 'New ICTs and Institutional Change: the Case of the Criminal Justice System' *International Journal of Public Sector Management*, 9(4).

Bellamy, C. and Taylor, J. A. (1998a) *Governing in the Information Age* (Buckingham: Open University Press).

Bellamy, C. and Taylor, J. A. (1998b) 'Understanding Government Direct' *Information Infrastructure and Policy*, 6(1).

Bennington, J.(1994) *Local Democracy and the European Union: The impact of Europeanisation on local government* (London: The Commission for Local Democracy).

Berry, L. L. (1980) 'Services Marketing is Different' *Business*, May—June, quoted in Lovelock, C. (1996) *Services Marketing* 3rd edn (London: Prentice Hall International).

Beveridge, Lord (1942) *Social Insurance and Allied Services* (Cmnd 6404) (London: HMSO).

Blair, T. (1987) Article in The *Guardian* quoted in Mandelson, P. and Liddle, R. (1996) The Blair Revolution: Can Labour Deliver? (London: Faber and Faber).

Blair, T. (1997) 'Next on the List: Clean up the Councils' The *Guardian*, 3 November, p. 17

Blair, T. (1998a) *The Third Way: New Politics for the New Century* (London: The Fabian Society).

Blair, T. (1998b) *Leading the Way: A New Vision for Local Government* (London: Institute for Public Policy).

Bloomfield, B. and Coombs, R. (1992) 'Information Technology, Control and Power' *Journal of Management Studies*, 29(4).

Booms, B. H. and Bitner, M. J. (1981) 'Marketing Strategies and Organisational Structures for Firms', in Donnelly, J. and George, W. *Marketing of Services* (Chicago: American Marketing Association) quoted in Zeithaml, V. and Bitner, M. (1996) *Services Marketing* (New York: McGraw-Hill).

Bovell, V., Lewis J. and Wookey, F. (1997) 'The Implications for Social Services Departments of the Information Task in the Social Care Market' *Health and Social Care in the Community*, vol. 5, no. 2.

Boyne, G. A. (1998a) 'Competitive Tendering in Local government: a review of theory and evidence' *Public Administration*, vol. 76.

Boyne, G. A. (1998b) 'Public Services Under New Labour: Back to Bureaucracy?' *Public Money and Management*, vol. 18 (3).

Bozeman, B. and Straussmann, J. (1990) *Public Management Strategies* (Oxford: Jossey Bass).

Brindle, D. (1995) 'NHS trust deal lost £3.5m' The *Guardian*, 6 October, p. 8.

Brindle, D. (1998a) 'Squeeze is betrayal, say unions' The *Guardian*, 30 January.

Brindle, D. (1998b) 'Health minister is jeered in row over private cash' The *Guardian*, 9 April.

British Medical Association (1998) Letter to chairman of Professional Regulation Working Group, 8 May, unpublished.

Brown, H. and Smith, H. (1993) 'Women caring for people: the mismatch between rhetoric and reality?' *Policy and Politics,* vol. 21, no. 3).

Bryson, C., Gallegher, J., Jackson, M., Leopold, J. and Tuck, K. (1993) 'Decentralization of Collective Bargaining: Local Authority Opt-outs' *Local Government Studies,* 19(4).

Bryson, J. (1988) *Strategic Planning for Public and Nonprofit Organizations* (Oxford: Jossey Bass).

Buchanan, M. (1975) *The Limits of Liberty* (Chicago: Chicago University Press).

Burch, M. and Holliday, I. (1999) 'The Prime Minister's and Cabinet Offices ' *Parliamentary Affairs,* vol. 52, no. 1.

Butcher, T. (1995) *Delivering Welfare* (Buckingham: Open University Press).

Butcher, T. (1998) 'The Blair Government and the Civil Service' *Teaching Public Administration,* vol. XVIII, no. 1.

Butler, P. and Collins, N. (1995) 'Marketing Public Sector Services: Concepts and Characteristics' in *Journal of Marketing Management,* vol. 11.

Butler, R. (1994) 'Reinventing British Government: A Symposium' *Public Administration,* vol. 72, no. 2.

Byrne, L. (1997) *Information Age Government: Delivering the Blair Revolution* (London: Fabian Society).

Cabinet Office (1984) *Programme of Action on Equal Opportunities for Women in the Civil Service* (London: HMSO).

Cabinet Office (1988a) *Equal Opportunities for Women in the Civil Service: Progress Report 1984-87* (London: HMSO).

Cabinet Office (1988b) *Improving Management in Government: The Next Steps* (London: HMSO).

Cabinet Office (1991) *The Government's Guide to Market Testing* (London: HMSO).

Cabinet Office (1996) *Government Direct* (Cm 3438) (London: HMSO).

Cabinet Office (1997a) *Next Steps Report* (Cm 3889) (London: HMSO).

Cabinet Office (1997b) *The Government's Response to Comments on the Green Paper, Government Direct* (London: The Stationery Office).

Cabinet Office (1998a) *Modern Public Services: Results of the Government's Comprehensive Spending Review* (London: The Stationery Office).

Cabinet Office (1998b) *Next Steps Briefing Notes* (September) (London: Cabinet Office).

Cabinet Office (1998c) (Samuels, M.) *Towards Best Practice: an evaluation of the first two years of the Public Sector Benchmarking project 1996-98* (London: Cabinet Office).

Cabinet Office (1998d) *Better Quality Services* (London: The Stationery Office).

Cabinet Office (1998e) *Service First: The New Charter Programme* (London: The Stationery Office).

Cabinet Office (1998f) *Better Government for Older People* (London: The Stationery Office).

Cabinet Office (1998g) *Modern Public Services for Britain: Investing in Reform* (Cm 4011) (London: The Stationery Office).

Campbell, A. and Alexander, M. (1997) 'What's Wrong with Strategy?' *Harvard Business Review,* vol. 75.

Cantor, L., Robert, I. and Pratley, B. (1995) *A Guide to Further Education in England and Wales* (London: Cassell).

Carr, F. and Cope, S. (1994a) 'Britain and Europe: from Community to Union' in Savage, S., Atkinson, R. and Robins, L. (eds) *Public Policy in Britain* (London: Macmillan).

Carr, F and Cope, S. (1994b) 'Implementing Maastricht: the Limits of European Union' *Talking Politics,* 6.

Carter, N., Klein, R. and Day, P. (1992) *How Organisations Measure Success. The Use of Performance Indicators in Government* (London: Routledge).

Cassells, J. (1983) *Review of Personnel Work in the Civil Service* (London: HMSO).

Castells, M (1996) *The Rise of the Network Society*, vol. I. (Oxford: Blackwells).

Caulfield, I. and Schulz, J. (1989) *Planning for Change: Strategic Planning in Local Government* (Essex: Longman).

CCTA (1994) *Information Superhighways. Opportunities for Public Sector Applications* (Norwich: CCTA).

CCTA (1995) *Information Superhighways. An Update on Opportunities for Public Sector Applications* (Norwich: CCTA).

Central Statistical Office (1998) *Economic Trends 1998* (London: The Stationery Office).

Cerny, P. (1993) 'Plurilateralism: Structural Differentiation and Functional Conflict in the Post-Cold War World Order' *Millenium*, 22(1).

Chapman, D. and Cowdell, T. (1998) *New Public Sector Marketing* (London: Financial Times Pitman).

Chapman, R. and O'Toole, B. (1995) 'The Role of the Civil Service: A Traditional View in a Period of Change' *Public Policy and Administration*, vol. 10, no. 2.

Charman, S., Savage, S. and Cope, S. (1999) 'Getting to the Top: Selection and Training for Senior Managers in the Police Force' (forthcoming in *Social Policy and Administration*).

Civil Service Statistics (1998) (London: HMSO).

Clarke, J. (1998) 'Making a Difference: Markets and the Reconstruction of Public Services in Britain'. Paper given at the British–German Workshop on Public Sector Modernisation, Humbold University, Berlin.

Clarke, J. (ed.) (1993) *A Crisis in Care? Challenges to Social Work* (London: Sage).

Clarke, J., Cochrane, A. and McLaughlin, E. (eds) (1994) *Managing Social Policy* (London: Sage).

Clarke, M. (1998) 'Governance and the European Union: A Discussion of Co Government' *Local Governance*, vol. 24, no. 1.

Clarke, M. and Stewart, J. (1991) *The Role of the Chief Executive* (Luton: Local Government Management Board).

Cm 1599 (1991) *Citizen's Charter: Raising the Standard* (London: HMSO).

Cm 1730 (1991) *Competing for Quality* (London: HMSO).

Cm 2540 (1994) *Second Report of Citizen's Charter Unit* (London: HMSO).

Cm 2627 (1994) *The Civil Service: Continuity and Change* (London: HMSO).

Cm 2748 (1995) *The Civil Service: Taking Forward Continuity and Change* (London: HMSO).

Cm 3370 (1996) *Citizen's Charter – Five Years On* (London: HMSO).

Cm 3818 (1997) *Your Right to Know (London:* HMSO).

Cm 4011 (1998) *Modern Public Services for Britain: Investing in Reform* (London: The Stationery Office).

Cm 4181 (1998) *Public Services for the Future* (London: The Stationery Office).

Cm 4310 (1999) *Modernising Government* (London: The Stationery Office).

Cmd 5174 Department of Education and Science (1992) *Education: A Framework for Expansion* (London: HMSO).

Cmnd. 8616 (1982) *Efficiency and Effectiveness in the Civil Service* (London: HMSO).

Cmnd. 9058 (1983) *Financial Management in Government Departments* (London: HMSO).

COI (1997) *Our Information Age. The Government's Vision.* (London: Central Office of Information).

Colling, T and Ferner, A. (1995) 'Privatization and Marketization' in Edwards, P. *Industrial Relations Theory and Practice in Britain* (London: Blackwell).

Collinge, C. and Leach, S. (1995) 'Building the Capacity for Strategy Formation in Local Government' *Local Government Studies*, 21(3).

Collins, J. (1994) 'Collegialism and managerialism: a new model of university governance?' An unpublished MA dissertation, University of Portsmouth.

Corby, S. (1992) 'Industrial relations developments in NHS trusts' *Employee Relations*, 14, 6.

Corby, S. (1993) 'How Big a Step is "Next Steps"? Industrial Relations Developments in Executive Agencies' *Human Resources Management Journal*, vol. 4, no. 2.

Corby, S. (1996) 'The National Health Service' in Farnham, D. and Horton, S. *Managing People in the Public Services* (London: Macmillan).

Corby, S. (1997) 'Industrial Relations in Civil Service Agencies' *Industrial Relations Journal*, vol. 24, pt 3.

Corby, S. and Higham, D. (1996) 'Decentralisation in the NHS: diagnosis and prognosis' *Human Resource Management Journal*, 6, 1, 49–62.

Crick, B. (1998) 'Still Missing: A Public Philosophy? *Political Quarterly*, vol. 68).

Croft, S. and Beresford P. (1996) 'Service user's perspectives' in M. Davies (ed.) *The Blackwell Companion to Social Work* (Oxford: Blackwell).

Crook, S., Pakulski, J. and Waters, M. (1992) *Postmodernization* (London: Sage).

Crouch, C. (1979) *The Politics of Industrial Relations* (London: Fontana).

CSSA (1997) The *Response of the Computing Services and Software Association to the Public Consultation on government.direct* (http://www.open.gov.uk/citu).

Dahrendorf, R. (1995) 'Preserving Prosperity' in *New Statesman & Society,* 15/29 December.

Davenport, T. H. (1993) *Process Innovation. Re-engineering Work Through Information Technology* (Boston, Mass.: Harvard Business School Press).

Davenport, T. H, Eccles, R. G. and Prusak, L. (1992) 'Information Politics' *Sloan Management Review*, Fall.

Davies, S. and Griffiths, D. (1995) 'Kirklees Metropolitan Council: Corporate Strategy in a Local Authority' in Clarke-Hill, C. and Glaister, K. *Cases in Strategic Management* 2nd edn (London: Pitman).

Davis, H. (ed.) (1996a) *Quangos and Local Government: A Changing World* (London: Frank Cass).

Davis, H. (1996b) 'The Fragmentation of Community Government', in S. Leach, H. Davis and Associates, *Enabling or Disabling Local Government* (Buckingham: Open University Press).

Davis, H. and Hall, D. (1996) *Matching Purpose and Task: The Advantages and Disadvantages of Single and Multi-Purpose Bodies* (University of Birmingham: Institute of Local Government Studies).

Davis, H. and Walker, B. (1998) 'Contracting for Best Value in Local Government: Some Research-Based Perspectives', unpublished conference paper, Seventh Quasi-Market Research Seminar 1998, London School of Hygiene and Tropical Medicine.

Day, P. and Klein, R. (1985) *Accountabilities* (London: Tavistock).

Day, P. and Klein, R. (1997) *Steering but not Rowing? The Transformation of the Department of Health* (Bristol: Policy Press).

Deakin, N. and Walsh, K. (1996) 'The Enabling State: The Role of Markets and Contracts' *Public Administration*, vol. 74.

Deal, T. and Kennedy, A. (1982) *Corporate Cultures* (Reading, Mass.: Addison-Wesley).

Dean, H. (1996) 'Who's complaining? Redress and social policy' in May, M., Brunsdon, E. and Craig, G. (eds) *Social Policy Review* 8 (London: Social Policy Association).

Department for Education (1993) Circular 93/12 *The Further Education Funding Council* (London: HMSO).

Department for Education and Employment (1997a) *Excellence in Schools* Cm 3681 (London: The Stationery Office).

Department for Education and Employment (1997b) *Targets for the Future* (London: The Stationery Office).

Department for Education and Employment (1998a) *The Learning Age* (Cm 3790) (London: The Stationery Office).

Department for Education and Employment (1998b) *Teachers Meeting the Challenge of Change* (Green Paper) (London: The Stationery Office).

Department of Education and Science (1983) *Teaching Quality* (Cmnd 8836) (London: HMSO).

Department of Health (1989) *Caring for People: Community Care in the Next Decade and Beyond* (London: HMSO).

Department of Health (1993) *Health and Social Services Statistics for England* (London: HMSO).

Department of Health (1995) *Local Authority Social Services Statistics: Staff of Local Authority Social Services Department at 30 September 1994, England* (S/F 94/1) (London: Government Statistical Service).

Department of Health (1997a) *The New NHS. Modern – Dependable* (Cm 3807) (London: HMSO).

Department of Health (1997b) *Social Services: Achievements and Challenges* (London: HMSO).

Department of Health (1997c) *Statistical Bulletin* (London: Department of Health).

Department of Health (1998a) *Personal Social Services Current and Capital Expenditure in England 1996–1997* (London: HMSO).

Department of Health (1998b) *Modernising Health and Social Services: National Priorities Guidance 1999/2000 – 2001/02* (London: The Stationery Office).

Department of Social Security (1998a) *A New Contract for Welfare* (Cm 3852) (London: The Stationery Office).

Department of Social Security (1998b) *New Ambitions for Our Country: A New Contract for Welfare* (London: The Stationery Office).

Department of Social Security (1998c) *The New Deal* (London: The Stationery Office).

Department of the Environment, Transport and Regions (1998a) *Modernising Local Government: Local Democracy and Community Leadership* (London: The Stationery Office).

Department of the Environment, Transport and Regions (1998b) *Modern Local Government: In Touch with the People* (London: Stationery Office).

Department of the Environment, Transport and Regions (1998c) *A Mayor and Assembly for London* (London: The Stationery Office).

Department of Trade and Industry (1998) *Fairness at Work* (Cm 3968) (London: The Stationery Office).

Doig, A. (1997) 'The Privatisation of the Property Services Agency: Risk and Vulnerability in Contract-Related Fraud and Corruption' *Public Policy and Administration*, vol. 12, no. 3).

Douglas, A. and Philpot, T. (1998) *Caring and Coping: A Guide to Social Services* (London: Routledge).

Downs, A. (1957) *An Economic Theory of Democracy* (New York: Harper and Row).

Drewry, G. (ed.) (1989) *The New Select Committees* (Oxford: Clarendon Press).

Drucker, P. (1954) *Principles of Management* (London: Heinemann).

Drucker, P. (1974) *Management: Tasks, Responsibilities, Practices* (London: Heinemann).

Drucker, P. (1989) *The Practice of Management* (Oxford: Heinemann).

Duff, A. (ed.) (1997) *The Treaty of Amsterdam: Text and Commentary* (London: The Federal Trust).

Dunleavy, P. and Hood, C. (1994) 'From Old Public Administration to New Public Management' *Public Money and Management,* 14 (3).

Dunleavy, P. (1994) 'The Globalization of Public Services Production: Can Governments be 'Best in World'? *Public Policy and Administration,* 9(2).

Dunsire, A. (1973) *Administration: The Word and the Science* (London: Martin Robinson).

Dyerson, R. and Roper, M. (1991) 'Managing Change in Britain. IT Implementation in the Department of Social Security and the Inland Revenue' *Informatization and the Public Sector,* 1.

Elcock, H. (1991) *Change or Decay? Public Administration in the 1990s* (London: Longman).

Elcock, H. (1993) 'Strategic Management' in Farnham, D. and Horton, S. *Managing the New Public Services* (London: Macmillan).

Elcock, H. (1996) 'Strategic Management' in Farnham, D. and Horton, S. *Managing the New Public Services* 2nd edn (London: Macmillan).

Ellis, K. (1993) *Squaring the Circle: User and Carer Participation in Needs Assessment* (York: Joseph Rowntree Foundation).

Enderby v Frenchay Health Authority (1993) *Industrial Relations Law Reports,* 591–600.

Engel, M. (1998) 'Hague and Co. Offer Music Hall Portrayal of Disintegration that Fails to Bring House Down' The *Guardian,* 10 October, p. 13.

European Commission (1995) *G7 Information Society Conference Pilot Projects. Chair's Summaries* (Brussels: European Commission).

Farnham, D. (1997a) 'New Labour, New Unions and New Labour Market' *Parliamentary Affairs,* 49 (4).

Farnham, D. (1997b) *Employee Relations in Context* (London: IPD).

Farnham, D. (ed.) (1999) *Managing Academic Staff in Changing University Systems: International Trends and Comparisons* (Buckingham: Open University Press/ Society for Research into Higher Education).

Farnham, D. and Giles, L. (1995a) *Pay, Contracts and Collective Organization of Departmental Heads in New Universities: A National Report, 1994–5* (London: NATFHE).

Farnham, D. and Giles, L. (1995b) 'Trade Unions in Britain: Trends, and Counter Trends since 1979' *Employee Relations,* vol. 17, no. 2.

Farnham, D. and Giles, L. (1996a) 'Education' in Farnham, D. and Horton, S. *Managing People in the Public Services* (London: Macmillan).

Farnham, D. and Horton, S. (1992) 'Human Resources Management in the Public Sector: Leading or Following the Private Sector?' Paper given at the 22nd Conference of the Public Administration Committee, University of York.

Farnham, D. and Horton, S. (eds) (1996a) *Managing the New Public Services* 2nd edn (London: Macmillan).

Farnham, D. and Horton, S. (1996b) *Managing People in the Public Services* (London: Macmillan).

Farnham, D. and Horton, S. (1997) 'Human Resources Flexibilities in the United Kingdom's Public Services: Typologies, Overview and Evaluation' in *Review of Public Personnel Administration,* summer 1997, vol. xvii, no. 3.

Farnham, D., Horton, S., Barlow, J. and Hondeghem, A. (eds) (1996) *New Public Managers in Europe* (London: Macmillan).

Farnham, D. and Jones, J. (1998) 'Who are the Vice Chancellors and Principals in the UK? An analysis of their professional and social backgrounds, 1990–97' *Higher Education Review,* 30(2), spring.

Farnham, D. and McNeill, J. (1997) 'Pay Delegation in Next Steps Agencies: Some Initial Research Findings' *Public Policy and Administration*, vol. 12 no. 4.

Farnham, D. and Pimlott, J. (1995) *Understanding Industrial Relations* 5th edn (London: Cassell).

Fayol, H. (1949) *General and Industrial Management* (London: Pitman).

FEFC (1992) 'Funding Learning' (Coventry FEFC) cited in Cantor, L., Roberts, I. and Pratley, B. (1995) *A Guide to Further Education in England and Wales* (London: Cassell).

FE Now (1998) no. 49 November.

Finn, D. (1998a) 'Labour's New Deal for the Unemployed and the Stricter Benefit System', *Social Policy Review*, 10 (London: Social Policy Association).

Finn, D. (1998b) 'Welfare to Work: Making it Work Locally', paper presented at the International Conference on the Local Dimension of Welfare to Work, OECD, Sheffield, November.

FITLOG (1998) *Community Governance in the Information Society* (London: Foundation for IT in Local Government).

Flynn, N. (1995) *Public Sector Management* 2nd edn (Hemel Hemptstead: Prentice Hall/ Harvester Wheatsheaf).

Flynn, N. (1997) *Public Sector Management* 3rd edn (London: Prentice Hall/ Harvester Wheatsheaf).

Flynn, N. and Williams, G. (eds) (1997) *Contracting for Health: Quasi-markets and the National Health Service* (Oxford: Oxford University Press).

Foster, C. and Plowden, W. (1996) *The State under Stress* (Buckingham: Open University Press).

Fowler, A. (1993) *Taking Charge* (London: IPM).

Fowler, A. (1995) *Human Resource Management in Local Government* (London: Pitman).

Foxall, G. (1986) 'Marketing and Matching' *Management Decision*, vol. 24.

Friedman, M. (1962) *Capitalism and Freedom* (Chicago: University of Chicago Press).

Fry, G. (1984) 'The Development of the Thatcher Government's "Grand Strategy" for the Civil Service: A Public Policy Perspective' *Public Administration*, 62 (3).

Fulton Report (1968) *The Civil Service, Vol. 1* (Cmnd 3689) (London: HMSO).

Gamble, A. (1985) *Britain in Decline* (London: Macmillan).

Gamble, A. (1988) *The Free Economy and the Strong State: The Politics of Thatcherism* (London: Macmillan).

Gamble, A. and Payne, A. (eds) (1996) *Regionalism and World Order* (London: Macmillan).

Gaster, L. (1995) *Quality in Public Services* (Buckingham: Open University Press).

Geary, J. (1993) 'A New Voluntarism or Trade Union Marginalization', paper presented at University College Cardiff, Employment Research Unit Conference, September.

George, S. (1990) *An Awkward Partner* (Oxford: Oxford University Press).

George, S. (1991) *Politics and Policy in the European Community* (Oxford: Oxford University Press).

Giddens, A. (1993) *Sociology* (Cambridge: Polity Press).

Giddens, A. (1994) *Beyond Left and Right* (Cambridge: Polity Press).

Giddens, A. (1998) *The Third Way*, (Cambridge: The Polity Press).

Glidewell, Sir Ian (1998) 'The Review of the Crown Prosecution Service: A Report' (Cm 3960) (London: HMSO).

Gore, A. (1993) *Creating a Government that Works Better and Costs Less* (New York: Plume Books).

Gostick, C., Davies, B., Lawson, R. and Salter, C. (1997*) From Vision to Reality in Community Care* (Aldershot: Gower).

Gould, P. (1998) *The Unfinished Revolution: How Modernisers Saved the Labour Party* (London: Little Brown).

GP (1998) 'We are facing chaos. . .',15 May, 36.

Gray, A. (1998) *Business-like But Not Like a Business: The Challenge for Public Management* (London: CIPFA).

Gray, A. and Jenkins, B (1995) 'From Public Administration to Public Management: Reassessing a Revolution' *Public Administration*, vol. 73.

Greenwood, J. and Wilson, D. (1994) *Public Administration in Britain Today* (London: Unwin Hyman).

Greer, A. and Hoggett, P. (1996) 'Quangos and Local Governance', in L. Pratchett and D. Wilson (eds) *Local Democracy and Local Government* (London: Macmillan).

Griffiths, R. (1983) *Report of the NHS Management Inquiry* (London: Department of Health and Social Security).

Griffiths Report (1988) *Community Care: An Agenda for Action* (London: HMSO).

Grønroos, C. (1994) 'From Marketing Mix to Relationship Marketing: Towards a Paradigm Shift in Marketing' *Management Decision*, vol. 32, no. 2.

Haas, E. B. (1964) 'Technocracy, Pluralism and the New Europe' in Graubard, S. (ed.) *A New Europe* (Boston: Houghton Mifflin).

Hadley, R. and Young, K. (1990) *Creating a Responsive Public Service* (Hemel Hempstead: Harvester Wheatsheaf).

Hall, S. (1998) 'The Great Moving Nowhere Show' *Marxism Today*, November/ December.

Hall, S. and Jacques, M. (1983) *The Politics of Thatcherism* (London: Lawrence and Wishart).

Hall, S. and Jacques, M. (eds) (1989) *New Times: The Changing Face of Politics in the 1990s* (London: Lawrence and Wishart).

Halsey, A. (1992) *Decline of the Donnish Dominium*. (Oxford: Clarendon).

Ham, C. (1998) 'Life at the limits' The *Guardian*, 1 July.

Hambleton, R., Essex, S,. Mills, L. and Razzaque, K. (1995) *The Collaborative Council: A Study of Inter-Agency Working in Practice* (York: Joseph Rowntree Foundation).

Hammer, M. and Champy, J. (1993) *Re-engineering the Corporation* (NewYork: Harper Collins).

Hansard (1979) *House of Commons Budget Statement* 12 June 1979, Parliamentary Debates Commons 1979–80, 968 (London: HMSO).

Harrison, S. (1988) *Managing the National Health Service* (London: Chapman and Hall).

Harrison, S., Hunter, D. J., Marnoch, G. and Pollit, C. (1992) *Just Managing: Power and Culture in the National Health Service* (London: Macmillan).

Hay, C. (1997) 'Blaijorism: Towards a One-Vision Polity' *Political Quarterly*, vol. 68.

Hay, M. and Williamson, P. (1997) 'Good Strategy: the view from below' *Long Range Planning*, vol. 73, spring.

Hayek, F. (1944) *The Road to Serfdom* (London: Routledge and Kegan Paul).

Hayek, F. (1973) *Law, Legislation and Liberty, Vol. 1: Rules and Order* (London: Routledge and Kegan Paul).

Held, D. and McGrew, A. (1993) 'Globalization and the Liberal Democratic State' *Government and Opposition*, 28(2).

Henkel, M. (1991) 'The New "Evaluative State"' *Public Administration*, vol. 69.

Hennessy, P., Hughes, R. and Seaton, J. (1997) *Ready, Steady, Go! New Labour and Whitehall* (London: Fabian Society).

Henwood, M. (1995) *Making a Difference? Implementation of the Community Care Reforms Two years On* (London: Kings Fund).

Herzberg, F., Mausner, B. and Synderman, B. (1959) *The Motivation to Work* (New York: Wiley).

Heseltine, M. (1980) 'Ministers and Management in Whitehall' *Management Services in Government*, 35.

Hetherington, P. and Atkinson, M. (1998) 'Upbeat Blair Pledges Help for Jobless' The *Guardian*, 17 September, p. 2.

Higher Education Funding Council (1996) *A Guide to Funding Higher Education in England: How the HEFCE Allocates its Funds* (London: HEFCE).

Hirst, P. and Thompson, G. (1996) *Globalization in Question* (Cambridge: Polity Press).

HM Treasury (1997) *National Assets Register* (London: The Stationery Office).

HM Treasury (1998) *Report on the Comprehensive Spending Review* (London: The Stationery Office).

HM Treasury and Cabinet Office (1991) *Pay and Management* (London: HMSO).

HMIC (1997a) *Devon and Cornwall Constabulary Inspection* (Home Office: HMSO).

HMIC (1997b) *Greater Manchester Police* (Home Office: HMSO).

HMIC (1997c) *Merseyside Police Inspection* (Home Office: HMSO).

HMIC (1997d) *North Yorkshire Police Inspection* (Home Office: HMSO).

HMIC (1997e) *Northumbria Performance Review Inspection* (Home Office: HMSO).

HMIC (1997f) *South Wales Police* (Home Office: HMSO).

HMIC (1997g) *Warwickshire Constabulary Inspection* (Home Office: HMSO).

HMIC (1997h) *West Midlands Police Inspection* (Home Office: HMSO).

HMIC (1998a) *Dorset Police Inspection* (Home Office: The Stationery Office).

HMIC (1998b) *Dyfed Powys Inspection* (Home Office: The Stationery Office).

HMIC (1998c) *Gwent Police* (Home Office: The Stationery Office).

HMIC (1998d) *Hampshire Constabulary* (Home Office: The Stationery Office).

HMIC (1998e) *Kent County Constabulary* (Home Office: The Stationery Office).

HMIC (1998f) *Lancashire Constabulary Inspection* (Home Office: The Stationery Office).

HMIC (1998g) *Lincolnshire Police Inspection* (Home Office: The Stationery Office).

HMIC (1998h) *Northamptonshire Police Inspection* (Home Office: The Stationery Office).

HMIC (1998i) *West Mercia Constabulary Inspection* (Home Office: The Stationery Office).

Hobsbawm, E. (1998) ' The Big Picture: The Death of Neo-Liberalism' *Marxism Today*, November/December.

Hoggett, P. (1991) 'A New Management in the Public Sector?' *Public Policy and Administration*, 69(4).

Hoggett, P. (1996) 'New Modes of Control in Public Service' *Public Administration*, vol. 74.

Hogwood, B. and Gunn, L. (1984) *Policy Analysis for the Real World* (Oxford: Oxford University Press).

Holliday, I. (1991) 'The Conditions of Local Change: Kent County Council Since Reorganisation *Public Administration*, 69(4).

Holloway, D. (1998) 'Accounting For The Audit Commission' *Educational Management and Administration*, vol. 26, no. 1.

Home Office (1989) Circular 87/1989 *Equal Opportunities: Policies in the Police Service* (London: HMSO).

Home Office (1993) Circular 39/1993 *Pert 1: The Future Management of Police Training* (London: HMSO).

Home Office (1996a) *Protecting the Public* (London: HMSO).

Home Office (1996b) *Joint Performance Measures* (London: HMSO).

Home Office (1998) *Annual Report* (Cm 3908) (London: The Stationery Office).

Home Office (1999) *The Stephen Lawrence Inquiry – Report of an Inquiry by Sir William MacPherson of Cluny* (Cm 4262/1) (London: The Stationery Office).

Hood, C. (1991) 'A Public Management for All Seasons' *Public Administration*, vol. 69 (1).
Hood, C. (1994) *Explaining Economic Policy Reversals* (Buckingham: Open University Press).
Hood, C. (1995a) 'Emerging Issues in Public Administration' *Public Administration*, vol. 73, spring.
Hood, C. (1995b) 'Contemporary Public Management: a New Global Paradigm' *Public Policy and Administration*, 10(2).
Hood, C., Jones, O. Scott, C. and Travers, T. (1998) 'Regulation Inside Government: Where New Public Management Meets the Audit Explosion' *Public Money and Management*, 18(2).
Horton, S. (1990) 'Local Government: A Decade of Change' in Savage, S. and Robins, L. *Public Policy under Thatcher* (London: Macmillan).
Horton, S. (1993) 'The Civil Service' in Farnham, D. and Horton, S. *Managing the New Public Services* (London: Macmillan).
Horton, S. (1996a) 'The Police' in Farnham, D. and Horton, S. *Managing People in the Public Services* (London: Macmillan).
Horton, S. (1996b) 'The Civil Service' in Farnham, D. and Horton, S. *Managing People in the Public Services* (London: Macmillan).
Horton, S. (1997) 'Next Steps Agencies and Accountability: Are Contracts the Answer?' Paper given at a conference organised by the Cardiff Business School, University of Wales, May 1997.
Horton, S. (1999a) Chief Executives in Next Steps Agencies: Self Perception of their Role *Public Policy and Administration*, forthcoming.
Horton, S. (1999b) 'The United States: Self-governed Profession or Managed Occupation?' in Farnham, D. *Managing Academic Staff in Changing University Systems: International Trends and Comparisons* (Buckingham: Open University Press/ Society for Research into Higher Education).
Horton, S. and Jones, J. (1996) 'Who are the New Public Managers? An initial analysis of "Next Steps" Chief Executives and their Managerial Role' *Public Policy and Administration*, vol. 11, no. 4.
House of Commons (1990) 'The new role for district health authorities' *Research note*, no. 252, July.
House of Commons (1995) *The Role of the Civil Service* Final Report of the Treasury and Civil Service Committee (London: HMSO).
House of Commons (1995–6) *Electronic Publication of House of Commons Document*. First Report of the Information Committee. HC 328 (London: HMSO).
House of Commons (1997) Home Affairs Committee Report *Police Disciplinary and Complaints Procedure* First Report (London: HMSO).
House of Lords (1996), *Information Society. Agenda for Action in the UK*. Report of the Select Committee on Science and Technology. HL 77 (London: HMSO).
Hudson, M. (1995) *Managing Without Profit: The Art of Managing Third Sector Organizations* (London: Penguin).
Hughes, G., Mears, R. and Winch, C. (1997) 'An Inspector Calls? Regulation and Accountability in Three Public Services' *Policy and Politics*, 25(3).
Hughes, O. (1994) *Public Management and Administration* (New York: St Martins Press).
Hutton, W. (1995) *The State We're In* (London: Cape).
Hutton, W. (1997) *The State to Come* (London: Vintage).
Hutton, W. (1998) 'The Big Bang' *Marxism Today*, November/December.
Incomes Data Services (1997) *Pay in the Public Services: review of 1996, prospects for 1997* (London: Incomes Data Services).
Incomes Data Services (1998) *Pay in the Public Services: review of 1997, prospects for 1998* (London: Incomes Data Services).

Inland Revenue (1994) *Electronic Lodgement Service.* Consultative Document (London: Inland Revenue).

Ironside, M. and Seifert, R. (1995) *Industrial Relations in Schools* (London: Routledge).

Isaac-Henry, K. (1997) 'Developments and change in the public sector', in Isaac-Henry, K., Painter, C., and Barnes, C. (eds) *Management in the Public Sector: Challenge and Change* (London: Chapman and Hall).

Isaac-Henry, K. (1999, forthcoming) 'Chief Executives and Leadership in a Local Authority: A Fundamental Antithesis', in K. Theakston (ed.) *Bureaucrats and Leadership* (London: Macmillan).

Isaac-Henry, K. and Painter, C. (1991) 'The management challenge in local government: emerging trends' *Local Government Studies,*17(3).

Jackson, P.M. (1993) 'Public service performance evaluation: A strategic perspective', *Public Money and Management,* vol. 8 (4).

Jackson, P.M. (1995) 'Reflections on Performance Measurement in Public Service Organisations' in Jackson, P.M. (ed.), *Measures of Success in the Public Sector* (London: CIPFA).

Jackson, P.M. (1998) 'Public Sector Value Added: Can Bureaucracy Deliver?', unpublished conference paper, Public Services Research Unit 1998 conference, Cardiff Business School.

Jackson, P.M. and Palmer, A. (1993) *Developing Performance Monitoring in Public Service Organisations* (Leicester: University of Leicester).

James, M. (1997) 'Grin and bear it' *Local Government Chronicle,* 25 July, p. 12.

Jarratt Report (1985) *Report of Steering Committee for Efficiency Studies in Universities* (London: Committee of Vice Chancellors and Principals Sir Alex Jarratt (Chairman)).

Jervis, P. and Richards, S. (1997) 'Public Management: Raising our Game'. *Public Money and Management,* vol. 17 (2).

Jessop, B. (1993) 'Towards a Schumpeterian Workfare State?' *Studies in Political Economy,* 40.

Johnson, G. and Scholes, K. (1999) *Exploring Corporate Strategy* (Hemel Hempstead: Prentice Hall).

Johnson, T. (1973) *Professions and Power* (London: Macmillan).

Jones, K. (1989) 'Community care: old problems and new answers' in P. Carter, T. Jeffs and M. Smith (eds) *Social Work and Social Welfare Yearbook 1* (Milton Keynes: Open University Press).

Jordan, G. (1993) *Next Steps: From Managing by Command to Managing by Contract* (Aberdeen Papers in Accountancy, Finance and Management: University of Aberdeen).

Juran, J.M. (1979) *Quality Control Handbook* 3rd edn (New York: McGraw Hill).

Kavanagh, D. (1987) *Thatcherism and British Politics* (Oxford: Clarendon Press).

Kay, J.A. (1993) *Foundations of Corporate Success* (Oxford: Oxford University Press).

Keeling, D. (1973) *Management in Government* (London: Allen and Unwin).

Keen, J. (1994) 'An Information Strategy for the NHS?' *Public Administration,* 72(1).

Kelliher, C. (1996) 'Competitive tendering in NHS catering: a suitable policy?' *Employee Relations,* 18, 3, pp. 62–76.

Kelly, A. (1991) 'The "new" managerialism in the social services' in P Carter, T. Jeffs and M.K. Smith (eds) *Social Work and Social Welfare Year Book 3* (Milton Keynes: Open University Press).

Keohane, R. and Hoffman, S. (1991) 'Institutional Change in Europe in the 1980s' in Keohane, R. and Hoffman, S. (eds) *The New European Community: Decision Making and Institutional Change* (Boulder: Westview Press).

Kerley, R. (1994) *Managing in Local Government* (London: Macmillan).
Kickert, W. J. M., Klijn, E. H. and Koppenjan, J. F . M. (eds) (1997) *Managing Complex Networks: Strategies for the Public Sector* (London: Sage).
Kirchner, E. (1992) *Decision Making in the European Community: The Council, Presidency and European Integration* (Manchester: Manchester University Press).
Kitchen, H. (ed.) (1997) *A Framework for the Future: An Agenda For Councils in a Changing World* (London: Local Government Information Unit).
Klein, R. and Redmayne, S. (1996) *Why Regulate? Residential Care for Elderly People* (Bristol: Polity Press).
Labour Force Survey Statistics (1994) (London: HMSO).
Labour Party (1997) *New Labour Because Britain Deserves Better* (Labour Manifesto) (London: Labour Party).
Labour Party (1998) *Building a Better Britain* (London: Labour Party).
Laming H (1997) *Better Management, Better Care* (London: The Stationery Office).
Langlands, A. (1994) Letter to chief executives of NHS trusts, 6 June, unpublished.
Lash, S. and Urry, J. (1994) *Economies of Signs and Space* (London: Sage).
Lawrence, P. and Lorsch, J. (1969) *Organization and Environment* (London: Irwin Dorsey).
Lawton, A. (1998) *Ethical Management for the Public Services* (Buckingham: Open University Press).
Lawton, A. and Rose, A. (1991) *Organization and Management in the Public Sector* (London: Pitman).
Le Grand, J. (1991) 'Quasi-Markets and Social Policy' *Economic Journal*, vol. 101.
Le Grand, J., Mays, N, and Mulligan, J. (1998) *Learning from the NHS Internal Market: A review of the evidence* (London: King's Fund).
Leach, S., Stewart, J. and Walsh, K. (1994) *The Changing Organisation and Management in Local Government* (London: Macmillan).
Leach, S. (1996) *Mission Statements and Strategic Visions: Symbol or Substance?* (London: LGMB).
Leat, J. and Perkins, E. (1998) 'Juggling and dealing: the creative work of care package purchasing' *Social Policy & Administration*, vol. 32, no. 2.
Legge, K. (1989) 'Human Resource Management: a Critical Analysis, in Storey, J. (ed.) *New Perspectives on Human Resouces Management* (London: Routledge).
Legge, K. (1995) *Human Resource Management* (London: Macmillan).
Lewis J. and Glennerster H. (1996) *Implementing the New Community Care* (Buckingham: Open University Press).
Likierman, A. (1993) 'Performance indicators: 20 early lessons from managerial use' *Public Money and Management*, vol. 8 (4).
Lilley, R. and Wilson, D. (1994) 'Change in the NHS, View From a Trust' *Personnel Management*, May.
Lindblom, C. (1977) *Politics and Markets* (New York: Basic Books).
Locke, M., Pratt, J. and Burgess, T. (1985) *The Colleges of Higher Education 1972–1982* (London: Critical Press).
Loveday, B. (1994) 'From Local Service to State Police?' *Political Quarterly*, Winter, 66.
Loveday, B. (1998) 'Waving Not Drowning: Chief Constables and the New Configuration of Accountability in the Provinces' *International Journal of Police Science and Management*, 1, no. 2.
Lovelock, C. (1996) *Services Marketing* 3rd edn London,: Prentice Hall International).
Lovelock, C. and Weinberg, C. (1978) 'Public and Non-Profit Marketing Comes of Age' in Zaltman, G. and Bonoma, T. *Review of Marketing* quoted in Kotler, P. (1984) *Marketing Management – Analysis, Planning and Control* 5th edn (London: Prentice Hall International).

Lowndes, V. and Skelcher, C. (1998) 'The Dynamics of Multi-Organisational Partnerships: An Analysis of Changing Modes of Governance' *Public Administration,* 76(2).

Ludlow, P. (1991) 'The European Commission ' in Keohane, R. and Hoffman, S. (eds) *The New European Community: Decisionmaking and Institutional Changes* (Boulder: Westview Press).

Luke, J. and Caiden, G. (1989) 'Coping with Global Interdependence' in Perry, J. (ed.) *Handbook of Public Administration* (San Francisco: Jossey Bass).

Macmillan, H. (1938) *The Middle Way* (London: Macmillan).

Mailly, R., Dimmock, S. J., and Sethi, A. S. (1989) 'Industrial relations in the National Health Service since 1979' in Mailly, R., Dimmock, S. J. and Sethi, A. S. (eds) *Industrial Relations in the Public Services* (London: Routledge).

Mandleson, P. and Liddle, R. (1996) *The Blair Revolution: Can Blair Deliver?* (London: Faber and Faber).

Mark, A. (1994) 'Demarketing – a strategy of rationing for equity' in Malek, M. (ed.) *Setting Priorities in Health Care* (London: John Wiley).

Marquand, D. (1988) *The Unprincipled Society* (London: Fontana).

Martin, B. (1993) *In the Public Interest: Privatization and Public Sector Reform* (London: Zed Books).

Marwick, A. (1968) *Britain in the Century of Total War* (London: Bodley Head).

Marwick, A. (1990) *British Society Since 1945* (London: Penguin).

Massey, A. (1993) *Managing the Public Sector* (Aldershot: Edward Elgar).

Mather, G. (1994) 'The Market, Accountability and the Civil Service' *Public Policy and Administration,* vol. 9, no. 3.

Mather, G. (1998) 'New Labour', talk given at the Public Administration Conference, University of Birmingham, September.

Maud, Sir John. (Chairman) (1967) *Committee on the Management of Local Government, Vol. 1: Report* (London: HMSO).

McGregor, D. (1960) *The Human Side of Enterprise* (New York: McGraw-Hill).

McGrew, A. (1992) 'A Global Society?' in Hall, S., Held, D. and McGrew, T. (eds) *Modernity and its Futures* (Cambridge: Polity Press).

McHugh, M. (1997) 'Trouble in Paradise: Disintegrated Strategic Change with a Government Agency' *International Journal of Public Sector Management,* 10(6).

McKevitt, D. (1992) 'Strategic Management in Public Services' in L. Wilcocks and J. Harrow *Rediscovering Public Services Management* (London: McGraw Hill).

McLeod, I. and Maude, A. (eds) (1950) *One Nation: A Tory Approach to Social Problems* (London: Conservative Political Centre).

McVicar, M. (1996) 'Education' in Farnham, D. and Horton, S. *Managing the New Public Services* 2nd edn (London: Macmillan).

Means, R. and Smith, S. (1998) *Community Care Policy and Practice* (London: Macmillan).

Megaw Report (1982) *Report of an Inquiry into the Principles and the System by which the Remuneration of the Non-Industrial Civil Service should be Determined* (Cmnd 8590) (London: HMSO).

Metcalfe, L. and Richards, S. (1990) *Improving Public Management* 2nd edn (London: Sage).

Middlemas, K. (1995) *Orchestrating Europe: The Informal Politics Of European Union 1973–1995* (London: Fontana).

Midwinter, A. and McGarvey, P. (1995) 'Problems with the New Management Agenda' *Local Government Policy Making,* 2(1).

Millward, N., Stevens, M. and Hawes, W. (1992) *Workplace Industrial Relations in Transition* (Aldershot: Dartmouth).

Milward, A. (1994) *The European Rescue of the Nation State* (London: Routledge).

Mintzberg, H. (1973) *The Nature of Managerial* Work (New York: Harper and Row).

Mintzberg, H. (1994) 'Rethinking Strategic Planning – Part 1: Pitfalls and Fallacies' *Long Range Planning*, 29(4).

Mintzberg, H. and Waters, J. (1994) 'Of Strategies, Deliberate and Emergent' in De Witt, B. and Meyer, R. *Strategy: Process, Content, Context* (New York: Western Publishing Company).

Moody, G. and Eustace, R. (1974) *Power and Policy in British Universities*. (London: Allen and Unwin).

Morgan, C. and Murgatroyd, S. (1994) *Total Quality Management in the Public Sector* (Buckingham: Open University Press).

Morgan, I. (1991) *Report on Safer Communities* (London: HMSO).

Morgan, I. and Newburn, R. (1997) *The Future of Policing* (Oxford: Oxford University Press).

Morley, D. (1993) 'Strategic Direction in the British Public Service' *Long Range Planning*, 26(3).

Morris, R. (1995) *School Choice in England and Wales: an Exploration of the Legal and Administrative Background* (Slough: National Foundation for Educational Research).

Mueller, D. (1979) *Public Choice* (Cambridge: Cambridge University Press).

Mueller Report (1987) *Working Patterns* (London: HMSO).

Mulgan, G. (1995) 'Myth of Withering Government' The *Independent*, 25 May, pp. 14–15.

Mulgan, G. (1998) 'Whinge and a Prayer' *Marxism Today*, November/December.

Murray, I. (1998) 'Curb on Caesarean births to save costs' *The Times*, 6 March.

National Committee of Inquiry into Higher Education (1997) *Main Report* (Chair Sir Ron Dearing) (Norwich: HMSO).

National Consumer Council (1989) *In the Absence of Competition* (London: HMSO).

Newburn, R. and Jones, S. (1997) *Policing After the Act* (London: PSI).

Newman, J. (1852) *The Idea of a University* (London: Doubleday).

Newman, J. (1997) 'The limitations of management: gender and the politics of change' in Clarke, J., Cochrane, A. and McLauughlin, E. (eds) *Managing Social Policy* (London: Sage).

Newman, J. and Clarke, J. (1994) 'Going about our Business? The Managerialization of Public Services' in Clarke, J., Cochrane, A. and McLaughlin, E. (eds) *Managing Social Policy* (London: Sage).

NHS Executive (1994) *Report of the working party on the review of the consultants' distinction awards scheme* (Leeds: unpublished).

NHS Management Executive (1990) *NHS trusts: a working guide* (London: HMSO).

Niskanen, W. (1971) *Bureaucracy and Representative Government* (Chicago: Aldine Atherton).

Nolan, Lord (Chairman) (1996) *Second Report of the Committee on Standards in Public Life: Local Public Spending Bodies, Vol. 1: Report* (London: HMSO).

Nolan Report (1997) *Standards in Public Life: Third Report of the Committee on Standards in Public Life* (London: HMSO).

Nora, S. and Minc, A. (1980) *The Computerization of Society* (Cambridge, Mass.: MIT Press).

Office of Public Service (1996) *The Civil Service Management Code* (London: HMSO).

Ohmae, K. (1995) *The End of the Nation State: The Rise of Regional Economies* (London: Harper Collins).

Oliver, I. (1996) 'Police Accountability in 1996' *Criminal Law Review*, September. Online (11/19/98) *http://www.open.gov.uk./citu/gdirect/govresp.htm*.

Online (11/20/98) *http://ssa.nics.gov.uk/assets/busiplan/strategy.hmtl* S.A.A. Strategic and Business Plan, 1997–8.

Osborne, D. and Gaebler, T. (1992) *Reinventing Government* (Reading, Mass.: Addison Wesley).

Painter, C. (1994) 'Public Service Reform: Reinventing or Abandoning Government? *The Political Quarterly*, 65 (3).

Painter, C. (1995) 'The Next Steps Reform and Current Orthodoxies' in O'Toole, B. and Jordan, G. *Next Steps: Improving Management in Government* (Aldershot: Dartmouth).

Painter, C. (1996) *Local Government and the Unelected State* (London: LGIU).

Painter, C. (1997) 'Management by the Unelected State: The Rise of Quangocracy', in K. Isaac-Henry, C. Painter and C. Barnes (eds) *Management in the Public Sector* (London: International Thomson Business Press).

Painter, C. (1999) 'From Thatcher to Blair: Public Service Reform – A Third Way' *Parliamentary Affairs*, vol. 52, no. 1.

Painter, C. and Clarence, E. (1998) 'Public Services Under New Labour: Collaborative Discourses and Local Networking' *Public Policy and Administration*, 13(3).

Painter, C., Isaac-Henry, K. and Chalcroft, T. (1994) *Appointed Agencies and Public Accountability* (Birmingham: University of Central England).

Painter C., Isaac-Henry K. and Rouse J. (1997) 'Local Authorities and Non-Elected Agencies: Strategic Responses and Organisational Networks' *Public Administration*, 75(2).

Painter, C. and Isaac-Henry, K. (1997) 'Relations with Non-Elected Agencies: Local Authority Good Practice' *Public Money & Management*, 17(1).

Painter, C. Rouse, J., Isaac-Henry, K. and Munk, L. (1996) *Changing Local Governance: Local Authorities and Non-Elected Agencies* (Luton: Local Government Management Board).

Panitch, L. (1994) ' Globalisation and the State' in Miliband, R. and Panitch, L. (eds) *Socialist Register 1994: Between Globalism and Nationalism* (London: Merlin Press).

Paterson, I.V. (Chairman) (1973) *The New Scottish Local Authorities: Organisation and Management Structures* (Edinburgh: Scottish Development Department).

Payne, A. and Gamble, A. (1996) 'Introduction: the Political Economy of Regionalism and World Order' in Gamble, A. and Payne, A. (eds) *Regionalism and World Order* (London: Macmillan).

Perri, 6 (1998a) *Holistic Governance* (London: Demos).

Perri, 6 (1998b) *The Future of Privacy* (London: Demos).

Perry, J. and Kraemer, K. (1983) *Public Management: Public and Private Perspectives* (California: Mayfield).

Peston, R. (1998) 'Nurses on lower pay in line for 5% increase' *Financial Times*, 14/15 November.

Peters, B.G. (1992)'Bureaucratic Politics and the Institutions of the European Community' in Sbragia, A. (ed.) *Euro-Politics: Institutions and Policymaking in the 'New' European Community* (Washington DC: Brookings Institution).

Peters, B.G. (1993) 'Managing the Hollow State' in Eliassen, K. and Kooiman, J. (eds) *Managing Public Organizations* (London: Sage).

Peters, T. (1987) *Thriving on Chaos* (New York: Harper Row).

Peters, T. and Austin, N. (1985) *A Passion for Excellence* (New York: Harper Row).

Peters, T. and Waterman, R. (1982) *In Search of Excellence* (New York: Harper Row).

Pettigrew, A., Ferlie, E. and McKee, L. (1992) *Shaping Strategic Change* (London: Sage).

Philpot, T. (1994) *Managing to Listen: A Guide to User Involvement for Mental Health Users* (London: King's Fund).

Pike, A. (1994) 'An Efficiency That Runs in the Blood – Public Services Management' *Financial Times*, 23 November.
Pike, A. (1998) 'The search for value in the town halls: A radical overhaul in managing services is being tested in pilot projects' *Financial Times*, 12 February, p. 10.
Pilbeam, S. (1998) 'Individual Performance-Related Pay (IPRP): Believers and Sceptics', *Croners Employee Relations Review*, No. ,June
Police Foundation (1998) *Annual Lecture*, Right Hon. Jack Straw MP, Merchant Taylors Hall, London EC2.
Polidano, C. (1999) 'The Bureaucrat Who Fell Under a Bus' *Governance* (forthcoming).
Pollitt, C. (1986) 'Beyond the Management Model: The Case for Broadening Performance Assessment in Government and the Public Services' *Financial Accountability and Management*, 2 (3).
Pollitt, C. (1990) *Managerialism and the Public Services* 1st edn (Oxford: Blackwell).
Pollitt, C. (1993) *Managerialism and the Public Services* 2nd edn (Oxford: Blackwell).
Pollitt, C. (1995) 'Justification by Works or by Faith: Evaluating the New Public Management' *Evaluation*, vol. 1(2).
Pollitt, C. and Bouckaert, G. (eds) (1995) *Quality Improvement in European Public Services* (London: Sage).
Pollitt, C. and Harrison, S. (eds) (1992) *Handbook of Public Services Management* (Oxford: Blackwell).
POST (1995) *Information Superhighways. The UK National Information Infrastructure* (London: Parliamentary Office of Science and Technology).
POST (1998) *Electronic Government* (London: Parliamentary Office of Science and Technology).
Power, M. (1997) *The Audit Society* (Oxford: Oxford University Press).
Pratt, J. (1997) *The Polytechnic Experiment*. (Buckingham: SHRE and Open University Press).
Price Waterhouse/Department of Health (1991) *Implementing Community Care: Purchaser, Commissioner and Provider Roles* (London: HMSO).
Priestley Report (1956) *Royal Commission on the Civil Service* (London: HMSO).
Prime Minister's Office (1991) *Citizen's Charter* (London: HMSO).
Prior, D. (1996) ' "Working the Network": Local Authority Strategies in the Reticulated Local State', in H. Davis (ed.) *Quangos and Local Government: A Changing World* (London: Frank Cass).
Raab, C (1998) 'Electronic Confidence. Trust, Information and Public Administration' in Snellen, I. and van de Donk, W. *Public Administration in an Information Age: A Handbook* (Amsterdam: IOS Press).
Ranson, S. and Stewart, J. (1994) *Management in the Public Domain: Enabling the Learning Society* (London: Macmillan).
Rao, N. and Young, K. (1995) *Competition, Contracts and Change: The Local Authority Experience of CCT* (London: LGC Communications).
Rear, T. (1994) 'Defender of academic faith' in *The Times Higher Education Supplment*, 2 December, p. 12.
Reich, R. (1998) 'Third Way Needs Courage' The *Guardian*, 21 September, p. 20.
Rhodes, R. (1994) 'The Hollowing Out of The State: The Changing Nature of the State in Britain' *Political Quarterly*, 65(2).
Rhodes, R. (1997) *Understanding Governance: Policy Networks, Governance Reflexivity and Accountability* (Buckingham: Open University Press).
Rice, A. (1963) *The Enterprise and its Environment* (London: Tavistock).
Richards, S. (1994) 'Devolving Public Management, Centralizing Public Policy' *Oxford Review of Economic Policy*, 10(3).
Riddell, P. (1983) *The Thatcher Government* (Oxford: Robertson).
Ridley, N. (1989) 'Controlling a Natural Monopoly' *Financial Times*, 6 November.

Rigg, C. and Trehan, K. (1997) 'Changing Management and Employment in Local Government', in Isaac-Henry, K., Painter, C. and Barnes, C. (eds) *Management in the Public Sector* (London: International Thomson Business Press).

Robbins Report (1963) *Committee on Higher Education, Report* (Chair: Lord Robbins) (London: HMSO).

Robertson, R. (1995) 'Globalization: Time–Space and Homogeneity–Heterogeneity' in Featherstone, M., Lash, S. and Robertson, R. (eds) *Global Modernities* (London: Sage).

Rose, R. and Peters, G. (1978) *Can Government Go Bankrupt?* (New York: Basic Books).

Rouse, J. (1997) 'Resource and Performance Management in Public Service Organisations', in Isaac-Henry, K., Painter, C., and Barnes, C. (eds) *Management in the Public Sector* (London: Chapman and Hall).

Savage, S. (1990) 'A War on Crime: Law and Order Politics in the 1980s' in Savage, S. and Robins, L. (eds) *Public Policy Under Thatcher* (London: Macmillan).

Savage, S. and Leishman, F. (1996) 'Managing the Police: A Force for Change' in Farnham, D. and Horton, S. (eds) *Managing the Public Services* (London: Macmillan).

Savage, S., Cope, S. and Charman, S. (1997) 'Reform through Regulation: Transformation of the Public Police in Britain' *The Review of Policing Issues*, 3(2).

Schein, E. (1985) *Organisational Culture and Leadership* (London: Jossey-Bass).

Scott, P. (1983) 'The state of the academic profession in Britain.' *European Journal of Education*, 18(3).

Scott, P. (1995) *The Meanings of Mass Higher Education* (Buckingham: Open University Press).

Scottish Office (1997) *Designed to Care* (Cm 3811) (Edinburgh: The Stationery Office).

Scott Report (1997) *Report of the Inquiry into the Export of Defence Equipment and Dual Use of Goods to Iraq and Related Prosecutions* House of Commons Paper 115 (Session 1995–6) (London: HMSO).

Scullard v Knowles (1996) *Industrial Relations Law Reports,* pp. 344–6.

Seccombe, I. and Smith, G. (1996) *In the balance: registered nurse supply and demand 1996*, Report 315 (Brighton: Institute for Employment Studies).

Seebohm Report (1968) *Report of the Committee on Local Authority and Allied Personal Services* (London: HMSO).

Seifert, R. and Ironside, M. (1993) 'Industrial Relations in State Schools'. Thames Business Paper No. 19, University of Greenwich Business School.

Self, P. (1965) *Bureaucracy or Management* (London: London School of Economic).

Shaoul, J. (1998) 'Charging for capital in the NHS: to improve efficiency?' *Management Accounting,* March.

Sheaff, M. (1987) 'NHS Ancillary Services and Competitive Tendering' *Industrial Relations Journal* 19(2).

Sheehy, Sir Patrick (1993) *'Inquiry into Police Responsibilities and Rewards* (London: HMSO).

Sheldrake, J. (1996) *Management Theory: from Taylorism to Japanization* (London: International Thomson Business Press).

Sinclair, J., Seifert,, R. and Ironside, M. (1994) ' The Restructuring of Non-Teaching Jobs in Schools: the Two-pronged Attack of CCT and LMS'. Paper presented at the University College Cardiff, Employment Research Unit Conference, September.

Sisson, K. (1994) *Personnel Management*, 2nd edn (Oxford: Blackwell).

Skelcher, C., McCabe, A., Lowndes, V. and Norton, P. (1996) *Community Networks in Urban Regeneration* (Bristol: The Policy Press).

Smith, M. J. (1998) 'Reconceptualizating the British State: Theoretical and Empirical Challenges to Central Government' *Public Administration*, 76(1).

Smith, R. (1994) *Strategic Management and Planning in the Public Sector* (London: Longman).

Snellen, I. And van de Donk, W. *Public Administration in an Information Age: A Handbook* (Amsterdam: IOS Press).

Social Services Inspectorate (1998a) *Social Services Facing the Future*. The Seventh Annual Report of the Chief Inspector, Social Services Inspectorate, 1997/98 (London: DoH).

Social Services Inspectorate (1998b) *They Look After Their Own, Don't They?* Inspection of Community Care Services for Black and Ethnic Minority Older People (London: DoH).

Social Services Inspectorate / Audit Commission (1997) *Reviewing Social Services* Annual Report 1997 (London: DoH).

Socialist Health Association (1998) *The private finance initiative in the NHS*. Pamphlet issued with The Centre for Public Service and *Health Matters* magazine.

SOCITM (1998) *Modernising Local Government. Embracing the Information Age* (Northampton: Society of Information Technology Management).

Stacey R. (1992) Management into the 21st Century: The End of the Stable Paradigm?' Paper prepared for the Sixth Annual Conference of the British Academy of Management.

Stacey R. (1996) *Strategic Management and Organisational Dynamics* (London: Pitman).

Steedman, H. and Green, A. (1996) *Widening Participation in Further Education and Training: A Survey of the Issues*. Report to the Further Education Funding Council (London: Centre for Economic Performance, London School of Economics).

Steel, D. and Heald, D. (1982) 'Privatising Public Enterprise: an Analysis of the Government's Case' *The Political Quarterly*, 53(3).

Stewart, J. (1993a) 'The Limitations of Government by Contract' *Public Money and Management*, vol. 13 (3).

Stewart, J. (1993b) *Accountability to the Public* (London: Policy Forum).

Stewart, J. (1995) *Local Government Today: An Observer's View* (Luton: Local Government Management Board).

Stewart, J. and Clarke, M. (1987) 'The Public Service Orientation: Issues and Dilemmas, *Public Administration*, 65(2).

Stewart, J. and Walsh, K. (1994) 'Performance Measurement: When performance can never be finally defined' *Public Money and Management*, vol. 14 (2).

Stewart, R. (1982) *Choices for the Manager: A Guide to Managerial Work and Behaviour* (London: McGraw-Hill).

Stoker, G. (1997) 'Quangos and Local Democracy' in M. Flinders, I. Harden and D. Marquand (eds) *How to Make Quangos Democratic* (London: Charter 88).

Stoney, C. (1997) 'Strategic Management in Local Government: a Theoretical and Empirical Investigation'. PhD thesis, Leeds Metropolitan University.

Storey, J. (1989) *New Perspectives in Human Resource Management* (London: Routledge).

Storey, J. (1992) *Developments in the Management of Human Resources* (Oxford: Blackwell).

Storey, J. (1996) *Human Resource Management: A Critical Text* (London: Routledge).

Stratta, E. (1990) 'A Lack of Consultation' *Policing*, 6, Autumn.

Talbot, C. (1997) 'UK Civil Service Personnel Reforms: Devolution, Decentralisation and Delusion' *Public Policy and Administration*, vol. 12 no. 4.

Talbot, C. (1998) *Public Performance: Towards a Public Service Excellence Model* (Monmouthshire: Public Futures).

Taylor, F. (1911) *Principles of Scientific Management* (New York: Harper Press).

Taylor, J. and Williams, H. (1989) 'Telematics, Organization and the Local Government Mission' *Local Government Studies*, May–June.

Taylor, P. (1996) *The European Union in the 1990s* (Oxford: Oxford University Press).

Teacher Training Agency (1997) *Proposals for the Future Use of TTA INSET Funding* (London: TTA).

Terry, F. (1997) 'Managing Relations with the European Union: the case of local government' in *Management in the Public Sector: Challenge and Change* (eds K. Isaac-Henry, C. Painter and C. Barnes) (London: International Thompson Business Press).

Terry, L. (1995*) Leadership in Public Bureaucracies – the Administrative Conservator* (London: Sage).

Theakston, K. (1998) 'New Labour, New Whitehall' *Public Policy and Administration*, vol. 13, no. 1.

Therborn, G. (1995) *European Modernity and Beyond* (London: Sage).

THES (1998) *Times Higher Educational Supplement*, 6 November.

Thompson, J. (1995) *Strategy in Action* (London: Chapman and Hall).

Thornley, C. (1998) ' "Cheap and flexible": perspectives on low pay, local pay and efficiency for NHS health care assistants'. Paper presented to the British Universities Industrial Relations Annual Conference, July.

Tomkins, C. (1987) *Achieving Economy, Efficiency and Effectiveness in the Public Sector* (London: Routledge).

Tomlinson, J. (1993) *The Control of Education* (London: Cassell).

Tonge, R. and Horton, S. (1996) *Financial Management* in Farnham, D. and Horton, S. *Managing the New Public Services* (London: Macmillan).

Townsend, P. *et al.* (1970) *The Fifth Social Service: Nine Fabian Essays* (London: Fabian Society).

Travers, T., Jones, G. and Burnham, J. (1997) *The Role of the Local Authority Chief Executive in Local Governance* (York: Joseph Rowntree Foundation).

Travis, A. (1998) 'Warning despite record fall in crime' The *Guardian*, 8 April, p. 8.

Trow, M. (1995) 'Comparative reflections on diversity in British higher education'. Paper prepared for CVCP seminar on diversity in higher education. London, September.

Trow, M. (1997) 'More trouble than it's worth' *The Times Higher Education Supplement*, 24 October.

Turnbull, P and Blyton, P. (1992) *Reassessing Human Resource Management* (London: Sage).

Turner, D. and Pratt, J. (1990) 'Bidding for funds in higher education'. *Higher Education Review*, 24(2).

Urwick, L. (1944) *The Elements of Administration* (London: Pitman).

Veljanovski, C. (1991) 'The Regulation Game' in Veljanovski, C. (ed.) *Regulators and Markets* (London: Institute of Economic Affairs).

Walker, A (1990) 'The Strategy of Inequality,: Poverty and Income Distribution in Britain 1979–89' in Taylor, I. (ed.) *The Social Effects of Free Market Policies* (Hemel Hempstead: Harvester Wheatsheaf).

Walsh, K. (1994) 'Marketing and Public Sector Management' *European Journal of Marketing*, vol. 28, no. 3).

Walsh, K. (1995) *Public Services and Market Mechanisms: Competition, Contracting and the New Public Management* (London: Macmillan).

Walsh, K., Deakin, N., Smith, P., Spurgeon, P. and Thomas, N. (1997) *Contracting for Change* (Oxford: Oxford University Press).

Warner, D. and Crosthwaite, E. (eds) (1995) *Human Resource management in Higher and Further Education* (Buckingham: The Society for Research into Higher Education).

Welsh Office (1998) *NHS Wales: Putting Patients First* (Cm 3841) (Cardiff: The Stationery Office).

West Midlands Police Authority (1997) *Annual Report of the Chief Constable* (Birmingam: West Midlands Police Authority).

Whitchurch, C. (ed.) (1994) *A Handbook for University Administrators and Managers* (Sheffield: Sheffield University Staff Development).

White, G. and Hutchinson, B. (1996) 'Local Government' in Farnham, D. and Horton, S. *Managing People in the Public Service* (London: Macmillan).

Widdicombe, D. (Chairman) (1986) *The Conduct of Local Authority Business:* (London: HMSO).

Wighton, D. (1998) 'NHS chief to face MPs' grilling over clinical codes' *Financial Times*, 12 March, 9.

Willcocks, L. (1994) 'Managing Information Systems in Public Administration: Issues and Prospects' *Public Administration*, 72(1).

Williams, R. (1997) *Performance Management* (London: International Thomson Business Press).

Williamson, O. (1975), *Markets and Hierarchies* (New York: The Free Press).

Wilson, D. (Former Head of Prison Officer and Operation Training for HM Prison Service) *Interview*, June.

Wilson, D. and Game, C. (1998) *Local Government in the United Kingdom* (London: Macmillan).

Winchester, D. and Bach, S. (1995) 'The State: the public sector' in Edwards, P. *Industrial Relations: theory and practice in Britain* (Oxford: Blackwell).

Wistow, G., Knapp, M., Hardy, B., Forder, J., Kendall, J., and Manning, R. (1996) *Social Care Markets: Progress and Prospects* (Buckingham, Open University Press).

Young, K. (1996) 'Reinventing Local Government' *Public Administration*, 74(2).

Zuboff, S. (1988) *In the Age of the Smart Machine. The Future of Work and Power* (Oxford: Heinemann).

Index